Matt Teuten / Novus Select

Vanie Poyey

LAURENCE TRIBE (*upper left*) has taught constitutional law at Harvard Law School for four decades and has written widely about the law—including the most frequently cited treatise on the U.S. Constitution. He has argued dozens of cases at the Supreme Court, including the first argument in *Bush v. Gore*.

JOSHUA MATZ (*upper right*), a graduate of Harvard Law School and a former contributor to *SCOTUSblog,* is a law clerk for Supreme Court Justice Anthony Kennedy.

Together, Tribe and Matz taught an acclaimed course at Harvard College about the Supreme Court and the Constitution.

Additional Praise for *Uncertain Justice*

"Tribe and Matz set out to portray the Roberts Court in what they see as its messy complexity. It is no doubt difficult to write with clarity about uncertainty, but Tribe and Matz largely succeed. Surveying a shifting legal landscape, they offer crisp accounts of key cases."
—*The New York Times Book Review*

"Marvelous . . . Tribe and Matz's insights are illuminating."
—*Chicago Tribune*

"An engaging and accessible history of the Court's major decisions . . . [Tribe is] among this nation's most sophisticated thinkers about constitutional law."
—*The New York Review of Books*

"By giving the Justices their due, this book reminds us what it really means to respect the Constitution and its mission."
—*The Los Angeles Review of Books*

"Laurence Tribe and Joshua Matz have produced a brilliantly layered account of the Roberts Court. Filled with memorable stories and striking references to literature, baseball, and popular culture, this book is a joy to read from start to finish—an irresistible narrative that will delight the general public as well as journalists and scholars."
—Doris Kearns Goodwin, author of
Team of Rivals and *The Bully Pulpit*

"Laurence Tribe, the foremost constitutional scholar and advocate of his generation, and Joshua Matz have written a brilliantly insightful and engaging account of the Roberts Court. Relentlessly fair-minded in its judgments about the justices and their work, *Uncertain Justice* is an indispensable guide to the Court's recent history and, more important, to its future."
—Jeffrey Toobin, author of *The Nine* and
senior legal analyst, CNN

"*Uncertain Justice* is a fascinating, penetrating, and highly readable analysis of the Supreme Court's jurisprudence. Anyone who aspires to understand how and in what ways the Court is influencing our lives and our laws will want to read this superb and evenhanded book."

—Theodore B. Olson, U.S. Solicitor General,
President George W. Bush

"No one knows the Supreme Court like Laurence Tribe, and no one brings its decisions to life like Tribe and Joshua Matz. *Uncertain Justice* is spellbinding—whether you care about gay marriage, health care, NSA surveillance, or gun control, this magnificent book will widen and deepen your understanding of our constitutional landscape."

—Kathleen M. Sullivan, Dean,
Stanford Law School (1999–2004)

"*Uncertain Justice* provides a uniquely valuable perspective on the often confusing swirl around the most divisive legal, social, and political issues of our time. Once I started reading it, I just could not stop."

—Ron Klain, chief of staff, Vice Presidents
Biden (2009–11) and Gore (1995–99)

"*Uncertain Justice* is must reading for anyone interested in the current unannounced agenda of the Supreme Court. Lucidly written and impeccably reasoned, this essential book documents the ways in which the Roberts Court has engaged in a wholesale revision of the Constitution."

—Scott Turow, author of *One L,*
Presumed Innocent, and *Identical*

"We need this book. It is a brilliant discussion of the murky, quirky, troubling, and uncertain Roberts Court. Written in simple, elegant prose for the general public, *Uncertain Justice* is the best explanation we have of how this Court reaches its most important decisions."

—John Jay Osborn, Jr., author of *The Paper Chase*

"*Uncertain Justice* offers a page-turning and accessible analysis of the Roberts Court and its individual justices. It illuminates the often sharp disagreements and occasionally surprising agreements that mark the Court's performance. For those seeking a thoughtful, bal-

anced, and fair-minded review of the Roberts Court, this is the book to read."   —Geoffrey Stone, Dean, University of
Chicago Law School (1987–94)

"Put simply, *Uncertain Justice* is a great book. Timely and important, it tells it like it is and captures the essence of the Court's changing role in American life. It is an amazing piece of work."
—Charles J. Ogletree, Jr., Jesse Climenko
Professor of Law, Harvard Law School

"A well-researched, unsettling investigation of recent trends in the nation's highest court . . . A near-forensic dissection of the Court's work under Roberts . . . Many of their conclusions will be eye-openers."
—*Kirkus Reviews*

"[An] insightful perspective on the Supreme Court . . . [and a] nuanced look at how the Court under Chief Justice Roberts has arrived at momentous decisions from *Citizens United* to support for Obamacare."
—*Booklist*

UNCERTAIN JUSTICE

THE ROBERTS COURT AND THE CONSTITUTION

LAURENCE TRIBE
AND JOSHUA MATZ

PICADOR   HENRY HOLT AND COMPANY   NEW YORK

UNCERTAIN JUSTICE. Copyright © 2014 by Laurence Tribe and Joshua Matz. All rights reserved. Printed in the United States of America. For information, address Picador, 175 Fifth Avenue, New York, N.Y. 10010.

www.picadorusa.com
www.twitter.com/picadorusa • www.facebook.com/picadorusa
picadorbookroom.tumblr.com

Picador® is a U.S. registered trademark and is used by Henry Holt and Company under license from Pan Books Limited.

For book club information, please visit www.facebook.com/picadorbookclub or e-mail marketing@picadorusa.com.

Designed by Kelly S. Too

The Library of Congress has cataloged the Henry Holt edition as follows:

Tribe, Laurence, author.
    Uncertain justice : the Roberts court and the constitution / Laurence Tribe, Joshua Matz.—1st ed.
        p. cm.
    Includes bibliographical notes and index.
    ISBN 978-0-8050-9909-6 (hardcover)
    ISBN 978-0-8050-9913-3 (e-book)
1. Constitutional law—United States.   2. Constitutional law—Social aspects—United States.
I. Matz, Joshua, author.   II. Title.
    KF4550.T789 2014
    342.73—dc23

                                                                                    2014002845

Picador Paperback ISBN 978-1-250-06935-1

Picador books may be purchased for educational, business, or promotional use. For information on bulk purchases, please contact the Macmillan Corporate and Premium Sales Department at 1-800-221-7945, extension 5442, or write to specialmarkets@macmillan.com.

First published by Henry Holt and Company, LLC

First Picador Edition: June 2015

10 9 8 7 6 5 4 3 2 1

CONTENTS

UNCERTAIN JUSTICE

PROLOGUE:

UNCERTAIN JUSTICE

H. L. Mencken reputedly said, "For every complex problem, there is a solution that is simple, neat, and wrong."[1]

Understanding the Supreme Court undoubtedly qualifies as a "complex problem."[2] The nine justices currently issue more than seventy opinions every year, some of them thunderbolts that rock American life and others rightly destined for obscurity. With a hand in nearly every major issue of our time, from privacy and affirmative action to gun rights and health care, the Court is inescapable. Yet it is also mysterious and secretive, committed to rituals and reasoning that even experts struggle to understand. Its opinions are poked and prodded, examined under a microscope and held up to the light. The public hangs on to rumors of backroom drama, while scholars read tea leaves and prophesy the future. Clear trends predominate in certain areas of law, but efforts to develop a unified field theory of the Court—to explain its work as the result of a particular clash of politics, personalities, or principles—inevitably fall short. Even in this age of statistical models that seek to wring hidden meaning out of human behavior, the nine men and women who make up the Court intrigue and surprise us.

Consider a handful of the Court's rulings since 2005, when John G. Roberts Jr. was appointed Chief Justice of the United States.[3] In 2008, faced with a challenge by detainees held at Guantánamo Bay, the Roberts Court struck down an Act of Congress regulating national security in wartime.[4] That same year, a narrow majority invoked the Constitution's "original meaning" to hold that the Second Amendment protects an individual's right to keep and bear arms.[5] In 2010, the Court issued *Citizens United v. Federal Election Commission*, triggering heated debate over corporate money in American politics.[6] Then, in 2012, the Court upheld Barack Obama's signature achievement—the Affordable Care Act.[7] Since 2012, this Court has also blocked state efforts to regulate immigration,[8] limited warrantless GPS surveillance,[9] invalidated part of the Voting Rights Act,[10] and held that part of the Defense of Marriage Act violates the rights of same-sex couples.[11] Trying to comprehend the legal precedents, constitutional philosophies, and judicial personalities that shape these wildly divergent decisions can seem overwhelming.

Of course, an effort to understand the Roberts Court—much like an effort to understand the Court at any point in history—must reckon with more than just its results. The Court issues opinions in which the justices grapple with fundamental principles, argue over what the Constitution means and what role they should play in giving it life, and offer signals of where they are heading. These opinions open a window into the justices' hearts and minds, giving us a glimpse of how they view the world. In many cases, the justices' decisions, as well as their concurrences and dissents, also exert a magnetic pull on American life, both in their practical effects and through their bold interventions in our discourse. When Justice Sandra Day O'Connor warned that "a state of war is not a blank check for the President,"[12] and when Roberts condemned the "sordid business" of "divvying us up by race,"[13] they spoke to the public about constitutional values in ways that can't simply be reduced to how they voted in those cases.

Judicial opinions, though, can defy easy comprehension. Far too often, their meaning is misunderstood. It doesn't help that in controversial cases, the Court frequently erupts in a confusing cacophony of competing writings. Nor do its opinions always offer a comprehensive and transparent view of the Court; sometimes they are downright misleading.

The complex problem, then, is that the Supreme Court presents many kinds of uncertainty: What is really going on within the Court? What moves the justices to take the actions they do? How will they resolve the issues that reach them in the future? What roles do they see for themselves? Are they achieving what the Constitution requires or justice demands?

To be sure, this uncertainty has its limits. The Court is not a legal randomizer, emitting new constitutional rules without rhyme or reason. In less than a decade, for instance, the Roberts Court has wrought remarkable and directed changes in many areas of the law, forever transforming how the Constitution is understood. Yet the shifting boundaries of what we can know about the Court, the futures that seem likely and the precedents not long for this world, tell a captivating story in their own right. As Carl von Clausewitz observed, "Although our intellect always longs for clarity and certainty, our nature often finds uncertainty fascinating."[14]

In some important domains of constitutional law, a majority of the Roberts Court stands on the brink of revolution yet seems profoundly uncertain about whether and how to proceed. In other domains, it has already initiated major changes whose long-term effects are clouded in mystery. Some of these developments reflect a desire by the justices to remake our constitutional understanding, while others have been forced by dramatic cultural, technological, and political upheaval. Although uncertainty is not unique to the Roberts Court—it is always part of life at the Marble Palace—it affords an especially helpful entry point to this Court.

Many of the most important stories of the Roberts Court consist not of definitive rulings but of the portents and fault lines that lurk in opinions and hint at what lies ahead. In this book, we show how conventional wisdom on these matters is often misleading, and we draw out the latent meaning of many of this Court's most important opinions to identify the uncertainties facing the nation and its justices.

To that end, we do not adopt a standard convention in books about the Court: the "deep explanation." We do not point to a strong left/right split, a partisan realignment, or a dispute over legal method and then argue that the life of the Court really boils down to *that* story. We do not claim that the Roberts Court is ultimately about a fight between "activism" and "judicial restraint," both of which are largely useless terms (all justices are "activists" in certain areas of constitutional law). We do not pick one or two justices and insist that their agendas or struggles fundamentally define the Court. Nor do we distill the Court down to "liberals" and "conservatives," explaining cases as the result of ideological blocs and agonizing over one or more inscrutable "swing voters."

There is, of course, much to be said for these approaches to the Court. Executed well, each can reveal important patterns, draw out the under-appreciated influence of a particular justice or idea, and identify overall coherence or contradiction in the Court's undertakings. Yet writing about the Court is not like examining the physical universe. Whereas scientists can at least strive for perfection in their models, only a madman or a fool would ever claim to have fully explained the Court.[15] At times, this realization can inspire an intense frustration: scholars of the Court inevitably feel as if they are trying to nail jelly to the wall, to borrow an apt phrase from Teddy Roosevelt.[16] In the end, though, accepting this limitation is liberating. It points the way toward a more ecumenical mind-set that can shed valuable light on the Court by approaching it from many angles at once.

Indeed, there are particularly good reasons to look skeptically on all of the leading deep explanations. They often overstate the determinate role of politics, principles, or personality and thereby squeeze out crucial elements of uncertainty and contingency. They certainly don't capture how the justices actually think about their work or their positions on a nine-member court. Justice Elena Kagan tends to lean left and Justice Samuel A. Alito Jr. tends to lean right, but neither of them would ever approach a case by saying, "I'm a [liberal/conservative], so what does that mean for my vote here?" Nor do any of the justices reflexively think in, say, activist or nonactivist terms when considering how to work through constitutional issues.

To the contrary, in deciding how to vote and what to say, the justices are moved by a dizzying array of considerations, only some of them apparent to the public.[17] First and foremost, the justices must account for what the Constitution requires. This may seem straightforward enough. But as Justice David Souter remarked after he resigned from the Court, "The Constitution is a pantheon of values, and a lot of hard cases are hard because the Constitution gives no simple rule of decision for the cases in which one of the values is truly at odds with another."[18] He explained, "We want order and security, and we want liberty. And we want not only liberty but equality as well."[19] Reconciling those values calls for brilliant legal analysis, but it also requires judgment.[20]

Charged with ascertaining what the Constitution means and then creating law to implement its commands, the justices necessarily draw on a wide range of tools. They look to the Constitution's text, how it was understood when it was ratified, our national history, judicial precedent, the Constitution's values, and the practical needs of our time.[21] No justice relies uniformly on one method of interpretation. They all practice the art and science of forging meaning from different materials, matching a timeless constitution to a changing world. In so doing, they are influenced by reason and principle, but also by their unique experiences and personal quirks.

Many other factors shape the Court's decisions. Like any branch of government, the Court cares deeply about its legitimacy and its role in our democratic society.[22] Blessed with tremendous power, cursed with great responsibility, and fated to serve in a cynical age, the justices of the Roberts Court know well that the power to persuade is among their mightiest weapons. Decisions on big data or gay rights, for example, interact with a quickly changing culture. That power, in turn, can affect the Court itself: the justices, after all, are very much a part of the culture they help shape. To study the Court is thus to examine an institution whose own rulings alter the path down which it travels.

The nine justices also practice their own form of politics. Not the low and occasionally demoralizing politics of our endless partisan struggle, but a high politics of constitutional principle, in which they compete to define the framework of our fundamental law.[23] That politics, like all politics, contains an irreducible human element. The justices approach their task from different backgrounds, and with different temperaments and predispositions. They have each given a great deal of thought to the Constitution and its long history. Yet even with all of them acting in good faith, major conflict is unavoidable. Those disagreements unfold in a shifting matrix of alliances, betrayals, and rivalries, as a succession of justices address myriad issues all at once and debate them through the decades.

In those contests, every justice matters. For that reason, any accounting of the Roberts Court must grapple with the uncertainty inherent in a Court steered not just by one chief but by nine unique individuals—each with a different vision and voice, each with just one vote, and each keen to take the lead on certain issues. Adam White has thus speculated in the *Wall Street Journal*, "Maybe we have a court without leaders."[24] That's an intriguing proposition, but we would amend it: the Roberts Court has *nine* leaders, not none.

Against this vibrant, complex reality of life at the Court, deep explanations usually flatten the justices into cardboard cutouts. In terms attributed to Mencken, these arguments are "simple, neat, and wrong," even though many of them are actually quite intricate. Sometimes they ignore or miss out on revealing stories and intellectual struggles that reflect the justices' worldviews; too often, they fail to take the justices' beliefs seriously. Worse, they elide the uncertainty so vital to any satisfactory account of the Roberts Court, whose work involves an ever-shifting mix of principle, ideology, statesmanship, and personality.

In lieu of a comprehensive theory that maps the grand meaning of it all, we approach nine areas of law with an eye to elements of intrigue and surprise—and an openness to different ways of illuminating the Roberts Court. Some chapters emphasize a clash of principles, while others highlight personalities or practicalities. We zoom in on some important decisions and then zoom out to afford a panoramic view when details obscure the big picture. At times we draw heavily on history to unmask hidden meanings; in other circumstances, we focus mainly on the future. Individual justices take center stage when their contributions have proved to be especially important, or when an opinion sheds valuable light on their personality and beliefs.

Throughout, we treat the Court's complexity not as an obstacle to be overcome but as a key to understanding why it has reached some surprising decisions and what its future holds. We aim to make useful generalizations about why the justices see things the way they do, what competing visions press against their core beliefs, and where their assumptions and aspirations are likely to lead them. To achieve that goal, we often focus on nodes of uncertainty—points where debate about the Constitution's meaning is particularly intense, the Court is torn about its role, the effects of its decisions remain obscure, or the justices' goals seem unclear or contradictory.

For centuries, Americans have looked to the Court with great expectation and even greater concern. As Justice Oliver Wendell Holmes Jr. remarked at a New York dinner party in 1913, "We are very quiet there, but it is the quiet of a storm center."[25] Public interest in the Court has spiked in recent years, as the justices have waded into debates over guns, privacy, health care, campaign finance, and many other controversial issues. Their pronouncements drive not only the daily headlines but also the moment-to-moment discourse that plays out online. This is as it should be. When the justices speak, our world changes. Whether lauded or scorned, their decisions shape our future.

This book is meant to help readers better understand their Court. By exploring the Roberts Court in all its wondrous complexity, we aim to bring to life the nine lawyers who gather in a conference room and create the rules by which we live. By charting uncertainty, we reveal possibility. Justice means something different to each of us; we will all evaluate the Court differently. But we can all agree that where the Court's future is most uncertain, so is the justice it will render.

There's a magic to it, a power that always sends a chill down one's spine. The bell chimes. The velvet curtain rustles. The Marshal chants, *"Oyez! Oyez! Oyez! . . . God save the United States and this Honorable Court!"* Nine black-robed justices appear, all together, arrayed behind an arced bench that lets every one of them face the lawyers lucky enough to argue at our highest court. The air thickens with tension, the journalists lean forward, and a few of the justices crack jokes under their breath and struggle not to laugh too loudly. Then the Chief Justice of the United States calls the room to order, and the proceedings—most commonly oral argument or the announcement of an opinion—commence.

By convention, and because many other ways of slicing up the flow of time would be even more arbitrary, periods of Supreme Court history are named after chief justices. That is why one calls the current Court the "Roberts Court" and why, in this book, we focus on decisions issued after Roberts was confirmed as the Chief. In fact, though, chief justices wield little formal power on the Court. Most of a chief's authority extends to the administration of the federal judiciary. Like his peers, a chief possesses only one vote in deciding cases and in selecting which cases the Court will hear. (The Court receives roughly eight thousand petitions for review per year and usually grants around seventy-five, with each grant requiring the vote of four justices.) Among his colleagues, the main perk of the job is the power to decide who writes the Opinion of the Court, at least when the Chief is in the majority. If he is not, then the most senior justice in the majority assumes the assignment power. The Chief also presides over oral argument and the post-argument conferences, during which the justices explain their views and cast tentative votes; in both capacities, he acts mainly as an evenhanded moderator.

Informally, though, the Chief can do a lot to set the tone at the Court. He is also the Court's main emissary to the public and the other branches of government. So when Chief Justice William H. Rehnquist passed away, in September 2005, the justices waited with bated breath to learn the identity of his successor. They did not have to wait long.

Two months earlier, on July 19, 2005, John G. Roberts Jr. had been nominated to the Court to replace Justice O'Connor, who had announced her resignation.[26] Two days after Rehnquist's death, George W. Bush withdrew that nomination and renominated Roberts for the position of Chief Justice. Roberts was confirmed on September 29, and the Roberts Court's first term got under way on October 3.

Widely considered the best Supreme Court advocate of his generation, Roberts was known before his ascension to the Court as a gifted writer, skilled strategist, and brilliant legal mind. He had represented a range of clients, though his ideology leaned firmly rightward—as evidenced by his work at Ronald Reagan's Department of Justice and the cases and clients he had accepted in private practice.

Nominated to the Court after a brief stint on the federal bench in Washington, D.C., Roberts displayed considerable modesty during his confirmation hearings, offering restraint and minimalism as watchwords of his judicial philosophy. He would be fair, like an umpire, and would strive to build consensus around narrow opinions that did not decide any more than each case required. At oral argument, he divides his time between acting as a traffic cop for the other justices and pressing the lawyers with all the skill of a former master of their craft.

Because the justices arrange themselves in order of seniority, Antonin Scalia sits immediately to Roberts's left (to a viewer facing the bench).[27] Scalia donned the robes of a justice on September 26, 1986, when he was elevated from a federal court in Washington, D.C. Before his judicial career, Scalia had been a law professor, a private practitioner, and a lawyer in the administrations of Richard Nixon and Gerald Ford.

Since his confirmation to the Court, Scalia has used his considerable wit, erudition, and rhetorical talents to leave an indelible mark on our jurisprudence. In his dazzling opinions and spirited lectures, he has evangelized originalism, arguing that constitutional interpretation is legitimate only when it is based on how Americans understood the Constitution at the time it was ratified. He usually leans strongly conservative, though his commitment to originalism and respecting the plain meaning of statutory text can lead him to support what are typically seen as liberal positions. More willing than any of his colleagues to wield an acidic pen, Scalia is known for a pugnacious and sometimes cutting style that alternately amuses and provokes the other justices. His personality carries through at oral argument, where his comments and questions have earned him the title of "funniest justice."[28]

Clarence Thomas sits to Scalia's left.[29] Whereas Scalia is originalism's greatest public advocate, Thomas is its most devoted practitioner, willing to reimagine whole fields of constitutional law from scratch. Thomas was confirmed on October 15, 1991, after the closest Senate vote in Supreme Court history: fifty-two to forty-eight. George H. W. Bush had appointed Thomas, then a judge in Washington, D.C., to replace Justice Thurgood Marshall, the liberal civil rights icon who had argued *Brown v. Board of Education* in 1952 and 1953. Critics complained, unfairly and incorrectly, that Thomas wasn't up to the task of being a justice. Opponents of the appointment also focused on his deeply conservative politics and the hotly disputed details of a sexual harassment scandal. Sickened by the whole experience, Thomas famously deemed the confirmation proceedings a "high-tech lynching for uppity blacks . . . who in any way deign to think for themselves . . . unless [they] kowtow to an old order."[30]

This was not Thomas's first painful encounter with the establishment; nor would it be his last. These experiences have led him to a fundamental distrust of what he views as the consensus of self-righteous (and often hypocritical) elites. That skepticism shines through in his opinions. Willing to go it alone, he frequently writes separately to propose innovative, originalist views of constitutional law. Unlike his invariably boisterous peers, Thomas is nearly always silent at argument. "Maybe it's the Southerner in me," he once commented. "Maybe it's the introvert in me, I don't know. I think that when somebody's talking, somebody ought to listen."[31]

Thomas's quest for originalist purity could not contrast more starkly with Stephen Breyer's love of compromise and devoted striving for workable, pragmatic solutions.[32] Seated to Thomas's left, Breyer was nominated by Bill Clinton and confirmed on August 3, 1994. Breyer has devoted his career on the Court to the principle of "active liberty"—the idea that, when deciding cases, courts should do what they can to foster democratic dialogue and public involvement in the political process.[33] He believes to his core that, with the right incentives and respect for technocratic expertise, government can play an essential role in enhancing society's welfare. This optimistic view of governmental processes is informed by his experience as a highly effective member of Senator Ted Kennedy's staff on the Judiciary Committee in the 1970s, where he saw true bipartisanship in action. It also reflects his formidable work on regulation as a scholar of administrative and antitrust law, technical fields that drew on Breyer's love of empirical research.

Allergic to bright-line rules and strict categories, Breyer almost always prefers that the Court identify all relevant considerations and then balance them to reach the right, workable result under the circumstances. At oral argument, this disposition (and his background as a law professor) makes him a master of hypotheticals. Unpacking one unlikely scenario after another—sometimes causing lawyers to lose track of which one they are addressing—Breyer enthusiastically probes the limits of legal arguments.

Sonia Sotomayor, nominated by Barack Obama and confirmed on August 6, 2009, anchors the left wing of the bench. The first Hispanic justice, Sotomayor was raised in public housing projects in the Bronx and overcame many daunting obstacles in the course of her remarkable career—a story she has told in a captivating memoir, *My Beloved World*.[34] After graduating from Princeton and Yale Law School, Sotomayor worked as a New York City prosecutor and then as a commercial litigator. She also associated with a Puerto Rican civil rights group and served as an active member of New York City's Campaign Finance Board. She sat as a federal trial judge in Manhattan from 1992 to 1998 and as an appeals court judge from 1998 to 2009. These experiences exposed her to an unusually diverse cross section of American law and society.

On the Court, Sotomayor has emerged as a voice for common sense. She has also displayed a keen sensitivity to the potential for injustice in law enforcement, calling attention to maltreatment in prisons, abuses of the death penalty system, dangers to privacy rights, and police and prosecutorial misconduct. In her questions and opinions, Sotomayor is a "judge's judge"—steeped deeply in the logic of law and the context in which cases arise. More than most of her colleagues, though, Sotomayor has also maintained an active public presence, dispensing wisdom on *Sesame Street*, trading jokes on *The Daily Show*, salsa dancing on Univision, and leading the 2014 New Year's Eve Countdown in New York City.[35] After publishing her best-selling memoir in 2013, Sotomayor traveled the country to share her inspirational story. "It is my great hope that I'll be a great justice," she remarked, but the "more important [measure of my life's meaning] is my values and my impact on people who feel inspired in any way by me."[36] In this sense, Sotomayor has bravely engineered a different kind of public niche for a justice—one that embraces the humanity and experiences that guide her hand and allows her to serve as a respected role model to others facing tough challenges in life.[37]

Swinging back across the bench, Anthony Kennedy, less senior only than Roberts and Scalia, sits to the Chief's right.[38] Nominated by Ronald Reagan from his post on the Ninth Circuit Court of Appeals in California, Kennedy was sworn in on February 18, 1988. Raised in Sacramento, Kennedy returned home to California after studying at Stanford, the London School of Economics, and Harvard Law School. Before his elevation to the bench, Kennedy pursued a successful career in private practice; as a lawyer and lower court judge, he taught constitutional law at the McGeorge School of Law, where his popular lectures were the stuff of local legend.

Energetic, friendly, and engaging, Kennedy is also a true humanist—a lover of history, literature, art, and science. He remains deeply attached to California, but he is also a world traveler, and he has spent many summers working with judges from foreign nations. Kennedy's politics tend rightward with a pronounced libertarian streak, especially on social issues, but they defy ready categorization (and therefore frustrate those who seem determined to force each justice into "left" or "right" voting blocs). An unmistakable constant, though, is that Kennedy is driven by strong beliefs about the Court's duty to protect liberty. In that project, Kennedy is a generative constitutional theorist, willing to work with raw principles of liberty, equality, and dignity to address the great questions of our age. He is also exquisitely attuned to ways in which the Constitution creates a structure of government meant to safeguard our freedom.

Ruth Bader Ginsburg sits to Kennedy's right. Appointed by Bill Clinton, Ginsburg moved across town from the D.C. Circuit Court of Appeals and took her seat on August 10, 1993. Ginsburg's judicial service capped a remarkable career as the nation's premier legal advocate for women's rights, a career in which she argued several Supreme Court cases that established the constitutional basis for rights to gender equality. It is especially fitting, then, that several of Ginsburg's most influential opinions on the Court have involved sex discrimination.[39] Yet Ginsburg's interests are wide ranging; before she became a judge, she taught civil procedure at Columbia Law School, and she remains keenly attuned to the mechanics of justice.

Ginsburg can be reserved and soft-spoken in public, but she is known and respected among her colleagues for her formidable intellect, boundless energy, and active exercise regimen. (Her trainer has been known to push other justices by pointing out that she lifts more than they do.) Though she has a lively sense of humor, Ginsburg is professional, polite, and extraordinarily precise in her opinions and questions. She cares deeply about the role of the Court and frequently speaks about the need to find a balance between advancing constitutional values and respecting the democratic process. Ginsburg is herself a vocal participant in a dialogue with the other branches; on several occasions, she has openly (and successfully) called on Congress to reverse what she sees as grievous errors in the Court's sex discrimination rulings. In recent years, as the senior left-leaning justice, Ginsburg has emerged as a savvy and respected leader—and has written a number of celebrated dissents in health care, affirmative action, and voting rights cases.

Next comes Samuel A. Alito Jr., who joined the Court on January 31, 2006, after George W. Bush nominated him to replace Sandra Day O'Connor. Alito was born in Trenton, New Jersey, and raised in a nearby suburb. A stellar career led him through Reagan's Department of Justice, the role of top federal prosecutor in New Jersey, and a federal appellate judgeship. Along the way, he developed a brand of cautious conservatism— a belief that law and practices developed in bygone eras merit substantial respect but should not be mindlessly embraced. He strongly respects tradition, though he acknowledges that distinctly modern challenges may call for innovations. He values individual rights, but he cares deeply about respecting community and inherited social structures. On the Court, Alito has emerged as an unabashed critic of overreliance on originalism and an advocate for "law and order" approaches to criminal justice. He is also a devastating questioner; in 2010, Jan Crawford of CBS wrote that "he's like a one-justice Delta Force: he's so quiet and low-key while draw-ing in the lawyers with his questions that he manages to plant several bombs before they even realize he's on the attack."[40]

Although usually serious and direct at argument, Alito is known for a gentle, pointed wit. At a highbrow dinner in 2012, for example, he deli-cately summarized the facts of a free speech case involving Nicole Richie, asking, "Have you ever tried to get cow bleep out of a Prada purse, it's not so bleeping simple."[41] Alito also has a gift for literary and artistic images that drive home his points. In a case about public monuments and the many messages they can simultaneously convey, he reached out to a famous cultural icon: the "Greco-Roman mosaic of the word 'Imagine' that was donated to New York City's Central Park in memory of John Lennon." Alito noted that some observers of that mosaic might "imagine" the "musical contributions that John Lennon would have made if he had not been killed." Others, though, might instead recall the lyrics of Lennon's famous song and "imagine" a world "without religion, countries, posses-sions, greed, or hunger."[42] Alito then used this double meaning to make a strong legal argument.

Seated at the far right side of the bench, Elena Kagan is the Roberts Court's junior justice. Appointed by Barack Obama and sworn in on August 7, 2010, Kagan is the only current justice who wasn't previously a judge, and she therefore brings valuable diversity to the Court. Kagan made her name as an adviser to Bill Clinton, the Dean of Harvard Law School, and the Solicitor General under Obama. In each capacity, she developed a reputation for brilliance, good judgment, and an uncanny ability to build bridges with those of different views. Her famous humor was on full display at her confirmation hearing, where she responded to a senator's question about where she was on Christmas: "You know, like all Jews, I was probably at a Chinese restaurant."

That poker-faced charm remains undimmed by Kagan's service on the Court; in 2011, she cheerfully introduced an intimidating opinion by observing, "If you understand anything I say here, you will likely be a lawyer, and you will have had your morning cup of coffee." Kagan has already earned plaudits for her straightforward, highly readable prose style and her streak of real-world pragmatism. Her views on many issues, though, remain unclear—partly because they are still developing and partly because Kagan has held her cards close to the chest, writing fewer separate opinions than any other justice each year since she joined the Court. The revelation of Kagan's principal concerns and distinctive views of constitutional law has only just begun.

This is a tale of nine powerful personalities, nine distinctive worldviews, all brought to bear on the triumphs and travails of the American people. Confirmed to the Court for life and vested with great influence over how we understand and implement the Constitution, the justices can frame the way we live. Through their votes and opinions, through acts of sheer lawmaking and the subtler powers of persuasion, they address many of the burning issues of our age. Their rulings reverberate backward and forward in time but also influence the most mundane aspects of the here and now: whom we can marry, what guns we can buy, where our children go to school, and whether we can be compelled to buy health insurance. They shape both global affairs and our most intimate privacy.

The story of the Roberts Court is thus more than just the narrative of a single institution. It is also essential to the story of "We the People" and our ongoing efforts to "form a more perfect Union, establish Justice, insure domestic Tranquility, provide for the common defence, promote the general Welfare, and secure the Blessings of Liberty to ourselves and our Posterity." It is a story marked by uncertainty, but one all the more thrilling for its lack of a predetermined outcome. As the justices of the Roberts Court sit around their conference table and make law, the destiny of millions of Americans—those who live today and those still to come—rests heavily on their shoulders. This is a mighty burden. But nobody ever said that establishing justice was easy.

1

EQUALITY:

ARE WE THERE YET?

On January 6, 2011, the Constitution of the United States was read aloud in the House of Representatives for the first time in American history. The text of our founding charter had been entered into the *Congressional Record* twice before, in 1882 and 1915, but never had it received spoken life. It was a marvelous scene to behold. As one observer described it, "Sentence by sentence, in accents that reflect the myriad districts that did not even exist when the document came into being, by women and African Americans whose full rights were not recognized at that time, the constitutional language fluttered through the chamber."[1]

This was an act of political partisanship, a showy statement by the newly elected Republican majority in the House that respect for law had been restored to the Capitol. But its symbolic power was too great for such a minor purpose. Not even blatantly partisan motives could break the spell of destiny that overcame the chamber as centuries-old words of creation echoed in the halls of Congress.

The moment was marred, however, by the House's decision to exclude sections of the Constitution that have since been superseded by amendment. This choice left whole swaths of America's past unmentioned. The most glaring omission was Article I, Section 2—the infamous "Three-Fifths Clause," which counted black slaves as "three fifths" of a person for purposes of deciding how many representatives in Congress each state received. The stormy days of Prohibition, an experiment that dramatically upended American life in the 1920s, also fell by the wayside.[2]

Derided by many as an inept concession to political correctness, this whitewashing of our basic charter betrayed a more profound error. It neglected the powerful truth expressed in Omar Khayyám's deathless lines: "The moving finger writes, and having writ, moves on. Nor all your piety nor wit shall lure it back to cancel half a line, nor all your tears wipe out a word of it."[3] Every letter of the Constitution is part of our national experience. As the Civil War drew to a bloody close, America did not erase references to its sins. Rather, it enacted new amendments to forever banish slavery and promise "equal protection of the laws." The very text of the Constitution admits abomination and strives toward redemption.[4]

Thus, when Justice Robert Jackson described the rejection of coerced orthodoxy as a "fixed star in our constitutional constellation," he suggested a many-layered truth.[5] The text of the Constitution, like the night sky, is composed of elements drawn from strikingly different eras in our history. Prohibition is imposed and repealed. Slavery is recognized, regulated, and abolished. The Fourteenth Amendment safeguards voting rights for "male[s] . . . being twenty-one years of age," while the Nineteenth Amendment protects women's suffrage and the Twenty-sixth Amendment lowers the voting age to eighteen. Article II provides that the runner-up in a presidential election becomes vice president—a rule altered by the Twelfth Amendment, passed after Thomas Jefferson was forced to serve under his rival, John Adams. Americans have not erased provisions that we have come to view as misguided; instead, we have added new amendments. As a result, the text tells a story. It may be only a small and selective part of our national tale, as we rarely amend the Constitution, but it's a powerful vision in its own right.

This uneasy coexistence of past and present has always been a fact of American life. The Constitution is not a thing of levers and pulleys, a clockwork universe that mechanically drives us along a predetermined path to a preselected future. Nor is it a flash-frozen remnant of history, reaching out with its dead hand to make sure we stick firmly to a path marked in 1789. Rather, it's the lived framework for an ongoing debate over how best to approximate our national ideals. It anchors us in the past, guides us in the present, and offers shared aspirations for the future.[6]

No issue poses harder questions about what the Constitution means than racial equality. George Santayana warned that "a country without a memory is a country of madmen,"[7] but where does that leave a country bristling with incompatible memories? Reflecting on slavery, Jim Crow, *Brown v. Board of Education*, and the civil rights movement, Americans often talk right past each other.[8] Is the lesson of our history that we must never allow government to classify based on race, or that we may recognize race in a benign manner to remedy past injustice and achieve diversity? Have we moved far enough past a legacy of racism that the federal government can no longer justify special measures to protect minority voters in the South? What does it mean to aim for equality under the law when people are still judged by the color of their skin? These questions divide the American public, as do questions about the scope of the problem: in 2013, 79 percent of blacks thought that America had to do "a lot more" to achieve racial equality, but only 44 percent of whites agreed with that assessment.[9]

Differences of opinion on these hard issues often reflect the fact that competing views of history shape the meaning we discern in current events. As Barack Obama explained in candid remarks after the Trayvon Martin trial in 2013, "I think it's important to recognize that the African American community is looking at this issue through a set of experiences and a history that doesn't go away."[10] His statement echoed William Faulkner's famous line "The past is never dead. It's not even past."[11] This is true for all Americans: our national experience of race, past and present, partakes of a history "that doesn't go away."

At the Court, partisans on every side of debates over affirmative action, school desegregation, and voting rights have long enlisted the Constitution in their cause. The justices, in turn, have fractured into camps that spare no quarter when combat is joined. In the first major affirmative action case, decided in 1978, Justice Harry Blackmun argued that "in order to get beyond racism, we must first take account of race."[12] His view has inherited powerful contemporary champions in Justices Ginsburg, Breyer, Sotomayor, and Kagan. Chief Justice Roberts, along with Justices Scalia, Thomas, and Alito, couldn't disagree more strongly. "The whole point of the Equal Protection Clause," Roberts declared in 2013, "is to take race off the table."[13] Justice Kennedy, meanwhile, has charted a third path focused on carefully limiting when and how government policies can invoke race.[14]

This struggle has unfolded alongside another chapter in our tale of equality: the progress of gay rights in American life and law. While the story of race in America stretches back centuries, the gay rights movement emerged and rocketed to prominence in little more than a generation. As Kennedy told a group of law students in 2013, "Most of us, even in your own young lifetimes, probably didn't talk much about it. . . . I think all of us were surprised at the speed of the thing."[15]

Now many gay rights advocates wonder when, not whether, they can persuade the Court to recognize a right to marriage equality. How much longer, they ask, will an issue implicating fundamental rights continue to be put up for a vote? Given that a majority of Americans supports same-sex marriage, why wait?[16] Many others feel differently. Moved by hostility to same-sex marriage or a belief that this question should be left to voters, they argue that the Court must not arrogate to itself the final word.

Equality is an explosive principle on the Roberts Court. Born in different eras and of different worlds, the justices disagree over where we have been, where we are, and where we should go. They also disagree over their legitimate role in bringing about an imagined future. These divisions have erupted in opinions striking down key parts of both the Voting Rights Act and the Defense of Marriage Act. They have also reshaped the rules that govern school desegregation and affirmative action.

Still, the story of equality and the Roberts Court has really only just begun. Ultimately, decisions made by this Court may define what "Equal Protection of the Laws" means in the twenty-first century.

Discrimination takes many forms, but in *Calhoun v. United States*, a federal drug case from 2011, it seemed unmistakable.[17] Frustrated with defendant Bongani Calhoun's evasive answers, the prosecutor had asked a shocking question during cross-examination: "You've got African-Americans, you've got Hispanics, you've got a bag full of money. Does that tell you—a light bulb doesn't go off in your head and say, This is a drug deal?" The Court refused to hear an appeal in *Calhoun*, but in a rare move, Sotomayor wrote a brief statement to emphasize that "such argumentation is an affront to the Constitution's guarantee of equal protection of the laws." The prosecutor, she warned, had "tapped a deep and sorry vein of racial prejudice." She added, "I hope never to see a case like this again."

The federal prosecutor in *Calhoun* drew Sotomayor's condemnation because he had invoked a pejorative racial stereotype that could inflame a jury into convicting. In general, such racial discrimination by any agent of the state prompts a straightforward resolution: we do not allow the government to deploy harmful racial classifications.

It's easy to take this principle for granted. Yet for most of American history, the law regularly discriminated on the basis of race. It did so not just in the era of slavery but well into the twentieth century—long after the Constitution was amended in 1868 to safeguard equality. As Obama recalled in 2008, change required "Americans in successive generations who were willing to do their part—through protests and struggle, on the streets and in the courts, through a civil war and civil disobedience and always at great risk—to narrow that gap between the promise of our ideals and the reality of their time."[18] Only in the mid-twentieth century, after a massive civil rights struggle, did America finally embrace the view that government may not invoke racial classifications to harm minorities.

That triumph, however, did not undo centuries of oppression.[19] To quote Obama again: "Many of the disparities that exist in the African-American community today can be directly traced to inequalities passed on from an earlier generation that suffered under the brutal legacy of slavery and Jim Crow." These disparities are, in part, the result of segregated and inferior schools, rules that prevented blacks from owning property or obtaining mortgages, race-based exclusions from universities, denials of social services, and abuses in the criminal justice system. They are also the result of subtler but no less invidious forms of discrimination that persist through the present day. This does not mean America is defined solely by its past, or that modern Americans lack responsibility for their fate. But it does mean that any realistic account of the racial divides in American life must account for the ripples and aftershocks of legalized prejudice.

This is especially true of racially segregated education. In 1954, the Court famously abolished "separate but equal" schools in *Brown*. But desegregation did not follow fast on *Brown*'s heels. Indeed, the Court intentionally allowed the South to move very slowly—"with all deliberate speed"—in desegregating its public schools.[20] Since then, the Court has walked a tortuous path.[21] After a general retreat that lasted until the late 1960s, it returned to the fray and told judges to integrate school districts as a remedy for official discrimination. In 1974, however, the Court limited school busing across city boundaries, a rule that stalled integration efforts at a time of rising residential segregation between inner cities and suburbs. Then, in the early 1990s, the Court signaled that lower courts ought to return such matters to local control.

These and other trends have led to re-segregation. As a landmark study concluded in 2007, "U.S. schools are becoming more segregated in all regions for both African American and Latino students."[22]

Some districts have responded to the perceived evils of segregation by adopting race-based integration plans. In 2007, the Roberts Court faced a challenge to programs in Seattle, Washington, and Jefferson County, Kentucky. Both districts allowed students to rank which schools they wished to attend. In Seattle, if a school was oversubscribed, race was used as a tiebreaker to keep each school close to the district's white-nonwhite racial balance. In Jefferson County, elementary school students listed preferences among a cluster of non-magnet schools. Students were then assigned schools based on those preferences, subject to the rule that each school had to maintain a black enrollment of between 15 and 50 percent.

In *Parents Involved in Community Schools v. Seattle School District No. 1*, the Court struck down both programs.[23] Roberts, Thomas, Kennedy, Breyer, and Stevens each wrote separately, turning *Parents Involved* into a landmark case on the true meaning of *Brown* and racial equality under the Constitution. Their opinions mark the broad outlines of where this Court may steer the nation in the years ahead.

Roberts has long frowned on race-conscious programs. As far back as the 1980s, he spoke warmly of the Reagan administration's "anti-busing and anti-quota principles," warning of "reverse discrimination" against whites.[24] On the Court, Roberts has forcefully condemned the "sordid business" of "divvying us up by race."[25] Whereas he usually prefers to write narrow rulings, Roberts has assigned himself most of the high-profile race cases and issued sweeping statements of principle.

In *Parents Involved*, Roberts championed a color-blind constitution, one that forbids government from using racial classifications—even when the goal is to benefit minorities.[26] Quoting precedent, Roberts argued that "distinctions between citizens solely because of their ancestry are by their very nature odious to a free people whose institutions are founded upon the doctrine of equality." Any use of race by government, he maintained, "reinforce[s] the belief, held by too many for too much of our history, that individuals should be judged by the color of their skin."

Claiming *Brown*'s mantle, Roberts insisted that "history will be heard." In his telling, *Brown* was not about "the inequality of the facilities but the fact of legally separating children on the basis of race." Seattle and Jefferson County had thus violated *Brown*'s core holding: "Before *Brown*, schoolchildren were told where they could and could not go to school based on the color of their skin. The school districts in these cases have not carried the heavy burden of demonstrating that we should allow this once again—even for very different reasons."

To Roberts, allowing schools to use race in assigning students, whatever the reason, would ensure that the "ultimate goal of eliminating entirely from governmental decisionmaking such irrelevant factors as a human being's race will never be achieved." There are many ways for American society to confront its legacy of racism, but the Chief sees in the Constitution a command that government be color-blind. In a memorable final line, Roberts summed up his view: "The way to stop discrimination on the basis of race is to stop discriminating on the basis of race."

As he so often does in race cases, Thomas wrote separately. Even those who disagree with him cannot deny that the Court has benefited from his remarkable string of solo opinions. In these essays, Thomas has drawn on a rich vein of American social thought to argue that even well-intentioned uses of race by the government ultimately harm minorities.

Parents Involved also evoked powerful memories for Thomas. In his gripping autobiography, *My Grandfather's Son*, he described his reaction to forced busing in the early 1970s: "As I watched TV pictures of black children being bused into South Boston, it was clear that the situation had reached the point of total absurdity. *I* wouldn't have gone to South Boston. It would have been taking my life into my hands for me to do so. Why, then, were innocent children being made to do what a grown man feared—and to what end?"[27] Even in his youth, it had been clear to Thomas that "once again blacks were being offered up as human sacrifices to the great god of theory. . . . In the seventies you rarely had to look very far to find a theory, or a black person on whom it was being tried out."[28]

In *Parents Involved*, Thomas warned that allowing even "benign" racial policies is an invitation to disaster: "If our history has taught us anything, it has taught us to beware of elites bearing racial theories. . . . Can we really be sure that the racial theories that motivated [segregationists] are a relic of the past or that future theories will be nothing but beneficent and progressive? That is a gamble I am unwilling to take, and it is one the Constitution does not allow." Thomas then likened the arguments in support of the challenged programs to those favored by segregationists and cuttingly replied that "what was wrong in 1954 cannot be right today." Seattle and Jefferson County "would permit measures to keep the races together and proscribe measures to keep the races apart." For Thomas, as for Roberts, the color-blind Constitution stripped them of that prerogative.

Although Thomas usually prides himself on a firm commitment to originalism, race cases direct his attention mainly to 1954. Employing what Stanford Law Professor Pam Karlan has described as "*Brown* originalism," Thomas, like many other justices, spends far more time exploring first principles as defined in *Brown* than he does explaining what Americans thought when they ratified the Equal Protection Clause in 1868.[29] This does not make his opinions any less powerful, but his approach may reflect the fact that many historians believe that the original understanding of the Equal Protection Clause is compatible with at least some benign race-based programs.[30]

On the day in June 2007 when *Parents Involved* was announced, Breyer read his dissent from the bench. The former law professor spoke for twenty-one minutes, his voice strained with fury. "The majority is wrong," he said. "This is a decision that the court and the Nation will come to regret."

The Chief's logic in *Parents Involved* offended Breyer on just about every level. To Breyer, only by mutilating the Constitution and stripping it of history could we make it color-blind. The Equal Protection Clause, he argued, "sought to bring into American society as full members those whom the Nation had previously held in slavery. . . . Those who drafted an Amendment with this basic purpose in mind would have understood the legal and practical difference between the use of race-conscious criteria in defiance of that purpose, namely to keep the races apart, and the use of race-conscious criteria to further that purpose, namely to bring the races together." Breyer reasoned that the Constitution protects against the subordination of minorities but permits government to invoke race when it has solid justifications and beneficial purposes.

In Seattle and Jefferson County, Breyer saw three overpowering reasons for the local policies: (1) a remedial interest in "setting right the consequences of prior conditions of segregation"; (2) an educational interest in "overcoming the adverse educational effects produced by and associated with highly segregated schools"; and (3) a democratic interest in "teaching children to engage in the kind of cooperation among Americans of all races that is necessary to make a land of three hundred million people one Nation." The Constitution, he argued, can tolerate a political choice to use racial tools in service to these worthy goals.

Breyer presented himself as *Brown*'s true heir: "*Brown* held out a promise. It was a promise embodied in three Amendments designed to make citizens of slaves. It was the promise of true racial equality—not as a matter of fine words on paper, but as a matter of everyday life in the Nation's cities and schools. It was about the nature of a democracy that must work for all Americans. It sought one law, one Nation, one people, not simply as a matter of legal principle but in terms of how we actually live."

Breyer viewed *Brown* through the lens of his yearning for workable principles in the face of real-world necessities. In much the same way, he saw *Parents Involved* as a case about much more than race, though racial equality was central to the outcome. It was a case about the very nature of the Constitution—and about the judicial role in making democracy work. Breyer was bracingly candid on this score: "I do not claim to know how best to stop harmful discrimination; how best to create a society that includes all Americans; how best to overcome our serious problems of increasing *de facto* segregation, troubled inner city schooling, and poverty correlated with race. But, as a judge, I do know that the Constitution does not authorize judges to dictate solutions to these problems."

Stevens joined Breyer's dissent and added a few trenchant, personal thoughts of his own. "It is my firm conviction," he wrote, "that no Member of the Court that I joined in 1975 would have agreed with today's decision." Stevens was particularly troubled by the "cruel irony" of Roberts's claim that *Parents Involved* was just like *Brown*, simply because in both cases "schoolchildren were told where they could and could not go to school based on the color of their skin." As Stevens remarked, "This sentence reminds me of Anatole France's observation: 'The majestic equality of the law, forbids rich and poor alike to sleep under bridges, to beg in the streets, and to steal their bread.' The Chief Justice fails to note that it was only black schoolchildren who were so ordered; indeed, the history books do not tell stories of white children struggling to attend black schools. In this and other ways, the Chief Justice rewrites the history of one of this Court's most important decisions."

While Roberts and Thomas preached the virtues of color blindness, and Breyer and Stevens pushed back, Kennedy charted a middle ground. Although he had historically taken a hard line against racial classifications, in *Parents Involved* he displayed considerable sympathy for the liberal positions. He acknowledged that, although "the enduring hope is that race should not matter, the reality is that too often it does." Then, faced with the Chief's call to simply ban all racial discrimination, Kennedy described it as "too dismissive of the legitimate interest government has in ensuring all people have equal opportunity regardless of their race." He added that "fifty years of experience since *Brown v. Board of Education* should teach us that the problem before us defies so easy a solution."

Kennedy voted to strike down the programs before the Court, but he could not agree with Roberts and Thomas that "the Constitution mandates that state and local school authorities must accept the status quo of racial isolation in schools." Wary of boundless justifications for racial balancing, however, Kennedy proposed a different sort of limit. While districts may not classify students based on race, they can use "indirect means," such as strategic choices about where to build new schools, race-conscious drawing of attendance zones, and targeted recruiting of students and faculty.

In sum, Kennedy agreed that schools have a compelling interest in avoiding racial isolation. But he disagreed with the methods used by Seattle and Jefferson County. As he explained, "The idea that if race is the problem, race is the instrument with which to solve it cannot be accepted." There are good reasons, he added, to look with particular skepticism on classifying individuals by race: "Crude measures of this sort threaten to reduce children to racial chits valued and traded according to one school's supply and another's demand." His proposed alternatives, which take race into account at a more general level, partly avoid that evil. To Kennedy, they ensure that "the individual, child or adult, can find his own identity, can define her own persona, without state intervention that classifies on the basis of his race or the color of her skin." None of the eight other justices, however, viewed this compromise as satisfactory.

In practice, *Parents Involved* did not radically alter the landscape of educational segregation in America.[31] Many districts had largely abandoned integration programs, focusing instead on closing the achievement gap, enhancing school choice, providing access to preschool, and undertaking other education reforms. Districts committed to racial integration, moreover, can still draw on the substantial tool kit described by Kennedy, though residential segregation remains a daunting barrier to any such integrative project.

Parents Involved is nonetheless profoundly important as a statement about the meaning of equality in the modern world. Roberts and Thomas believe that state-sponsored integration is reminiscent of segregation, a comparison that has inspired fury and sadness in many civil rights leaders.[32] These justices see a clear, color-blind line that runs from *Brown* toward a future free of race-based policies. They see a society that has made enough progress to close the door on race-based remedies for past discrimination. They know where America is going, where the Constitution *requires* it to go, and will use every power at hand to make that future a reality. Breyer's mighty dissent challenges this vision of America's past, present, and future. He and those who share his view maintain that to overcome racism, and to build a decent society on the ruins of what a history of discrimination has left us, we may first need to account for race.

Each side in this contest sees itself as the inheritor of a grand historical project through which America may find redemption for its original sins—and each thinks the other side may return us to the evils of that demon-haunted past. At its heart, *Parents Involved* is a case about the Roberts Court grappling with the uncertain aim of our national trajectory.

In June 2003, Justice Sandra Day O'Connor wrote for a bare majority in *Grutter v. Bollinger* to uphold affirmative action under the Equal Protection Clause.[33] Although schools may not use race quotas, she ruled, they may consider a student's race as part of a holistic inquiry designed to achieve diversity by enrolling a critical mass of minority students. But O'Connor did not think her opinion would be the final word on affirmative action. In a coda, she warned that such programs are justified by interests that will not last forever: "We expect that 25 years from now, the use of racial preferences will no longer be necessary."

In June 2013, one day after *Grutter*'s ten-year anniversary, the Court announced its ruling in *Fisher v. University of Texas at Austin*.[34] The university admitted most students without any express consideration of race and achieved a measure of diversity by accepting all Texas students who graduated in the top 10 percent of their high school class. To secure what it considered to be a "critical mass" of diversity, the university then used race as one of several factors when it filled the rest of its class. Abigail Fisher argued that the university thereby violated the Equal Protection Clause. She had good reason to expect a warm reception at the Court. Since *Grutter*, Alito had replaced O'Connor, creating a five-justice block of votes for a narrowing—or outright elimination—of affirmative action.

The instant Roberts called the case, spectators gripped their seats. *Fisher* had been argued in October; every other case heard that month had been decided by late April. Court watchers speculated about behind-the-scenes maneuvering, perhaps even a reversal of *Grutter*.[35] Indeed, at oral argument, Breyer had pressed Fisher's lawyer, nervously joking that "*Grutter* said it would be good law for at least 25 years . . . and I know that time flies, but I think only nine of those years have passed."

With Kagan recused, the best the university could hope for was a four-to-four tie, which would affirm the lower court ruling in its favor. But all signs pointed toward a loss. The only questions seemed to be how big a loss and why was it taking the Court so long to decide. The Court's drawn-out struggle with *Fisher*, though, should not have been surprising, especially since affirmative action hits several justices close to home.

In his memoir, Thomas offers a scathing indictment of affirmative action. Acknowledging that race played a role in his admission to Yale Law School, Thomas describes the experience as a painful one: "I felt as though I'd been tricked, that some of the people who claimed to be helping me were in fact hurting me."[36] The "paternalistic big-city whites," he adds, "offered you a helping hand so long as you were careful to agree with them, but slapped you down if you started acting as if you didn't know your place."

At Yale, Thomas worked hard to "vanquish the perception that [he] was somehow inferior to [his] white classmates." Nonetheless, he recalls that "it was futile for me to suppose that I could escape the stigmatizing effects of racial preference, and I began to fear that it would be used forever after to discount my achievements."[37] Thomas blames affirmative action for these humiliations; "racial preference had robbed [his] achievement of its true value."[38] In interviews, Thomas has said that this stigma pursued him onto the Court. "Once it is assumed that everything you do achieve is because of your race," he warns, "there is no way out."[39]

Sotomayor also benefited from race-conscious admissions when she applied to Princeton and Yale Law School. She has described herself as "a product of affirmative action," recognizing that she was admitted despite lower standardized test scores.[40] But unlike Thomas, she does not disparage that outcome: "I had no need to apologize that the look-wider, search-more affirmative action that Princeton and Yale practiced had opened doors for me. That was its purpose: to create the conditions whereby students from disadvantaged backgrounds could be brought to the starting line of a race many were unaware was even being run."[41] To Sotomayor, affirmative action is not to blame when others diminish her accomplishments. Rather, "to doubt the worth of minority students' achievement when they succeed is really only to present another face of the prejudice that would deny them a chance even to try."[42] While Sotomayor recognizes that race-conscious admissions policies present hard questions, she has emphasized that "for me, it was a door-opener that changed the course of my life."[43]

Sotomayor, though, faced painful challenges. Reflecting on Princeton in the 1970s, she described it as "an environment where an undercurrent of hostility often belied the idyllic surface."[44] The campus paper "routinely published letters to the editor lamenting the presence on campus of 'affirmative action students,' each one of whom had presumably displaced a far more deserving affluent white male and could rightly be expected to crash into the gutter built of her own unrealistic aspirations." With these "vultures circling," Sotomayor recalls facing "relentless" pressure to succeed.

Alito, who graduated from Princeton in 1972, just four years before Sotomayor, also developed views on affirmative action early in his career. Just over a decade after graduating, in a bid for promotion at the Reagan

Department of Justice, Alito wrote that he was "particularly proud" of his work developing arguments "that racial and ethnic quotas should not be allowed."[45]

Of course, affirmative action isn't always about race. While Alito and Sotomayor were still undergraduates, Ginsburg argued a series of Supreme Court cases that first established constitutional rights to sex equality. As co-founder and director of the Women's Rights Project at the ACLU, she spent much of her career championing equal rights for women—an issue that has, for the most part, remained conspicuously absent from the Roberts Court docket of constitutional cases.

After O'Connor retired in 2006, Ginsburg was the only woman left on the Court, an experience she has since described as "almost like being back in law school in 1956, when there were 9 of us in a class of over 500."[46] After Obama nominated Sotomayor, Ginsburg acknowledged that she would be thrilled not to "be the lone woman around this place."[47] And when asked about Sotomayor's self-description as a product of affirmative action, Ginsburg pointedly replied, "So am I." After all, she explained, "I was the first tenured woman at Columbia." She had been hired because of pressure to add women professors. "But when I got to Columbia," she recalls, "I was well regarded by my colleagues. . . . They backed me up."

Spectators and journalists alike were surprised by the Court's ruling in *Fisher* on that June day in 2013: by a vote of seven to one, the justices refused to render a final verdict on the university's admissions program. Rather, in an opinion by Kennedy, the Court ruled that a lower court had erred when it had deferred to the university's insistence that consideration of race was necessary to achieve diversity. Under *Grutter*, courts defer to a university's "educational judgment" that diversity is "essential to its educational mission." But once a university decides to pursue diversity, *Fisher* requires it to prove in court "that the means chosen by the University to attain diversity are narrowly tailored to that goal." Specifically, judges must "ultimately be satisfied that no workable race-neutral alternatives would produce the educational benefits of diversity." With this new statement of the law, Kennedy sent *Fisher* back to the Fifth Circuit Court of Appeals so that lower court judges could reevaluate the university's admissions policy.

Fisher afforded Kennedy an opportunity to turn part of his *Grutter* dissent into a majority opinion. In *Grutter*, he had explained that forcing schools "to seriously explore race-neutral alternatives" would focus their "talents and resources" on "devising new and fairer ways to ensure individual consideration." These race-neutral programs, he argued, might achieve diversity while avoiding "preferment by race," which "can be the most divisive of all policies, containing within it the potential to destroy confidence in the Constitution and in the idea of equality."

In *Grutter*, *Parents Involved*, and *Fisher*, Kennedy rejected absolute arguments for a color-blind constitution. He recognized that ensuring diversity and thwarting racial isolation are important enough interests to sometimes outweigh a presumption against racial classification. But his openness to "benign" classifications came with a catch: because, as he sees it, governmental use of race is *always* dangerous, the Constitution imposes a harm-mitigation rule. Government must prove that the use of race to achieve its goals is strictly necessary—and that it has made as indirect and minor a use of race as possible. In Kennedy's view, this requirement mitigates the damage of invoking race and it sets government on a path toward little or no use of race-based measures at all.

Kennedy's opinion attracted some surprising signatories: Roberts, Alito, Breyer, and Sotomayor. This unusual coalition suggests that Kennedy's draft may have emerged from tense internal negotiations as the only one that could win five votes, and that his colleagues on the left and right joined it to avert a cacophony of separate, divisive writings.

Thomas and Scalia joined Kennedy's majority too, but they wrote separately to clarify that they still believe government must be color-blind. Scalia kept his concurrence to three sentences, but his views are well-known from earlier opinions: "To pursue the concept of racial entitlement—even for the most admirable and benign of purposes—is to reinforce and preserve for future mischief the way of thinking that produced race slavery, race privilege and race hatred. In the eyes of government, we are just one race here. It is American."[48] Faced with affirmative action cases, Scalia has displayed particular sensitivity to the race-based resentment that such discrimination engenders among whites. Thus, at argument in *Grutter*, he remarked, "The people you want to talk to are the high school seniors who have seen people visibly less qualified than they are get into prestigious institutions where they are rejected. If you think that is not creating resentment, you are just wrong."

Thomas's opinion in *Fisher* offered further evidence of his deep-seated opposition to all affirmative action. "Every time the government places citizens on racial registers," he wrote, "it demeans us all." No court, he added, "would accept the suggestion that segregation is permissible because historically black colleges produced Booker T. Washington, Thurgood Marshall, [or] Martin Luther King, Jr." And rightly so: "No benefit in the eye of the beholder can justify racial discrimination."

In a section likely shaped by his own experiences, Thomas ripped into "the benighted notion that it is possible to tell when discrimination helps, rather than hurts, racial minorities." In his words, "The worst forms of discrimination in this Nation have always been accompanied by straight-faced representations that discrimination helped minorities." Here Thomas invoked history: "Slaveholders argued that slavery was a 'positive good' that civilized blacks and elevated them in every dimension of life," and segregationists said that "separate schools protected black children from racist white students and teachers." Then, as now, advocates of discrimination were wrong: "Racial discrimination is never benign." It results, Thomas argued, in the admission of students who struggle to compete and emerge with tainted accomplishments.

Even as her left-leaning colleagues joined Kennedy, almost certainly for tactical reasons, Ginsburg would have none of it. Drawing a line in the sand, she composed a powerful dissent.

Ginsburg has long supported affirmative action. In 2003, she argued that "we are not far distant from an overtly discriminatory past, and the effects of centuries of law-sanctioned inequality remain painfully evident in our communities and schools."[49] Against that historical background, "actions designed to burden groups long denied full citizenship stature are not sensibly ranked with measures taken to hasten the day when entrenched discrimination and its aftereffects have been extirpated." Quoting Judge John Minor Wisdom, a civil rights hero and an iconic jurist, Ginsburg reasoned that "the Constitution is both color blind and color conscious. To avoid conflict with the equal protection clause, a classification that denies a benefit, causes harm, or imposes a burden must not be based on race. In that sense, the Constitution is color blind. But the Constitution is color conscious to prevent discrimination being perpetuated and to undo the effects of past discrimination."

In *Fisher*, Ginsburg attacked Kennedy's compromise position. She had spent her career trying to persuade the Court to speak openly about a form of discrimination once shrouded in silence. Kennedy's insistence on what she saw as deliberate obfuscation struck her as absurd. "Only an ostrich," she caustically remarked, "could regard the supposedly race neutral alternatives as race unconscious." Driving home the point, Ginsburg borrowed sarcasm from 1935: "The notion that Texas' Top Ten Percent Law is race neutral calls to mind Professor Thomas Reed Powell's famous statement: 'If you think that you can think about a thing inextricably attached to something else without thinking of the thing which it is attached to, then you have a legal mind.' Only that kind of legal mind could conclude that an admissions plan specifically designed to produce racial diversity is not race conscious." Surely, Ginsburg exclaimed, we should favor honest dialogue about race over "camouflage."

Indeed, Ginsburg might have added that true race neutrality could well prove impossible. In telling their story, applicants of all sorts (and their recommenders) draw on personal experiences. In some cases, those experiences include overcoming racial discrimination, navigating issues of race and identity, or celebrating racial self-understanding. Students may be drawn to law, for example, after seeing too many people who look like them get "randomly" stopped and frisked. Forcing schools to blind themselves to any hint of race could push them to distort their review of applications. In a world that still sees, feels, and cares about color, court-ordered color blindness can produce awkward, race-conscious results.

Kennedy's opinion, though, is now the law of the land. It allows race-based affirmative action, but only when a school can prove that race is critical to achieving diversity. Schools must prove that point, moreover, to federal judges—plenty of whom will look doubtfully on their position and require them to disprove the adequacy of other methods. This may be hard to do, especially when available data are inconclusive.

The main effect of *Fisher* will therefore be to direct attention toward race-neutral means of ensuring diversity. Common proposals include preferences for low-income students or students from low-income neigh-borhoods, partnerships between colleges and disadvantaged high schools, the elimination of legacy-based admissions, expanded financial aid bud-gets, and top 10 percent programs like the one reviewed in *Fisher*. Many of these options seek to exploit correlations between race and income or race and geography. A scholarly battle already rages over whether income and geography are close enough proxies for race, and whether any of the leading alternatives to race-based affirmative action will suffice to create a "critical mass" of racial diversity.[50]

Some see *Fisher* as an opportunity to enshrine a new era of durable programs that ensure diversity and focus on economic disadvantage.[51] These commentators point out that race-based affirmative action is deeply unpopular and has already been banned in several states. Others warn, as the *New York Times* did, that replacing race with class "may simply reinforce stereotypes within the student body that will equate minority students with poverty, masking both the economic (and ideological) diversity within minority communities but also the challenges that con-front white working-class students."[52] Race, many add, cannot simply be reduced to class. Race has its own history, meaning, and importance.[53]

Whatever its promise and pitfalls, *Fisher* marks a turning point for affirmative action. It allows schools to value racial diversity but scowls at explicit consideration of race. Ginsburg saw this as Janus-faced logic, and her dissent offers a strong case for candor. Kennedy, though, did not see it that way. As he explained in *Parents Involved*, "If this is a frustrat-ing duality of the Equal Protection Clause it simply reflects the duality of our history and our attempts to promote freedom in a world that some-times seems set against it." Given the strong probability that Roberts and Alito would follow Scalia and Thomas to end all affirmative action, Ken-nedy's view is likely to be the one that matters most on the Court for the foreseeable future.

The Voting Rights Act of 1965 was more than a mere statute. By the early 1960s, America had endured nearly two hundred years of bitter struggle over race and the right to vote. Although the Fifteenth Amendment, rat-ified after the Civil War, commanded that the right to vote not be denied on account of race, bigoted laws and brutal repression in the South had nullified this rule for much of the twentieth century. Even after *Brown*, the right to vote remained off-limits for many southern blacks. Poll taxes, literacy tests, absurd registration rules, and dozens of other horrid innovations stood in the way, as did the threat of violent reprisal. One of the great ambitions of the 1960s civil rights movement was to shatter barriers between blacks and voting booths. At stake was more than individual dignity and America's democratic legitimacy; armed with the right to vote, blacks could empower and protect themselves through the political process.[54]

At first, though, the best efforts of civil rights activists and their allies in the federal government came to naught. It was like battling the Hydra: every law struck down was replaced by one, two, or three more. As civil rights advocates waged a war of attrition against devious and persistent racism, they realized that to win they had to change the state of play.

Against this background, Congress passed the Voting Rights Act (VRA). It was no ordinary law. Men and women had died for it. They had fought on bridges and in churches and in their homes. They had been firebombed and beaten, blasted with water and savaged by attack dogs. Etched into the United States Code by a heady mixture of blood, politics, and principle, the VRA was the crown jewel of the civil rights movement, its best hope for redemption of American democracy. Through it, Congress finally gave life to the Fifteenth Amendment—and to the promise of equal protection embodied in the Fourteenth Amendment. As Lyndon Johnson told Congress in a heartfelt plea for legislation, "Should we defeat every enemy, should we double our wealth and conquer the stars, and still be unequal to this issue, then we will have failed as a people and as a nation."[55]

The VRA was exceptional not only in its birth but also in its method. Its most important provision—Section 5—required certain jurisdictions, mostly in the South, to obtain permission from the federal Department of Justice before putting election laws into effect. This creative "preclearance" rule was meant to prevent local officials from outmaneuvering civil rights litigation. And in most respects it succeeded, as did the rest of the law.[56] A Department of Justice study estimated that in the five years after the VRA was passed, nearly as many blacks registered to vote in Georgia,

Alabama, Louisiana, North Carolina, Mississippi, and South Carolina as in the entire century before 1965.[57] On nearly every front—including registration rates, voter turnout, and minority representation—the VRA achieved its goals.

In 1970, the Court upheld the VRA as an exercise of Congress's power under the Fifteenth Amendment to protect minority voting rights by "appropriate legislation."[58] Congress itself then reconsidered the VRA on several occasions, reauthorizing the law after extensive hearings in 1970, 1975, and 1982. In 2006, Congress again considered reauthorization of the VRA. Since 1982, the Court had narrowed its view of Congress's power to enforce the post–Civil War amendments—the constitutional basis for Section 5 of the VRA.[59] Congress therefore amassed a huge factual record and held extensive hearings to determine whether it should once again reauthorize the VRA preclearance formula and rule.[60] Despite some warnings that the law might be unconstitutional if left unchanged, Congress reauthorized both of those sections of the VRA for another twenty-five years by an overwhelming majority.[61]

By the time he arrived on the Court, Roberts had long opposed the VRA; he had openly professed that view while working for Ronald Reagan's Department of Justice in 1982.[62] To Roberts, Section 5 imposed a substantial burden on covered states that was no longer justified. In the 2009 case of *Northwest Austin Municipal Utility District No. 1 v. Holder* ("*NAMUDNO*"), his opinion for eight justices fired off a warning flare: "Things have changed in the South. Voter turnout and registration rates now approach parity. Blatantly discriminatory evasions of federal decrees are rare."[63] Acknowledging that "these improvements are no doubt due in significant part to the Voting Rights Act itself," Roberts cautioned that "the Act imposes current burdens and must be justified by current needs."

Although the Chief ultimately decided *NAMUDNO* on narrow grounds, he put Congress on clear notice that the VRA's preclearance rule was in peril. He also laid down a cache of legal tools for the future if Congress failed to act. Creating new doctrine, Roberts asserted that America has maintained a "historic tradition that all the States enjoy 'equal sovereignty.'" He then declared that "a departure from the fundamental principles of equal sovereignty requires a showing that a statute's disparate geographic coverage is sufficiently related to the problem that it targets." In other words, Roberts objected that Section 4 of the VRA—its coverage formula—singled out certain states for a weighty burden even though "the evil that Section 5 is meant to address may no longer be concentrated" there. Against claims that the VRA preclearance rule was essential for racial equality in voting rights, Roberts interposed a different kind of equality argument, one focused on equal treatment of the sovereign states at the hand of the federal government.

Congress did not modify the VRA to bring it into line with Roberts's view of the nation's "current needs." Its inaction set the stage for a high-stakes showdown that reached the Court in 2013: *Shelby County v. Holder.*[64]

Viewed as the last stand of Section 5, *Shelby County* unleashed raw emotions on the Court. At argument, the right-leaning justices assailed the VRA coverage formula. Roberts bluntly challenged Solicitor General Don Verrilli, asking, "Is it the government's submission that the citizens in the South are more racist than citizens in the North?" Kennedy, too, made his skepticism plain: "If Alabama wants to have monuments to the heroes of the Civil Rights Movement, if it wants to acknowledge the wrongs of its past, is it better off doing that if it's [its] own independent sovereign or if it's under the trusteeship of the United States Government?" Scalia, though, raised the most eyebrows when he charged that the 2006 reauthorization of Section 5 was "very likely attributable" to "perpetuation of racial entitlement." He added, "I am fairly confident it will be reenacted in perpetuity unless a court can say it does not comport with the Constitution. Even the name of it is wonderful: The Voting Rights Act. Who is going to vote against that in the future?"

The left-leaning justices struck back, accusing their colleagues of overstepping judicial bounds. Sotomayor pressed a lawyer on whether "the right to vote is a racial entitlement in Section 5," adding later, "Why should we make the judgment, and not Congress, about the types and forms of discrimination and the need to remedy them?" Kagan echoed this point while questioning Shelby County's attorney: "Well, that's a big, new power you are giving us, that we have the power now to decide whether racial discrimination has been solved? I did not think that that fell within our bailiwick." Breyer, in turn, bristled at the suggestion that it was improper to target southern states: "What do you think the Civil War was about? Of course it was aimed at treating some States differently than others."

Oral argument in *Shelby County* was heated and dramatic. It was also marked by a profound irony: when Debo Adegbile of the NAACP stood to argue that race discrimination persists in America, his eleven minutes at the podium were the only time a black lawyer addressed the Court in the seventy-five total hours of oral argument it held during the 2012 term.[65]

Unlike *Fisher*, there was no great mystery about *Shelby County*. It was clear that the VRA preclearance requirement was doomed. Roberts wrote the majority opinion and held that the VRA's coverage formula was unconstitutional. Conceding that the VRA had achieved great things, he condemned its heavy and persistent burden on the equal sovereignty of the states: "History did not end in 1965. By the time the Act was reauthorized in 2006, there had been 40 more years of it. In assessing the current need for a preclearance system that treats States differently from one another today, that history cannot be ignored." Now that we are beyond a world of voting tests and poll taxes, Roberts argued, Congress could justify burdening states with a preclearance rule only by first finding that "current conditions" warranted it. Congress cannot, he instructed, "rely simply on the past." Yet that, he concluded, was precisely what it had done.

Joined by Breyer, Sotomayor, and Kagan, Ginsburg dissented. In reauthorizing the VRA, she wrote, Congress had acted properly to enforce the post–Civil War amendments, whose purpose was to "arm Congress with the power and authority to protect all persons within the Nation from violations of their rights by the States." The Constitution, she added, entrusted such enforcement to Congress, and it was not the Court's role to second-guess the legislature on how to get there. Ginsburg added that the Chief's reliance on a "fundamental principle of equal sovereignty" was wholly misplaced—that principle, she retorted, had never been applied to limit Congress's power to create "remedies for local evils."

Unmoved by the Chief's insistence that the South has come a long way, Ginsburg drew her reply from Shakespeare's *The Tempest*: "What's past is prologue." She explained: "Throwing out preclearance when it has worked and is continuing to work to stop discriminatory changes is like throwing away your umbrella in a rainstorm because you are not getting wet." Pointing to Congress's vast evidentiary record, Ginsburg reasoned that Congress was within its rights to conclude that the covered states remain uniquely troubled by new forms of voting discrimination. These "second generation barriers," she observed, include racial gerrymandering and burdensome voter ID laws.[66] And the VRA preclearance rule thus "remains vital to protect minority voting rights and prevent back-sliding." Making her views crystal clear, Ginsburg concluded, "In my judgment, the Court errs egregiously by overriding Congress' decision."

The disagreement in *Shelby County* unfolded on many levels. It reflected a debate over the Court's role in ensuring that Congress respect the Constitution's structure of federalism. It mirrored varying levels of concern on the Court about alleged violations of voting rights. It tapped into long-running debates over federal power under the post–Civil War amendments to protect individual rights from recalcitrant states. And it revealed a sharp, if familiar, split in the justices' solicitude for burdens on state sovereignty.

But the most striking disagreement in *Shelby County* involved the arc of American history. In 2013, the Chief Justice of the United States held that the South had moved far enough past its legacy of racial discrimination that extraordinary measures to protect voting rights in that region were no longer justified. His opinion was a self-conscious landmark. It focused nearly all of its attention on the equality of the sovereign states, remarking upon the equality concerns that birthed Section 5 of the VRA only to deem them surpassed or geographically dispersed. Just as O'Connor charted a line in *Grutter* and guessed that we would need twenty-five more years of affirmative action, so did Roberts take the measure of our past and present to conclude that Congress must lay down its arms. The future of race and voting rights, Roberts announced, is here. In that sense, *Shelby County* echoed *Parents Involved*: both opinions call on the nation to move beyond its legacy of racism and the special measures supposedly justified by that tragic inheritance.

Ginsburg's dissent came from a different place. It offered a story of imperfect advances and occasional backsliding, not a self-confident tale of transcendence. It drew out the reality of persistent racial division and the potential for tragic irony in declaring victory in a war that rages subtly all around us. It marked the need for sentinels against a past that may return again and the cautious wisdom of leaving successful walls standing. In *Shelby County*, Ginsburg looked out and observed a society in which covered jurisdictions remain afflicted by innovative discrimination— and thus saw the very evil that Section 5 was designed to prevent. To Roberts's celebratory account, Ginsburg replied, *No, we are not there yet.*

Her dissent saw grave error in so sharply separating our past and present—an error, she warned, that may embarrass the future.

The Roberts Court's engagement with racial equality has been forged in the crucible of competing visions of America's course through history. The opinions in *Parents Involved*, *Fisher*, and *Shelby County* are shot through with incompatible lessons from our past and prescriptions for the future. Even as they disagree over the moral of our national story, the justices debate their role in moving us along and deciding what the Constitution requires in light of current conditions. Race, however, is not the only domain in which the Court has faced these difficult questions while implementing the Constitution's promise of equal protection.

Love, they quickly learned, is not a constitutional argument.

Richard and Mildred Loving were born to families that had lived in the rolling hill country around Caroline County, Virginia, for generations.[67] To the Lovings, Caroline County was a friendly and familiar place, lit by their childhood memories and the warmth of family. They first grew close when Richard was seventeen and Mildred was eleven. He was white, she was part black and part Cherokee, and Caroline County—located just north of Richmond—was known for an unusually easygoing attitude toward issues of race. After a roughly seven-year courtship, in 1958 Richard and Mildred decided to travel to Washington, D.C., to get married.

Five weeks later, acting on an anonymous tip, three police offers burst into their home at two A.M. and arrested them for violating Virginia's Racial Integrity Act, which banned interracial marriages. With police flashlights shining in his face, Richard pointed to their marriage certificate. But the county sheriff replied, "That's no good here." After a brief stint in jail, the couple pleaded guilty before Leon Bazile, a judge of the Caroline County Circuit Court. Bazile later wrote, "Almighty God created the races white, black, yellow, Malay and red, and he placed them on separate continents. . . . The fact that he separated the races shows that he did not intend for the races to mix." To avoid a one-year prison sentence, the Lovings agreed to leave Virginia and not return together for twenty-five years. Felons in the eyes of the law, they built a life in exile, bearing and raising three children in Washington, D.C. Far from the world they knew best, the Lovings struggled to get by financially and endured a terrible loneliness. As Mildred told a friend years later, "I missed being with my family and friends. . . . I wanted my children to grow up in the country, where they could run and play, and where I wouldn't worry about them so much. I never liked much about the city."[68]

Unable to tolerate total separation from their true home, the Lovings began sneaking back into Virginia; usually, Mildred arrived in open daylight and then Richard drove down under cover of darkness. This was no way to live. By 1963 they could not take it any longer. Desperate, they wrote a letter to Attorney General Robert Kennedy, imploring him to help. Kennedy responded by referring the Lovings to the American Civil Liberties Union, which agreed to take their case and filed suit in 1964.

The Lovings were neither activists nor radicals. Their lawyer once remarked that they were "very simple people, who were not interested in winning any civil rights principle. . . . They just were in love with one another and wanted the right to live together as husband and wife in Virginia, without any interference from officialdom." Faced with such raw bigotry and the high price it had exacted, however, they appealed to the courts. When the Supreme Court in 1966 agreed to hear their case, a lawyer asked Richard if he had anything to say to the justices. Richard replied, "Tell the court I love my wife, and it's just unfair that I can't live with her in Virginia."

Three years earlier, at a restaurant called Portofino in New York's Greenwich Village, Edith Windsor had met Thea Spyer.[69] Portofino was known for attracting a lesbian crowd on Friday nights, free of anti-gay entrapment. Windsor, a brilliant thirty-four-year-old computer programmer and divorcée eager to pursue her true romantic interests, was immediately captivated by Spyer, a charismatic PhD in psychology more familiar with New York's lesbian scene. They danced, and then kept on dancing until Windsor ripped a hole in her stocking. "We immediately just fit, our bodies fit," Spyer later recalled. They started dating, and four years later Spyer proposed—with a pin, not a ring, to avoid questions. They moved in together near Washington Square Park, bought a house on Long Island, traveled the world, and proudly marched for civil rights.

In 1977, tragedy struck: Spyer, aged forty-five, was diagnosed with chronic progressive multiple sclerosis. Windsor eventually became Spyer's full-time caregiver, tending to her every need. When, in 2007, Spyer's doctors warned her that she had just one year to live, she woke up the next morning and asked Windsor, "Do you still want to get married?" Windsor did, so they flew to Canada with close friends and were wedded in Toronto in a ceremony officiated by Canada's first openly gay judge. Windsor was seventy-seven, Spyer was seventy-five, and it was their last trip together. They got married, Windsor recalls, because "marriage is different."[70] As Windsor told a crowd at City Hall in New York, with Spyer by her side, "Thea looks at her ring every day, and thinks of herself as a member of a special species that can love and couple 'until death do them part.'"[71]

Two years after their wedding, Spyer died. Devastated, Windsor suffered a heart attack a few weeks later—the result of what doctors informally call "broken-heart syndrome." Once she recovered, Windsor soon realized that despite the life they had built together, "the federal government was treating us like strangers." She owed a huge estate tax while living on a fixed income, a burden imposed solely because the federal Defense of Marriage Act (DOMA), which had been enacted in 1996, said her marriage was worthless in the eyes of federal law. Windsor disagreed and filed suit in federal court.

These two couples, one of different races and one of the same gender, sought equal recognition before the law. Separated by half a century, they stood united in a belief that the Constitution protects their dignity, liberty, and equality. Each couple—one in life, one in death—found its way to the Court. And each won an opinion vindicating their rights. But, as is so often true at the Court, there is more to these tales than meets the eye.

Challenges to bans on interracial marriage had reached the Court long before the Lovings' case. Just one year after *Brown v. Board of Education* was decided in 1954, in fact, a case called *Naim v. Naim* squarely presented the issue. Reeling from the massive backlash to *Brown* and aware that over 90 percent of whites opposed interracial marriage, the Court fabricated an excuse to duck the issue.[72] It kept on ducking until 1967, by which point the number of states with laws banning it had fallen to sixteen, even though most whites still opposed interracial marriage.[73] Only after the nation had made a measure of progress would the justices intervene. The same year that Spyer covertly proposed to Windsor, the Court decided *Loving v. Virginia.*[74]

In a unanimous opinion, Chief Justice Earl Warren celebrated liberty and equality, constitutional values that the Court finally enforced. "There can be no doubt that restricting the freedom to marry solely because of racial classifications violates the central meaning of the Equal Protection Clause," he held. "The freedom to marry has long been recognized as one of the vital personal rights essential to the orderly pursuit of happiness by free men."

Two years after *Loving*, police officers raided the Stonewall Inn, a gay bar in New York City.[75] Raids were a fact of gay life after World War II. Around the country, police arrested thousands of men for lewdness, loitering, vagrancy, and sodomy. Known and suspected homosexuals were banned from federal employment, dishonorably discharged from the military, stripped of medical and legal licenses, denied the right to adopt children, and subjected to brutal "treatment" for their "disease." Gay foreigners were denied permission to enter the country. Despite the emergence of early civil rights efforts, the public looked on gays and lesbians with fear and disgust.[76] State-sanctioned discrimination was widely accepted; when IBM hired Windsor, it unknowingly violated an executive order barring companies with federal contracts from employing homosexuals.

The Stonewall raid in 1969 unleashed pent-up fury in the gay community. Angry crowds marched, drag queens assembled for a chorus line rally, a firebomb exploded, and "Gay Power" graffiti appeared throughout New York City. Protests spread across the nation, launching a wave of gay rights activism and a push for social acceptance. The movement built momentum through the 1970s and '80s, scoring remarkable victories in dark times. As people came out of the closet to friends and family, attitudes started changing. The emergence of AIDS, a tragedy of unspeakable sadness, led to rapid political organization in the face of initial apathy from public health officials. In 1986, however, the movement encountered a major setback when the Court heard *Bowers v. Hardwick*, a landmark gay rights case that arose in Georgia. Split five to four, the Court ruled that the Constitution did not prohibit states from making consensual gay sex a crime.[77]

In 1996, with the cultural ground shaking beneath its feet, the Court once again heard a case about gay rights. By a six-to-three vote in *Romer v. Evans*, it struck down Amendment 2, an amendment to the Colorado constitution that banned any branch or political subdivision of the state from prohibiting discrimination based on sexual orientation.[78] Writing for the Court and invoking the Equal Protection Clause, Kennedy noted that Colorado had withdrawn "from homosexuals, but no others, specific legal protections from the injuries caused by discrimination." As Kennedy saw the matter, "It is not within our constitutional tradition to enact laws of this sort. . . . A law declaring that in general it shall be more difficult for one group of citizens than for all others to seek aid from the government is itself a denial of equal protection of the laws in the most literal sense." Reaching the "inevitable inference" that Colorado's amendment was "born of animosity" toward gays and lesbians, Kennedy deemed it unconstitutional.

The Court next heard a gay rights case, *Lawrence v. Texas*, in 2003.[79] By then, American attitudes toward gays and lesbians had been transformed, and it seemed almost comical to insist that a Texas ban on consensual gay sex was all about "sodomy." This absurdly archaic term sounded more like a disease than something practiced by millions of Americans, gay and straight. It also distracted attention from what nearly everyone understood to be the true purpose of the Texas law: to criminalize homosexuality and express moral disapproval of gay and lesbian intimacy. Although this message would have been utterly unremarkable just a few decades earlier, in the early 2000s it struck many Americans as brutal and discriminatory. The law's challengers called out its anti-gay animus, adding that it was bizarre and tyrannical for Texas to use its criminal law to control ordinary sex between two adult men.

Six justices voted to strike down the Texas law, but Kennedy faced a delicate task in explaining its constitutional flaw. In *Bowers* the Court had mockingly dismissed as "facetious" the notion that the Constitution protects a "right to engage in homosexual sodomy." For nearly two decades, *Bowers* had loomed like a thundercloud over claims to gay and lesbian equality. The Court's blessing of laws that treated gays and lesbians as criminals was invoked to justify discrimination in adoption hearings, deportation proceedings, dishonorable discharges from the military, and many other contexts.

O'Connor, a repentant member of the *Bowers* majority, favored a narrow ruling against Texas that would technically leave *Bowers* standing.

But Kennedy disagreed. The occasion called for more, much more—an opinion that would recognize and repair the terrible insult wrought by *Bowers*. As Kennedy put it, *Lawrence* called upon the Court to protect "spheres of our lives and existence . . . where the State should not be a dominant presence." It also encompassed the "more transcendent dimensions" of an "autonomy of self that includes freedom of thought, belief, expression, and certain intimate conduct." Modern understandings of liberty and equality were simply incompatible with what the Court had said in 1986. The right at issue was not just about engaging in "homosexual sodomy." Kennedy decided to address *Bowers* head-on and destroy it utterly.

He did not disappoint. Composing an opinion that was half wrecking ball, half olive branch, Kennedy wrote: "*Bowers* was not correct when it was decided, and it is not correct today. . . . The petitioners are entitled to respect for their private lives. The State cannot demean their existence or control their destiny by making their private sexual conduct a crime. . . . As the Constitution endures, persons in every generation can invoke its principles in their own search for greater freedom." Women and men, gay and straight alike, wept openly in the courtroom. A new age had dawned in the Marble Palace.

Lawrence slammed the door shut on Court-sanctioned hostility to the equal dignity of gays and lesbians, at least in regard to their most private affairs. But hot on the heels of this landmark case, a new issue took center stage: same-sex marriage. Just a decade after *Lawrence*, Windsor's challenge to DOMA would reach the Court.

Scalia harbored few doubts about what *Lawrence* meant for the question of marriage—and even fewer reservations about expressing them. In dissent, he charged Kennedy with signing on to the "homosexual agenda," blasting him for "dismantl[ing] the structure of constitutional law that has permitted a distinction to be made between heterosexual and homosexual unions, insofar as formal recognition in marriage is concerned." This opinion, which belongs to the "sky is falling" genre of dissents, added laws against bigamy, incest, and bestiality to the list of statutes supposedly endangered by *Lawrence*. Yet at least with respect to marriage, Scalia was right about the ruling's potential. The merged threads of liberty, equality, and dignity that constituted the core of Kennedy's reasoning could easily be read as gesturing toward marriage equality.[80]

Marriage, though, raised difficult questions, extending far beyond disputes over whether doctrines of liberty or equality compel recognition of same-sex marriage rights. The most challenging issues concerned the Court's role at a moment of rapid change in public beliefs about how the Constitution's principles apply to gays and lesbians.[81]

All nine justices on the Roberts Court agree that discrimination on the basis of race is unconstitutional and must be subjected to the strictest judicial scrutiny. Its recent disputes have turned mainly on how to square affirmative action and race-conscious integration with that principle. In contrast, the role of the Court and Constitution in thwarting discrimination based on sexual orientation remains deeply unsettled. Even after *Romer* and *Lawrence*, the justices openly debate whether we have yet reached a point—or will ever reach a point—where the Equal Protection Clause is understood to require searching scrutiny of discrimination against gays and lesbians. (The originalists, Scalia and Thomas, likely believe that this question was settled against same-sex marriage over a century ago, when the Fourteenth Amendment was ratified.) Questions about the social meaning of discrimination against gays and lesbians, and about the propriety of a judicial intervention that might compel an answer to the same-sex marriage issue, still loom large. So do disputes about the role of other constitutional values, including liberty, dignity, intimate association, and religious freedom. These debates, in turn, are caught up in disagreements over whether gays and lesbians can protect themselves adequately through the political process, whether sexual orientation is an immutable trait, and whether any credible social scientific evidence supports the anti–gay rights view.

The Court is sensitive to these developments. As exemplified by the delay between *Naim* and *Loving*, the Court sometimes seeks to avoid a backlash and to respect democracy by staying its hand while the nation deliberates.[82] By stepping gently into cultural wars, the Court may preserve its legitimacy and ensure that its interventions are respected. But as the justices know well, such logic, taken too far, can lead them to abdicate their role. It is the Court's sworn duty, after all, to protect even unpopular minorities when the Constitution so requires—and delay may come at the price of terrible suffering and rank injustice. The Court, moreover, can play a vital role in public debate by reminding Americans of shared constitutional principles. Considerations of this sort often influence whether and when the Court gets involved in high-profile issues, how broadly it decides to rule when addressing them, and what principles it lays down for the future.

Mere months after Kennedy issued his remarkable *Lawrence* opinion, the marriage question assumed new and pressing importance when the highest court of Massachusetts held that its state constitution compelled recognition of same-sex marriages. Citing *Lawrence*, the court explained, "Whether and whom to marry, how to express sexual intimacy, and whether and how to establish a family—these are among the most basic of every individual's liberty and due process rights."[83] In words now recited at many weddings, Chief Justice Margaret Marshall described why marriage is so important: "Civil marriage is at once a deeply personal commitment to another human being and a highly public celebration of the ideals of mutuality, companionship, intimacy, fidelity, and family. It is an association that promotes a way of life, not causes; a harmony in living, not political faiths; a bilateral loyalty, not commercial or social projects. Because it fulfils yearnings for security, safe haven, and connection that express our common humanity, civil marriage is an esteemed institution, and the decision whether and whom to marry is among life's momentous acts of self-definition."

Like a firebolt, the Massachusetts ruling ignited national debate.[84] Previously, many gay rights litigators had avoided the issue of marriage, fearful of triggering a backlash, and focused on other important objectives. Their caution was grounded in experience: when Hawaii's top court had first raised the issue of same-sex marriage rights in 1993, it had caused a national furor. In the ensuing uproar, Congress had passed—and Bill Clinton had signed—DOMA.[85] This law provided that the federal government recognized *only* opposite-sex marriage; as a consequence, a same-sex couple treated as married in their home state was viewed as two single people by Congress.

Massachusetts, though, made the marriage issue unavoidable. The nation's political parties took up the debate, initially spurred by Republicans eager to exploit divided sentiment among Democrats and mobilize their socially conservative base. States began voting on (and passing) constitutional amendments enshrining a "traditional" definition of marriage. Initially caught somewhat off guard, gay rights groups turned considerable attention and resources to the fight. Marriage ultimately became the premier gay rights issue of the early 2000s, the focus of intense social, cultural, and political energy. In a remarkably short time span, public opinion on the marriage question moved sharply in favor of same-sex marriage rights. Partly as a result, after a series of devastating losses in 2004 and 2005, marriage equality advocates scored huge victories near the end of the decade. By the early 2010s, they were winning one legislative and judicial victory after another in a massive state-by-state civil rights campaign.

In 2012, faced with important and controversial decisions by the lower federal courts, the Roberts Court plainly had no choice but to enter the fray. It ultimately agreed to hear two cases. One of them involved a challenge to California's Proposition 8, a statewide referendum that had reversed a California Supreme Court ruling recognizing same-sex marriage rights. With state officials unwilling to defend Proposition 8, the Court ultimately dismissed this case on procedural grounds.[86] That dismissal left in place a lower court ruling that struck down Proposition 8 and led California to conclude that it must allow same-sex marriages. The other case that the Court granted in 2012 was a direct constitutional attack on DOMA. It had been filed in New York by Edith Windsor.

United States v. Windsor reached the Court in a strange posture.[87] The Department of Justice would ordinarily have defended DOMA as a law duly enacted by Congress, but in this instance it filed briefs on Windsor's side of the case.[88] Obama had concluded that DOMA violated the Constitution and that he could not in good faith order his lawyers to defend it. In response, Republicans in the House of Representatives instructed an entity called the Bipartisan Legal Advisory Group to defend DOMA. Whereas the political branches usually stand united in their defense of federal statutes, in *Windsor* the Court was well aware of their bitterly divided opinion. That split offered an apt metaphor for the rest of the nation.

The Court was also intimately familiar with the stakes of the case. Back in 1986, Justice Lewis Powell—the swing vote in *Bowers*—told a clerk,

"I don't believe I've ever met a homosexual."[89] As a result, he confessed, he simply did not understand the stakes of the case, or why anyone would even want to engage in "sodomy." By 2013, nobody on the Court could credibly suggest that gays and lesbians were beyond their comprehension—not least because plenty of openly gay young lawyers had clerked for the justices.[90] Nor was the Court a bastion of so-called traditional marriage: reflecting the diversity of America's family life, its members had experienced divorce, adoption, singledom, and widowhood.[91] Obliged to decide what the Constitution says about the right to marry, the Roberts Court boasted a wealth of perspectives.

In *Windsor*, Kennedy—joined by Ginsburg, Breyer, Sotomoyor, and Kagan—held that DOMA cannot stand. But rather than rule broadly that the Constitution protects a right to same-sex marriage, he limited the direct holding of his opinion to the federal law under review.

Kennedy acknowledged that "until recent years, many citizens had not even considered the possibility that two persons of the same sex might aspire to occupy the same status and dignity as that of a man and woman in lawful marriage." But challenges to this belief, he wrote, had led some to "the beginnings of a new perspective, a new insight" that bans on same-sex marriage cause an "unjust exclusion." Accordingly, "slowly at first and then in rapid course, [states like New York] came to acknowledge the urgency of this issue for same-sex couples who wanted to affirm their commitment to one another before their children, their family, their friends, and their community." In so doing, they "sought to give further protection and dignity" to "a personal bond that is more enduring." Here Kennedy quoted and cited *Lawrence*, linking his powerful ruling on private intimacy to the fundamental principles at stake in *Windsor*.

DOMA, however, prohibited federal recognition of these new marriages. It did so despite a "history and tradition" of treating "the definition and regulation of marriage" as "within the authority and realm of the separate States." Far exceeding any previous federal regulation of marriage, DOMA ranged widely and crudely over one thousand unrelated federal benefits, stripping them from "a class of persons that the laws of New York . . . have sought to protect." Drawing on his deep concern for federalism, Kennedy made clear that this singular act of disregard for state law raised gravely troubling questions in its own right.[92]

But the true heart of his opinion was its conclusion that DOMA

violated fundamental rights to equality and dignity: "The avowed purpose and practical effect of the law here in question are to impose a
disadvantage, a separate status, and so a stigma upon all who enter into
same-sex marriages." Through DOMA, Kennedy observed, Congress
intended to express "moral disapproval of homosexuality, and a moral
conviction that heterosexuality better comports with traditional (especially Judeo–Christian) morality." DOMA wrote "inequality into the
United States Code," divesting "married same-sex couples of the duties
and responsibilities that are an essential part of married life and that
they in most cases would be honored to accept." This bare desire to harm
a minority group, Kennedy wrote, rendered DOMA unconstitutional.

And as he explained, DOMA's harms were substantial: "By creating
two contradictory marriage regimes within the same State, DOMA forces
same-sex couples to live as married for the purpose of state law but
unmarried for the purpose of federal law, thus diminishing the stability
and predictability of basic personal relations the State has found it proper
to acknowledge and protect. By this dynamic DOMA undermines both
the public and private significance of state-sanctioned same-sex marriages;
for it tells those couples, and all the world, that their otherwise valid marriages are unworthy of federal recognition. This places same-sex couples in
an unstable position of being in a second-tier marriage. The differentiation
demeans the couple, whose moral and sexual choices the Constitution
protects, and whose relationship the State has sought to dignify. And it
humiliates tens of thousands of children now being raised by same-sex
couples. The law in question makes it even more difficult for the children
to understand the integrity and closeness of their own family and its con-
cord with other families in their community and in their daily lives."

In conclusion, Kennedy wrote, "The federal statute is invalid, for no
legitimate purpose overcomes the purpose and effect to disparage and to
injure those whom the State, by its marriage laws, sought to protect in
personhood and dignity."

Alito, Roberts, and Scalia dissented separately, accusing the Court of
terrible error. Roberts and Scalia (joined by Thomas) first argued that
the Court lacked the power to decide *Windsor*, arguing that Obama's
agreement with Windsor meant that there was no real "case" or "con-

troversy" between the named parties.[93] But all three dissenters went further and insisted that, on the merits, the Court should have upheld DOMA.

Alito directly attacked the notion that the Constitution protects any right to same-sex marriage. Reflecting his deep social conservatism and wariness of meddling with tradition, Alito emphasized not only the novelty of any such right but uncertainty about what might result from change to "ancient" family structures. "No one," he argued, "can predict with any certainty what the long-term ramifications of widespread acceptance of same-sex marriage will be." Gesturing to debates among theologians, social scientists, historians, and philosophers, he described two competing visions of marriage—one based on "consent," the other based on "procreation and biological kinship"—and concluded that "the Constitution does not codify either of these views." Rather than deem traditionalists "bigots or superstitious fools," he cautioned, "unelected judges" should acknowledge "the silence of the Constitution on this question."

Roberts focused on DOMA, arguing that Congress had reasonably passed it to ensure "uniformity and stability" by retaining "the definition of marriage that . . . had been adopted by every State in our Nation, and every nation in the world." Anticipating the likely next case, Roberts then emphasized that *Windsor* focused *only* on DOMA—a federal law—and did not address state-level bans on same-sex marriage. Highlighting Kennedy's references to Congress intruding on the prerogatives of the sovereign states, the Chief proposed a reading of *Windsor* that would leave it largely speechless on the ultimate question of same-sex marriage.

While Roberts tried his hand at damage control, Scalia reprised the tone of his *Lawrence* dissent, warning that *Windsor* would lead inevitably to recognition of same-sex marriage rights. He even copied and lightly edited a section of Kennedy's opinion to show just how readily it could be adapted to that purpose. Scalia didn't mince words in condemning the majority for what he saw as a gross abuse of power: "Few public controversies will ever demonstrate so vividly the beauty of what our Framers gave us, a gift the Court pawns today to buy its stolen moment in the spotlight: a system of government that permits us to rule *ourselves*." Celebrating the "plebiscites, legislation, persuasion, and loud voices" that marked the debate over same-sex marriage, Scalia mourned *Windsor* as "a tragedy for our democracy." He also denounced the majority's holding that DOMA reflected prejudice and animus: "[DOMA] did no more than codify an aspect of marriage that had been unquestioned in our society for most of its existence. . . . It is one thing for a society to elect change; it is another for a court of law to impose change by adjudging those who oppose it *hostes humani generis*, enemies of the human race."

Few rulings are more uncertain than *Windsor*. Scalia saw a future foreordained, while Roberts saw a one-off ruling on federal power. Commentators are deeply fractured in their views of the decision. This was no doubt intentional: Kennedy drew on principles of federalism, equality, and dignity to produce an opinion appropriate to what he saw as the evolving needs of our time. While it cannot be doubted that *Windsor* takes a forceful step toward recognition of same-sex marriage rights, and several lower courts have already read it that way,[94] the Court left the door open just wide enough to retreat from the field if it so chooses when it accepts another same-sex marriage case.

When Edith Windsor heard the news that her challenge to DOMA had succeeded, she burst into screams and sobs—and immediately cried out, "I wanna go to Stonewall right now!" Then she called a friend and said, "Please get married right away!" About an hour later, the phone rang. It was the President. When Windsor took the phone, she said, "Hello, who am I talking to? Oh, Barack Obama? I wanted to thank you. I think your coming out for us made such a difference throughout the country."[95]

These three sets of cases—*Naim* and *Loving*; *Bowers, Lawrence*, and *Windsor*; *Fisher, Parents Involved*, and *Shelby County*—instruct us that timing can be everything in asking the Court to enforce the Constitution's promise of equal protection. How the Court sees history unfolding and what role it chooses for itself in that tale is sometimes more important than the facts of the particular case at hand. Tellingly, in a 2013 speech to an audience of law students, Kennedy mused aloud about the Court's reluctance to render a marriage equality ruling that goes "too broad and deep" to let democracy run its course.[96] But in the very next breath, he added that to him it seemed unjust for any court faced with a person suffering a real injury to turn the litigant away on the theory that he or she had the misfortune to arrive at court too soon.

At argument in the Proposition 8 case from California, Scalia posed an unusual question to Ted Olson, the lead attorney arguing for marriage equality: "I'm curious, when did it become unconstitutional to exclude homosexual couples from marriage?" On the Roberts Court, the answer to that question still looms on the horizon.

2

HEALTH CARE:

LIBERTY ON THE LINE

In April 2013, Barack Obama declared broccoli his "favorite food."[1] It was a bold choice. By selecting broccoli, he directly repudiated the official White House policy established by George H. W. Bush in 1990: "I do not like broccoli and I haven't liked it since I was a little kid and my mother made me eat it. I'm the President of the United States and I'm not going to eat any more broccoli."[2] Obama's announcement also signaled a touching act of forgiveness for a maligned vegetable. Not since George W. Bush choked on a pretzel in 2002 had a food come closer to destroying a presidency.[3] In conservative hands, this humble member of the cabbage family nearly hobbled Obama's signature domestic achievement: national health care reform, as embodied in the Affordable Care Act (the ACA, a.k.a. Obamacare).

In their crusade against the law, which began its tortuous path through Congress in 2009, the ACA's opponents rallied support by conjuring an improbable nightmare: Obama, barely masking a self-righteous smirk, ramming leafy greens down our national throat and insisting that it is all for our own good. If the government could make each of us buy what it deemed adequate health care, what *couldn't* it make us do? Did the federal government's power to issue commands have no constitutional limit? The prospect of mandatory broccoli familiarized these fears. It sparked frustrated memories of being told to "eat your veggies" and of parents insisting "we know what's best."

The image of a force-fed vegetable soon assumed a life of its own.

Pollsters asked Americans about hypothetical mandates to purchase broccoli.[4] Senator Tom Coburn asked Elena Kagan during her confirmation hearing in 2010 about a law requiring Americans to eat three fruits and three vegetables every day. (She politely replied, "Sounds like a dumb law.")[5] The *New Yorker* published a cartoon in which a precocious child sits with his arms crossed and declares, "I say it's government-mandated broccoli, and I say the hell with it."[6] Broccoli was everywhere—even the hallowed halls of the Court, where it would be mentioned twelve times in written opinions assessing the ACA. Justice Ginsburg, the ACA's most eloquent champion when the law came before the Court, scornfully derided this argument as "the broccoli horrible."

The legal challenge to the ACA was no standard "slippery slope" argument. It did not warn that the principles underlying the ACA, taken to a logical conclusion, might someday lead to trouble. The ACA *was* trouble. Its opponents argued that it was the bottom of the slope, an evil of constitutional dimension. Now that we had fallen so far, nothing stood between vulnerable citizens and federal broccoli mandates. By 2012, the law's critics turned their full attention to the Court. Congress had erred by passing the ACA, Obama by signing it, and now only the justices could save us from this unprecedented bout of political insanity.

But how? The Court is not a superlegislature. Its reasoning and the authorities on which it can legitimately rely are unique. Although it seemed clear that at least five justices would have voted against the ACA if they had been senators, its adversaries needed a *constitutional* argument.

This is when things got interesting. Challenges to the ACA channeled and magnified demands that the Court restore the Constitution to a role it hadn't played in more than seventy-five years: the source of robust, judicially enforced limits on federal power to regulate the economy. That call to battle echoed amid Tea Party activism, Occupy Wall Street protests, and election year politics.

Legal arguments against the ACA that initially struck many experts as far-fetched benefited from fierce partisan debate over the federal government's role in stabilizing a post-recession economy. Controversy over creating jobs, protecting consumers, overseeing banks, and honoring entitlements while addressing public debts soured many on federal regulation. Reacting with alarm to Obama's pursuit of progressive economic policies, a coalition of conservatives and libertarians objected in the language of constitutional law.[7]

Their attacks captured creeping anxiety about the use of federal power, by celebrating the importance of "structural limits" on the powers Congress may wield. Structural limits result from how the Constitution maps out the government and constrains its authority—the separation of powers and federalism, for example. Respect for constitutional limits on federal power, the law's challengers argued, is vital to the preservation of American freedom. The vision behind the attack on the ACA was thus part of a broader legal and political assault on federal power to regulate the economy, the judicial front in a wider war over national policies and values.

Although the Court tried a century ago to aggressively police the boundaries of federal power and economic liberty, it largely abandoned that effort in the late 1930s. Since then, it has mostly left these matters to the political safeguards of democracy. In the course of reviewing the ACA, though, a majority of the Roberts Court signaled its openness to a project of reviving and enforcing constitutional limits on federal power. This was striking because the Court has refused every request to invalidate major social legislation since Franklin Delano Roosevelt's New Deal. If pursued, that undertaking could draw the Court into a more active, if haphazard, role in reviewing policies that affect our national life. It's thus remarkable that the ACA survived only by a single vote.

That vote, cast by Chief Justice Roberts, forestalled a momentous clash between the Court and the political branches. Yet a close reading of his opinion strongly suggests that the Chief shares his right-leaning colleagues' desire to limit the scope of federal power—and to craft new constitutional law in order to do so. The ACA survived, but the *way* it survived left no doubt that five justices on the Roberts Court are sympathetic to those who survey the vast scope of federal regulation and declare, "Enough!".

National Federation of Independent Business v. Sebelius, a.k.a. the *Health Care Case*, ranks among the most anticipated and controversial decisions in American history.[8] It is also one of the most misunderstood. Too many observers treat the Court's ruling as if it erupted out of nowhere and tells us little about the future of the Roberts Court. True, the story of the *Health Care Case* is fascinating in its own right. But the ACA ruling should not be seen as a one-off event. Nor should so much attention be consumed by attempts to divine the Chief's personal and political motives for upholding the law. [9] The decision's value as a sign of things to come is far more important.

A panoramic view of the *Health Care Case* reveals that the Roberts Court is poised at the intersection of centuries-old debates over American freedom and its relation to American federalism. As the Court stands at that crossroads, its opinions upholding the ACA reveal its uncertainty about how best to move ahead. Although the Court (barely) left Obama's most important law standing, it sent an unmistakable message: change looms on the horizon.

By the time its opponents asked the Court to serve as executioner, the ACA had already come back from the dead once. And in the century before the Court ruled, the liberal dream of providing affordable, universal health coverage had survived countless deaths.[10]

That story stretches back to 1912. During his unsuccessful run for a third term as president, Teddy Roosevelt delivered a fiery speech on social policy to the Progressive Party convention. In words that resonated for decades, he argued that "the hazards of sickness, accident, invalidism, involuntary unemployment, and old age should be provided for through insurance."[11] Twenty years later, when FDR followed through on Teddy's call, universal health care was left out of the legislation that established Social Security because of concerted political and professional opposition.[12] Harry Truman championed a national health-insurance program, but the closest he came to success was watching Lyndon B. Johnson—in an act of tribute—sign Medicare into law at the Truman Presidential Library.[13] In the 1970s, Richard Nixon and Senator Edward Kennedy tried to reach a compromise that would guarantee health coverage for every American, but the talks fizzled and were eventually overshadowed by Watergate.[14] Two decades later, Bill Clinton's attempt to reform health care crashed and burned after Clinton suffered what he later called "a good shellacking" in the 1994 midterm elections.[15]

When Obama took up the torch, his push to create universal coverage was never supposed to hinge on a mandate that every individual obtain insurance. The individual mandate was originally a conservative idea, cooked up by right-wing policy wonks in the late 1980s as an alternative to a government-run health care system.[16] During the 2008 Democratic primary, Obama had even criticized Hillary Clinton's plan for including a coverage mandate.[17] Soon after taking office, though, Obama changed his mind. He was persuaded by Democrats in Congress, the cold logic of budget projections, and evidence suggesting that a mandate could best achieve increased coverage and reduced cost.[18]

That switch in Obama's position was just one of many twists and turns in the struggle to enact the ACA. The battle was epic in scope and ferocity. It consumed nearly two years of the federal government's attention and led both sides to extreme measures. The drama reached a fever pitch in January 2010, when Republican Scott Brown was elected by Massachusetts voters to replace the late Senator Ted Kennedy, a liberal lion who had devoted his career to universal health care. Brown's election deprived Democrats of the sixty votes in the Senate they would need to overcome an assured Republican filibuster. Many pundits issued yet another death certificate for health care reform.[19]

Obama and his Democratic allies, however, responded to this setback with steely resolve. After tense negotiations, the House agreed to pass the Senate's bill. The Senate later used a special budgetary procedure that required only fifty-one votes to pass the changes House Democrats had demanded. Republicans cried foul, but the Democrats hadn't violated any Senate rules. On March 23, 2010, Obama proudly affixed his signature to the ACA.[20]

The new law is nothing if not complex. It contains thousands of moving parts and touches nearly every aspect of the health care system. Many of its provisions are still being interpreted and implemented, a process that will continue for years to come and affect virtually every patient, doctor, hospital, and branch of government. As the difficulties that plagued the law's rollout revealed, implementation will be a formidable challenge in its own right.

The legislation finally delivered to Obama's desk, though, rested on three simple pillars. First, the ACA aimed to secure universal coverage. To achieve that goal, it required states to expand their Medicaid programs (mostly at federal expense); provided subsidies for middle-income Americans to buy insurance; created government-run "exchanges" on which people could shop for policies; and penalized large employers who

failed to provide affordable insurance to their employees. Second, to promote affordability, the law restricted practices by health-insurance companies that had excluded millions of Americans from the market. Most
important, the ACA's "guaranteed issue" provision banned insurers from
denying coverage to people with preexisting medical conditions, and
its "community rating" rule prohibited insurers from charging those
people higher premiums. Finally, the law mandated that people who
could afford a qualified health-insurance plan on the private market buy
one, unless they were otherwise covered by Medicaid, Medicare, or their
employer. Failure to comply with this "individual mandate" would result
in the imposition of a "shared responsibility payment," adjusted by income
and levied as part of the annual federal income tax.

The ACA included an individual mandate because its guaranteed
issue and community ratings initiatives created a dire risk: if Americans
did not have to pay higher costs even if they had preexisting conditions,
and thus could wait to purchase health insurance until they were already
sick, many might decide against coverage while healthy. This could be
especially true of young people, who often view insurance as a burdensome cost and make relatively little use of it. The resulting insurance
"death spiral" would be cataclysmic. Insurers rely on a large population of healthy people to fund the steep costs of sick plan members. If
everyone in a plan were sick, premiums would skyrocket—forcing many
Americans out of the market and compelling the government to pick up
the ever-growing tab.[21] Though in theory we could simply leave sick people to their own devices, America long ago rejected such a miserly view
of its shared social responsibilities. The Emergency Medical Treatment
and Active Labor Act, passed in 1986, made that rejection manifest by
requiring hospital emergency rooms to treat anyone seeking medical
help.

By mandating that virtually all Americans obtain coverage, the ACA
sought to protect the safety net it created from potential ruin. In practice, the law essentially offered a choice: either pay for health insurance
or pay a "shared responsibility" tax designed to compensate, in part, for
the costs that the class of uninsured people inevitably impose on others,
including taxpayers. After all, deciding to self-insure is risky. Everyone
eventually uses health care, and the evidence shows that, as a group,
those who self-insure often end up unable to pay for the cost of their

care, forcing the rest of us to cover a big part of their bill. For example, Congress found that, in 2008, hospitals, physicians, and other professionals received no compensation for $43 billion worth of the $116 billion in care they administered to the uninsured. The resulting increase in health care costs, Congress discovered, was partly passed on through insurers and raised annual family premiums by an average of more than $1,000. In a sense, the coverage mandate was a conservative policy that forced Americans to take responsibility for the consequences of their choices.

The ACA's opponents saw it differently. They saw an unwieldy and harmful law that would wreak havoc on a national scale. They saw an effort to manage the American economy with a form of discredited central planning. And the closer they looked, the more they saw a use of federal power with socialist or even tyrannical implications: a requirement that all Americans buy something on the private market. A libertarian drive to prevent government control over basic economic choices merged with a distinct fear of federal power to propel a ferocious legal assault.

Almost before the ink of Obama's signature could dry, Florida's attorney general filed suit in federal court. He challenged the mandate and the Medicaid expansion, but his broader aim was to see every page of the new law burned. Eventually, twenty-five other states joined Florida's suit. Private plaintiffs filed their own cases. From the outset, it was obvious that only our highest court could settle this momentous conflict.

At about ten o'clock in the morning on June 28, 2012, Obama stepped out of the Oval Office and stood before a bank of four televisions in the adjoining vestibule.[22] He knew the Court would rule on the ACA in just a few minutes. It was the last day of the Court's term, and the justices were sure to release all their remaining opinions. Soon, he would learn if his law had survived.

Across town, Roberts gathered with his colleagues in the Court's oak-paneled robing room to don his black, priestlike vestments. Following time-honored custom, each justice shook hands with every other justice—an affirmation of mutual purpose and respect that must have carried particular weight before the Court announced its bitterly divided opinion.[23] A moment later, the Chief and his colleagues appeared in the great courtroom, sliding quickly through red velvet drapes and establishing themselves around the imposing curved bench. The justices were visibly exhausted. Each—except for Roberts—had suffered at least one bruising defeat in the *Health Care Case*. And even the Chief's victory was bitter-sweet.

For a long moment, the nine justices looked out over the audience. The air grew thick with tension. The justices knew the result, but the rest of the world was still in the dark. Unlike most other Washington institu-tions, the Court maintains a strict "no snitches" policy—creating a rare cone of silence in a city of sieves. Its self-imposed secrecy largely sur-vived even the pressure brought to bear in this historic case; only a few outsiders appear to have had any sense of the machinations within the Court.[24] Bereft of smoke signals, the nation had endured a roller-coaster ride of shifting expectations.

In the legal challenge's early days, nearly every scholar and politician who reviewed the case considered it frivolous.[25] When asked about her constitutional authority in 2009, Speaker of the House Nancy Pelosi incredulously replied, "Are you serious?"[26] Mere days before oral argu-ment in March 2012, Linda Greenhouse, writing in the *New York Times*, reaffirmed this conventional wisdom: "The constitutional challenge to the law's requirement for people to buy health insurance—specifically, the argument that the mandate exceeds Congress's power under the Commerce Clause—is rhetorically powerful but analytically so weak that it dissolves on close inspection. There's just no there there."[27] Con-gress, she explained, enjoys broad power to regulate economic activity. And what could be more economic than the multibillion-dollar health care market? It seemed to her, and many others, like an open-and-shut case.

On March 27, 2012, everything changed. During one of the longest arguments in living memory, the five right-leaning justices unleashed a devastating barrage of questions upon the ACA's defender, Solicitor Gen-eral Don Verrilli. Decrying the ACA's threat to personal freedom, they jabbed at every pressure point in Verrilli's argument. Paul Clement, one of the leading oral advocates of his generation, assailed the law in a vir-tuoso performance that stoked the justices' fear of tyranny. A majority of the Court clearly took the challenge very seriously. Halfway through the proceedings, Jeffrey Toobin of CNN raced from the Court to publicly prophesy the mandate's demise.[28]

After argument, the nation eagerly awaited the Court's decision. Rumors swirled of shifting votes and shady, behind-the-scenes efforts to sway the justices.[29] Obama jousted with Mitt Romney over the ACA, and public opinion polarized around its legal merits. Republicans repeatedly called for bills to defund or repeal the law. The website Intrade even hosted bets on whether the mandate would survive. The morning of the decision, it posted odds in favor of invalidation ranging from 66.2 percent to 72.9 percent.[30]

As Intrade users placed their final bets and Obama waited anxiously in the White House, Roberts took his seat in the great courtroom.

At 10:07:39 on the morning of June 28, 2012, Fox and CNN broke the silence with headline news: the individual mandate had fallen. In the White House, Obama stared at the screen, undoubtedly dumbfounded. But before the news could sink in, White House Counsel Kathy Ruemmler appeared with a broad smile and a double thumbs-up. Confused, Obama glanced back at the screen. Ruemmler reassured him; she had seen a dispatch at 10:08:30 from Tom Goldstein and Amy Howe on *SCOTUSblog*, the first site to correctly report the ruling.[31] The Court had issued a complicated opinion. Eager to break the news, several journalists had filed stories prematurely. In fact, the individual mandate—and thus most of the ACA—had survived.

But not all of it. Seven justices—the five conservatives, joined by Justices Breyer and Kagan—had struck down a central part of the ACA's Medicaid expansion, which required states to cover everyone with incomes up to 33 percent above the poverty line. The ACA punished noncompliant states by stripping away all their existing Medicaid funding, which made up an important part of many state budgets. The Court held that this rule constituted impermissible coercion by the federal government, even though the Medicaid expansion was almost entirely federally funded. This part of the decision received relatively little attention at the time, but it eventually allowed roughly half the states to depart from the ACA's Medicaid expansion. The resulting coverage gap remains a subject of intense political dispute in many states.[32]

When Roberts announced his ruling, though, the mandate's bright future took center stage. Obama had just scored a decisive constitutional victory. As he absorbed the news, the president grabbed Ruemmler and enveloped her in a bear hug.

The day after he announced his ruling in the *Health Care Case*, Roberts prepared to vacation in Malta, a getaway that he cheerfully described as "an impregnable island fortress."[33] He added, "It seemed like a good idea."

The Chief's vote to uphold the ACA will go down as one of the most consequential acts of his tenure on the Court—and one of the most controversial. Hailed by some as King Solomon and denounced by others as Benedict Arnold, the Chief was deemed an idiot, a genius, a statesman, and a canny strategist.[34] Liberals heralded a great triumph but worried that the opinion was a Trojan horse. In op-eds and interviews, they warned that it could provide legal firepower to conservatives in the future and confer undue credibility on Roberts as he pursued a radical right-wing agenda.[35] Most libertarians and conservatives, meanwhile, bemoaned the ACA's new lease on life, even as some proponents of the challenge discerned victories in the ashes of defeat.[36]

Of course, any considered assessment of the ruling must start with the opinion itself. The main legal issue in the *Health Care Case* was whether Congress exceeded its powers under the Constitution in enacting the mandate. It's a fundamental principle of American constitutionalism that the federal government has limited powers. Congress does not enjoy a freestanding authority, often dubbed a "police power," to legislate on any matter affecting public morals, safety, health, or welfare. Instead, it must always act pursuant to a grant of power set forth in the Constitution.

In defending the ACA, the Department of Justice invoked three great delegations of power in Article I of the Constitution as sources of authority to impose the mandate: Congress's power to "regulate Commerce . . . among the several States," its power to pass "all Laws . . . necessary and proper" to carrying into effect its other powers, and its power to tax and spend for the "general Welfare of the United States." The law's challengers pushed back, arguing that the power to regulate commerce doesn't reach citizens who aren't already participating in the relevant market—here, citizens who are "inactive" in the market for insurance. The mandate, they added, was not really a "tax." In an avalanche of briefs, the government, the challengers, and other interested parties laid out intricate arguments about how the precedents and principles governing Congress's power should apply to the ACA.

In a ruling aptly described by Stanford Law Professor Pam Karlan as the "most grudging opinion ever to uphold a major piece of legislation," Roberts concluded that Congress lacks the power to impose true mandates.[37] He then saved the ACA, however, by reasoning that the law could be read as not *really* imposing a mandate at all. This was a prospect that some observers thought the Chief had signaled on the first day of argument, though it had escaped most Court watchers.[38] With four justices voting to uphold the mandate outright and four justices voting to strike it down, the Chief's vote—which is rumored to have shifted after a post-argument conference—controlled the outcome.[39]

In his opinion, Roberts immediately distanced himself from the ACA's alleged virtues: "We do not consider whether the Act embodies sound policy choices. That judgment is entrusted to the Nation's elected leaders . . . [and] it is not our job to protect the people from the consequences of their political choices." In style and substance, the Chief made clear his disdain for the law that he had stoically set about rescuing.

Roberts began his analysis by embracing wholesale one of the main critiques of the mandate: it regulated decisions *not* to buy health insurance. Roberts did not question precedents establishing that the Commerce Clause empowers Congress to regulate essentially all economic *activity*, but he argued that it did not encompass power over economic *inactivity*: "Construing the Commerce Clause to permit Congress to regulate individuals precisely because they are doing nothing would open a new and potentially vast domain of congressional authority. . . . That is not the country the Framers of our Constitution envisioned. Congress already enjoys vast power to regulate much of what we do. Accepting the Government's theory would give Congress the same license to regulate what we do not do, fundamentally changing the relation between the citizen and the Federal Government." Plainly offended by the ACA's intrusion on liberty, Roberts ridiculed the law as an attempt to "regulate an individual from cradle to grave."

Roberts also rejected arguments that the mandate could be saved by the Constitution's "Necessary and Proper" Clause, a catchall provision authorizing Congress to "make all Laws which shall be necessary and proper for carrying into Execution" other constitutional powers. Invoking this clause, the government sought to justify the mandate as an indispensable means of ensuring that the ACA's guaranteed issue and community ratings provisions did not cause an insurance death spiral.

The Chief conceded that the mandate would achieve that goal and, thus, was "necessary," but he held that it was not a "proper" means of doing so. The mandate, he reasoned, represented a kind of bootstrapping by Congress, which had itself created the problem that the mandate was supposedly necessary to solve. Further, he warned that a mandate was a "great substantive and independent power" in its own right.[40] Holding that federal authority to pass the rest of the ACA impliedly conferred power to impose something as huge as a mandate would be like letting the tail wag the dog. It just wouldn't do.

This left only the taxing power. Invoking the long-recognized judicial duty to save a law if any fair means of doing so can be found, Roberts held that the "mandate" need not be understood as a mandate at all. Rather, it could reasonably be read as requiring only that certain people pay a tax if they decline to buy insurance. The Solicitor General had aggressively pressed this argument, assuring the Court that those who chose to pay the penalty would not be treated as outlaws. And the Court has long recognized that the taxing power can legitimize laws when, in practice, they function as taxes.

Roberts noted that the mandate operates mainly through the tax system: "The 'shared responsibility payment,' as the statute entitles it, is paid into the Treasury by 'taxpayers' when they file their tax returns. It does not apply to individuals who do not pay federal income taxes. . . . For taxpayers who do owe the payment, its amount is determined by such familiar factors as taxable income, number of dependents, and joint filing status." The IRS, Roberts added, "must assess and collect [the payment] 'in the same manner as taxes,'" and this process "yields the essential feature of any tax: it produces at least some revenue for the Government . . . about $4 billion per year by 2017."

"Because the Constitution permits such a tax," the Chief concluded, "it is not our role to forbid it, or to pass upon its wisdom or fairness." Construed as a tax, the "mandate" survived.

Prudent as ever, though, Roberts added a qualifier: even if the policy operated as a tax, it would be deemed unconstitutional if it became the functional equivalent of a mandate. Thus, if the penalty on failing to purchase insurance were to be set so high that it would leave uninsured Americans with no rational alternative to making the purchase, it could not stand. As the Chief sternly admonished, quoting from a canonical 1928 case, "'the power to tax is not the power to destroy while this Court sits.'"[41]

The Chief's careful threading of the constitutional needle managed to infuriate all eight of his peers.

Ruth Bader Ginsburg is not given to the scornful, combative dissenting style that has become Scalia's trademark. She typically sticks to respectful, restrained disagreement with the majority.[42] Occasionally, she bluntly calls on Congress to overrule what she views as a serious mistake.[43] In rare instances, she shares with reporters her belief that an "activist" majority led the Court astray.[44] Only once in a great while does she cast her polite tone aside, tear a majority opinion apart, and remind us that she has within her all the ferocity that was needed in her role as field marshal of the legal movement for sex equality.[45]

In the *Health Care Case*, joined by Breyer, Sotomayor, and Kagan, Ginsburg unloaded on the Chief's anti-mandate ruling. Before publishing her dissent to this part of the Court's decision, the ever-savvy Ginsburg hosted a special strategy session with the other left-leaning justices to make sure they were all on the same page.[46]

Denouncing the Chief's logic as "stunningly retrogressive," Ginsburg likened it to rulings from the widely condemned pre–New Deal period. Roberts's "crabbed reading of the Commerce Clause," she wrote, "harks back to the era in which the Court routinely thwarted Congress' efforts to regulate the national economy in the interest of those who labor to sustain it." Lining up cases, Ginsburg explained that "our precedent has recognized Congress' large authority to set the Nation's course in the economic and social welfare realm." Thus, "whatever one thinks of the policy decision Congress made, it was Congress' prerogative to make it." In the Chief's analyses of the Commerce Clause and the Necessary and Proper Clause, Ginsburg saw the specter of a world in which courts ride roughshod over Congress. Worse, in her view, Roberts not only overstepped the judicial role but also erred in his Commerce Clause reasoning: the decision to self-insure in the face of inevitable need for medical services is surely "economic activity" and is therefore properly subject to federal regulation, even by Roberts's logic.

Ginsburg displayed little patience for the libertarian core of Roberts's opinion—and even less patience for his allusion to broccoli. "When contemplated in its extreme," she observed, "almost any power looks dangerous. The commerce power, hypothetically, would enable Congress to prohibit the purchase and home production of all meat, fish, and dairy goods, effectively compelling Americans to eat only vegetables. Yet no one would offer the hypothetical and unreal possibility of a vegetarian state as a credible reason to deny Congress the authority ever to ban the possession and sale of goods. The Chief Justice accepts just such specious logic when he cites the broccoli horrible as a reason to deny Congress the power to pass the individual mandate."[47] To Ginsburg, it was silly to conjure extreme examples and insist that they showed why the Court must fabricate implausible limits on federal power over commerce. Inevitably, democracy—rather than judge-made law—is the real limit on what Congress can do, she argued.

Without so much as acknowledging the Chief's opinion, Scalia, Kennedy, Thomas, and Alito assailed their erstwhile ally from the right. Rather than rally behind an opinion written by a single justice, they composed a joint dissent listing all four of them as its authors. This remarkable tactic invoked *Cooper v. Aaron*, a case from 1958 in which the Court reaffirmed its power to compel desegregation in a single opinion listing all nine justices as the authors—the only such opinion ever published.[48] "Justice SCALIA, Justice KENNEDY, Justice THOMAS, and Justice ALITO, dissenting" sent a powerful message: this case strikes to the heart of the Court's role and the most basic principles of our Constitution.

The four dissenters pulled no punches. They articulated in clear and passionate terms the visions of liberty and federalism that required them to invalidate the ACA outright: "The Constitution, though it dates from the founding of the Republic, has powerful meaning and vital relevance to our own times. The constitutional protections that this case involves are protections of structure. Structural protections—notably, the restraints imposed by federalism and separation of powers—are less romantic and

have less obvious a connection to personal freedom than the provisions
of the Bill of Rights or the Civil War Amendments. Hence they tend to
be undervalued or even forgotten by our citizens. It should be the responsibility of the Court to teach otherwise, to remind our people that the
Framers considered structural protections of freedom the most important ones, for which reason they alone were embodied in the original
Constitution and not left to later amendment. The fragmentation of power
produced by the structure of our Government is central to liberty, and
when we destroy it, we place liberty at peril."

The joint dissent pilloried the Chief's view of the taxing power issue:
the mandate imposed what the law called a "penalty" on those who failed
to comply; Obama had publicly insisted that it was *not* a tax; and the
ACA served a manifest regulatory purpose. In the dissent's view, "to say
that the Individual Mandate merely imposes a tax is not to interpret the
statute but to rewrite it." And that would be uniquely illegitimate, the
dissenters opined, for "imposing a tax through judicial legislation inverts
the constitutional scheme, and places the power to tax in the branch of
government least accountable to the citizenry." Pronouncing a harsh verdict on the Chief's handiwork, the dissenters concluded that "the Court
today decides to save a statute Congress did not write."

As Harvard Law School Dean Martha Minow has observed, reading
the joint dissent and Ginsburg's opinion is "a bit like traveling between
two countries speaking different languages."[49] The justices disagree at a
fundamental level about the meaning of the Constitution and the Court's
role in enforcing limits on federal power. Rarely do factions on the Court
find themselves so far apart.

What, then, to make of the Chief's opinion?

In many respects, Roberts aligns himself with the joint dissent. He
repeatedly assails the mandate for its intrusion on liberty and violation
of federalism. Unlike Ginsburg, he valorizes the judicial role in policing
limits on federal power to regulate the economy. And he creates new
doctrine to limit the Commerce Clause and the Necessary and Proper
Clause, seeding land mines for future Congresses to avoid. As Karlan
wrote in the *New York Times*, "Anton Chekhov once remarked that 'one

must not put a loaded rifle on the stage if no one is thinking of firing it.' . . . In [the *Health Care Case*] the conservative majority also laid down a cache of weapons that future courts can use to attack many of the legislative achievements of the New Deal and the Great Society—including labor, environmental, civil rights and consumer protection laws."[50]

But the Chief's decision to characterize the mandate as a tax and thereby save it creates another kind of opportunity as well. Unwilling to sanction a true mandate, and disdainful of the command-and-control vision that mandates represent, Roberts leaves room for incentive-based and indirect forms of federal regulation. The government can use the tax code to nudge people to buy insurance, though it cannot use taxes to effectively coerce choice. As Columbia Law Professor Gillian Metzger writes of the Chief's opinion, "how the government regulates is as important as whether it regulates."[51]

In this respect, the Chief, like the dissenters, adheres to a view of liberty that consists of freedom *from* government. As a matter of the judicial role, however, he is open to allowing Congress to use choice-respecting methods of regulation. By encouraging Congress to adopt incentive-based tools, Roberts may hope to avoid even larger regulatory impositions, such as a single-payer public health care system. As Metzger explains, Roberts repeatedly "downplay[s] the collective and redistributive aspects" of the ACA. He thus transforms the law into one aimed at "informing and empowering individuals more than affirming societal responsibility for meeting a basic human need."

Roberts may have favored such an approach for any number of reasons. Most obviously, and quite respectably, he may have thought that it is right as a matter of constitutional law. From a certain perspective on judicial legitimacy, he may also have deemed it best to avoid a clash with the President on the eve of an election; in this cynical view, the course Roberts chose was the narrowest way to achieve that goal while remaining true to his principles. Another possible explanation is that Roberts agreed with Judge Brett Kavanaugh, who surmised in a lower court opinion that "we may be on the leading edge of a shift in how the Federal Government goes about furnishing a social safety net for those who are old, poor, sick, or disabled and need help."[52] If the trend is toward privatizing social services, and away from a model of heavy taxation linked to government-provided benefits, it could be wise to ensure that Congress has the powers necessary for that shift (which, as a matter of policy, Roberts would likely favor).[53]

Lest anyone think he hadn't considered the issue carefully, Roberts took pains to explain why libertarians should not fear the taxing power. After acknowledging that it is broader than the commerce power—since taxes, unlike regulations, can be imposed on people merely for existing—Roberts reasoned: "The taxing power does not give Congress the same degree of control over individual behavior. Once we recognize that Congress may regulate a particular decision under the Commerce Clause, the Federal Government can bring its full weight to bear. Congress may simply command individuals to do as it directs. . . . By contrast, Congress's authority under the taxing power is limited to requiring an individual to pay money into the Federal Treasury, no more." Taxes, moreover, generate a degree of political accountability unmatched by anything else in the policy universe.

The Chief's opinion, Ginsburg's partial dissent, and the joint dissent rest on contradictory views of American freedom and federalism. They also evince radically opposed beliefs about the Court's role in deciding issues that involve these fundamental principles, many of which significantly affect economic policy. Even beyond its importance as a milestone in our national journey, the *Health Care Case* thereby reveals fault lines that divide not only the Roberts Court but the broad expanse of American history.

Americans love liberty. It's our political oxygen, a source of our great strength, and a guiding light of the Constitution. Like most national values, though, its meaning is hotly disputed. As Abraham Lincoln wisely observed in 1864, "We all declare for liberty; but in using the same word we do not all mean the same thing."[54] Laws that strike some as abusive may offer others the promise of long-sought freedom. Caught at the intersection of competing accounts of American liberty, the ACA was fated to be a lightning rod for charges of unbounded government power.

At its core, the constitutional challenge to the ACA was mainly about protecting individual liberty to make basic economic decisions.[55] Congress could educate us about buying health insurance, nudge us to buy it, and tax us to create a single-payer national system of the sort represented by Medicare. But mandating that we buy insurance on the private market was a step too far, said its detractors. Even the Court's expansive precedents upholding federal laws, argued Georgetown Law Professor Randy Barnett, the main academic architect of the challenge to the ACA, involved regulation of existing economic activity. Those precedents did not uphold compulsion of new activity by those who had chosen to remain outside the regulated economic market.[56]

This argument, however, rests on a particular vision of what it means to be free. That vision has deep roots in our history and constitutional traditions but is at odds with the account of human liberty that animates much of the modern welfare state.

American political thought, stretching back to the framers, has been heavily influenced by a libertarian streak that defines liberty as the absence of government.[57] Whether stemming from moralistic accounts of natural law or efficiency-based beliefs about achieving the greatest good for the greatest number, libertarian theories maintain that government action usually makes us less free. They therefore warn that the state should generally stick to basics, like ensuring security and enforcing contracts, and mostly leave individuals to act as they see fit so long as they're not hurting anyone else. Broadly speaking, libertarians frown on laws that impose morality, limit choice to "protect" people from themselves, redistribute wealth, or regulate economic actors to advance subjective notions of fair and equal opportunity.[58]

To many people of a libertarian bent, the ACA appeared un-American and downright tyrannical. The law, they believed, was a brutal exercise of federal power to manipulate the health care market. Its vow to commandeer every citizen's most basic economic choices, they argued, was unprecedented. To drive home their point, the justices who voted to strike down the mandate borrowed their warning of its peril from a revered Founding Father, Alexander Hamilton. Federal power, the dissenters intoned with citations to his writings in *The Federalist Papers*, must not become a "hideous monster whose devouring jaws . . . spare neither sex nor age, nor high nor low, nor sacred nor profane."[59]

The Obama administration felt otherwise. When he rose to defend the ACA, Solicitor General Verrilli invoked a very different account of liberty: "We have been talking about [provisions of the ACA] in terms of

their effect as measures that solve . . . problems in the economic marketplace, that have resulted in millions of people not having health care
because they can't afford insurance. There is an important connection, a
profound connection between that problem and liberty. . . . There will be
millions of people with chronic conditions like diabetes and heart disease, and as a result of the health care that they will get, they will be
unshackled from the disabilities that those diseases [impose] and have
the opportunity to enjoy the blessings of liberty."

With that gauntlet thrown down, Verrilli's challenge to libertarian
logic was clear. Government, the Solicitor General insisted, is not only
capable of enhancing freedom; government is essential to freedom. The
Court, he might have added, has long upheld programs enacted to realize that ideal: Social Security, Medicaid, and Medicare, to name just a
few.[60]

This progressive account of liberty emerged in the early twentieth
century, when reformers from many walks of life questioned received
truths about the role of the state.[61] They pointed out that rights are not
just abstractions; rather, rights are caught up in debatable choices about
how society organizes itself and how the state exercises power. These
progressives explored the role social structures play in shaping human
lives, recognizing that liberty can be lost to accidents of birth, social
conditions that stifle success, and the invisible hand of a free market.
Recognizing so many species of un-freedom, progressives charted a new
approach. As the historian Eric Foner writes, "to traditional notions of
individualism and autonomy, Progressives wedded the idea that such
freedom required the conscious creation of the social conditions for full
human development."[62]

The Great Depression, like no event before or since, revealed the stark
contrast between libertarian and progressive accounts of freedom.[63]
Whereas Herbert Hoover remained wedded to traditional views and
adopted a fairly passive approach to the nation's economic crisis, FDR
leapt into the breach with the New Deal, which forever transformed the
role of the federal government.

In his 1944 State of the Union Address, delivered as World War II
drew to a close, FDR crystallized his thinking by proposing a Second Bill
of Rights.[64] Arguing that familiar "political rights" had "proved inadequate," he explained that "true individual freedom cannot exist without

economic security and independence." After all, he said, "necessitous men are not free men." FDR's remarkable list included the right "to a good education," the right "to earn enough to provide adequate food and clothing and recreation," and the right to "adequate protection from the economic fears of old age, sickness, accident, and unemployment." It also included "the right to adequate medical care and the opportunity to achieve and enjoy good health." FDR's bold vision was never implemented as a matter of constitutional law; unlike some other liberal democracies, such as South Africa, the United States does not have a tradition of recognizing welfare rights. Many of FDR's ideals, however, have since been realized in landmark social legislation.

Self-consciously in step with that liberal tradition, the ACA's proponents viewed themselves as inheritors of a march toward securing the Constitution's "blessings of liberty." Immediately after the House had passed the ACA, Speaker Pelosi exulted that "this bill tonight [creates the] opportunity for affordable health care for all Americans [to] have the freedom to have a happier life [and] to have the liberty to pursue their own happiness."[65]

That vision of liberty was completely foreign to the ACA's challengers. They thought it absurd to proclaim that such a manifestly invasive law would be a boon to liberty. As Paul Clement remarked at oral argument, "The mandate's threat to liberty is obvious," adding that "it's a very funny conception of liberty that forces somebody to purchase an insurance policy whether they want it or not." Such a command, he declared, "is a revolution in the relationship between the central government and the governed."

The *Health Care Case*, then, triggered a war of ideological worlds. The law's challengers worried—and its supporters hoped—that judicial ratification of the ACA would inaugurate a historic change in our social compact.[66] In truth, it was inevitable that a great battle over American freedom would unfold in the Roberts Court as it weighed Obama's signature achievement.

Observed broadly, the *Health Care Case* thus appears as but a snapshot of a centuries-old struggle. The joint dissenters unabashedly embrace a libertarian perspective on the ACA. Their opinion suggests that they see little redeeming virtue in the alternative vision advanced by FDR and those who followed in his footsteps. Indeed, several of these justices hinted at argument that they viewed the mandate as entirely illegitimate, the moral equivalent of highway robbery. Ginsburg's opinion, in contrast, says little about grand principles of freedom. Instead, it stands as a statement in its own right about the Court's limited role in selecting among accounts of liberty. To Ginsburg, that task is reserved mainly to Congress, though her partial dissent occasionally gestures toward an embrace of the progressive theory that animates the ACA. Roberts, meanwhile, walked a libertarian-inflected middle ground. He examined the powers that Congress invoked to justify the mandate, testing each to see how it could be used to burden liberty. In the end, he concluded that Congress may wield choice-respecting tools but not pure mandates.

The ACA managed to withstand a withering legal challenge, but liberty's soul remains up for grabs in the Roberts Court.

The *Health Care Case* turned heavily on what it means to be free, but the lawyers and justices lavished attention on the balance between the states and the federal government. This may seem peculiar: why didn't the lawyers challenging the ACA forthrightly argue that the law violated an individual's fundamental right to control personal economic decisions? It's a question worth asking, because the answer illuminates the basic architecture of modern constitutional law and sheds light on how that body of law affects our lives.

Although the framers were influenced by many social and economic considerations, their final product was shy on details about how the United States must order its economic affairs.[67] Wisely appreciating how much they could not anticipate, the framers left most economic issues for democracy to address. The Constitution specifically protected certain property and contract rights, and it enshrined free speech and due process safeguards central to a free market, but it enumerated no general right to economic liberty.

This does not necessarily mean that the Constitution is wholly silent on economic freedom. Most of the current justices (although not Scalia and Thomas) acknowledge that the Constitution protects rights other than those specifically listed in the amendments. Many see this view reflected in the Constitution's history and structure—and in the Ninth Amendment, which instructs that the "enumeration in the Constitution, of certain rights, shall not be construed to deny or disparage others retained by the people."[68] Invoking various amendments, but relying ultimately on its power to recognize new rights, the Court has struck down laws banning same-sex intimacy, burdensome limits on contraception and abortion, bans on interracial marriage, and bans on sending one's own children to private schools.[69] When the Court recognizes a right not expressly stated in the Constitution—a so-called unenumerated right—it limits both the state and federal governments.

For a time in American history, the Court aggressively protected an unenumerated right to economic liberty.[70] In the late nineteenth and early twentieth centuries, it enforced an unwritten "liberty of contract" and struck down scores of progressive laws. Nowadays this period— dubbed the "*Lochner* era" after one of its leading cases—is widely condemned.[71] Laws that are today considered unimpeachable were then thought to stand on shaky ground. In 1923, for example, the Court struck down minimum-wage laws because they interfered with employees' rights to contract with employers for lower wages.[72]

In the late 1930s, after a conservative Court relied partly on *Lochner*-style doctrines to strike down key New Deal laws, FDR went to war with the Court.[73] He directly challenged its power and appointed liberal justices to replace retiring members of the conservative Old Guard. In most of these efforts, he enjoyed robust legislative and popular support, although his attempt to pack the Court by persuading Congress to expand the number of justices met with resounding defeat. By 1937, the Court had abandoned its insistence that the Constitution requires libertarianism, ending the era of judicial protection for unenumerated economic liberties.[74] Since then, the justices have left most fights over economics to the democratic process.

As every lawyer involved in the *Health Care Case* knew, no member of today's Court is willing to recognize a free-floating judicial power to strike down statutes that violate some supposed right of economic freedom. The only justice who has even gestured in that direction is Thomas, and on this point he is a true outlier.[75] Indeed, the entire armature of modern constitutional law reflects active judicial protection of political and social rights, and minimal judicial involvement in economic affairs.

Although some view this as an odd structure, arguing that "economic rights" and "civil rights" are of equal worth, it has long been accepted as a constitutionally required limit on the judicial role. Laws that burden economic choice alone—however important that choice might be in people's lives—need only be supported by a conceivable rational basis. The Court has repeatedly declined to recognize a wide-ranging right to be free of regulation.[76]

Decades of precedent therefore prevented the ACA's challengers from translating their libertarian objections directly into constitutional arguments. After all, the individual mandate didn't force anyone to eat healthfully, ingest medications, or submit to regular physical exams. Had it done so, the mandate would likely have violated a fundamental right to have control over one's own body.[77] Instead, the mandate merely required Americans to obtain health insurance or pay a penalty. Because it burdened only economic freedom, the ACA wasn't vulnerable to direct assault for violating a protected right. Its challengers had to rely instead on principles of federalism.

Federalism is a key element of the American constitutional order. In agreeing to form a union, the thirteen original states ceded only some powers to the federal government, reserving all other powers to themselves. The Tenth Amendment confirms this understanding: "The powers not delegated to the United States by the Constitution . . . are reserved to the States respectively, or to the people." It does not, however, say anything about the scope of the powers delegated or identify exactly which powers the Constitution leaves *un*delegated.[78] The Constitution thus creates, but incompletely describes, the federal system. The scope of federal power has long been defined by tradition, politics, and structural inference more than analysis of any textual blueprint.[79]

Questions about state and federal power sometimes seem obscure and technical, far removed from daily life. Many of these issues belong to the province of legal experts, government insiders, and undergraduate political science majors. But it would be a mistake to lose sight of the important role played by federalism in our lives and our law. As the Court has repeatedly observed, there is a deep connection between the state-federal balance and individual rights, a link essential to understanding the *Health Care Case*.

More than any recent litigant, Carol Anne Bond has brought the relationship between freedom and federalism into stark relief.[80] Bond once loved her friend Myrlinda Haynes like a sister, but that didn't stop Bond from trying to poison her. A thirty-four-year-old Pennsylvanian, Bond learned one day that Haynes had become pregnant after sleeping with Bond's husband. Furious, Bond hatched a plan to burn Haynes by spreading toxic chemicals on Haynes's mailbox, car door handle, and doorknob. Bond's scheme, though, had a fatal flaw: the chemicals were bright orange and hard to miss. Even so, after Bond attempted to poison her more than twenty-four times in several months, Haynes slightly burned her thumb. After local police and prosecutors dropped the ball, the United States Attorney charged Bond with federal criminal offenses under an anti-terrorism law that implements the Chemical Weapons Convention. When Bond argued that the Constitution did not endow Congress with the power to pass such a sweeping criminal law, the federal government replied that she had no right to assert that claim. In its view, only a state could raise Bond's federalism argument.

As *Bond v. United States* proved, transgressions of limits on federal power do not affect only states. Bond faced imprisonment under a law of questionable constitutionality. In 2011, writing for a unanimous Court, Kennedy rejected the government's argument. He explained that "the individual liberty secured by federalism is not simply derivative of the rights of the States. . . . When government acts in excess of its lawful powers, that liberty is at stake." It was precisely this fusion of freedom and federalism that formed the vanguard of the attack on the ACA.

The central insight regarding limits on federal power, credited to James Madison, is that the Constitution protects rights in more ways than one. Its most direct method of protection is to say something such as "Congress shall make no law respecting an establishment of religion, or prohibiting the free exercise thereof." By recognizing a right, the Constitution creates a strong presumption in favor of that kind of liberty. It tells Americans that we value this right; it also tells politicians to respect it and courts to guard its boundaries.

Madison, one of the most brilliant framers, nonetheless doubted that rights alone would control political majorities. In a letter to Thomas Jefferson, he argued that "experience proves the inefficacy of a bill of rights on those occasions when its control is most needed. Repeated violations of these parchment barriers have been committed by overbearing majorities in every State."[81]

That is where the Constitution's structural provisions, those that define the separation of powers and federalism, become vital to any account of liberty.[82] As Madison recognized, the rules that establish government also define its ability and incentives to ride roughshod over individual freedom. The diffusion of power within and across levels of government is one of the Constitution's most ingenious designs. Even as the Constitution creates and empowers a national government, it also establishes safeguards designed to prevent that power from getting out of hand. Some of those fail-safes take the form of rights, while others take the form of structural limits on where and how and by whom power can be exercised. With this political architecture in mind, Hamilton once remarked that "the Constitution is itself, in every rational sense, and to every useful purpose, a bill of rights."[83]

In *Bond*, Kennedy extolled the genius of our system. "Federalism has more than one dynamic," he explained. "The allocation of powers in our federal system preserves the integrity, dignity, and residual sovereignty of the states . . . but that is not its exclusive sphere of operation." Rather, "federalism secures to citizens the liberties that derive from the diffusion of sovereign power." It permits "local policies more sensitive to the diverse needs of a heterogeneous society . . . enables greater citizen involvement . . . [and] makes government more responsive by putting the States in competition for a mobile citizenry." This, Kennedy explained, is the "counterintuitive insight" of federalism: "Freedom is enhanced by the creation of two governments, not one." He added, "By denying any one government complete jurisdiction over all the concerns of public life, federalism protects the liberty of the individual from arbitrary power."

Scalia echoed these views at a public lecture in 2013, noting that "every banana republic, every president-for-life could boast a bill of rights. . . . The former Evil Empire, the Union of Soviet Socialist Republics, had a wonderful bill of rights."[84] It is the "distribution of power," he added, that separates our Constitution. These remarks accorded with

Scalia's earlier confession that Bill of Rights cases are not the ones "I live or die for," as it is the structure of government that ensures that laws are "not just words on paper."[85]

These powerful points raise a deep question about the Court's duty in our constitutional system, a question at the heart of the *Health Care Case*: what role should judges play in interpreting and enforcing structural limits on federal power? This is a deceptively hard issue. After all, limits on Congress that protect individual liberty can take forms other than judicially enforced rules. And more often than not, that is exactly what happens: a combination of politics, practicalities, and custom usually keeps the federal government from coloring outside constitutional lines.

From time to time, though, the federal government is accused of crossing a constitutional limit. On those occasions, the Court may be called upon to issue a final judgment and to offer broader pronouncements on the scope of federal power. Since the 1930s, the Court has generally taken a cautious view of its role in this endeavor, emphasizing that the federal government enjoys broad powers under the Constitution. As a result, political and practical checks are often the only game in town. (As we have learned in recent years, though, politics—and particularly partisanship—can provide a more than formidable check on Congress's ability to exercise power.[86])

The Court's broad view of federal power dates back to the early Republic, when a series of famous cases firmly settled that the Constitution permits a vital national government. As Chief Justice John Marshall wrote in 1819 in *McCulloch v. Maryland*, "the sword and the purse . . . and no inconsiderable portion of the industry of the nation are intrusted to its Government. . . . A Government intrusted with such ample powers, on the due execution of which the happiness and prosperity of the Nation so vitally depends, must also be intrusted with ample means for their execution."[87] This is not to say that the early Court gave Congress and the President carte blanche. But it did adopt a generous view of most federal powers, including all of the powers at issue in the *Health Care Case*: the regulation of commerce, taxing and spending, and Necessary and Proper Clause authority.

From the mid-nineteenth century through the 1930s, around the same time it recognized rights to economic liberty, the Court tried to manufacture and enforce stricter limits on the federal government. It quickly discovered, though, that creating such rules is a challenging task. The Court came to rely on arbitrary and even bizarre doctrine; for example, in striking down federal laws, it reasoned that agriculture, manufacturing, and mining do not constitute "commerce" within the meaning of the Commerce Clause.[88] In the end, the Court's attempt to parse the interconnected national economy and render segments of it off-limits to Congress proved ill-fated. In the late 1930s, the whole project collapsed in acrimony, battered by its collision with FDR and his New Deal. The current justices know this history well: while criticizing Roberts's refusal to uphold the mandate under the Commerce Clause, Ginsburg bluntly pointed out that "this Court's former endeavors to impose categorical limits on the commerce power have not fared well."

From the mid-1930s to the late 1980s, the Court consistently upheld federal actions against claims that they overstepped limits set forth in the Constitution. Its rulings etched into precedent a virtually unlimited view of the federal government's power to craft policy, subject to the formidable check of politics.[89] Then, in the 1990s and early 2000s, five conservative justices handed down a series of rulings that began to identify judicially enforceable limits on federal authority.[90] These opinions, none involving major legislation, portended substantial future constraints on federal power. Shying away from systemic statements of new rules, they struck at particular federal acts while emphasizing the dignity of the states—all to the end of implementing what Chief Justice William Rehnquist once called "the tacit postulates" of "the constitutional plan."[91] The Rehnquist Court stepped toward a more vigorous account of federalism mainly by identifying "non-economic" conduct that the Commerce Clause does not empower Congress to regulate and by giving new meaning to the Tenth Amendment's protections of state sovereignty (including, for example, limits on federal commandeering of state agencies).

Even so, these rulings did not significantly disturb the received wisdom that the modern federal government wields broad power, only marginally limited by the Court and the Constitution, in presiding over the American economy. The Court expressed a mood, but one without much doctrinal force. As soon became clear to many scholars and judges, the Commerce Clause is not a workable tool for a federalism renaissance—

not least because efforts to limit Congress's power over "commerce" have always collided with the manifest implausibility of parsing domains of American life and deeming some of them noncommercial. (After all, most behavior, in the aggregate, has a substantial economic effect.) Some scholars turned to history or formal theory to help in that effort, but the difficulties of translating even purportedly clear original understanding to the modern world posed a daunting obstacle.[92] Legal rules built around state sovereignty encountered problems of their own. For one thing, many potentially troubling uses of federal power don't involve a direct assertion of federal power over state governments. Further, the federal and state governments have created elaborate and innovative cooperative federalism schemes, in which they share power in novel and sometimes beneficial ways that the Court is reluctant to disrupt by imposing rigid constitutional rules.[93] In those sorts of relationships, states can wield a wide range of tools to protect their prerogatives other than the threat of judicial intervention.[94]

Notwithstanding some of the limits of then-existing doctrine, in the *Health Care Case*, the ACA's opponents, moved mainly by beliefs about liberty, struck at the mandate using the language of federalism. They knew that a majority of the Roberts Court spoke this language fluently and was open to innovative doctrinal arguments. Extolling the liberty-protecting virtues of limited national government, they argued that Congress had exceeded its powers, and they called on the Court to offer the Obama administration a lesson in basic civics. Most radically, they asked the Court to fashion new constitutional law limiting the federal government.

That is exactly what Roberts and the joint dissenters did, embracing arguments about the scope of the Commerce Clause and the Necessary and Proper Clause that had never before been invoked to strike down an Act of Congress. This is why Ginsburg's opinion goes on at such length about the judicial role: her colleagues had ventured into new and treacherous territory. Summoning decades of history, she protested that the Court had no business in such rocky waters.

Sometimes the trick to defeating legal arguments is finding their limiting principle—or their lack of one. In debates over the ACA, opponents of the law relied on this strategy to brilliant effect, criticizing the law's defenders for failing to identify any worthwhile limit on Congress's power to regulate American life. If the Constitution means anything, they argued, surely it means that Congress cannot have a full-blown police power. Yet only such an unbounded power, they insisted, could possibly support the mandate.[95]

This was a strong argument, so far as it went. Ultimately, however, it turned on the hotly disputed question of whether to describe self-insurance as economic *activity* that could be regulated or as economic *inactivity* that should be off-limits to the government. (And on whether the supposed line between economic activity and inactivity makes any sense as a limit on the scope of Congress's authority under the Commerce Clause.) Given that the battle took this form, the Solicitor General's refusal to identify other limits on federal power made tactical sense: why concede today a power you might need tomorrow?

The attack on the mandate, meanwhile, faced its own difficulty: it could prove too much. As a general proposition, denying the federal government power to regulate will almost always increase liberty, at least from a libertarian point of view. But that doesn't tell us *which* federal laws we should find to be prohibited by the Constitution's structure of federalism. Nor does it tell us which powers it would make sense to deny to Congress even as we otherwise allow the national government a wide range of authorities. Federalism can protect liberty, but a workable theory of federalism must do more than say that every Act of Congress that burdens individual liberty should be prohibited by the Constitution's state-federal structure. Instead, it must afford an explanation of why, as a matter of constitutional history and principle, a challenged law relies on power that should be deemed distinctly dangerous at the federal level. If we are to deny Congress certain powers but allow states to wield those same powers, we can reasonably ask why they pose a unique threat in the hands of one legislature and not the other.

Bond is illustrative. It involved a federal prosecution for a failed attempt to poison a romantic rival, brought under a law Congress had passed to enforce an international chemical weapons treaty. The law did appear to cover Bond's conduct, but few could ever have imagined it being used to prosecute a garden-variety local offense. More important, we have good reason to worry about the federal government stepping out of bounds when exercising a wide-ranging "police power" through criminal law. As compared to local, elected prosecutors, vast centralized bureaucracies like the Justice Department may be less accountable. The enforcement of criminal law, moreover, often embodies moral judgments and decisions about priorities that vary dramatically from community to community. Partly for that reason, America enjoys a strong tradition of reserving most criminal justice functions to local and state officials. Nor is criminal law the only field we mostly leave to states: family law, which governs such matters as divorce, marriage, and adoption, has long been the nearly exclusive province of state government. Few would disagree that local control over legal issues involving families is generally desirable.

Seen in this light, the *Health Care Case* presented difficult questions for those eager to dismantle the ACA. Is it uniquely troubling for the federal government to control basic economic decisions, such as whether Americans buy insurance on the private market? Is it less troubling if Americans are not compelled to buy insurance by the federal government but simply face a modest tax penalty if they decline to do so? Finally, against a background of broad federal authority—which includes the power to ban goods, regulate virtually all commerce, levy substantial taxes, and create schemes like Welfare and Medicaid—what about the ACA's purchase mandate made it a singularly dire threat to the liberty guarded by constitutional structure?

The ACA's foes spent little time explaining why mandates, in particular, are acceptable at the state level but unacceptable at the federal level. They noted that state-level mandates, unlike federal mandates, can be escaped simply by moving to another state, though the difficulty of uprooting one's life makes this a pretty unlikely option.[96] They described the mandate as "unprecedented," though that, too, is a relatively weak attack, since there must be a first time for any new kind of federal policy. And they warned of a fundamental change in the relationship between governed and government, though this objection seems equally applicable to many other tools of federal power. (Indeed, that precise objection was raised in response to the initial exercise of many federal powers that we now take for granted, including the power to prohibit commerce altogether and the power to establish welfare schemes.)

Federalism is a marvelous thing, but structural arguments require coherent explanations of why certain kinds of decisions should be denied to particular levels of government. Apart from repeating the mantra that self-insurance is best viewed as inactivity and that regulating inactivity is uniquely threatening to liberty, the ACA's critics struggle to offer a fully reasoned account of why it is especially threatening for Congress, in particular, to compel us into action to address a national problem. And the activity/inactivity line doesn't hold up terribly well on close inspection; it turns out a lot of behavior can fairly be characterized in either manner.[97]

In many ways, then, the strongest glue holding this attack together was a libertarian belief in a right to personal control over economic decisions. It was the ACA's violation of this right, a right that dare not speak its name, that made its "unprecedented" nature and effect on the social contract so troubling. In the eyes of many of its challengers, the federal government had to be denied the power to mandate the purchase of insurance because *no* government should have it. As a legal matter, their argument would have held little sway if directed at a state law, given judicial unwillingness to protect unenumerated economic rights. But when aimed at Congress, the argument gained traction because it found natural expression in the language of limited federal powers. Congress must not have all powers—and given its sweeping implications, this power, perhaps more than any other, must qualify as beyond the pale.

Although the argument made by the ACA's opponents was ultimately unsuccessful, five justices looked kindly on it. This was itself a remarkable sign of things to come. Since the New Deal, advocates of limited federal authority have watched helplessly as the Court conferred nearly boundless power on Congress. Yet over the past several decades, many Americans have grown insistent that constitutional limits on federal power vis-à-vis the states exist; that they must be enforced by the Judiciary; and that they serve vital functions. In their case against the ACA, conservative and libertarian litigators saw a rare opportunity to vindicate core premises of the federalist vision. If they lacked a complete account of why purchase mandates should be prohibited, even as other vast federal powers are allowed, that is not a fatal objection. Indeed, many of these litigators would likely take issue with other powers that Congress currently enjoys clear authority to exercise. And a last stand is rarely the most elaborately designed battle maneuver. Although they went down in defeat, the attack on the ACA offered its challengers a chance to rally believers in state-centric governance by letting loose the war cry of "Federalism" just at the moment when the nation's ears were most carefully attuned.

In the *Health Care Case*, five justices accepted versions of the challengers' arguments. In so doing, they signaled a willingness, perhaps even an eagerness, to resume a judicial role in limiting federal economic regulations that the Court had largely abandoned in 1937. They also suggested an inclination to take a harder look at laws affecting economic liberties.

The Court's long-standing reluctance to intervene in economic policy is no guarantee that it will remain forever dormant. For the time being, though, the Court seems entirely unwilling to return to a world of *Lochner*-style liberty of contract. In 2013, for example, Scalia emphatically rejected such a project: "I have long been an advocate of the proposition that it is not for judges to write their own policy preferences into the Constitution. . . . Economic liberty is not an exception to this rule. In a democracy, if the basic law so permits, the legislature may decide to replace the free market with central planning, however unwise it may be."[98] It seems clear that Scalia's peers on the Roberts Court share his disinclination to open that can of worms.

Yet in a series of rulings involving other constitutional rights, this Court has gently tiptoed toward a bolder role in economic matters. *Sorrell v. IMS* is a prime example of this trend.[99] In *Sorrell*, the Court struck down a Vermont law designed to lower prescription drug prices. Vermont had tried to prevent pharmacies from giving drug companies detailed information about the prescription practices of individual doctors—data that drug companies used to tailor their marketing tactics to convince doctors to prescribe pricier drugs. The Vermont law, like the ACA, sought to leverage principles of economics to deliver effective health care at a lower cost. Joined by Roberts, Scalia, Thomas, Alito, and Sotomayor, Kennedy saw not simply an economic regulation but an abridgment of free speech. Invoking decades of precedent treating commercial advertising as a form of protected expression, he put the law under an unforgiving First Amendment microscope and declared it invalid.

In an anxious dissent joined by Ginsburg and Kagan, Breyer cited

Lochner and cautioned that the Court was expanding the First Amendment into new and inappropriate terrain. In his view, Vermont's law was merely a regulation of economic activity and should have been tested under a far more forgiving judicial standard. To Breyer, the First Amendment's potent limits on government simply didn't apply here.[100]

Breyer's fear was understandable. To protect the public and ensure fair markets, economic regulations often govern the exchange of information—its timing, form, accessibility, and content. We tell drug makers what they can say on labels and financial institutions what they must disclose to investors. We limit access to medical data and require corporations to disclose key facts to shareholders. In an information age, as the line between economic transactions and speech blurs, the *Sorrell* approach might imperil whole swaths of financial, corporate, consumer, and medical regulation. Aggressively pursued, it might lead the Court to a far more prominent position in regulating transactions central to the modern marketplace and, thus, expand the judicial role in shaping ground rules for vital segments of the American economy.[101]

Sorrell is part of a line of Roberts Court cases suggesting an appetite for a more active judicial role in overseeing economic affairs. Individually they may not say much, but viewed together they point the way toward more assertive use of constitutional law by a majority of the Court to advance deregulatory economic beliefs.

In 2010, for example, in a case about who owns the pricey real estate created by Florida's beach-restoration programs, Scalia urged the Court to adopt a very broad view of when the state has "taken" property and must therefore pay fair compensation.[102] Two years later, invoking the First Amendment, Alito limited the procedures by which any public sector union could adjust the mandatory fees it collected periodically from all the workers in the bargaining unit it represents. Alito strongly implied that the Court is on the verge of imposing additional rules that would limit the ability of unions to prevent nonmembers from "free-riding on the union's efforts, sharing the employment benefits obtained by the union's collective bargaining without sharing the costs incurred"—rules that would strike at the heart of public sector unions' ability to form and thrive.[103] That same year, in a case arising from a sinfully boring fight over sewer improvements in Indianapolis, Roberts dissented and invoked equal protection principles to explain why he would invalidate the city's unusual method of financing its project.[104] As Linda Greenhouse noted in the *New York Times*, this was one of exceptionally few cases not involving race in which the conservatives saw a violation of the Equal Protection Clause and the liberals did not.[105] The Chief conceded in his dissent that equality-based judicial intervention in matters of taxation and regulation "is and should be" rare. "But," he added, "every generation or so a case comes along when this Court needs to say enough is enough, if the Equal Protection Clause is to retain any force in this context."

Judicial cries of "enough is enough" that claim to be once-in-a-generation events have a way of recurring sooner than expected. When such cries invoke an important principle, predictions that they will not become part of a pattern should be viewed with skepticism. And in this instance, it's worth noting that the claim was issued by a youthful chief justice of the United States, just three weeks before his landmark opinion in the *Health Care Case*.

More notable still is the way in which all these cases—involving Vermont drug laws, Florida beach-nourishment programs, a public sector union in California, and sewer financing in Indianapolis—signal a loosely unified project. It is increasingly evident that the Roberts Court is prepared to more closely scrutinize economic regulation, both state and federal, with an eye toward protecting a wide range of related individual rights.

This trend has been accompanied by a heightened willingness to explore constitutional limits on federal power in particular. Thomas has spent decades writing separately on this point, but now his right-leaning colleagues are also taking pains to disapprove of anything that looks like a federal "police power."

Thus, in *United States v. Comstock*, a 2010 case about a law that permits the civil commitment of sexually dangerous criminals beyond the date they would otherwise be released from jail, the Court engaged in a heated debate over limits on the Necessary and Proper Clause.[106] Breyer upheld the law, adopting a broad view of Congress's lawmaking powers. But Kennedy and Alito, in concurrences, and Scalia and Thomas, in dissent, firmly resisted Breyer's expansive reasoning. Invoking the Constitution's structure of federalism, they argued that the Court should more carefully and critically scrutinize Congress's claim that its law really was both *necessary* and *proper* to carry into effect its other powers. A similar debate played out two years later in *United States v. Kebodeaux*, an otherwise minor case about sex offender registration requirements. Breyer once again wrote for a majority to uphold federal power, but Scalia and Thomas forcefully objected in dissent that Congress had taken a step too far. Strikingly, Roberts wrote separately, joined by Alito, to prevent "incautious readers [from thinking] they have found in the majority opinion something they would not find in either the Constitution or any prior decision of ours: a federal police power."[107] Such a power, he added, "does not exist." The Chief rarely writes concurrences; he wrote only two of them in the whole 2012 term. His decision to write in *Kebodeaux* revealed his sustained interest in federalism.

Together, *Comstock*, *Kebodeaux*, and the *Health Care Case* mark a new and momentous development in conservative efforts to articulate judicially enforceable constitutional limits on Congress. The Commerce Clause and the Tenth Amendment remain important, but now the Court is building jurisprudence to narrow Congress's power under the Necessary and Proper Clause, which serves the vital role of allowing Congress leeway to effectuate all its other grants of power.[108] In the *Health Care Case*, the dissenters also placed Congress's power to tax and spend for the general welfare under a microscope, hinting at the need for a reevaluation. Thus, in opinions haunted by fear of a federal "police power," the Court has shifted its focus away from protecting traditional spheres of state sovereignty and is now engaged directly with questions of when Congress is empowered to regulate at all, regardless of any intrusion on the states. Dosing their writings with unsubtle concern about the danger of federal tyranny, the five right-leaning justices have undertaken a lawmaking project with the potential to launch the Court into a more prominent—and disputed—role in policing its coordinate branches.[109]

The *Health Care Case* thus perfectly captures what might best be imagined as a double helix of increased judicial oversight. One strand involves the direct protection of personal freedom in economic affairs from all levels of government. The other strand involves a restriction of federal power, invoked in no small part to back up that protection of individual economic liberty. Each strand of this double helix incorporates a vision of liberty *from* government, not liberty *enabled by* government, and each augurs a more active role for the Court in matters that it once left mainly to democracy.

In recent years, some scholars have warned that the Roberts Court stands poised to revive the ghost of an ancient enemy: *Lochner*-style doctrines of economic liberty. Their concerns are almost certainly exaggerated. Nobody on this Court seems eager to return to the pre–New Deal age of judicial recognition of a vague, unenumerated right to be free of regulation. Nor is the Roberts Court likely to return us to the maze of arbitrary doctrines that once limited federal power to preside over an interconnected national economy.

But this does not mean that scholars who see echoes of the past are wholly off base. In its own way, the Roberts Court has conjured the spirit and spell of a pre-1930s world, moving sporadically but unmistakably toward greater solicitude for economic liberty and judicial limits on federal power. The *Health Care Case*, a remarkable ruling in its own right, is the most significant sign yet of what may wait ahead. In truth, the specter haunting the regulatory state is not a ghost returned from pre–New Deal days. It may just be the Roberts Court.

3

CAMPAIGN FINANCE:

FOLLOW THE MONEY

In 2011, one of America's most powerful institutions laid siege to the Supreme Court. This was never a fair fight. The Court ranks among the most sacrosanct centers of influence in the United States. It has withstood confrontations with presidents, Congresses, and whole sections of the nation determined to defy it. And the Roberts Court justices are extremely smart and politically savvy. But they could bring only knives to what turned out to be an intensely public gunfight.

Stephen Colbert, more famous than any justice, had decided to use his national platform on Comedy Central's *The Colbert Report* to make the Court look utterly absurd. Bound by traditions of decorum and unwilling to descend into unseemly brawls with critics, the justices endured one blow after another for months on end. Meanwhile, they could hit back against Colbert and his ilk only indirectly and occasionally in suitably high-minded public speeches.

Colbert focused his comedic wrath on the Roberts Court's most controversial ruling to date: *Citizens United v. Federal Election Commission*.[1] In that instantly famous case, the Court held that corporations and unions have a First Amendment right to spend as much money as they choose when advocating the election or defeat of political candidates, so long as they do not coordinate their advertising with the candidates' campaigns. *Citizens United* provoked a storm of protest from Americans convinced that it would irreparably harm our political system.

Colbert's comic genius and unparalleled flair for spectacle had received a gift in *Citizens United*'s assertion that "independent expenditures, including those made by corporations, do not give rise to corruption or the appearance of corruption." Aided and abetted by Jon Stewart of *The Daily Show*, whose impeccable sense of irony has made him the leading source of news for a cynical generation, Colbert wreaked nightly havoc on national television. In an elaborate, deadly serious parody, Colbert staged a string of devious campaign stunts designed to prove the unbearable wrongness of *Citizens United*. His vision was clear: "Colbert Nation could have a voice, in the form of my voice, shouted through a megaphone made of cash."[2] For Colbert, it was all about the "American dream . . . that anyone, no matter who they are, if they are determined, if they are willing to work hard enough, someday they could grow up to create a legal entity which could then receive unlimited corporate funds, which could be used to influence our elections."[3]

To realize that dream, Colbert hired Trevor Potter, a former chairman of the Federal Election Commission (FEC). Colbert and Potter spent much of 2011 arguing a single point: the Roberts Court had completely underestimated how easy it is for groups with corporate funds to covertly coordinate "independent" activities with candidates. This secret coordination, they implied, would make it stunningly simple for big money to corrupt and capture our officials. Casting himself as a Mr. Smith for our postmodern era, Colbert went to Washington and soberly testified before the FEC on behalf of his request to found a Super PAC[4]—a kind of political action committee that, thanks to *Citizens United*, can accept unlimited contributions from any source and spend them to support or oppose any candidate (so long as they don't formally coordinate expenditures with candidates). After the FEC gave him the nod in June 2011, Colbert brightly explained to his fans that by "PAC," he didn't mean "political action committee"; what he had in mind was "plastic and/or cash."[5] In tune with the doublespeak conventions that govern such things, Colbert named his Super PAC Americans for a Better Tomorrow, Tomorrow, Inc.

Starting that fall, Colbert aired segments showing how anonymous millionaires were quietly funding Karl Rove's secretive Super PAC, Crossroads GPS. Colbert explained how to manipulate disclosure rules, smirking as he declared that "I am opaque . . . yo' motha' gave me my money."[6] And, to prove that "shady, out of state group[s] whose intentions are not clear" can influence elections, he ran ads in the Iowa primaries that called on voters to support "Rick Parry," not Texas Governor Rick Perry.[7] "You can feel confident *he's* not asking us to do that," Colbert explained helpfully.

After actually outpolling several candidates in the South Carolina Republican primary, Colbert doubled down on this mad-eyed gambit by turning his Super PAC over to Stewart and exploring a presidential run.[8] Presidential candidates can't oversee their own Super PACs, but in reality the lines between independence and coordination are paper thin—yet another exploitable gap between optimistic law and dispiriting reality. As *Politico* reported, "Night after night, Stewart and Colbert have appeared together on one another's shows, giggling and biting their knuckles about how they are 'not coordinating' even as they plot the next steps in Colbert's not-yet-officially-announced campaign."[9] Colbert took every chance to explain that Mitt Romney, Newt Gingrich, and Rick Perry were all supported by Super PACs founded by their allies. By turning his Super PAC over to Stewart, Colbert was merely following conventional practice.

Not content to play a mere supporting role in this act, Stewart went rogue. He ran ads attacking "Mitt the Ripper," recalling presidential candidate Mitt Romney's claim on the stump that "corporations are people" and charging that "as head of Bain Capital, [Romney] bought companies, carved them up and got rid of what he couldn't use."[10] He endorsed former Godfather Pizza Chairman Herman Cain even after Cain had withdrawn, explaining that Cain is "such a Washington outsider, he's not even running for president."[11] And for the coup de grâce, he enlisted movie star Samuel Jackson to narrate an attack ad targeting Colbert.[12]

Priceless, one might say. One would be wrong. Colbert reported to the FEC in early 2012 that his Super PAC had raised $1,023,121.[13]

If this extended Colbert episode reveals the First Amendment at its best, many Americans seem to believe that *Citizens United* portrays it at its worst. To them, the case marked a turning point in our history, a deadly threat to America's centuries-old experiment in democracy.

The truth, as usual, is more complicated. It's easy to lose sight of the fact that *Citizens United* posed incredibly difficult questions about free speech, popular sovereignty, and political equality. Deciding when Congress can ban certain disfavored speakers from the marketplace of ideas or limit how much they can speak is no easy task. It certainly isn't out-landish to conclude, as the Court did, that free speech rights must pre-vail over hard-to-document fears that corporate wealth will distort public discourse or corrupt politicians. Indeed, almost four years have passed since *Citizens United* was decided, and it has yet to rend the fabric of American life.

In an age of disenchantment with politics and stark economic ine-quality, *Citizens United* became a focal point for debates about the evap-oration of faith in responsive government. This is understandable, but *Citizens United* simply cannot bear all that weight. Money in politics is only one part of our era's story of corruption and dysfunction—and *Citizens United*, in turn, is only one part of the story of money in politics. The wealthy have always found ways to convert economic might into political power. The real question is what role government should be trusted to play in efforts to affect how and where money flows through the electoral system.

This perspective directs attention to the Roberts Court's broader agenda of deregulating campaign finance. Five justices—Roberts, Scalia, Kennedy, Thomas, and Alito—have voiced grave doubts about the legiti-macy of most efforts by government to dictate how money may be spent in elections. By reshaping the architecture of money, influence, and political organization, the Roberts Court is transforming how America conducts—and funds—politics.

On January 21, 2010, the justices took their seats and gazed solemnly out at their majestic courtroom. Chief Justice Roberts said simply, "In case 08-205, *Citizens United versus the FEC*, Justice Kennedy has the Opinion of the Court." Kennedy then announced the majority's holding. Within days, an astonished outcry against the Court echoed across the nation.

Its decision, though, came as no surprise to Court watchers. The case had arisen from efforts by Citizens United, a nonprofit corporation that accepted funds from for-profit corporations, to promote a documentary attacking Hillary Clinton, who was then seeking the Democratic presi-dential nomination. Citizens United wanted to distribute *Hillary: The Movie* through video-on-demand and promote it on TV, but federal law prohibited "electioneering communications" backed by corporate general treasury funds for thirty days before a primary election. When its law-suit first reached the Court, Citizens United mainly argued that *Hillary: The Movie* wasn't a prohibited electioneering communication because it didn't expressly urge viewers to vote against Clinton. Several justices, though, seemed much more interested in broader questions about the government's powers over campaign speech. Alito engineered a particu-larly devastating exchange in which a federal lawyer conceded that, under the government's theory, Congress could even ban books about candidates for political office. Roberts followed up: "It's a five-hundred-page book, and at the end it says, 'And so vote for X,' the government could ban that?" Yes, the lawyer replied. A few months later, the Court ordered re-argument of the First Amendment issues.

Jeffrey Toobin, a journalist, has since revealed that Scalia, Kennedy, Thomas, and Alito were willing to decide the big constitutional ques-tions right away. [14] They saw no need for re-argument. Outraged by their willingness to rule on broader issues that Citizens United's lawyers had barely raised, Justice David Souter drafted a biting dissent charging the majority with illegitimate activism. Roberts, who had originally voted for Citizens United on the narrow ground that its movie wasn't an elec-tioneering communication, worried that Souter's dissent would badly dent the Court's credibility. The re-argument was his ingenious sug-gestion: the more conservative justices knew they had already won, but a second hearing would nullify some of the most damaging of Souter's accusations.

The Department of Justice wasn't privy to these backstage maneu-vers, but the order calling for re-argument was hardly a subtle message. Acknowledging the obvious importance of the case, then Solicitor Gen-eral Elena Kagan personally re-argued it. In one of the twists of fate that occur with intriguing regularity at the Court, *Citizens United* afforded Kagan her first argument as solicitor general—and gave Sonia Soto-mayor, who had since replaced Souter, her first major argument as a jus-tice. (Sotomayor, however, already had a deep background in the subject from her time on New York's Campaign Finance Board, where she force-fully warned against the danger of too much unsupervised money in politics.[15]) Kagan fought valiantly for what she surely knew to be a doomed cause. Urging her future colleagues to uphold a law plainly lack-ing five votes, Kagan all but conceded defeat. Angling for a narrow loss, she told the Chief, "As to whether the government has a preference as to the way in which it loses . . . the answer is yes."

Kennedy wrote for the majority. Few topics inspire Kennedy more than the First Amendment, which enjoys a special place in his libertarian jurisprudence. In *Citizens United*, he composed an opinion extolling the value of unfettered expression. Warning against the perils of even well-intentioned government censorship, he invoked a wide range of free speech precedents to explain that core principles of liberty and democracy required protection of Citizens United.

Roberts wrote separately to explain why his vote in *Citizens United* was consistent with the values of judicial modesty, restraint, and unanimity that he has publicly championed. He argued that Kennedy's result—which struck down a federal law and reversed two Supreme Court precedents—was both unavoidable and manifestly justified. In a show of solidarity with his fellow President George W. Bush appointee, Alito joined Roberts's concurrence.

Scalia also wrote separately. He has long opposed the Court's willingness to uphold campaign finance laws and reveled in the chance to destroy some nettlesome precedents.[16] True to form, though, he thought the Court needed more than the soaring principles and precedents that formed the backbone of Kennedy's opinion. It needed originalism. With a few centuries-old dictionaries in tow, Scalia composed a lengthy lesson in eighteenth-century history to explain "the conformity of today's opinion with the original meaning of the First Amendment."

Finally, Thomas suggested in his own opinion that the Court should go even further. Invoking the First Amendment right to anonymous speech, he argued that Congress had no power even to require public disclosure of campaign expenditures, a power that Kennedy's majority expressly upheld. In Thomas's view, the right to speak on political affairs encompasses the right to speak behind a veil of anonymity. After all, retaliation by the public and elected officials against unpopular speakers can chill First Amendment rights as surely as an outright ban. No other justice agreed with him, but it's hardly unusual for Thomas to use his solitary writings to propose innovative conservative approaches to constitutional law.

Presented with four right-leaning opinions, the more liberal justices all rallied in dissent behind Justice John Paul Stevens, a moderate and in many ways apostate Republican whose appointment by Gerald Ford in 1975 seemed to many the finest achievement of that brief presidency. By 2010, the Court had moved so sharply to the right that Stevens, whose own views had moved only slightly to the left, found himself cast in the unexpected role of liberal hero.[17] Fast approaching the end of his long and storied career on the Court, Stevens composed a ninety-page dissent that besieged every factual premise, procedural device, and legal argument in *Citizens United*. The final lines of this epic opinion foreshadowed the coming conflict: "While American democracy is imperfect, few outside the majority of this Court would have thought its flaws included a dearth of corporate money in politics."

The rage that crackled beneath Stevens's genteel prose erupted in raw form throughout the country. The White House immediately denounced *Citizens United* as "a major victory for big oil, Wall Street banks, health insurance companies and the other powerful interests that marshal their power every day in Washington to drown out the voices of everyday Americans."[18] Wisconsin Senator Russ Feingold, the coauthor, with Arizona Senator John McCain, of the bipartisan federal law that *Citizens United* struck down, condemned this "terrible mistake."[19] Congress debated responsive legislation, and liberals started forging constitutional amendments that could negate *Citizens United*—efforts that quickly progressed toward implausible calls for a constitutional convention, the first since 1787.[20]

It was as though people were genuinely shocked by the sudden discovery that moneyed interests, including corporations, powerfully influence American politics. A Supreme Court ruling that could have provided a rare opportunity to debate long-simmering, systemic issues was instead portrayed as alarming news and treated as a whipping boy for all the flaws in contemporary politics. Perhaps this was inevitable in the context of a terrifying recession blamed by many on big banks, heated public debate over economic inequality, and a spike in populist anti-corporate sentiment. Opinion polls marked widespread hostility to the decision.[21] Reformers channeled and stoked these energies. And when Colbert took up the cause, he struck comic gold.

The justices are not shrinking violets; hate mail and vicious op-eds come with the territory. The main rationale for entrusting a group of unelected, life-tenured judges with so much power is that they can stand up for the Constitution against heated political opposition. True to form, if any justices were surprised by the backlash to *Citizens United*, they withstood the vicious criticism of their handiwork with characteristic aplomb.

At times, though, the mask slipped. The biggest breakdown occurred at the 2010 State of the Union Address, six days after *Citizens United* was announced. In a tense moment almost without parallel in our history, the President criticized the justices as they sat arrayed in stony silence just feet away: "The Supreme Court reversed a century of law that I believe will open the floodgates for special interests—including foreign corporations—to spend without limit in our elections. I don't think American elections should be bankrolled by America's most powerful interests, or worse, by foreign entities."[22] While his colleagues marshaled their willpower and remained still, Alito visibly mouthed, "Not true." This silent objection was caught on camera and dissected in frame-by-frame detail. One year later, after a series of public speeches by justices in which they described the recurring awkwardness of attending State of the Union Addresses, Alito skipped the event altogether. Instead, he delivered a speech of his own entitled "Top Things You May Not Know About the U.S. Supreme Court" to a standing-room-only crowd at the Hawaii Supreme Court, far from the drama transpiring in D.C.[23]

The President's high-profile critique of the Court and Alito's reaction would have been enough to make *Citizens United* exceptional. But the justices also continued their debates in public, joined by retired colleagues. Discussing judicial elections, retired Justice Sandra Day O'Connor warned that "if both sides unleash their campaign spending monies without restrictions, then I think mutually assured destruction is the most likely outcome."[24] After retiring in June 2010, Stevens declared, "I think they made a serious mistake."[25] Justice Breyer echoed these remarks, warning that the people who "want to spend lots of money on a candidate" can "drown out the people who don't have a lot of money."[26] This may sound timid next to the daily screaming matches we witness on TV, but for the justices, this sort of commentary is the rough equivalent of slamming down a gauntlet.

The *Citizens United* majority defended its position. Thomas argued in a public lecture that the fact of incorporation shouldn't silence political speech: "If 10 of you got together and decided to speak, just as a group, you'd say you have First Amendment rights to speak."[27] Why, he asked, should use of the corporate form suddenly strip away those rights? Scalia took a different tack in remarks to the South Carolina Bar Association, bluntly explaining, "I don't care who is doing the speech. The more the merrier. . . . People are not stupid. If they don't like it, they'll shut it off."[28] Alito expressed his feelings about the debates over *Citizens United* when he lamented that judicial opinions are "reduced to a slogan that you put on a bumper sticker, and that's very frustrating."[29] He added, "Campaign finance is very complicated, so it's easy to get it wrong, and sometimes people get it wrong inadvertently. . . . We speak through our opinions [and] can't engage in a back-and-forth with people."

Alito was right. Campaign finance *is* complicated. And *Citizens United* is often deeply misunderstood. A closer look at the decision is in order, one that begins with a step back in time to another landmark precedent.

In the 1970s, Watergate sent Americans reeling. The scandal and its aftershocks revealed a dark rot of corruption at the core of our political system. In 1974, Gerald Ford signed the most far-reaching campaign finance reform law ever to emerge from Congress. As Congressman Bill Frenzel put it, "We couldn't go back to the American people and tell them that we had no answer to the abuses that they had seen. This is our answer, and we have to make it work." To some, campaign finance reform emerged as a beacon of light in one of our democracy's darkest hours.[30]

Congress sought to foster a new culture of public integrity by creating public financing for presidential elections, expanding disclosure of donations, and limiting the flow of money. Specifically, Congress capped how much each candidate could spend overall, how much an individual could donate directly to candidates ("direct contributions"), and how much an individual could spend independently to support candidates ("independent expenditures"). These rules were meant to achieve Congress's goal by regulating money donated and money spent.

New York Senator James Buckley, brother of the legendary conservative thinker William Buckley, would have none of it. He accused his peers of carelessly crafting a law that he dubbed "the Incumbent Protection Act of 1974."[31] Identifying a danger of campaign finance reform,

Buckley predicted that the new rules would make it more difficult for challengers to raise enough money to unseat incumbent officeholders. Incumbents, he noted, often enjoy easy access to campaign funds and the substantial benefit of name recognition. Joined by 1968 anti-war presidential candidate Eugene McCarthy, Buckley sued to invalidate the new law. Although Buckley relied on the First Amendment free speech guarantee, one of his main concerns was electoral competition.[32]

In *Buckley v. Valeo*, the Court carved out an unstable middle ground.[33] It upheld the public financing scheme, disclosure rules, and limits on direct contributions to campaigns. But it struck down the rules constraining the amounts campaigns could spend and the limits on independent expenditures for ads supporting or opposing candidates.

To explain why Congress could limit direct contributions but could not limit independent expenditures, the Court focused on the risk of corruption. *Buckley* reasoned that direct contributions create a serious risk of the reality or the appearance of quid pro quo corruption—as in *I'll give you $500,000 if you make me an ambassador*. It concluded that independent expenditures, in contrast, pose no such risk: "The absence of prearrangement and coordination of an expenditure with the candidate or his agent not only undermines the value of the expenditure to the candidate, but also alleviates the danger that expenditures will be given as a *quid pro quo* for improper commitments from the candidate."[34]

Buckley provides a crucial context for *Citizens United*. By asserting that independent expenditures do not cause corruption, *Buckley* forced the government to fight an uphill battle in explaining why corporate expenditures are different. Indeed, rightly understood, the real issue posed by *Citizens United* was not whether government efforts to limit corporate or union speech in elections raise serious First Amendment concerns: they clearly do. The real issue was what interests the government may legitimately advance to overcome those burdens on speech and how the Court should evaluate such arguments.

Buckley also made it harder to insist in 2010 that bans on corporate funds are an effective way to prevent a flood of corrupting expenditures. It did so by unleashing forces that caused a deluge long before *Citizens United*. When *Buckley* held that candidates have a right to spend as much as they want, while upholding limits on how much money they could accept, it destroyed the delicate balance Congress had sought to strike.

As Yale Law Professor Heather Gerken put it, "The Supreme Court created a world in which politicians' appetite for money would be limitless but their ability to get it would not. Two of my colleagues analogized it to giving fat, hungry politicians access to an all-you-can-eat financial buffet but insisting they can only serve themselves with a teaspoon."[35] The inevitable search for loopholes through which to funnel money to candidates, she added, turned campaign finance into a "regulatory equivalent of Whac-a-Mole."

The regulators couldn't keep up. By 2010, American politics was already awash in money, including corporate funds. Even before *Citizens United*, corporations and unions were allowed to spend money on election issues so long as they did not expressly encourage people to vote for or against a named candidate. They could also use their resources without limit in other ways, including lobbying legislators and regulators. *Citizens United* thus addressed a landscape in which the surviving loophole-ridden ban on electioneering communications by corporations was hard to justify as a uniquely effective bulwark against the potentially corrupting effects of money. That fox was already inside the henhouse.[36]

The thought of allowing limitless corporate expenditures nonetheless disturbed many observers—and had done so for a long time.[37] In 1907, President Teddy Roosevelt presided over passage of the first law that banned corporate campaign contributions. In 1947, Congress prohibited even independent campaign expenditures by corporations and labor unions. After *Buckley*, Congress reaffirmed the position that corporations may not use general treasury funds to finance independent expenditures— a provision that Congress updated again in 2002. Time and again, our politicians had warned that corporate money *does* pose a singular danger, a conviction born of their considerable experience. But could this intuition translate into constitutional law?

Writing for the Court in 1990, Justice Thurgood Marshall, who had argued *Brown v. Board of Education* decades earlier, offered an influential argument for special limits on corporate speech.[38] He invoked an interest in preventing corporations from using their unparalleled wealth to monopolize and distort political discourse. In 2003, a badly fractured Court relied in part on Marshall's logic to uphold an updated federal campaign finance law.[39]

Marshall's "anti-distortion" theory rested on a deep concern for political equality: in what sense are we really equal when corporations can use their wealth and legal advantages to exert extraordinary control over the marketplace of ideas?[40] His argument resonated with an egalitarian school of American political theory that frowns on the translation of economic power into political influence.[41] This thesis tends to be particularly attractive to those who start from the premise that the distribution and privileges of wealth are, themselves, products of our history and politics.[42] Equality is hardly foreign to the First Amendment: the Court has long invoked egalitarian ideals to preserve public spaces for speech by those without substantial resources and to protect ideological dissidents.[43] Drawing on these traditions, Marshall argued that we do not violate First Amendment rights by denying corporations, which have reaped the benefits of our social order, the chance to use their economic gains to benefit even more by distorting political discourse with their unparalleled wealth.[44]

This argument, though, stood in tension with a premise of modern First Amendment law: although government enjoys broad power to adjust our economic arrangements using such tools as progressive taxation, we should rarely trust it to decide outright whose views to amplify or muffle. Even if opportunities to engage in influential speech are unfairly distributed because of income inequalities, and even if government can directly redistribute wealth, the cure of allowing government to directly "adjust" the distribution of speech is worse than the disease. We are not a symphony for Congress to conduct according to its view of fair speech rights.

In *Citizens United*, Kennedy rejected Marshall's anti-distortion defense of campaign finance laws. "The First Amendment," he declared, "prohibits Congress from fining or jailing citizens, or associations of citizens, for simply engaging in political speech." This rule does not change "simply because the speaker is an association that has taken on the corporate form." Just as the Court (sometimes) protects unpopular groups whose speech seems dangerous, so too must it protect corporations—another sometimes unpopular group—against charges that their speech is too harmful. Linking corporate speech to classic First Amendment safeguards, Kennedy warned that the "troubling assertion of brooding governmental power" to ban political books "cannot be reconciled with the confidence and stability in civic discourse that the First Amendment must secure." Kennedy also noted that anti-distortion logic endangered our free press, since most media are corporate and it can be hard to define who counts as "the press."[45]

Quoting *Buckley*, Kennedy then challenged Marshall's account of political equality: "The concept that government may restrict the speech of some elements of our society in order to enhance the relative voice of others is wholly foreign to the First Amendment." If politicians could manipulate electoral speech by supposedly dangerous speakers, Kennedy observed, they might use that power to secure their own positions—hardly an equality-enhancing outcome. Further, given that wealthy corporations already have ample access to methods of political influence, Kennedy argued that *Citizens United* would benefit "smaller or nonprofit corporations [that] cannot raise a voice to object when other corporations, including those with vast wealth, are cooperating with the Government." Finally, Kennedy rejected the claim that there is something uniquely illegitimate about corporations using their funds to speak—or about translating wealth into political speech: "All speakers, including individuals and the media, use money amassed from the economic marketplace to fund their speech. The First Amendment protects the resulting speech, even if it was enabled by economic transactions with persons or entities who disagree with the speaker's ideas."

Kennedy concluded his opinion by turning from speakers to listeners, drawing on a tradition that protects our right to hear political messages and "judge what is true and what is false." Even if corporations have no independent right to speak, he argued, the public has a right to hear their ideas. As Kennedy explained it, "When Government seeks to use its full power . . . to command where a person may get his or her information or what distrusted source he or she may not hear, it uses censorship to control thought."

Citizens United decisively rejected the anti-distortion justification for campaign finance laws. In truth, though, the anti-distortion view had already lost many adherents since the early 1990s; not even Kagan or Stevens made much use of it in *Citizens United*.[46] This is likely for the best. To be sure, money can powerfully advantage a speaker in the marketplace of ideas (though so can celebrity, beauty, and intelligence). And concentrated wealth, left unregulated, can create a risk that most headlines and TV ads will be controlled by a small group (though the Internet has broken down some monetary barriers to influential speech). Still, it would be a mistake to leave judgments about the "proper" distribution of speech to politicians. Arming them with a roving license to level the playing field by silencing or adjusting the volume of disfavored speakers is an invitation to self-serving behavior and, ultimately, tyranny. The anti-distortion argument can too easily lead down this dangerous path, and *Citizens United* rightly discarded it.

In preparing for argument, Kagan knew that an anti-distortion approach would not sway the Roberts Court. Instead, she relied mainly on the well-established government interest in preventing corruption. Protection of political integrity, she reasoned, justifies a limited burden on union and corporate free speech rights. This argument has considerable intuitive appeal, and it captures what many Americans perceive to be the essential wrongness of the Court's ruling. But even though he agreed that an anti-corruption interest may sometimes justify campaign finance rules, Kennedy rejected Kagan's argument. His analysis of what corruption means for First Amendment purposes is the most important legacy of *Citizens United*.[47]

Corruption, Kennedy wrote, consists only of quid pro quo deals, in which someone spends money in exchange for a particular favor from a politician. It does not include "influence over or access to elected officials" or anything equally expansive. With this narrow definition in place, Kennedy concluded that independent expenditures—which by definition are not coordinated with candidates—"do not give rise to corruption or the appearance of corruption." As a result, the limit on expenditures by unions and corporations could not stand.

As commentators immediately pointed out, Kennedy's account of "corruption" as a basis for justifying campaign finance laws is hardly self-evident. To many, the Court's narrow focus on quid pro quo deals— and its insistence that a supposed lack of coordination prevents any corruption by independent expenditures—is simply mistaken. Lobbyists and politicians can read the writing on the wall. If a politician strongly suspects that a donor will spend a lot of money to buy helpful ads if he votes a certain way, a subtler form of corruption may come into play.

This is a world of winks, nods, and systemic influence.[48] When campaigns are expensive, lobbyists seem ubiquitous, and a small number of well-known donors provide a major portion of the funding, politicians and their staff can grow more dependent on these "special interests" than on their own voting constituents. A shift in priorities may sometimes occur subconsciously, as politicians start anticipating how a select number of wealthy purchasers of independent ads will react to their decisions. Such capture is all the more likely when "independent" groups are run by former advisers to candidates and share staff members, media contacts, and even offices with their favored campaigns. As Colbert's fiendishly clever barbs demonstrated, independence in the real world bears only a passing resemblance to independence in *Citizens United*, a widely recognized fact that has undercut public faith in responsive governance.

Building off that concern, Harvard Law Professor Lawrence Lessig has argued that the Court should accept prevention of this sort of "dependence corruption" as a justification for campaign finance laws. As he explains, our entire constitutional system rests on the premise that representatives will depend for their election and reelection on "We the People." But when representatives depend on those who fund their campaigns and political projects instead of on their constituents, popular sovereignty is threatened or altogether lost. In Lessig's view, the Constitution thus allows Congress to regulate corporate speech to protect the Republic.[49]

A separate critique of *Citizens United*, although one whose empirical foundations have been called into question by recent scholarship,[50] emphasizes that even the appearance of corruption can undermine democracy. In this view, when ordinary people, confronted by a world of special interests, lose faith that their voices and votes really matter, our democracy is imperiled. Citizens may lose respect for decisions made by elected officials and thus either decline to participate in government or take part halfheartedly, triggering a breakdown of our political system. Further, as New York University Law School Professor Adam Samaha has explained, the appearance of corruption can actually *create* corruption: if corrupt behavior seems acceptable, lobbyists will feel pressure to compete in the perceived market for special treatment.[51]

Many critics of *Citizens United* deploy these kinds of arguments, invoking more sophisticated accounts of corruption than mere quid pro quo deals as a justification for limits on independent expenditures by unions and corporations. There is great force to some of their objections, but that is not the end of the discussion. *Citizens United* was a hard case because the Court faced a choice among evils. Attacks on the opinion emphasize inequality and corruption, values that the Court did not fully acknowledge, but critics too often disregard the other side of the equation, which includes weighty free speech and democratic concerns. To be sure, the Court enters treacherous waters when it sets about defining corruption, an undertaking that requires it to make controversial assumptions about how our democracy ought to work when uncorrupted. And there may be wisdom to leaving many decisions about our democratic order to the public and its representatives. The Constitution, though, requires judges to play a role in reconciling competing values and ensuring that those representatives respect certain ground rules—and in modern constitutional law, they do so by defining the anti-corruption interest.[52]

Kennedy tacitly acknowledged that some might consider his definition of corruption artificially narrow. Tipping his hat to the opposing view, he allowed that "if elected officials succumb to improper influences from independent expenditures; if they surrender their best judgment; and if they put expediency before principle, then surely there is cause for concern." He went on to explain, though, that the First Amendment constrains how far we can let these concerns carry us as justifications for limiting speech. "It is our law and our tradition," he wrote, "that more speech, not less, is the governing rule." Before the Court allows Congress to pick a class of speakers and strip down their rights, it needs an unusually compelling justification.

Here, Kennedy alluded to the fact that broad accounts of the anti-corruption interest pose significant difficulties of their own. For one thing, he pointed out, it's hard to identify boundaries on the laws that a "generic favoritism or influence theory" can justify. After all, "it is in the nature of an elected representative to favor certain policies, and, by necessary corollary, to favor the voters and contributors who support those policies." Allowing Congress to silence speakers whenever some think the game is rigged could blast a hole in the First Amendment. While empirical evidence might, in theory, help establish some limits, disputes over the relevant facts and how to interpret them have kept this debate anchored mostly in speculation.

In addition, it's extremely hard to determine whether any given campaign finance rule has a big enough impact to survive judicial scrutiny. Judges have long implemented the First Amendment by requiring—among other things—that restrictions on speech demonstrably achieve a legitimate goal. The causes of political corruption in America and the reasons why politicians act the way they do, however, are many and complex. Money in politics is only one part of that story, which also includes minimally regulated lobbying, incumbent-protective gerrymandering, a revolving door between government and private industry, and a breakdown of civility in political culture. In turn, the rules governing expenditures by unions and corporations are only one part of the story of money in politics, which also includes direct contributions, lobbying, and a dizzying array of loopholes. As Kennedy noted, billionaires, unincorporated associations, and the corporate news media were already free to spend vast sums before *Citizens United*. This makes a constitutional difference because, to pass muster under the First Amendment, a campaign finance law must prevent enough corruption to justify its burden on speech—and must not constrain more speech than is necessary to achieve that goal. *Citizens United* suggests judicial skepticism of efforts by Congress to single out speakers, blame them for corrupting our politics, and muffle their voices.

This skepticism may flow, in part, from fear that anti-corruption arguments sometimes bleed into anti-distortion concerns. Many attacks on *Citizens United* highlight its potential to give corporations undue influence in the marketplace of ideas and skew policy outcomes in government. "Corruption," in this view, occurs when politicians become dependent on a wealthy clique and government is no longer responsive to the public interest. As Rick Hasen, a professor at the University of California, Irvine School of Law, observes, some arguments of this type can be characterized as political equality arguments; they seek "to justify campaign finance laws on grounds that the laws distribute political power fairly and correct a distortion present in an unregulated (or less regulated) system."[53] Kennedy and his colleagues are unreservedly hostile to such arguments. They worry that noble-sounding rationales for campaign finance laws can too easily conceal efforts by incumbents to protect themselves and punish their enemies.

The *Citizens United* majority did not adopt a narrow definition of corruption because it is naïve or apathetic. It did so because it doubts that the Court can otherwise create workable First Amendment law that adequately guards against abuse by politicians. Embracing a broader view of the anti-corruption interest risked creating an exception that swallowed the rule. Kennedy's libertarian streak and devotion to the First Amendment as a safeguard against tyranny shone through in his opinion, which put a heavy thumb on the scale in favor of allowing too much "dangerous" speech in the face of outright government censorship.

This is a powerful argument, though it is certainly reasonable to disagree with the Court's suggestion that it would be impossible or improvident to establish a middle-ground position. If a majority of the justices thought the Court had invoked anti-corruption reasoning to uphold too many campaign finance laws in the past, they might instead have used *Citizens United* to make a modest course correction. Such an approach would have left more room for politicians to use campaign finance laws, carefully reviewed by courts, as one tool among many in their efforts to restore public confidence in government integrity. Instead, the Court issued a wide-ranging ruling that stands as an imposing and—for now, at least—insuperable obstacle to most campaign finance regulations. Unsurprisingly, its decision remains hotly disputed.

In an age of political dysfunction, the extraordinary sums of money that candidates avidly pursue present hard questions about how to reconcile competing national values. *Citizens United* made clear that a majority of the Roberts Court is prepared to come down firmly on one side of that balance. As a result, even as the issue of money in politics looms ever larger in American life, the First Amendment as interpreted by the Roberts Court will prohibit most efforts—by the public and by politicians—to seek reform through campaign finance laws.

Many reactions to *Citizens United* mixed prophecies of doom with urgent calls for reform. Meaningful democracy has come to an end, pundits insisted; corporations must be stripped of their rights, and money must not be equated to speech. Speculation about the ruling's implications fueled proposals to "fix" the Court's alleged error. In time, however, it became clear that the most gloomy of these predictions fell wide of the mark. Although *Citizens United*'s effects are still rippling outward, early assessments suggest a more nuanced picture.

One of the main implications of *Citizens United* was the blessing of Super PACs in *SpeechNow.org v. FEC*.[54] This case was brought by Speech-Now.org, a nonprofit group that uses independent expenditures to promote candidates who favor free speech. SpeechNow.org had been told by the FEC that it had to register as a PAC, which meant that it could receive no more than $5,000 annually from any given donor, even corporate donors. SpeechNow.org objected to this limit and filed suit. Invoking *Citizens United*, the U.S. Court of Appeals for the D.C. Circuit agreed and struck down the regulation. As Chief Judge David Sentelle observed, "The Court held that the government has *no* anti-corruption interest in limiting independent expenditures. . . . Given this analysis from *Citizens United*, we must conclude that the government has no anti-corruption interest in limiting contributions to an independent expenditure group such as SpeechNow." *SpeechNow.org* encouraged the rise of Super PACs as a vehicle for the aggregation of independent expenditures, since these groups can raise unlimited sums of money from individual, corporate, and union donors. The FEC ultimately codified *SpeechNow.org* and sanctioned Super PACs.

In short order, the Super PACs that followed close on *Citizens United*'s heels were joined by groups organized under sections 501(c)(4) and 501(c)(6) of the tax code, which govern not-for-profit corporations. Because of *Citizens United*, these groups can accept huge contributions from corporations and then allocate those sums to independent expenditures. They also have the added virtue—in donors' eyes—of secrecy. Whereas the sources of monies donated to Super PACS are generally revealed pursuant to FEC regulations, the 501(c) entities are usually not compelled to provide information about donors. They have thus become key actors in the rise of secretive election funding, often called "dark money." Although *Citizens United* allowed disclosure rules, it didn't mandate them, and neither did the preexisting law governing 501(c) entities. As a result, one of the most striking features of the post–*Citizens United* landscape is a lack of transparency. Even as vast sums pour into the system from new sources, it can be nearly impossible for the public to determine who is spending money to influence votes.[55]

Together, Super PACs and 501(c) groups have transformed political fund-raising and thereby affected the organization of our electoral politics. As outside groups become more attractive to major donors, the political parties and individual campaigns have been forced to adapt. Their new relationships take many forms. Sometimes there is extensive informal coordination between outside groups and the political parties, a state of affairs facilitated by significant personnel overlap. These arrangements present their own tensions, but they often mirror familiar party structures. As Gerken notes, their principal oddity is that the outside groups are usually staffed mainly by experienced political operatives—a group that is a world away from the party faithful, who have traditionally supplied a "bridge between the elites and the voter, between the party and the people," as well as "an institutional check on the bargains that the elites can strike, some brake on how many principles will get compromised along the way."[56]

In other cases, though, outsiders wielding independent funds have clashed with each other and with the establishment. Even after the party elite coalesced around Mitt Romney, for example, the 2012 Republican primaries turned into a shooting gallery of rogue billionaires.[57] As party leaders watched in horror, the establishment's chosen son was pummeled by ferocious attack ads in a longer primary season than anyone had anticipated, partly because figures like billionaire Sheldon Adelson helped keep Newt Gingrich's campaign alive far past its expected expiration date. This pattern is likely to repeat itself in the years ahead, as ideological factions within each party jockey for control of the ticket—a trend witnessed most recently in an open conflict between Republican incumbents and Tea Party challengers. Experiences like this may lead parties to seek laws to help them control the outside groups that have become both vital and potentially fatal to their agendas. Those laws, in turn, may raise new constitutional concerns.

The questions that loomed largest after *Citizens United* focused on how it would affect electoral outcomes and policy choices. These concerns were justified, but they were often overstated. When the Court announced its holding, for instance, many liberals openly worried that big corporations would use their newfound "liberty" to buy the 2012 election for Republicans. That fear proved unfounded: even though roughly 70 percent of all disclosed outside spending came from conservative groups, Mitt Romney lost the presidential race and Republicans fared poorly overall—even the candidates backed by outside interests.[58] Sheldon Adelson, for example, gave more than $53 million to Super PACs, but all eight of the candidates he supported lost.[59] Karl Rove, a strategic mastermind who won fame advising George W. Bush, oversaw groups that spent $175 million and still lost twenty-one out of thirty elections.[60] Seemingly overnight, claims of potential corporate domination were replaced with dismissive shrugs. Robert Schlesinger of *U.S. News & World Report* went so far as to suggest that Super PACS are a "giant waste of money."[61] Supporters of *Citizens United*, meanwhile, claimed vindication. Allen Dickerson of the Center for Competitive Politics concluded that "the major takeaway is that voters are still sovereign."[62]

The truth is somewhere in the middle: if critics of *Citizens United* were unduly worried about its effects before the 2012 elections, pundits were too quick to deem it irrelevant after Election Day. Of course, to the extent the point was ever in doubt, the 2012 elections proved that winning takes more than an edge in independent expenditures. But while money can't guarantee a candidate victory, a serious absence of money may guarantee defeat or force a candidate to change positions to attract support. This is particularly true in hard-fought, close elections, as well as in lower-profile state and local elections where a big infusion of cash from national groups can flatten a smaller donor base. Further, using a single election as a test might obscure important effects of *Citizens United*: as Rove was quick to note, the flood of Super PAC money in 2012 may have helped thwart steeper Republican losses.[63] By broadening and altering the channels of campaign finance, *Citizens United* has almost certainly affected some electoral outcomes.[64]

Apart from any effects on particular elections, *Citizens United* has likely also affected some policy outcomes by causing an across-the-board realignment of government priorities toward interests backed by big money.[65] Favoritism and access may not constitute corruption as the Court defines it, but they undoubtedly influence policy. Every capable politician has an eye on the next election and a keen sense of who provided support last time, who didn't, who might be persuaded to shift their opinions, and how that might be achieved. *Citizens United* and the changes it triggered have bolstered this economy of money and influence. As politicians and their staffers spend more time on the fundraising trail wooing a select number of donors, and as legislators make decisions in the shadow of predictable reactions by key outside groups, it's hard to imagine that their policies won't be affected. Given the ease with which lawmakers can reward donors at little personal cost—details left out of a draft, bills killed in committee, small favors tucked into laws—the temptation to attract funds by currying favor will be ever present.

The relatively small audience of major donors contributes to the probability that *Citizens United* will ultimately affect outcomes. The Center for Public Integrity points out that just three GOP-aligned groups accounted for nearly one-third of all disclosed outside spending in the 2012 national election, and that more than half of all disclosed outside spending was controlled by ten groups.[66] Of the roughly $859 million total raised by Super PACs during that election, more than $505 million came from only 159 donors, each of whom donated at least $1 million.[67] In a study by Demos, the contrast is stark: whereas the two presidential candidates raised a total of $313 million from more than 3.7 million small donors giving less than $200 each, Super PACs exceeded that amount with donations from just 32 big donors (who gave an average of $9.9 million each).[68] The landscape of Super PACs and 501(c) groups is still in flux, but one key fact is holding constant: a small group of entities has control over a lot of money. And politicians want that money, badly.

Citizens United is therefore likely to trigger a self-reinforcing cycle. It has unleashed forces that will cause politicians, parties, and donors to organize relationships around groups like Super PACs and 501(c) entities. As that happens, and as the group of victorious candidates comes to consist mainly of politicians who can successfully navigate these new structures and depend on them for reelection, the impetus for change among officeholders will fade. Barack Obama's 2012 campaign provides just one example: although it signaled opposition in June 2011 to any involvement with Super PACs, his campaign later embraced a Super PAC called Priorities USA Action, which ultimately spent more than $65 million in support of his reelection.[69] Since then, Obama's once-outspoken opposition to *Citizens United* has grown awfully faint. As *Citizens United* becomes part of the accepted background, the question will be how to improve the world it has helped bring about, not how to restore a past that is quickly receding.

This doesn't mean that critics of *Citizens United* should just pack up and call it a day, but it does suggest that reformers concerned with money in politics should focus on the path ahead. Since 2010, however, many critics have either called for a return to the past or detoured into unproductive channels.

Some of the ruling's critics, for example, have aimed to change the Court's mind. The main push on this front occurred in early 2012, after the Montana Supreme Court defied *Citizens United* on the ground that Montana's sordid political history required recognition of a broader anti-corruption interest.[70] When the Court put Montana's ruling on hold, Ginsburg and Breyer wrote separately to suggest that an appeal could "give the Court an opportunity to consider whether, in light of the huge sums currently deployed to buy candidates' allegiance, *Citizens United* should continue to hold sway."[71] The two justices added that events since *Citizens United* "make it exceedingly difficult to maintain that independent expenditures . . . do not give rise to corruption or the appearance of corruption."

Accepting this invitation, legislators, states, citizens' groups, and former FEC officials flooded the Court with briefs urging a step back from *Citizens United*. These briefs, citing examples that supposedly proved corruption by independent expenditures, transformed the dispute into an unmistakable test of the majority's conviction. Would the majority abandon its statement of First Amendment principle in the face of a political and judicial backlash?

Not a chance. Fashioning ice-cold prose into a clear message, the *Citizens United* majority reversed Montana's highest court in a single paragraph without even hearing argument. Breyer dissented, joined by Ginsburg, Sotomayor, and Kagan. This was a fortunate turn of events for critics of *Citizens United*: the majority could have used the Montana case to expand on its holding. Barring a change in the Court's membership, additional attempts to persuade the Court to reconsider *Citizens United* are likely to meet similar ends.[72]

Channeling a populist impulse echoed in the Occupy Wall Street movement, many critics of *Citizens United* have also attacked the rule that says corporations enjoy First Amendment rights.[73] At first glance, corporate personhood may seem like a tempting target. As Senator Elizabeth Warren proclaimed to thunderous applause at the 2012 Democratic National Convention, "Corporations are not people. People have hearts, they have kids, they get jobs, they get sick, they cry, they dance. They live, they love, and they die. And that matters. That matters because we don't run this country for corporations, we run it for people."[74] In a witty protest of *Citizens United*'s treatment of corporations, Angela Vogel of Seattle married one.[75] Her stunt nicely complemented Jon Stewart's biting observation on *The Daily Show* that "corporations now have more rights than gay people" because "corporations can merge—gay people can't."[76]

Nonetheless, this focus on the inhumanity of corporations is misguided. As Harvard Law Professor Mark Tushnet notes, although constitutional rights belong to people, courts have long recognized that "corporations are one of the ways the law allows people to organize themselves to accomplish what they want."[77] Corporations don't *always* have the same status as natural persons, of course. In a case about access to government records, for instance, Roberts held that a rule about "invasion of personal privacy" does not cover corporations, cunningly adding, "We trust that AT&T will not take it personally."[78] But it does make sense for corporations, as associations of individuals, to enjoy certain constitutional rights, including the right to speak about public issues that may control the outcome of their ventures.

A successful assault on corporate personhood, moreover, would fail to address many concerns raised by *Citizens United*.[79] Even though the Court dealt with corporate and union speech, it has since become clear that such organizations aren't entirely (or even mostly) to blame for the recent spike in disclosed outside spending. That honor belongs to super-rich individuals, who were free to spend money long before 2010 but who benefited from the post–*Citizens United* transformation in campaign finance law. Large businesses, after all, tend to be cautious. As one election lawyer observed, "If you've got a bank on every corner, if you've got stores in every strip mall, you don't want to be associated with a social cause."[80] The national retailer Target learned this lesson the hard way in 2010, when it contributed to a group opposing same-sex marriage and was pummeled by consumers in a national backlash. Not surprisingly, then, corporations have mostly stuck to less risky forms of political influence—such as lobbying—and avoided significant participation in the post–*Citizens United* campaign finance system.

Many of the ruling's opponents also suggest that we should amend the Constitution to state that spending money does not qualify as "speech" under the First Amendment. True, money isn't speech. But it often costs money to speak effectively to more than just a few people at once, and allowing government to control who can spend enough to get heard on a grander scale would render freedom of speech illusory. Imagine a world in which people are free to talk and sing and write and publish—but only if they spend no money and charge nothing for their efforts. Acutely aware of how absurd that world would be, the Court has rightly decided lots of cases that protect people's rights to use their money to reach the broader public.

To the extent they are concerned with combating various kinds of corruption in our political system, critics of *Citizens United* would be well served to move past issues like corporate personhood and money's status as speech. Instead, they might aim to ensure greater transparency in our brave new world of Super PACs and 501(c) organizations.

Disclosure has long been a cornerstone of campaign finance law.[81] As *Buckley* recognized, disclosure informs voters about the interests to which candidates may be most responsive. It also "allows voters to place each candidate in the political spectrum more precisely than is often possible on the basis of party labels and campaign speeches." Moreover, by exposing funds to public view, disclosure can deter all kinds of corruption. *Citizens United* reaffirmed that "the public has an interest in knowing who is speaking about a candidate shortly before an election." As Kennedy noted, "Prompt disclosure of expenditures can provide shareholders and citizens with the information needed to hold corporations and elected officials accountable for their positions and supporters." He added, "Transparency enables the electorate to make informed decisions and give proper weight to different speakers and messages." Under both *Buckley* and *Citizens United*, these interests usually outweigh burdens on campaign speech.

Because other anti-corruption rules have been invalidated and our political system is rife with dark money, disclosure is now more important than ever. Billionaires and corporations secretly funneling massive expenditures through opaque 501(c) entities is an invitation to shady dealing, loss of public faith in politics, and unresolvable skepticism about the sources of political speech. In the post–*Citizens United* era, transparency would provide at least a measure of reassurance; as Justice Louis D. Brandeis wrote in 1913, "Sunlight is said to be the best of disinfectants; electric light the most efficient policeman."[82] And transparency would provide those benefits at relatively low cost. Unlike many other rules, disclosure requirements avoid limits on how and when people can spend money. Instead, as former Stanford Law Dean Kathleen Sullivan observes, they enable "the distribution of political influence to be treated as a political rather than a constitutional question."[83] They do so by placing "the question of undue influence or preferential access in the hands of voters, who, aided by the institutional press, can follow the money and hold representatives accountable for any trails they don't like."

Recently, however, disclosure rules have come under constitutional attack by groups eager to keep their political activity private.[84] These groups argue that compelled disclosure can result in retaliation that chills speech—especially in the Internet age, as even low-level donors may find themselves lambasted online or plugged into searchable maps.[85] Opponents of disclosure often cite examples from the same-sex marriage struggle. In *Citizens United*, for instance, Thomas argued that he would strike down disclosure rules governing corporate and union independent expenditures, pointing to a backlash in California against supporters of a measure to end recognition of same-sex marriages. "I cannot endorse a view of the First Amendment," he wrote, "that subjects citizens of this Nation to death threats, ruined careers, damaged or defaced property, or pre-emptive and threatening warning letters as the price for engaging in core political speech."

A similar issue reached the Court in *Doe v. Reed*, decided mere months after *Citizens United*.[86] *Doe* arose from efforts in Washington State to overturn a law extending benefits to same-sex couples. A group called Protect Marriage Washington circulated a petition and successfully collected enough signatures to force a referendum. Several groups then invoked Washington public records laws to request copies of that petition—and two of them publicly stated their intent to post signatories' names online, in searchable format. Alarmed, the petition sponsor and several signers filed suit under the First Amendment.

By a vote of eight to one, the Court held in an opinion by Roberts that disclosure of such petitions does not, in general, violate the First Amendment. It then sent the case down for further proceedings. Roberts instructed the lower court to determine if the sponsors and signers could show "a reasonable probability that the compelled disclosure of personal information will subject them to threats, harassment, or reprisals from either Government officials or private parties." If they could make that showing, he stated, they could avoid disclosure.[87]

Consistent with his position in *Citizens United*, Thomas dissented and warned that Washington's public records law "severely burdens [First Amendment] rights and chills citizen participation in the referendum process." Alito seemed sympathetic to Thomas's view and wrote separately to signal his belief that the signers' rights to "privacy of belief and association" must be protected. But Thomas and Alito stood alone: in a rare display, Breyer, Sotomayor, Stevens, and Scalia each wrote separately to cast doubt on the asserted grounds for evading disclosure. Scalia, in particular, took direct aim at Thomas and Alito: "There are laws against threats and intimidation; and harsh criticism, short of unlawful action, is a price our people have traditionally been willing to pay for self-governance. Requiring people to stand up in public for their political acts fosters civic courage, without which democracy is doomed." A democracy stripped of public scrutiny and the accountability of criticism, Scalia added, "does not resemble the Home of the Brave."

This Court's apparent belief in the constitutionality of disclosure rules, however, only means that such laws are likely to be upheld. For that to happen, they must first be legislated into existence: the First Amendment *allows* campaign finance disclosure rules, but it does not *impose* any. For national elections, this leaves the ball in Congress's court, which does not bode well for disclosure reform. Congress has twice tried to pass a law called the DISCLOSE Act, but those efforts collapsed in partisan acrimony in 2010 and then again in 2012.[88] The more recent DISCLOSE Act would have required corporations to report funds spent on campaign-related activity, identify themselves in ads, and notify shareholders of political spending. Opponents attacked the bill on several grounds, charging that it unfairly exempted certain special interests, imposed onerous reporting requirements on political speech, and subjected donors to harassment. Their view ultimately carried the day; the law failed to overcome a filibuster after the Senate split along purely partisan lines (with Democrats in favor, Republicans opposed). This does not mean, though, that disclosure reform is forever off the table. To those concerned by *Citizens United*, disclosure is likely to remain the most promising and realistic reform option.

Finally, *Citizens United* has also prompted attention to the corporate law rules that define when and how corporations can "speak," leading some to call for reform in this field.[89] A model for such changes would be unions. The Court has ruled that the First Amendment, which protects people against forced political speech and association, bans unions from spending any part of an employee's dues on politics if that employee objects. Thus, unions cannot force employees to financially support a political cause as a condition of employment; employees must be allowed to opt out of such activity. The Roberts Court reaffirmed—and expanded— this rule as recently as 2012.[90]

In contrast, corporations can spend huge sums of general treasury funds on political speech without seeking shareholder approval. The Court sees no First Amendment problem here because shareholders are always free to sell their stock and walk away. But Harvard Law Professor Ben Sachs rightly asks whether it makes sense, as a matter of constitutional law and public policy, to force shareholders to choose between making profitable investments and avoiding support for certain messages.[91] In buying a share of stock, should we have to accept a company's anti-gay or pro-choice political contributions along with its huge profit margins? Building on classic work by Harvard Law Professor Victor Brudney, who suggested in 1981 that corporate law should be modified to require shareholder approval of political spending,[92] Sachs makes an interesting case for allowing shareholders to opt out of such politics or for requiring majority shareholder approval of political expenditures. These proposals lack political support and would likely face crippling opposition from corporate directors with sway in key state legislatures, but they direct attention to important issues in shareholder rights in the wake of *Citizens United*.

Although often described as a bolt from the blue, *Citizens United* is part of a significant line of Roberts Court campaign finance cases. Several of these rulings—involving public funding of campaigns, contributions by foreigners, and judicial elections—provide valuable context to *Citizens United* by filling out this Court's vision of democratic politics.

A year after *Citizens United*, the Court returned to the fray in a case that addressed yet another pillar of campaign finance law: public funding. By providing candidates with public money to run their campaigns, these programs aim to keep politics clean by reducing dependence on wealthy donors and improving transparency.[93]

Thirty-five years earlier, in *Buckley*, the Court upheld a modest federal financing scheme for major-party presidential candidates. It explained that reliance on public money can "reduce the deleterious influence of large corporations on our political process," "facilitate communication by candidates with the electorate," and "free candidates from the rigors of fundraising." The Court concluded that "public financing as a means of eliminating the improper influence of large private contributions furthers a significant governmental interest."

In 1998, after suffering a wave of corruption scandals involving its governor, many of its legislators, and both of its U.S. senators, Arizona took the Court at its word—and added a twist to traditional public financing programs. Its Clean Citizens Elections Act awarded participating candidates a substantial lump sum of public money. In exchange, candidates promised not to fund their campaigns through private contributions, not to exceed a statutory limit on personal funds, and to return all unused public funds. For each dollar above the initial grant spent by a nonparticipating opponent or by an outside group supporting such an opponent, a participating candidate received an additional ninety-four cents. Arizona thus sought to ensure that candidates who received public funds were not later outspent by wealthy opponents and their supporters, an approach that encouraged use of the system and thereby helped secure the recognized benefits of public funding.

In *Arizona Free Enterprise Club v. Bennett*, decided in 2011, the Court struck down the act in an opinion described by Gerken as a "doctrinal death match between two incompatible world views."[94] Roberts wrote for a five-justice conservative majority; Kagan wrote for the more liberal dissenters. Their opinions spared no quarter. The Chief Justice and his most junior colleague battled over every premise and precedent, spicing their opinions with uncharacteristic sarcasm. To the Chief's warning that "in a democracy, campaigning for office is not a game," Kagan replied, "Arizonans deserve a government that represents and serves them all . . . truly, democracy is not a game." To the Chief's claim that Arizona might *discourage* speech by giving money to a speaker's opponent, Kagan pointed out that those candidates "could have received (but chose to spurn) the same financial assistance." She added: "Some people might call that *chutzpah*." Summing up her view, Kagan remarked that "if an ordinary citizen, without the hindrance of a law degree, thought this result an upending of First Amendment values, he would be correct." In the shadow of *Citizens United*, such hostility was understandable: the Court saw *Bennett* as yet another battle in the struggle over democracy and the First Amendment.

As his opinion made clear, Roberts saw a law that discouraged speech by imposing a harsh choice on privately funded candidates: either keep expenditures below a certain amount or trigger a flood of state funds to your rival. Worse, such candidates sometimes couldn't even prevent that distribution of additional state funds, since outside groups beyond their control might spend above the cap. This burden on speech—punishing each dollar spent with aid to the enemy—required weighty justification, something more than a forbidden effort to level the playing field. But Arizona lacked any such justification, since its law did little to thwart corruption. As Roberts explained, "The fact that burdening constitutionally protected speech might indirectly serve the State's anticorruption interest, by encouraging candidates to take public financing, does not establish the constitutionality of the matching funds provision." In his view, the harm to speech outweighed any remote benefits of making public funding desirable.

Kagan, in contrast, saw an admirable law that enhanced First Amendment values by encouraging more political speech, not less. She also saw an attack by opportunists who had spurned the state's financial assistance and now sought to silence public debate: "Petitioners are able to convey their ideas without public financing—and they would prefer the field to themselves, so that they can speak free from response." In her forceful, plainspoken dissent, Kagan assailed the majority for confining Arizona to the same laws that had failed so miserably to prevent corruption in the past. In her view, this creative state program had restored integrity to elections. "Except in a world gone topsy-turvy," Kagan observed, "additional campaign speech and electoral competition is not a First Amendment injury." Arizona's triggering mechanism, in turn, made sense as a "Goldilocks solution." Because it was hard to guess in advance how much money to give candidates but vital to give enough for publicly funded candidates to remain competitive, Arizona provided them with a lump sum and evened out the difference mid-campaign. Since the state was free simply to start with a higher lump sum, Kagan saw little virtue in punishing Arizona for fine-tuning its contributions this way.

In *Bennett*, the Roberts Court foreclosed a promising approach to public funding. Its ruling forced a number of cities and states to reconsider their campaign finance laws, and triggered heated debate over the future of public finance.[95] Although the Chief Justice insisted that his ruling did not address the constitutionality of *all* public financing schemes, some commentators saw dark omens. As Duke Law Professor Guy-Uriel Charles wrote, "A significant purpose of a public finance system is to subsidize candidates who opt into that system to compete with candidates who did not opt in. [*Bennett*] raises doubts about that very purpose."[96] Little wonder, then, that the Chief and Kagan broke out their heavy rhetoric: in a single stroke, *Bennett* invalidated one of the country's more effective public finance systems and called into question a potentially significant path toward campaign finance reform.

One year after *Bennett*, the Court addressed an important question raised by *Citizens United*: can foreign corporations spend money on American elections? Obama had expressed concern about this issue in his 2010 State of the Union Address; Alito mouthed the words "Not true" in apparent response to that comment. Yet, as Justice Stevens has observed, *Citizens United* signals hostility to laws that regulate speech based on the speaker's identity, whether that of a natural person or a wealthy corporation.[97] And the Court has long emphasized that the First Amendment protects more than just *speakers*: it protects *speech* and all those whom it might reach. The logic of this argument seems unassailable, but if taken seriously, it suggests that we should not deny citizens access to political ideas that happen to be expressed by noncitizens.

In the end, the Court essentially ducked the issue. A lower court upheld federal rules that limit campaign expenditures by noncitizens, explaining that we "may exclude foreign citizens from activities that are part of democratic self-government in the United States."[98] The question, of course, is what "activities" meet that definition. Voting clearly does, for example, but the law specifically excluded *speech* by foreigners, which might be thought to pose a harder question if a speaker's identity can't usually justify a ban on speech.[99] The Court never weighed in on this dilemma with an opinion of its own; instead, it simply affirmed the lower court's ruling.[100]

A case that suggests just a bit of leeway in *Citizens United* arose from judicial elections.[101] In 2007, Justice Brent Benjamin of the Supreme Court of Appeals of West Virginia cast the deciding vote to overturn a $50 million verdict against Massey Coal Company. He was in a position to vote for Massey Coal because he had been elected in 2004, after the verdict but before the appeal. In that election, Don Blankenship, the CEO of Massey Coal, donated $1,000 to Benjamin's campaign. Blankenship then spent $2.5 million on a PAC called And for the Sake of the Kids, which aggressively supported Benjamin. On top of this, he spent $500,000 on independent expenditures, including direct mailings, TV ads, and newspaper promotions. This $3 million of independent expenditures topped the total amount spent by all other Benjamin supporters combined. Benjamin ultimately beat his opponent 53 percent to 47 percent, but two years later he refused to recuse himself from the appeal of the $50 million verdict against Massey Coal, insisting that, notwithstanding Blankenship's expenditures, he was not biased.

In *Caperton v. A. T. Massey Coal Co.*, split five to four, the Court reversed West Virginia's Supreme Court of Appeals. Writing for the majority, Kennedy explained that "there is a serious risk of actual bias—based on objective and reasonable perceptions—when a person with a personal stake in a particular case had a significant and disproportionate influence in placing the judge on the case by raising funds or directing the judge's election campaign when the case was pending or imminent." The unacceptable risk of such bias in *Caperton*, Kennedy held, triggered a violation of the right to a fair trial. To avoid a flood of challenges to every ruling by an elected judge, he then emphasized that *Caperton* truly was an extraordinary case.

Caperton suggests that massive independent expenditures can, in some cases, help create the appearance—and perhaps the reality—of quid pro quo corruption: my money for your vote. In that respect, it varied slightly from the firm rule of *Citizens United*. This helps explain why Roberts and Scalia both published forceful dissents. While the Court is clearly in no hurry to expand the logic at the heart of *Caperton*, the case provides an important counterpoint to *Citizens United* and may someday be invoked to limit that opinion's strongest claims.[102]

For now, however, the Roberts Court stands at a crossroads. Whereas the Court once allowed Congress some latitude to limit speech by invoking a broad anti-corruption interest, the twilight of that era is upon us. In the First Amendment's name, a five-justice majority is handing down opinions that foreclose most efforts to regulate campaign finance. These justices firmly trust voters to sort out their beliefs in the marketplace of ideas and fear that politicians will censor speech to rig the electoral game in their favor. The more liberal justices have protested at every turn, arguing that politicians must be given room to protect government integrity, but to no avail. Unless the Court's membership changes, the vision of free speech and democratic politics embodied in *Citizens United* will hold steady at the Roberts Court, moving us ever closer to a world in which government is stripped of nearly all power over money in politics.

4

FREEDOM OF SPEECH:
SEX, LIES, AND VIDEO GAMES

Throughout the late 1960s, the justices of the Supreme Court spent at least one day each year in the basement watching porn together. By all accounts, it was fantastically awkward. Unable to define "obscenity" but convinced that the First Amendment couldn't protect unduly dangerous and morally corrupting expression, the Court was forced to create constitutional law one sex scene at a time.

These films ranged from scientific documentaries to the improbable escapades of lesbian nymphomaniacs. Justice Thurgood Marshall, a civil rights hero, took merciless pleasure in narrating the clips for the special benefit of Justice John Marshall Harlan II, an elegant former Wall Street lawyer who was by then losing his eyesight. Mocking Justice Potter Stewart's insistence that "I know it when I see it," clerks would call out in the dark, "I see it, I see it!" In 1968, some twenty years after serving in the U.S. Navy, a still youthful Stewart reflected on more adventurous times and confided in a particularly curious clerk that he had indeed seen it: "Just once, off the coast of Algiers."[1]

For years, the justices struggled to explain what made frank depictions and descriptions of sex dangerous. What was so harmful about obscenity? At what point, or with what body part, did a book or film land outside the First Amendment? The Court's logic fluctuated wildly from case to case. Such instability is uniquely troubling for free speech because excessive uncertainty about the limits of the criminal law can chill even innocent expression.[2]

Conventional wisdom tells us that these dark days of uncertain free speech law are long gone. Editorials regularly praise the Roberts Court for its unwavering dedication to free speech.[3] Floyd Abrams, a renowned First Amendment attorney, explains that "it is unpopular speech, distasteful speech, that most requires First Amendment protection, and on that score, no prior Supreme Court has been as protective as this."[4] Rarely does an American stand silent or speak in whispers for fear of punishment. Liberty towers above all other values. Or so the story goes.

This picture obscures more than it reveals. Forty years ago, the Court failed because it couldn't reliably define the First Amendment's limits. Today, the Roberts Court risks a different kind of misstep. On the one hand, it has rigidly adhered to categorical rules that broadly protect certain kinds of speech but occasionally undermine core First Amendment values by protecting speech that really is harmful enough to justify restrictions. On the other hand, even as it insists that those rigid rules are necessary to protect speech, it has displayed a taste for flexibility while creating new gaps in the First Amendment's canvass. Thus, even as it takes liberty too far in some cases, in others it seems openly skeptical of claims to First Amendment freedom. These rulings reveal a Court divided over its vision of why and how we should protect speech.

In short, there is more to the Roberts Court's First Amendment cases than meets the eye. The Court's voice booms forcefully when it vindicates borderline free speech claims, marginalizing the other values at stake in those cases. Meanwhile, much more quietly, it denies protection to some of those who most need its help to share in America's rich First Amendment tradition. The culprit is an approach that too rigidly categorizes certain speakers or types of speech as either completely protected by the First Amendment or barely protected at all—and that prevents the Court from candidly acknowledging its role in reshaping our liberties.

This tale of free speech has much in common with America's long, complicated love affair with the First Amendment. And it points the way to a future in which fundamental questions about what it means to protect free speech are hotly disputed in the Roberts Court.

Speech is powerful. It's the lifeblood of democracy, a precondition for the discovery of truth, and vital to our self-development. But speech is also dangerous. It can corrupt democracy, enable or incite crime, encourage enemies, and interfere with government. It can be wielded as a weapon and deployed against unwilling targets. Some speech, like pornography involving children, is created by inflicting terrible harm on innocents. Whole forests have been sacrificed to learned tomes that try to balance these benefits and perils.[5] Yet the First Amendment is no complex work of theory. It spends only ten words establishing one of our most important rights: "Congress shall make no law . . . abridging the freedom of speech."

Americans have built a vast edifice atop this brief command. Our commitment to protecting even dangerous speech is exceptional.[6] It sets us apart from other democracies in ways that sometimes leave them mystified, and on occasion it triggers riots in foreign capitals. But this wasn't always true. Our history is replete with examples of suppression, much of it sanctioned by the courts. The robust protection that we now afford to speech is the product of what lawyers call a common law process, in which the courts, in dialogue with each other and American society, shaped and reshaped the rules by which we live.[7]

It's easy to overestimate the guidance provided by the apparently airtight constitutional text. Absolutists ask, "What is it you don't get about the words 'no law'?" In their view—famously championed on the mid-twentieth-century Court by Justice Hugo Black[8]—the First Amendment is plenty clear about the scope of its prohibitions.

The absolutist stance provides potent rhetoric but weak analysis. "Speech," for instance, is not a self-defining term. It doesn't self-evidently include silent films, virtual reality simulations, or abstract art, let alone the decision to protest with a burning cross, a black armband, or an anti-gay jacket. Lots of conduct expresses a message; does the First Amendment cover people who publicly urinate on courthouses to protest injustice?

Then there is the matter of "abridging" speech. Does *any* restriction on free speech qualify as an abridgement? Surely it would be crazy to invalidate any law that might adversely affect speech. After all, the federal income tax leaves us with less money to spend broadcasting our views. The trademark and copyright laws protect intellectual property by limiting speech. Laws against extortion and blackmail prohibit certain uses of words. And the classic question about free speech still holds: what if you falsely scream "Fire" in a crowded theater?

Finally, the text says that we can't abridge the "freedom of speech." Does that "freedom" necessarily include hateful invectives shouted in another's face? Holocaust denial? Speech designed to undermine democracy itself?

Asking what the framers of the Constitution thought or what the public understood at the time the document was written and ratified is not very helpful when it comes to freedom of speech.[9] When the First Amendment was adopted, in 1791, it was widely understood to prohibit mainly "prior restraints" on speech, such as an insistence on preapproval of published works.[10] The government generally remained free to punish speech with a "bad tendency" to endanger public morals, health, welfare, or security. This rule was used to justify many limits. A lot of expression that we now protect—including scandalous art, advertisements, religious blasphemy, frank expressions of sexuality, and even some political commentary—could be prohibited if we were strict originalists.

To avoid these results, originalists often recast the original understanding in broader terms, trying to identify principles the public understood the First Amendment to embody. Of course, they must then explain how expansively we can define those principles and how to translate them into the modern world. That inquiry, in turn, usually defeats one of the supposed virtues of originalism: well-defined historical limits that control constitutional interpretation and prevent subjective judgments.

Moreover, Americans have *always* struggled over free speech.[11] Soon after the nation ratified the First Amendment, the Federalists who controlled Congress passed the Alien and Sedition Acts to punish dangerous speech and antagonize Thomas Jefferson's opposition party.[12] In the 1830s, the North and South clashed over Southern laws that made abolitionist speech a capital offense.[13] During the Civil War, Abraham Lincoln invoked his emergency powers as Commander in Chief to suppress dissident expression.[14] Matters grew worse in the 1880s and 1890s; our Gilded Age triggered a wave of new laws that empowered prosecutors to combat the "abuse" of speech rights by anarchists, socialists, immigrants, free lovers, and unions.[15] This pattern continued well into the early twentieth century.[16]

Most American citizens, of course, have enjoyed robust speech rights throughout our history. But until the mid-twentieth century, certain groups outside the mainstream risked deportation, persecution, and imprisonment when they expressed unpopular messages. During World War I, Woodrow Wilson relied on this absence of strong constitutional protections to persecute pacifists, anti-war demonstrators, and political opponents.[17] The Court repeatedly upheld Wilson's campaign of suppression, but a faction of the legal elite revolted and began to articulate a modern vision of free speech.[18]

This modern view was championed on the Court in the early twentieth century by two of our most brilliant justices: Oliver Wendell Holmes Jr. and Louis D. Brandeis. Grounded largely in the pragmatic belief that truth emerges from a market of ideas, a fear of government suppression, and a commitment to protecting democracy, this approach to free speech eventually sank deep roots on the Court.

In his most famous opinion, Holmes articulated a core principle of modern First Amendment law: the best way to root out bad ideas is to force them to survive on their own, not for government to ban them.[19] As Holmes put it, "The best test of truth is the power of the thought to get itself accepted in the competition of the market."[20] "We should be eternally vigilant," he elaborated, "against attempts to check the expression of opinions that we loathe and believe to be fraught with death." Both an act of faith and an empirical claim, this ideal remains enormously influential. It enjoys pride of place in modern legal thought, alongside Brandeis's argument that free speech is vital to democratic self-governance: "Those who won our independence," he instructed, "believed that the final end of the State was to make men free to develop their faculties . . . They believed that freedom to think as you will and to speak as you think are means indispensable to the discovery and spread of political truth; that, without free speech and assembly, discussion would be futile; that, with them, discussion affords ordinarily adequate protection against the dissemination of noxious doctrine; that the greatest menace to freedom is an inert people; that public discussion is a political duty, and that this should be a fundamental principle of the American government."[21]

By 1943, at the height of World War II and after more than a decade of dramatic development in free speech doctrine, Justice Robert H. Jackson captured the insurgent wisdom when he struck down a law compelling mandatory flag salutes—and added his own poetic twist in emphasizing individual conscience: "If there is any fixed star in our constitutional constellation, it is that no official, high or petty, can prescribe what shall be orthodox in politics, nationalism, religion, or other matters of opinion, or force citizens to confess by word or act their faith therein."[22]

The Cold War, however, reignited calls for suppression amid palpable danger.[23] In 1951, the Court sharply shifted its emphasis by asking whether "the gravity of the 'evil,' discounted by its improbability, justifies such invasion of free speech as is necessary to avoid the danger."[24] The Court then repeatedly "balanced" the value of communist speech against the danger of radical revolution—solving an impossible equation to limit free speech in a world darkened by fear.

The Court fully embraced robust protections of free speech only in the 1960s and '70s, when famous cases arose from efforts to conceal the Pentagon Papers, silence Vietnam War protesters, crush the civil rights movement, and suppress the sexual revolution.[25] The battle-scarred justices of that era chiseled a broad view of First Amendment liberty into constitutional law. As with its case-by-case attempt to define obscenity, the Court did not always live up to the promise of the values it espoused. But those justices, including William O. Douglas, Hugo L. Black, and William J. Brennan Jr., did more than any of their predecessors to transform into constitutional dogma the ideals we now know well—many of which first took shape in dissents by Holmes and Brandeis. Although free speech doctrine has evolved in significant ways since then, it is no exaggeration to say that we live in the free speech world that those justices forged from fragments of text and history, their own experiences, and some bold ideals.

Adhering to customs of judicial rhetoric, the Roberts Court's free speech rulings tend to sideline this messy history of judge-made law. Instead, the justices are deliberately selective in their collective memory. When they talk about the framers, they often borrow mythical narratives that their predecessors fabricated decades ago to justify doctrinal innovation—narratives like this one from 1927:

> Those who won our independence by revolution were not cowards. They did not fear political change. They did not exalt order at the cost of liberty. To courageous, self-reliant men, with confidence in the power of free and fearless reasoning applied through the processes of popular government, no danger flowing from speech can be deemed clear and present, unless the incidence of the evil apprehended is so

imminent that it may befall before there is opportunity for full discussion.[26]

Here we see Brandeis, writing at the peak of his powers. In his soaring rhetoric, the framers are cast in a suitably modern light and gifted
with all the right values: courage in dark times, faith in democracy, trust
that truth can defeat falsehood, and an abiding love of liberty. This is an
inspiring tale. It tells us why we protect speech and offers a model of
American citizenship. The story isn't very strong on specifics, but the gist
is clear: protect *a lot* of speech and look skeptically on claims that any
particular speech is too dangerous. To this day, stories like Brandeis's
help anchor the Court's account of First Amendment rights.

Whatever their drawbacks as accounts of what really happened in
the 1790s, these stories offer valuable lessons. And nowhere are those
insights more vital than in cases involving vulnerable members of our
society or dissenters from the ideological mainstream. It's easy to protect speech with which we agree and speakers who look like us. When
speech seems dangerous or valueless, however, and the speaker doesn't
seem like the kind of person we should protect, our First Amendment
beliefs face a true test. Those are the cases that force us to return to first
principles.

Modern free speech doctrine was forged in the crucible of two world wars,
the Red Scare, the Cold War, and conflicts in Vietnam and Korea. One of
its most resonant lessons is that the stress of wartime can seduce us into
equating speech by activists at home with the genuine threat posed by enemies abroad; thus, opinions upholding censorship during World War I
and the Red Scare are now regarded as errors to avoid. In contrast, cases
vindicating the rights of pacifists, protesters, and journalists are celebrated
as triumphs of principle—including a Vietnam War case in which a pro-
tester in a courthouse wore a jacket emblazoned with the words "Fuck the
Draft."[27]

Given the Roberts Court's strong free speech reputation, one might
have expected it to boldly reaffirm the continuing vitality of this national
commitment in our age of terror. On June 21, 2010, however, it did just
the opposite.

Four months earlier, the Court heard argument in *Holder v. Humanitarian Law Project* (*HLP*), a case testing the federal law that bans provision of "material support or resources" to any terrorist group.[28] This law mainly targets assistance to terrorists in the form of money, supplies, and weapons. *HLP* was brought by American human rights activists who wanted to assist the humanitarian and nonviolent political activities of two groups: the Kurdistan Workers' Party, which seeks an independent Kurdish state in Turkey, and the Liberation Tigers of Tamil Eelam, who seek an independent Tamil state in Sri Lanka. Both groups had bloody histories, including massacres of civilians, and had been designated foreign terrorist organizations by the Secretary of State.

Fearing criminal prosecution and imprisonment if they rendered assistance, the activists sought a ruling to protect their peaceful activities from the material support law. In the activists' view, this was a simple case: they wanted to train people in how to petition for relief before the United Nations, use international law to resolve disputes, present claims for tsunami-related aid, and negotiate peace treaties. Surely, they insisted, this political expression—designed not to facilitate violence but to discourage it—fell within the First Amendment's compass.

The Department of Justice disagreed. At argument, with the justices arrayed before her, then–Solicitor General Elena Kagan opened with the government's most effective trump card: the law criminalizing "material support," she declared, "is a vital weapon in this nation's continuing struggle against international terrorism." Kagan proceeded to challenge the activists' contention that support of peaceful activities and support of terror-related activities could be neatly distinguished. Any support to a terrorist organization might aid the whole entity, she explained, since money and skills are transferable: "Hezbollah builds bombs. Hezbollah also builds homes. What Congress decided was when you help Hezbollah build homes, you are also helping Hezbollah build bombs. That's the entire theory behind this statute, and it's a reasonable theory."

Writing for the Court, as he so often does in First Amendment cases, Chief Justice Roberts agreed that the theory was reasonable enough. So did five of his colleagues: Justices Stevens, Scalia, Kennedy, Thomas, and Alito. Support of any kind *could* free up resources to be used for terrorism, Roberts speculated. Assistance from American human rights activists, moreover, *could* "help lend legitimacy to foreign terrorist groups—legitimacy that makes it easier for those groups to persist, to recruit members, and to raise funds." Because the case involved "sensitive and weighty interests of national security," a field in which the Court lacked expertise, Roberts thought that "respect for the Government's conclusions is appropriate." The Executive Branch agencies with a detailed knowledge of the relevant facts had concluded that the activists' speech could cause the kind of harm that Congress sought to prevent with its material support statute. That was enough for Roberts.

To be sure, this is a powerful argument. But it must have its limits. In dangerous times, the political branches often overreact to innocent speech. Moments of crisis therefore demand careful scrutiny of Congress's assumptions by a branch of government unconcerned with reelection and charged with special solicitude for civil rights. Absent such probing scrutiny, liberty may be too readily lost to paranoid fears, political agendas, or a desire by the political branches to protect themselves against accusations of being insufficiently aggressive. In fact, judicial trust in the political branches at times of crisis has sometimes led the nation to catastrophe.

Most ignominiously, in a case that arose during World War II, *Korematsu v. United States*, the Court deferred to government assertions that the forced relocation of Japanese-Americans across the West Coast to internment camps was essential to national security.[29] Its opinion in *Korematsu* was wrong for many reasons, but one of its main errors was uncritical faith in factual claims by government lawyers about the threat posed by Japanese-American spies and saboteurs—claims that flatly contradicted confidential reports by high-level military and intelligence officials, and that were deliberately misrepresented to the Court by the Department of Justice.[30] While the Court undoubtedly owes the political branches a substantial measure of deference, out of respect for both their constitutional role and their expertise, that deference can go only so far.

In *HLP*, the Court embraced a narrow view of its own role in evaluating the justifications for a speech-restrictive law. It did not simply defer to a questionable finding of fact by Congress or the Executive Branch about the dangers of speech; rather, it didn't require any factual findings at all. Acknowledging that "whether foreign terrorist organizations meaningfully segregate support of their legitimate activities from support of terrorism is an empirical question," Roberts conceded that Congress hadn't offered "concrete evidence" that the activists' proposed speech posed any threat. But this was okay, he argued, because "the Government, when seeking to prevent imminent harms in the context of international affairs and national security, is not required to conclusively link all the pieces in the puzzle before we grant weight to its empirical conclusions." He was willing to accept the "informed judgment" of the Executive Branch.

This reasoning suggests that in national security cases, Congress and the Executive enjoy a form of super deference that can paper over notable empirical gaps in their justifications for limiting speech. In the future, *HLP* will therefore make it much harder to challenge national security laws on First Amendment grounds, as courts take a narrow view of their role in testing the strength of the government's factual claims. This part of the *HLP* opinion was all the more remarkable given that the Court implied that it was using "strict scrutiny"—normally the *least* forgiving form of judicial review.

In a muscular dissent, Justice Breyer, joined by Justices Ginsburg and Sotomayor, charged the majority with abdicating the judicial role. This was a case about political speech, the very stuff of democracy. Some of that speech was directed at Americans, placing it at the heart of the First Amendment. The activists had advocated nothing lawless or violent. As a result, Breyer concluded, censorship required weighty and precise justification.

In Breyer's view, the government fell far short of that standard. He did not see it as obvious that peaceful advocacy skills were "fungible" or that the terrorist groups would otherwise have paid for training in international law. "The Government," he remarked, "has provided us with no empirical information that might convincingly support [its] claim." Instead, it offered only "highly general support" in the form of evidence that the provision of goods and money to terrorists would pose a threat—proof that said little about the supposed dangers of training in United Nations petitions. Whereas Roberts called for deference, Breyer highlighted "the Court's own obligation to secure the protection that the Constitution grants to individuals."

Breyer also assailed Roberts's claim that "support" in the form of political speech can be banned to ensure that it does not "legitimize" terrorist groups. Because "speech, association, and related activities on behalf of a group will often, perhaps always, help to legitimate that group," he reasoned, the Chief's logic could mean that "the First Amendment battle would be lost in untold instances where it should be won." By Roberts's reasoning, even if a respected domestic organization merely *praised* a terrorist group, the organization would help "legitimate" the terrorists and could thus raise national security concerns. While Roberts limited his logic to "coordinated" support between Americans and terrorist groups, Breyer warned that the government's case against conferring "legitimacy" was a slippery slope.

Ultimately, Breyer's dissent in *HLP* marked the treachery of "arguments that would deny First Amendment protection to the peaceful teaching of international human rights law on the ground that a little knowledge about 'the international legal system' is too dangerous a thing." Innocent speech, he noted, can *always* be put to evil use. Yet we rightly allow a veritable deluge of potentially dangerous speech, requiring strong evidence of imminent danger before banning it.

As the landmark Roberts Court case about free speech in wartime, *HLP* sends a clear signal: judges must defer, and then defer again, to the government when it seeks to justify bans on speech. So long as the "informed judgment" of the government, some fact-finding on the general subject, and abstract reasoning all support the censorship as a tool against terrorism, it may well survive review. While judicial second-guessing of the political branches is always perilous in international conflicts, *HLP* elevates that concern to a new level. As a result, *HLP* will likely marginalize the Judiciary in protecting free speech in the national security field for many years to come.[31]

Not all threats to free speech implicate weighty matters of national security. Some are simpler and more mundane and affect populations whose rights it's easy to forget about. But those are exactly the cases that cast revealing light on our beliefs about the First Amendment.

Introduced in 2000, Pennsylvania's Long Term Segregation Unit (LTSU) was reserved for the most dangerous prisoners. Inmates were denied access to newspapers, magazines, and photos, locked in their cells twenty-three hours a day, allowed only one visitor each month, banned from all use of phones, and forbidden to watch TV or listen to the radio.

They were limited to minimal correspondence and reading material. Good behavior could result in transfer to a slightly less restrictive unit.

To many outside observers, these conditions were exceptionally and unjustifiably punitive. In 2009, Atul Gawande made a forceful case in the *New Yorker* that long-term solitary confinement—which, he noted, often drives inmates mad—should be considered a form of torture.[32] In 2012, the *Nation* discussed the LTSU and other segregated units in an essay whose title posed a troubling question: "Why Are Prisoners Committing Suicide in Pennsylvania?"[33]

Ronald Banks, an LTSU inmate, sued Pennsylvania in 2001. He charged that the ban on newspapers, magazines, and photographs violated his First Amendment rights. When *Beard v. Banks* reached the Court five years later, Pennsylvania offered a grab bag of justifications for its rule.[34] Its main point, though, concerned the social psychology of behavior modification: this deprivation, the state argued, encouraged inmates in the LTSU to improve and discouraged other inmates from engaging in behavior that would land them in the LTSU. No single opinion held a majority of the Court, but six justices voted for Pennsylvania.

Thomas, joined only by Scalia, expressed a view that, in practice, would leave prisoners with almost no constitutional rights at all. This narrow view of prisoners' rights dates back to Thomas's earliest days on the Court and initially scandalized left-leaning commentators; in response to one of his first rulings on the subject, the *New York Times* pejoratively called Thomas the "youngest, cruelest Justice."[35] His skepticism of inmate rights reflects a firm belief that the Eighth Amendment, which prohibits "cruel and unusual punishment," affords the states vast leeway to define conditions of incarceration. So long as those conditions don't violate the Eighth Amendment itself, he maintains, they are permissible.[36] Unimpressed by the Court's unsteady effort to identify a middle ground for inmate rights, Thomas warned in *Beard* that "judicial scrutiny of prison regulations is an endeavor fraught with peril."

Breyer, who is often inclined to defer to technical expertise, spoke for the rest of the majority. He ruled against Banks on the ground that Pennsylvania's behavior-modification logic justified its severe restrictions on First Amendment rights. Breyer characteristically emphasized the "professional judgment" and "experience-based conclusion[s]" in play. Persuaded by the Pavlovian logic of a deprivation scheme that encouraged good behavior and discouraged backsliding by using rights as both carrots and sticks, he scolded a lower court for imposing "too high an evidentiary burden" on Pennsylvania. Ultimately, Breyer thought that it would be unfair to require more than coherent logic and a dash of experience-based evidence to justify substantial limits on First Amendment rights in prison.

This view represents the flip side of his *HLP* dissent, where he thought logic and some informed judgment fell short. Part of the explanation for this switch is doctrinal: the burden for limiting First Amendment rights in *Beard* was less demanding because the case involved inmates. But part of it is personal: Breyer usually feels more at ease deferring to technocrats than to politicians. That sentiment, linked to his own background as a member of the United States Sentencing Commission, may explain Breyer's allowance of stronger deference to the state in *Beard*.

Breyer's opinion in *Beard* was hardly radical. It extended decades of Supreme Court precedent holding that inmates have far fewer constitutional rights than the rest of us—and that the rights inmates do enjoy are significantly watered down.[37] Nonetheless, it did *extend* that doctrine, and did so at the expense of free speech protections for prisoners by deferring to questionable justifications for censorship offered by Pennsylvania's prison administrators.

Castigating the Court for ignoring its duty to ensure that inmates receive ethical treatment, Stevens—joined by Ginsburg in dissent—decried this transformation of First Amendment freedoms into an elaborate psychology experiment. In his view, the state's strict policy struck at "First Amendment rights to receive, to read, and to think." Its most worrisome danger was the lack of any plausible limiting principle. What other rights may prisons strip away in an effort to rehabilitate? Marriage? Religious liberty? After all, wrote Stevens, "the more important the constitutional right at stake (at least from the prisoners' perspective), the stronger the justification for depriving prisoners of that right."

Worse, he wrote, Pennsylvania's rule verged "perilously close to a state-sponsored effort at mind control." Stevens explained, "The complete prohibition on secular, nonlegal newspapers, newsletters, and magazines prevents prisoners from receiving suitable access to social, political, esthetic, moral, and other ideas, which are central to the development and preservation of individual identity, and are clearly protected by the

First Amendment." Of course, prisoners are frequently deprived of important rights. But the rights to read and think are so fundamental to our humanity, Stevens argued, that the Court must require a particularly well-substantiated governmental justification for their denial. To a technocrat, the use of rights as behavior-modifying bargaining chips might seem the epitome of logic. To a humanist, it signals our collective descent down a frightening path.

To ward off such tyranny, Stevens called for "especially cautious" review of deprivation-based prison policies. He clearly believed that Pennsylvania flunked such analysis. Given the presence of many other incentives for rehabilitation, the absence of any real empirical evidence of the policy's success, and data showing that over 75 percent of prisoners never left the LTSU, Stevens argued that Pennsylvania's denial of First Amendment rights was indefensible.

Only Stevens and Ginsburg, though, rejected Pennsylvania's logic. Only they refused to accept the dark irony of cloaking in the mantra of rehabilitation the prison's decision to deny these men and women access to materials essential to psychological self-development. Here, as in *HLP*, a majority of the Roberts Court invoked a rule of deference to the government and mightily weakened free speech for a whole class of people—in this case, a class for whom few might feel much sympathy, and thus a class in particular need of judicial protection.

Justice Brandeis famously described free speech as an essential part of democratic self-government. He was right for many reasons, one of them being the role of free speech as a vital mechanism of accountability. The Roberts Court, though, has stripped speech protections from many public employees who are uniquely well positioned to convey to the public valuable information about government institutions.

In 2000, a Los Angeles prosecutor named Richard Ceballos suffered workplace retaliation for carrying out his professional duties as he understood them. Ceballos disclosed to a defense attorney—and testified at trial—that he had discovered serious misrepresentations in a search warrant crucial to a criminal prosecution. In his view, these disclosures of misconduct were ethically required after his superiors refused to take action. For his troubles, Ceballos was denied a promotion and transferred, which prompted him to file a suit alleging retaliation. At the time, the First Amendment protected public employees with a balancing test: does the value of the speech to the employee and society outweigh its harm to the government?[38]

This test was a major improvement on the Court's early brush with free speech claims by government workers. Justice Holmes, during his time on the Massachusetts Supreme Judicial Court and prior to his libertarian turn, summed up conventional wisdom in 1892: "[A policeman] may have a constitutional right to talk politics, but he has no constitutional right to be a policeman."[39] Public employees simply had no protections against being fired for their beliefs.

In the 2006 case *Garcetti v. Ceballos*, a bare majority of the Court took a step back toward that world.[40] Kennedy's opinion fashioned a new rule: when public employees speak as "citizens," they retain full First Amendment rights, but when they speak within the scope of their official responsibilities, their speech falls entirely outside the First Amendment. Kennedy made a strong argument for this innovation, emphasizing that public employers require discretion to manage staff entrusted with the authority to speak for the government: "Official communications have official consequences, creating a need for substantive consistency and clarity. Supervisors must ensure that their employees' official communications are accurate, demonstrate sound judgment, and promote the employer's mission. . . . If Ceballos' superiors thought his memo was inflammatory or misguided, they had the authority to take proper corrective action."

In dissent, Stevens went straight for the linchpin of Kennedy's logic: "The notion that there is a categorical difference between speaking as a citizen and speaking in the course of one's employment is quite wrong." In his view, it was "senseless to let constitutional protection for exactly the same words hinge on whether they fall within a job description." It was passing strange, Stevens remarked, that Ceballos could air his concerns in an op-ed in the *Los Angeles Times* but not in a court of law to safeguard the constitutional rights of the accused.

Justice David Souter, who retired from the bench three years later to return home to his beloved New Hampshire farmhouse, also assailed the majority's logic. He emphasized that, regardless of a government paycheck, employees retain a natural interest in sharing ideas—and the public enjoys a vital interest in hearing their considered thoughts, especially on matters about which they are the most knowledgeable. The balance between these values and bureaucratic efficiency shouldn't be resolved by a rule that denies to public servants the "poet's 'object ... to unite my avocation and my vocation.'" (Souter, a consummate New Englander, borrowed here from Robert Frost.) His dissent also warned that, without strong whistleblower protections for employees who reveal corruption, we will all suffer from less accountability in government.

In *Garcetti*, public employees lost some of their First Amendment freedom to share uniquely well-informed views with the public. This result was driven mainly by an understandable concern that such speech is dangerous because it can harm government efficiency. In most cases, after all, silencing a squeaky wheel is easier than replacing it, and employers are undoubtedly entitled to a measure of control over their staff. Indeed, for government employees who, like Ceballos, speak and write for a living, employer judgments about the quality and appropriateness of their speech are inevitable and will often be legitimate. Still, as a case that creates a general rule, *Garcetti* heavily weighted the scale in favor of preventing these perils of employee speech—and largely dismissed its social and individual worth. The result is that other constitutional values, including employee speech rights, public accountability, and transparency, were relegated to the sidelines.[41]

"BONG HiTS 4 JESUS" reached the Roberts Court in 2007. The case, *Morse v. Frederick*, began when Joseph Frederick, an adventurous high school senior, displayed a fourteen-foot banner bearing the words "BONG HiTS 4 JESUS" while the Olympic Torch Relay passed outside his school in Juneau, Alaska.[42] Principal Deborah Morse saw a pro-drug message and demanded that Frederick remove the banner. Frederick refused and was suspended. He promptly filed suit.

Morse involved wonderfully bizarre facts and sparked intense interest on the Court. Nobody really knew what the sign meant or why Frederick had waved it. At argument, Kennedy asked about "Rape Is Fun" signs and Scalia suggested "Extortion Is Profitable" banners. Souter wondered how disruptive it would really be "if the kids look around and they say, well, so-and-so has his bong sign again ... [and] they then return to

Macbeth." *Morse* had all the makings of a one-off case—and yet it prompted five heated opinions and dramatically limited student speech rights.

Speaking for a bare majority of the Court, Roberts concluded that Frederick had to lose because school officials may "restrict student speech at a school event, when that speech is reasonably viewed as promoting illegal drug use." This conclusion, in his view, followed from cases limiting in-school student speech rights—and from cases effectively creating a Constitution-free zone around any facts involving drugs in schools. Displaying his preference for narrow, careful rulings, the Chief then devoted several pages to downplaying the significance of his own decision: "Stripped of rhetorical flourishes . . . [this case] is less about constitutional first principles than about whether Frederick's banner constitutes promotion of illegal drug use." *Morse* was an easy and fact-bound decision, he insisted, adding that there was no need to sound "the First Amendment bugle." Most of his colleagues, however, disagreed.

Inspired by the topic, and ever willing to venture off alone in the name of originalism, Thomas wrote a lengthy historical essay to prove that students have no First Amendment rights at all: "In the earliest public schools, teachers taught, and students listened. Teachers commanded, and students obeyed." Mocking the Court's more nuanced rule, which "says that students have a right to speak in schools except when they do not," Thomas argued that the Judiciary should let democracy determine school policies. Unhappy parents, he pointed out, can always move, switch to a private school, or seek redress before school boards. There was no need for judicial intervention. Thomas concluded with a swipe at young Frederick: "To elevate such impertinence to the status of constitutional protection would be farcical and would indeed be to surrender control of the American public school system to public school students."

Disturbed, Alito drafted a sharp response to Thomas. Whereas Thomas claimed that public schools act *in loco parentis* (in place of parents), Alito warned that "when public school authorities regulate student speech, they act as agents of the State." Therefore, "it is a dangerous fiction to pretend that parents simply delegate their authority—including their authority to determine what their children may say and hear—to public school authorities." Alito rarely speaks out in favor of broad free speech rights in cases like this one. The fact that he did so here may be a sign of just how off-the-wall Thomas's originalist reasoning seemed to him. It may also reflect the concern Alito voiced in oral argument that schools could "suppress all sorts of political speech and speech expressing fundamental values of the students, under the banner of getting rid of speech that's inconsistent with educational missions." Alito likely had in mind friend-of-the-court briefs filed by Christian groups highlighting the rights of religious students.[43]

While the Court's right-leaning justices argued over the implications of their ruling against Frederick, Stevens, joined by Souter and Ginsburg, forcefully blasted the "First Amendment bugle." Echoing a point familiar from *HLP*, Stevens charged the conservative majority with abdicating its judicial role. Whereas Roberts saw no violation because the principal had "reasonably viewed" the banner "as promoting illegal drug use," Stevens disagreed that such incomprehensible and harmless speech as "BONG HITS 4 JESUS" could be punished based on what *someone else* might reasonably believe it means. This analysis, he warned, was an invitation to censorship of valuable expression.

Stevens also worried about the big picture: "The Court's ham-handed, categorical approach is deaf to the constitutional imperative to permit unfettered debate, even among high school students, about the wisdom of the war on drugs or of legalizing marijuana for medicinal use." If Frederick's "stupid reference to marijuana" is punishable, students might be "forgiven for zipping their mouths about drugs at school lest some 'reasonable' observer" censor them. The Court's rule, Stevens added, might even fail to protect "WINE SIPS 4 JESUS" banners.

Breyer echoed this concern, even while refusing to embrace Stevens's attack unreservedly. Gifted with an endless supply of hypotheticals, which alternately dazzle and disorient at oral arguments, Breyer let loose: "What about a conversation during the lunch period where one student suggests that glaucoma sufferers should smoke marijuana to relieve the pain? What about deprecating commentary about an anti-drug film shown in school?"

To Stevens, "although this case began with a silly, nonsensical banner, it ends with the Court inventing out of whole cloth a special First Amendment rule permitting the censorship of any student speech that mentions drugs, at least so long as someone could perceive that speech to contain a latent pro-drug message." Although he was by far the oldest of the justices, John Paul Stevens may have been the youngest at heart in his recognition that each generation has something to teach its elders. While school officials need tools to maintain control, *Morse* exalted the need for order over weighty First Amendment concerns.

Stevens's dissent proved prophetic. Since *Morse*, the Roberts Court has functionally banished certain groups of speakers to the sidelines—occasionally at the expense of other First Amendment values. Although *HLP*, *Beard*, *Garcetti*, and *Morse* presented hard choices, in each case the Court decided against the pro-speech view. And each time, it advantaged the powerful over the comparatively powerless: students, prisoners, public employees, and human rights activists have all seen their speech protections against the government weakened.

The creation of these new silos of largely unprotected speech was not required by precedent. Instead, the Court made judgments about how to reconcile competing values. One might take issue with how the Court balanced free speech against other considerations in these cases, but at least the Court's method of analysis was capable of accounting for the wide array of values at stake when we create First Amendment law.

In contrast, when it has upheld even questionable free speech claims, the Roberts Court has ardently disavowed *any* power to recognize new kinds of unprotected speech or to account for the dangers some speech might pose. It has insisted instead that speech gets either vast protection or nearly none at all—and that most of these decisions are wholly beyond its control. It has added that values other than liberty have little role to play in First Amendment calculus. Even to the extent that its position is plausible as a matter of hypertechnical doctrine, there is surely a hint of irony in the Court's solemn denial of any power, any power at all, to adopt a more nuanced approach to the First Amendment.

Cases involving children have a way of revealing the justices' distinct worldviews. In a ruling that expanded the circumstances in which kids must receive *Miranda* warnings ("You have the right to remain silent . . ."), Sotomayor displayed her pronounced bent toward "common sense" by invoking it repeatedly.[44] When Kagan held that it would be "cruel and unusual punishment" to impose mandatory life-without-parole sentences on kids, she employed a powerful, plainspoken style: "If death is different," she wrote, "children are different too."[45] In *Morse*, each of the justices who wrote an opinion divulged his most definitive traits—from the Chief's taste for narrow rulings to Thomas's tour of colonial classrooms.

Brown v. Entertainment Merchants Association proved to be equally illuminating.[46] Decided in 2011, *Brown* struck down a California law restricting the sale or rental of violent video games to minors without parental approval. At argument, California relied on precedents that allow states to treat adults and children differently when regulating the sale of pornographic material. It argued that "there is no sound basis in logic or policy for treating offensively violent, harmful material with no redeeming value for children any different than sexually explicit material." The *Washington Post* nicely summarized this argument: "If States can prohibit minors from buying *Penthouse, Hustler*, and *Playboy*, why not 'Grand Theft Auto' or 'Mortal Kombat'?"[47] California also emphasized its goal of helping parents to better monitor their children's formative gaming habits, citing studies that, in the state's view, proved a correlation between violent video games and violent behavior.

Scalia, joined in an unusual alliance by Kennedy, Ginsburg, Sotomayor, and Kagan, struck down the California law in a sweeping opinion. Scalia began by agreeing with the law's backers that the unprotected obscenity of *Hustler* was no different in principle from the violence of Mortal Kombat. But according to Scalia, the two types of speech did differ on the basis of history—and that was enough.

Whereas Americans have long limited the provision of obscenity to children, Scalia explained that there is no "tradition" of treating violent speech aimed at kids as unprotected by the First Amendment. If anything, he insisted, the opposite is true: "Grimm's Fairy Tales, for example, are grim indeed. . . . Hansel and Gretel (children!) kill their captor by baking her in an oven." He added: "Golding's *Lord of the Flies* recounts how a schoolboy called Piggy is savagely murdered *by other children* while marooned on an island." This section of Scalia's opinion mirrored the oral argument, where Sotomayor feared the loss of popular rap music and Kagan added that half the Court's law clerks had likely played Mortal Kombat while growing up. The Chief had pushed back on this history at argument, noting that "we do not have a tradition in this country of telling children they should watch people actively hitting schoolgirls over the head with a shovel so they'll beg [for] mercy," but the majority read the lessons of our past differently.

To Scalia, the fact that we have traditionally protected some violent speech directed toward children meant that all speech of that sort was entitled to the highest level of First Amendment protection. (And video games, he held, *do* qualify as speech.) California's decision to target a new medium didn't, in Scalia's view, make our traditions any less applicable. Surveying efforts to "protect" children from films, comics, television, and music, Scalia emphasized that fear of corrupting the young has repeatedly been invoked without success to permit censorship of new forms of expression. Unimpressed by studies purporting to show a link between interactive video games and violent behavior, and doubtful that California's law would effectively prevent minors from accessing other violent materials, Scalia shot it down.

Thomas, Alito, and Breyer strongly disagreed with Scalia. Each of their opinions says a lot about its author—and those by Alito and Thomas are a bracing reminder of oft-overlooked differences among the more conservative justices.

Thomas, still walking the lonely path he marked in *Morse*, composed an essay about the colonial period to explain why the First Amendment "does not include a right to speak to minors . . . without going through the minors' parents or guardians." A true believer in originalism, Thomas is willing to reimagine whole fields of law in ways that disturb even Scalia, who once described himself as a "faint-hearted originalist."[48] Scalia has since repudiated that much-cited moniker and affirmed his originalist bona fides, but, when asked in 2008 how he differs from "more extreme judges"—a reference that in context suggested Thomas—Scalia replied, "I'm an originalist and a textualist, not a nut."[49]

Alito, joined by Roberts, assailed Scalia from the opposite direction. As with Thomas, when Alito was first nominated, some ill-informed critics derisively suggested that he was little more than a Scalia clone— "Scalito." That is (and always was) an absurd claim. In recent years, Alito has emerged as a deep thinker about the role of new technology in constitutional law and a powerful critic of originalism.

Quite simply, Alito is a different kind of conservative. Hewing to a school of thought associated with Edmund Burke, he is protective of traditional values, sensitive to community-based norms, and skeptical of grand statements of principle that hover far above real-world implications.[50] He is also respectful of the need for judges to reflect carefully on a changing world and cautiously develop new legal rules. This perspective is born of a streak in conservative thought committed to free markets and public enforcement of conservative values—a streak that reached its heyday in the 1970s as Republicans reacted with disgust to 1960s counterculture.

While speaking at Columbia Law School in 2012, Alito offered thoughts on Burke that illuminate his own beliefs: "One of Burke's core insights was that the individual is foolish but the species is wise. Society is so incredibly complex that the solitary human mind is incapable of understanding how all the pieces fit together. Because the various components of the social order are interrelated in ways that are subtle and innumerable, it is almost impossible to predict all the consequences that will result from a rule. As a general matter, we can have greater confidence in established rules that have been tested and refined over time."[51]

This mentality sets Alito apart from Scalia, who wields his brand of originalism with inexhaustible self-assurance and skepticism about the supposedly distinct perils of modernity. Whereas Alito wants the Court to examine how First Amendment values are implicated in each case, Scalia sees nothing but danger in that project. When Scalia charged at argument in *Brown* that California wanted to create an exception that Americans "never ratified when they ratified the First Amendment," Alito shot back, "Well, I think what Justice Scalia wants to know is what James Madison thought about video games. Did he enjoy them?"

As Alito explained in *Brown*, the interactive nature of some video games is truly unprecedented: "If the technological characteristics of the sophisticated games that are likely to be available in the near future are combined with the characteristics of the most violent games already marketed, the result will be games that allow troubled teens to experience in an extraordinarily personal and vivid way what it would be like to carry out unspeakable acts of violence." These unique features of video games may require different rules, he suggested.

Alito ultimately voted to strike down California's statute because he viewed it as impermissibly vague, but he expressed profound disagreement with Scalia's core holding: "In considering the application of unchanging constitutional principles to new and rapidly evolving technology, this Court should proceed with caution. We should make every effort to understand the new technology. . . . And we should not hastily dismiss the judgment of legislators, who may be in a better position than we are to assess the implications of new technology."

While Alito urged caution and Thomas recounted colonial tales, Breyer mounted the most direct assault on Scalia's reasoning. Calling upon the Court to forthrightly balance the benefits and evils of speech, Breyer saw "no more than a modest restriction on expression." After all, he noted, the California law came nowhere close to banning the games. It merely required parental approval.

As usual, Breyer was excited by the chance to dive into a pile of social science research, which he lovingly detailed in a nine-page appendix to his opinion. While Scalia cavalierly dismissed California's empirical basis for treating video games differently from Grimm's fairy tales, Breyer exhaustively fact-checked the state's case. In it he found a solid argument, not the kind of self-serving hunch the political branches sometimes employ to justify suppressing speech they deem threatening. Breyer was especially impressed by expert opinions from public health professionals and other disinterested social science organizations.

Breyer also challenged the rigid doctrinal distinction that allowed kids to access violent speech but not obscenity, a line that Scalia merely chalked up to history. Here Breyer delivered a truly memorable critique: "What kind of First Amendment would permit the government to protect children by restricting sales of [an] extremely violent video game *only* when the woman—bound, gagged, tortured, and killed—is also topless?"

Finally, Breyer highlighted the values other than liberty that the Court had simply disregarded in *Brown*: "This case is ultimately less about censorship than it is about education. Our Constitution cannot succeed in securing the liberties it seeks to protect unless we can raise future generations committed cooperatively to making our system of government work. Education, however, is about choices. Sometimes, children need to learn by making choices for themselves. Other times, choices are made for children—by their parents, by their teachers, and by the people acting democratically through their governments."

By any measure, *Brown* was a hard case. Violent expression, no less than sexual expression, can be artistic and educational. (Consider Quentin Tarantino's *Inglourious Basterds* or Steven Spielberg's *Saving Private Ryan*.) But it can also be uniquely traumatizing and destructive, especially to children and especially when experienced in virtual reality. There's a good argument, then, for affording it a strong measure of First Amendment protection while also recognizing that reasonable restrictions supported by credible justifications may still pass muster. In *Brown*, Breyer and Alito both seemed to favor such an approach to the free speech question, one that would acknowledge the particular dangers posed by violent video games and carefully evaluate how those dangers should affect tolerable limits on the First Amendment rights of children. To them, California's regulation—which did not ban the sale or use of games but merely required parental approval—raised tough questions.

Scalia, in contrast, saw a request for the Court to manufacture a broad new category of totally unprotected violent speech—a request, he said, the Court would not tolerate. History and history alone, he declared, decides whether we protect a category of speech from regulation. Since *Brown* involved violent speech, a historically protected category, he reasoned that the most rigorous First Amendment scrutiny applied to California's law. There was no room in this all-or-nothing analysis for any reconsideration of the architecture of free speech rights, a bold assertion that, to some, may ring a bit hollow in light of the Court's creativity in *HLP*, *Beard*, *Garcetti*, and *Morse*.

Scalia's approach, if consistently applied, would have its virtues. Most important, it could prevent us from succumbing to our fears and blasting holes in the First Amendment at times of crisis. But it also has serious flaws, including a tendency to simply ignore new circumstances or competing values that deserve a home in the First Amendment.[52] In *Brown*, Scalia embraced a rigid line between leaving speech out in the cold and fortifying it with our most unyielding doctrine, a choice that Breyer and Alito refuse to make. That struggle will shape the future of free speech at the Roberts Court—and beyond.

States v. Stevens. Kitten murder!!

Scalia's strict historical reasoning in *Brown* hearkened back to *United States v. Stevens*, a case decided in 2010.[53] There, speaking for eight justices, Roberts struck down a federal law designed to thwart the manufacture and sale of "crush videos," which document gruesome displays of animal torture. Alito colorfully summarized a sample crush video in his solo dissent: "A kitten, secured to the ground, watches and shrieks in pain as a woman thrusts her high-heeled shoe into its body, slams her heel into the kitten's eye socket and mouth loudly fracturing its skull, and stomps repeatedly on the animal's head. The kitten hemorrhages blood, screams blindly in pain, and is ultimately left dead in a moist pile of blood-soaked hair and bone."

The federal law, however, was poorly drafted. It criminalized the commercial creation, sale, or possession of "animal cruelty," defined as works "in which a living animal is intentionally maimed, mutilated, tortured, wounded, or killed," if that conduct violates federal or state law where "the creation, sale, or possession takes place." By its literal terms, the law may have reached even the creation of hunting magazines or the surreptitious recording of abusive slaughter techniques.

To Roberts, *Stevens* was therefore an easy case: the law could not survive because it criminalized far too much constitutionally protected speech. (Congress ultimately responded to *Stevens* by passing a more carefully drafted law, though its new statute has also been challenged on First Amendment grounds.[54])

First, though, Roberts had to overcome an argument advanced by then–Solicitor General Kagan. Representing the government, she argued that the banned depictions of animal cruelty did not enjoy First Amendment protection. To support that position, Kagan defended a broad view of the Court's power to fashion exceptions: "This Court has recognized that some categories of speech lack First Amendment protection, because the speech has little or no expressive value and causes serious societal harms. Whether a given category of speech enjoys First Amendment protection depends upon a categorical balancing of the value of the speech against its societal costs."[55] In other words, when deciding whether a category of speech is covered, the Court should balance its benefits against its harms. Under that approach, Kagan argued, speech depicting illegal animal cruelty would surely qualify as unprotected. The federal statute would then survive, at least in most applications.

Kagan's argument struck a nerve. Icily rejecting her proposal to recognize a "'First Amendment Free Zone,'" Roberts called this "free-floating test for First Amendment coverage" "startling and dangerous." The Chief argued that Kagan's position would install too much power in the Judiciary to restrict speech by weighing malleable virtues and vices on an indeterminate scale. He noted that tradition already defines a small set of unprotected categories, such as obscenity, and strongly implied that the list is now closed. Then, in an unusually originalist turn, Roberts maintained that these limited exceptions have *always* been part of the Constitution: "The First Amendment itself reflects a judgment by the American people that the benefits of its restrictions on the Government outweigh the costs." Scalia later relied on these statements in *Brown* to more firmly nail the door shut on recognizing new categories of unprotected speech—in that case, violent speech aimed at minors.

The history underlying the approach taken by Roberts and Scalia, however, is questionable: the obscenity exception, for example, took shape in the Eisenhower and Nixon eras and mostly in the Court's own basement, not through a series of big, public decisions in 1791. More important, while it's true that judges unmoved by legitimate free speech claims pose a threat to liberty, insisting on a closed list of unprotected categories is not necessarily a real safeguard. If five justices want to weaken free speech rights *within* a category of protected speech, they have plenty of options. They might say that the government gets unusually broad deference in that area (*HLP*), or that the capacity in which the speech occurred matters (*Garcetti*), or that the institutional context changes things (*Beard*), or that the speech can reasonably be interpreted as unprotected (*Morse*). Indeed, these Roberts Court rulings are all, at bottom, about varieties of balancing within categories of protected speech. The Chief's powerful rhetoric in *Stevens* aside, the "judgment" made by "the First Amendment itself" has always been subject to an evolutionary common law process in which the Court plays a key role.

The flip side of this point is that even "unprotected" speech sometimes gets protection. Defamation, for example, was long considered "unprotected," until Southern states levied trumped-up libel judgments against Northern newspapers during the civil rights movement. With its First Amendment guns blazing, the Court stepped in and imposed new constitutional limits.[56]

This historical background doesn't mean the Court should have adopted Kagan's proposal, of course. Well-defined categories of intensely protected speech can occasionally constrain judges in ways that matter, whereas opening the door to all sorts of new categorical exclusions from the First Amendment could rock our free speech landscape. Further, given the Constitution's commitment to free speech, any such "balancing" must surely start with a heavy thumb on the scale in favor of speech—at least when government is censoring because of the ideas expressed or its fear that the speech will persuade. (In *Stevens*, by contrast, Congress aimed at crush videos because the act of creating them inflicted terrible harm.)

Together, *Stevens* and *Brown* cemented a rigidly categorical approach to the First Amendment. Kagan played a key role in both cases: in *Brown*, she provided Scalia with a critical fifth vote for his rejection of the position she had advanced just a year earlier in *Stevens*. Perhaps, if pressed, Kagan would resort to a time-honored quip made famous by Justice Robert Jackson in 1950, after he repudiated positions he had supported as attorney general: "The matter does not appear to me now as it appears to have appeared to me then."[57]

"Lying was his habit," explained Kennedy. "[He] lied when he said that he played hockey for the Detroit Red Wings and that he once married a starlet from Mexico." Thanks to an opinion bearing his name, Xavier Alvarez is destined to become the most famous liar in all of constitutional law. A dubious honor, but at least it's based in fact—unlike the Medal of Honor he claimed to possess when he lied yet another time while speaking to the Three Valleys Municipal Water District Board in Claremont, California, in 2007. This lie ultimately led to a prosecution under the perfectly named Stolen Valor Act, which Alvarez unabashedly contested by insisting that he enjoyed a First Amendment right to lie about possessing military medals.

In a witty opinion agreeing with Alvarez, Chief Judge Alex Kozinski of the Ninth Circuit Court of Appeals described a state-imposed "ever-truthful utopia" as "terrifying": "If false factual statements are unprotected, then the government can prosecute not only the man who tells tall tales of winning the Congressional Medal of Honor, but also the JDater who falsely claims he's Jewish or the dentist who assures you it won't hurt a bit. Phrases such as 'I'm working late tonight, hunny,' 'I got stuck in traffic' and 'I didn't inhale' could all be made into crimes. Without the robust protections of the First Amendment, the white lies, exaggerations and deceptions that are an integral part of human intercourse would become targets of censorship."[58] In Kozinski's view, "If the First Amendment is to mean anything at all, it must mean that people are free to speak about themselves and their country as they see fit without the heavy hand of government to keep them on the straight and narrow."

Kozinski did indeed describe a terrifying world. But was it truly a world threatened by the Stolen Valor Act? When *United States v. Alvarez* reached the Court, only four justices agreed with Kozinski's broad denunciation of the law.[59] Kennedy led Roberts, Sotomayor, and Ginsburg in this expansive approach. Invoking *Brown*, he held that the list of categorical exceptions to free speech protection does not include false statements. The Stolen Valor Act therefore faced (and flunked) exacting scrutiny. Kennedy reasoned, "the remedy for speech that is false is speech that is true."

Echoing Kozinski, who is both a friend and a former law clerk of his, Kennedy forcefully warned that "permitting the government to decree [Alvarez's] speech to be a criminal offense, whether shouted from the rooftops or made in a barely audible whisper, would endorse government authority to compile a list of subjects about which false statements are punishable." Citing George Orwell's classic dystopian novel *1984*, Kennedy declared that "our constitutional tradition stands against the idea that we need Oceania's Ministry of Truth." He added, "Suppression of speech by the government can make exposure of falsity more difficult, not less so. Society has the right and civic duty to engage in open, dynamic, rational discourse. These ends are not well served when the government seeks to orchestrate public discussion through content-based mandates." Kennedy's powerful and engaging opinion on the nature of false speech and freedom will undoubtedly become a classic of the First Amendment canon.

Even though *Alvarez* is his only recent writing on the topic apart from cases involving campaign finance or commercial speech, Kennedy has played a pivotal role in the Roberts Court's free speech cases. Whereas Ginsburg has reliably voted for free speech claims (except in campaign finance and commercial speech cases) and Alito has reliably voted against free speech claims (with the same caveat), Kennedy is the only justice to have voted with the winning side every time.

Kennedy's argument in *Alvarez* left Alito unmoved. He dissented, joined by Thomas and Scalia—further demonstrating the persistent instability of First Amendment voting patterns. Pointing to a "long line of cases recognizing that the right to free speech does not protect false factual statements that inflict real harm and serve no legitimate interest," Alito argued that *Alvarez* fell squarely into an unprotected category. Emphasizing the unique role played by the military, Alito then derided fears that upholding the Stolen Valor Act would lead Congress to go on a bender and pass similar laws for "Super Bowl rings, Oscars, or Phi Beta Kappa keys." "The safeguard against such laws," he wrote, "is democracy, not the First Amendment." In *Alvarez*, Alito was happy to work with strict rules, but only after he formulated an unprotected category that also suited his preference for allowing democracy to prohibit what he saw as valueless, harmful speech.

Breyer, as usual in free speech cases, wrote separately. He thought the Stolen Valor Act posed a difficult choice between free speech rights and preventing liars from diluting military medals. With these values in mind, Breyer offered his most developed challenge to the approach cemented in *Brown* and *Stevens*. He argued that the First Amendment must offer "proper protection" when a law "adversely affects constitutionally protected interests but warrants neither near-automatic condemnation . . . nor near-automatic approval." In other words, Breyer urged his colleagues not to lose sight of values underlying the First Amendment, calling on them to assess in each case whether those values would be vindicated or undermined. The ultimate question, in his view, was "whether the statute works speech-related harm that is out of proportion to its justifications."[60]

In *Alvarez*, Breyer ultimately came down against the Stolen Valor Act. But he emphasized the importance of Congress's goal—which had nothing to do with suppressing disapproved ideas—and suggested that a new iteration of the law could survive judicial scrutiny. That new version, he remarked, should require specific proof of harm from an imposter's lies. Breyer's concurrence suggested a real struggle with the case, a suggestion he confirmed at a recent conference at Harvard Law School. Speaking with unusual candor, Breyer voiced uncertainty that his vote had been correct and emphasized that a narrower law protecting the Medal of Honor should probably be upheld.[61]

Stolen Valor Act

Breyer's *Alvarez* opinion was classic Breyer, which makes it surprising (and intriguing) that Kagan joined it—and did so just one year after going along with Scalia's entirely incompatible opinion in *Brown*. This pattern of votes strongly hints that Kagan's vision of the First Amendment is still evolving and that she cannot yet be counted as a reliable vote for any particular approach to free speech issues.

Snyder v. Phelps

It was inevitable that our age of international conflict would generate hard free speech cases. Wars always do. In *HLP*, the Roberts Court dealt with pressing questions about civil liberties in wartime and the government's management of foreign affairs. Several years later, in *Snyder v. Phelps*,[62] the Court turned its focus from Turkey and Sri Lanka to a small funeral in Westminster, Maryland.

In 2006, marine Lance Corporal Matthew Snyder was killed in the line of duty in Iraq. His parents prepared a funeral for their fallen son at a Catholic church in Westminster. The Westboro Baptist Church, a small group of bigots who tour the country in search of high-profile venues at which to spew hatred, decided to transform Snyder's funeral into a platform for their venom. The day of the funeral, Westboro protested, taking care to do so in full compliance with local law. Its placards read, "God Hates the USA / Thank God for 9/11," "Thank God for IEDs," "Semper Fi Fags," "Thank God for Dead Soldiers," and "Priests Rape Boys."

Albert Snyder, Matthew's father, saw only the tops of these signs during the funeral, but he learned the full story that night. Five weeks later, Albert discovered an online "epic" posted by Westboro that savagely attacked him, his ex-wife, and his recently buried son. Soon he plunged into a severe depression, with serious physical symptoms. Fred Phelps, the leader of Westboro, was held liable by a jury for intentional infliction of emotional distress and other torts, and the trial court ordered Phelps to pay more than $2 million in damages. In short order, this case reached the Court.

Roberts, joined by seven of his colleagues, came to view *Snyder* as a test of our "profound national commitment to the principle that debate on public issues should be uninhibited, robust, and wide-open." His opinion relied heavily on precedent affording strong protection to speech on matters of "public" concern, which he called the "essence of self-government." Acknowledging that Westboro's messages "may fall short of refined social or political commentary," the Chief argued that "the issues they highlight—the political and moral conduct of the United States and its citizens, the fate of our Nation, homosexuality in the military, and scandals involving the Catholic clergy—are matters of public import." The fact that Westboro "spoke in connection with a funeral," and thereby "added to Mr. Snyder's already incalculable grief," did not alter this analysis. As Roberts explained, "On the facts before us, we cannot react to . . . pain by punishing the speaker. As a Nation we have chosen a different course—to protect even hurtful speech on public issues to ensure that we do not stifle public debate."

Snyder reasoned that speech cannot be punished if it relates to "public issues," which occurs when a speaker mentions a subject of "public import" and does so in a "manner designed . . . to reach as broad a public audience as possible." Given this logic, the Court might still permit the punishment of a speaker who commits the same degree of verbal assault as Westboro and causes the same degree of injury to a victim—so long as the verbal attack does not touch issues of public debate or the speaker targets his victims without first alerting the media.

Snyder thus involves a mismatch: it protects speech for one reason (its context and content) against punishment imposed for a wholly different reason (its impact on listeners). This rule has much to commend it from a theoretical view: expression concerning public issues is vital to democracy and merits extra protection. But it may seem cruel to victims of verbal assaults who don't care about the public character of the speech that is designed to hurt them. Albert Snyder surely felt no better knowing that his tormentors were also being viewed and debated on CNN. If anything, it's easy to imagine such publicity making things worse.

The reaction to *Snyder*, though, marginalized these sorts of concerns.[63] Indeed, *Snyder* prompted a wave of editorials breathlessly congratulating the Court for resisting the temptation to punish Westboro. As the *Washington Post* brightly opined, "The beauty of the First Amendment is often most vibrantly expressed under the ugliest of circumstances."[64]

Alito viewed the case differently. He saw the father of a fallen soldier, standing amid the dead, being attacked. "Our profound national commitment to free and open debate," he cautioned in a powerful opinion, "is

not a license for the vicious verbal assault that occurred in this case."
After all, Albert Snyder wanted only "the right of any parent who experiences such an incalculable loss: to bury his son in peace." Alito therefore dissented, adding that the First Amendment's values would remain secure if Westboro lost: "Allowing family members to have a few hours of peace without harassment does not undermine public debate. . . . In order to have a society in which public issues can be openly and vigorously debated, it is not necessary to allow the brutalization of innocent victims like petitioner."

Snyder's practical impact is likely to be limited. The Chief virtually invited legislatures to enact general rules restricting *any* protesting at funerals. Many states took the hint. Then, in 2012, Barack Obama signed a new statute barring protests within three hundred feet of military funerals. These laws often suffice to protect veterans' families.

Practicalities aside, though, *Snyder* reminds us that unsuspecting innocents are occasionally forced to bear the brunt of a First Amendment whose benefits are diffuse and collective. The Court took an aggressive stand, essentially stating that the victims of this savagery must be left without protection as the price of our shared liberty. Whether one agrees or not, it is unsettling to be reminded of freedom's steep cost.

Nobody would nominate "simplicity" as a defining virtue of the First Amendment. The Court has long struggled to divine the many purposes of free speech and to reconcile them with the complex and often uncertain demands of security, privacy, order, and efficiency. From Holmes and Brandeis defending anti-war activists, to Marshall narrating elaborate orgies, to Roberts refusing to protect "BONG HITS 4 JESUS," the legal meaning of free speech has been hammered out in a series of profoundly difficult cases. The justices play a vital role in this ongoing process, whether or not they admit it. Their opinions decide whether new realities require new legal rules, how to adapt general principles to unforeseen circumstances, and what role judges will play in protecting minorities against calls for suppression. They shape our lived experience as well as our law.

Partly because of rulings like *Brown* and *Snyder*, the Roberts Court enjoys a strong "pro-speech" reputation. Appearances deceive. A closer look reveals that the Court is deeply torn over its vision of free speech. In many ways, the Court is not as libertarian as it sometimes seems.[65]

In particular, this Court has significantly weakened free speech rights in cases touching national security, schools, prisons, and public employment. These cases rest ultimately on a willingness to balance the costs and benefits of speech—with an occasional thumb on the scale *against* open expression because of where the speech is occurring or who is speaking to whom. In the same breath, however, the Court has insisted that the major outlines of First Amendment law are defined entirely by tradition, cannot be changed, and leave no room to balance competing values. That line of cases adopts an all-or-nothing rule: speech is either fully protected by the First Amendment or entirely excluded. If speech does make the cut, values such as self-development, education, and public accountability are all swept under the rug. If speech doesn't make the cut, nearly anything goes. There is little room to be found in these majority opinions for alternative views of free speech rights.

That may soon change. Each in his own way and for his own reasons, Thomas, Breyer, and Alito have openly expressed deep unease with the Court's current approach to free speech issues. When Roberts joined Alito in *Brown*, and when Kagan joined Breyer in *Alvarez*, they hinted at reservations of their own about some of the Court's most pronounced trends.

Indeed, the key opinions in *Morse*, *Garcetti*, *Brown*, and *Alvarez* each prevailed by a single vote. Because the line of cases *rejecting* free speech claims has usually split the Court along left/right ideological markers, it is likely to remain stable unless the Court's composition changes decisively. But the line of cases *upholding* free speech claims has fractured the Court in unusual ways. In those rulings, only Kennedy, Ginsburg, and Sotomayor have consistently voted with the majority. As a result, there appears to be room for more substantial realignment—though it's impossible to predict what that would look like, since the justices who seem wary of this Court's overarching free speech dogma hardly present a unified front.

Meanwhile, the First Amendment beats on, a sometimes skipperless boat drifting deeper into uncertain waters, ruddered only imperfectly by selected values and stories drawn from our murky past.

5

GUN RIGHTS:

ARMED AND DANGEROUS

Death and mayhem in a pitch-black theater. Terrified cries, bodies life-less on the floor, the crush of humanity in a frantic escape.

Almost a century ago, Justice Oliver Wendell Holmes Jr. conjured this image to mark a line in the sand. The First Amendment, he explained, offers no shield to a man who falsely cries "Fire" in a crowded theater.[1] Such wanton creation of danger, devoid of redeeming social value, merits no constitutional protection.

On July 20, 2012, Justice Holmes's "'Fire' in a crowded theater" took on a grotesque modern meaning. Shortly after midnight, a twenty-four-year-old named James Holmes entered a packed screening of *The Dark Knight Rises* in Aurora, Colorado. Encased in armor, shielded by a mask, and sporting a shock of orange hair, he opened fire and killed twelve people.[2] Young Holmes gave new and tragic significance to an image that captures a sensible intuition: the Constitution is not a suicide pact. Tradition doesn't require us to read our founding document in a way that would condemn us to self-destruction. Thus "'Fire' in a crowded theater" now does double duty as the limiting metaphor for our First *and* Second Amendments, for freedom of speech and freedom of armed self-defense at the same time.

Of course, the two scenarios differ in important respects. We deal with the false inciter by stripping him of constitutional protection for just a fleeting moment. That single speech act is punishable, but his First Amendment rights remain otherwise undisturbed. We need not go back in time and figure out how much speech he should have been allowed in the first place. For the crazed gunman, however, the question is how to prevent such carnage, not whether to strip away his firearm at the cinema door. Answering that question requires a close examination of the system of laws that govern gun ownership, particularly limits on who can purchase guns and how much firepower they can obtain.

In 2008, the Court ruled for the first time that a federal firearms law violated the Second Amendment, which states, "A well regulated Militia, being necessary to the security of a free State, the right of the people to keep and bear Arms, shall not be infringed." From that moment on, gun policy had to reckon directly with the Constitution. Justice Scalia's opinion in *District of Columbia v. Heller* held that the Second Amendment protects an individual right to keep and bear arms against federal regulation—a conclusion that enjoyed little credibility until the late 1900s but had attracted robust support by 2008.[3] Two years later, in *McDonald v. Chicago*, the Court extended this newly recognized right to armed self-defense into a shield against state and local gun laws.[4] *Heller* and *McDonald* now anchor an evolving body of constitutional law that safeguards gun rights.

These rulings broke new ground and count among the Roberts Court's most important decisions. Yet for all the rhetorical pyrotechnics they displayed, *Heller* and *McDonald* are narrow and cautious opinions. Disowning any effort to "clarify the entire field" of Second Amendment law, the Court struck down two of the most restrictive gun laws in the country, the District of Columbia's handgun ban in *Heller* and Chicago's similar law in *McDonald*. At the same time, the Court emphasized that many of the most common gun laws are "presumptively" valid. Even more striking, the Court declined to offer guidance on how Second Amendment analysis works when a gun regulation is challenged in court. We know that a complete ban on the private possession of handguns by law-abiding adults in their homes for self-defense is unacceptable. But we can be absolutely certain of little more.

Judges are acutely aware of the possible consequences when they craft doctrine to govern firearms. Capturing a common sentiment, Judge J. Harvie Wilkinson III, appointed to the Fourth Circuit Court of Appeals by Ronald Reagan, has explained that "we do not wish to be even minutely responsible for some unspeakably tragic act of mayhem because in the peace of our judicial chambers we miscalculated as to Second Amendment rights."[5] So a measure of caution in creating this law is reasonable. Even more so than in the First Amendment context, the Court's decisions about gun rights will take shape in the shadow of terrible danger. All rights present a threat, but the price of too much (or too little) Second Amendment liberty can be counted in bullet-ridden corpses.

Yet hard choices can be deferred for only so long. The American public enjoys a newly acknowledged right but can only guess at the full scope of this protection; politicians, meanwhile, have struggled to negotiate policy in the uncertain shadow of new constitutional limits. Even as the nation engaged in fierce debate over gun regulation in 2013, *Heller* and *McDonald* hovered like the Sword of Damocles over innovative policy solutions. The Court must at some point offer greater clarity.

When that day comes, if the justices stick to the path marked in *Heller* and *McDonald*, the Roberts Court will leave the democratic process broad latitude to address gun-related danger effectively and creatively. This would anger some on the right, who view in the Second Amendment a promise from the framers that we can strap on AK-47s and carry them wherever we wish. It would anger some on the left, who view our Second Amendment as the unfortunate and vestigial remnant of a lost world. But it would suit most Americans just fine. The political constraints imposed by democracy, rather than constitutional rights of gun ownership, would remain the primary source of limits on gun regulation—even as courts played a critical role by protecting the core of a fundamental right to armed self-defense.

Guns divide the American people; for decades, we have struggled to fashion laws that balance safety against a rich tradition of gun ownership.[6] To many, possession of firearms is indelibly linked to a long history of self-defense, hunting, and opposition to tyranny. Weapons are closely connected to American ideals of self-reliance and liberty, particularly in our shared mythology of militiamen and cowboys, and gun owners have long feared calls for disarmament. Yet to others, particularly city dwellers, gun culture can appear alien, antiquated, and barbaric in its seeming disregard for the value of human life. Some strive for a middle ground, though the political center is besieged on both sides.

The mere mention of guns often incites hot-tempered debate and more talking than listening among otherwise reasonable people.

Compared to the private citizens of other developed nations, Americans are heavily armed. Approximately a quarter of American adults own guns, and more than a third of American households contain a working firearm; there are an estimated 200 million to 300 million guns in private circulation.[7] These firearms are concentrated more heavily in certain demographics. As Harvard Professor Jill Lepore notes, "Gun ownership is higher among whites than among blacks, higher in the country than in the city, and higher among older people than among younger people."[8] (She also notes that men are more likely to own guns than women.) Although the figure is hotly disputed, Americans use guns for self-defense hundreds of thousands—perhaps even millions—of times every year.[9] But, of course, guns serve many lawful purposes other than self-defense, including hunting and target shooting.

Not coincidentally, our heavily armed nation also suffers from an epidemic of gun-related violence. The numbers are chilling. On an average day, 33 Americans are slain by assailants with guns, which translates into roughly 12,000 firearm homicides each year.[10] Guns are also used in nearly 19,000 suicides per year. As one scholar notes, "Americans under age 40 are more likely to die from gunfire than from any specific disease."[11] In 2010, America also endured nearly 338,000 nonfatal crimes committed with guns and over 73,000 emergency room visits for nonfatal gunshot wounds.[12]

In our darkest moments, we may be tempted to chalk these tragedies up to failings of human nature. Guns facilitate evil, but they are merely tools in human hands. To put that point in more familiar terms: Guns don't kill people, people kill people. As Bruce Wayne's butler, Alfred, warns in *The Dark Knight*: "Some men aren't looking for anything logical, like money. They can't be bought, bullied, reasoned, or negotiated with. Some men just want to watch the world burn." Indeed, James Holmes seemed like a Batman supervillain given awful life, an agent of terror, nihilism, and chaos seeking only destruction. His rampage in Aurora appeared to be entirely inexplicable; the mystery of his actions led Americans to fill that void with frightful imaginings. Nonetheless, law and policy can play a vital role in regulating which people have access to the firepower that can transform evil impulses into bouts of carnage. They can also affect whether we have the capacity to defend ourselves against such threats and modify the likelihood of tragic accidents.

Until late 2012, a combination of partisan politics and pro-gun public opinion thwarted many efforts to pass laws that sought to reduce violence by limiting access to guns.[13] Even after the massacre in Aurora, bold calls for action by political leaders turned to ashes the moment they were uttered. As the film critic Roger Ebert wrote despairingly in July 2012, "The endless gun control debate will begin again, and the lobbyists of the National Rifle Association will go to work, and the op-ed thinkers will have their usual thoughts, and the right wing will issue alarms, and nothing will change. And there will be another mass murder."[14]

Ebert's morbid prophesy was fulfilled on December 14, 2012, when Adam Lanza entered Sandy Hook Elementary School in Newtown, Connecticut, and gunned down twenty-six people, including twenty first-grade children. Visibly moved by this unspeakable act, Barack Obama launched a massive effort to curb gun-related violence. "No single law, no set of laws can eliminate evil from the world or prevent every senseless act of violence in our society, but that can't be an excuse for inaction," he declared.[15] "Surely we can do better than this." Public opinion, largely unmoved by earlier tragedies, appeared for a brief time to be galvanized by an almost primal recoil against the mass slaughter of young children. The nation spent months engaged in intense political debate over the future of efforts to curb gun-related violence.

As soon became painfully clear to politicians and the public, however, the causes of gun violence are many and complex—and so are our policy options in responding to it. Obama, among others, has called for improvements in the diagnosis and treatment of mental illness.[16] Some have urged transformation of cultural norms, gesturing to the violent video games granted First Amendment protection by the Court in 2011.[17] Offering a different perspective, Yale Law Professor Dan Kahan has argued that legalizing marijuana and cocaine would substantially diminish drug-related cycles of urban gang violence.[18]

Many reform proposals, however, focus squarely on guns.[19] The most prominent options include: (1) universal, loophole-free background checks for all gun transfers, coupled with waiting periods that would limit who can buy guns; (2) firearm labeling and registration rules that would make it easier to catch shooters; (3) limits on the manufacture and

sale of assault weapons, armor-piercing rounds, high-capacity magazines, and other forms of heavy firepower; (4) prohibitions on or permit
requirements for concealed or public carrying of guns; (5) bans on guns
in bars, churches, schools, and other sensitive places; (6) requirements of
safe storage in the home; (7) closing loopholes that allow the unregulated
sale of firearms at gun shows or over the Internet; and (8) creating and
enforcing new criminal laws to punish illegal gun trafficking and straw
purchasing. Experts have also explored new ideas, such as personalized
firearms with thumbprint technology to help ensure that the lawful
owner is the user and insurance requirements to encourage lawful owners to secure and safely store their weapons.[20] Like everything else relating to gun regulation, however, the efficacy of these proposals is bitterly
disputed. Advocates of gun control argue among themselves over which
of these proposals is most likely to reduce violence. Gun rights supporters counter that safety is best enhanced through *wider* availability of
firearms, warning that these "reforms" would infringe on liberty and
offer only illusory benefits.[21]

How are we to adjudicate these competing claims? To Americans on
all sides of this debate, it seems obvious that the data support their position. That sentiment leads to charges that the other side is acting irratio-
nally. And perhaps it is. After all, it is easy to cherry-pick data, especially
when each side reads its own blogs and is inclined to trust "facts" that
confirm deeply held views. Hard evidence still has a role to play, and
certain arguments are clearly specious (e.g., the claim that background
checks substantially undermine gun rights). But in gun politics we cannot easily escape the clash of competing cultures.[22]

These disagreements are reflected in the variety of gun laws that dot
the American landscape. Some states heavily regulate guns. Others favor
the equivalent of an open-air market in heavy weaponry. These regional
variations generate intense conflict, particularly when the federal government tries to craft national gun control laws. A flood of gun-related
campaign cash, brutal lobbying tactics, and shameless efforts on both
sides to demonize the enemy have further embittered and fractured
national gun politics.

Before 2012, the national trend bent toward deregulation. In 2004, for
example, the federal government declined to renew a decade-old ban on
the possession of semiautomatic assault weapons. After Sandy Hook,

however, public opinion shifted at least temporarily toward greater support for modest, safety-oriented limits on gun possession, even as burdensome laws aimed at handguns and hunting rifles remained deeply
unpopular.[23] The moment of heightened political awareness and democratic deliberation that followed Sandy Hook thus raised hard questions
about the efficacy and political feasibility of leading gun reform proposals.[24] It also posed in stark relief a simple question: what limits, if any, does
the Second Amendment impose?

Until 2008 and *Heller*, the correct answer to this question as a matter of
judicial precedent was "none." No federal court had ever struck down a
statute under the Second Amendment. To the contrary, back in 1939 the
Supreme Court had supported America's first major experiment in gun
control. In that case, *United States v. Miller*, a unanimous Court upheld
what was in effect a federal ban on sawed-off shotguns, explaining that
the "obvious purpose" of the Second Amendment was to "assure the
continuation and render possible the effectiveness of [state militias]."[25]
Miller was widely understood to endorse a "collective rights" interpretation, which holds that the Amendment is concerned only with collective
defense and security from federal tyranny, not with individual self-
protection or hunting. In that view, states and the federal government do
not violate the Second Amendment by limiting private gun possession
unrelated to state militias. The collective rights model dominated legal
thought for most of the twentieth century.

In the 1960s, America lost John F. Kennedy, Robert F. Kennedy, and
Martin Luther King Jr. to assassins' bullets.[26] Tragedies like these sparked
decades of aggressive gun control efforts—but also generated a law-and-
order backlash to the growing menace of crime. Around the same time,
a nation weary of grand-style liberalism turned toward Richard Nixon's
brand of conservatism, which looked coldly on urban unrest and street
violence. As conservative social movements swept the country and
Americans grew more skeptical of government, support for a handgun
ban dropped from 60 percent in 1959 to 41 percent in 1975. Self-defense
emerged as a priority in those unsettled times. By the late 1970s, a cadre
of hard-line conservatives had seized control of the NRA and adopted
a firm anti-regulation position. Their push toward a new vision of the

Second Amendment also drew strength from an increasing focus on personal freedom.

The 1980s proved to be golden years for the gun rights movement. Utah's conservative Senator Orrin Hatch took charge of the Senate Subcommittee on the Constitution and oversaw production of an influential report entitled *The Right to Keep and Bear Arms*. Published in 1982, this report argued that "the second amendment to our Constitution was intended as an individual right of the American citizen to keep and carry arms in a peaceful manner, for protection of himself, his family, and his freedoms." In 1986, Congress passed the Firearms Owners Protection Act, citing a right to bear arms. Ronald Reagan insisted that "law-abiding people who want to protect their home and family" enjoy a "right to own guns," and his Department of Justice's *Guidelines on Constitutional Litigation* included a "right to keep and bear arms."

This individualist turn in Second Amendment views coincided with the rise of originalism as conservatives' preferred method of constitutional interpretation, lending a distinctly historical cast to calls for an individual right to bear arms. At the same time, a drop in public support for gun control and the growth of the NRA forged a mutually beneficial link between new constitutional theory and transformed political reality.[27]

Along the way, however, several distinct versions of the individual rights view came into focus. Harvard Law Professor Mark Tushnet has described three variants.[28] One model holds that we each enjoy a personal right to keep and bear arms that we can exercise for any reason, subject only to regulation tailored to pressing social need. A second model links gun rights to an armed citizenry resisting oppressive government. And a third model focuses on individual self-defense against crime. Each of these models draws upon different traditions and suggests different permissible limits on gun control. Nonetheless, in the 1980s and '90s, advocates declined to prioritize any single vision of the Second Amendment. Self-defense and opposition to tyranny, with hunting and recreation cast in supporting roles, merged into a single, broadly defined gun right.

It may seem odd that a single, relatively specific Amendment could support so many positions, but the grammatically adventurous Second Amendment is not a model of clarity. To quote it again: "A well regulated Militia, being necessary to the security of a free State, the right of the people to keep and bear Arms, shall not be infringed." Lawyers on all sides, employing grammatical and interpretive jujitsu, struggled in the 1990s and early 2000s to land a knockout blow in support of their favored interpretation.

These rapid and radical transformations in beliefs about the Second Amendment attracted fierce criticism, including attacks by leading conservatives. In 1989, former Solicitor General Robert Bork argued that the Second Amendment protects only "the right of states to form militia."[29] Two years later, former Chief Justice Warren Burger publicly denounced the emerging individual rights view as "one of the greatest pieces of fraud, I repeat the word 'fraud,' on the American public by special interest groups that I have ever seen in my lifetime."[30] These dismissive remarks were not well received. The struggle within conservative circles to articulate an originalism-based, individual gun right had been swift and brutal. Whereas Burger and Bork spoke the common sense of a prior decade, by the early 1990s many conservatives considered their remarks akin to blasphemy.

Around the same time, the individual rights view spread from gun enthusiasts and Republican lawyers to the academy. In 1989, University of Texas Law Professor Sanford V. Levinson published a famous article, "The Embarrassing Second Amendment," that chastised his colleagues for dodging the Amendment; in Levinson's view, they were motivated by a mixture of opposition to private gun ownership and fear that the best arguments might actually favor robust Second Amendment rights.[31] Over the next two decades, lawyers and historians produced a flood of scholarship in which the collective and individual rights views grappled for supremacy.[32] By 2000, one of this book's authors (Larry Tribe) could be counted cautiously among the "individual rights" supporters.[33]

In a political debate marked by extremes, moderate constitutional views are often misunderstood. Charlton Heston, the late Hollywood actor and NRA spokesman, phoned Tribe in 2000 to express delight at discovering a new "ally" and proposed a meeting on Heston's private plane to "put our heads together on strategy." Flustered, Tribe confessed to being a fan of Heston's movies (especially *Planet of the Apes*) but clarified his continued support for reasonable gun control. Needless to say, the conversation ended awkwardly. Heston never called again.

Before long, these developments in the political arena and the legal academy attracted judicial notice. In 1997, a sharply divided Court struck down a key provision of the Brady Handgun Violence Prevention Act, a federal statute that required state officials to conduct background checks on prospective handgun purchasers.[34] Writing for the Court, Scalia reasoned that this law, by forcing state officials to act as agents of a federal scheme, violated states' rights. The majority opinion made no mention of the Second Amendment, but Thomas, who often plays a key role in pushing the Court toward innovative conservative doctrine, added a prescient observation. "If . . . the Second Amendment," he wrote, "is read to confer a *personal* right to 'keep and bear arms,' a colorable argument exists that the Federal Government's regulatory scheme . . . runs afoul of that Amendment's protections." Thomas bolstered his point in a footnote laced with citations to law review articles, pointing out that "a growing body of scholarly commentary indicates that the 'right to keep and bear arms' is, as the Amendment's text suggests, a personal right."

Three years later, Justice David Souter gently pushed back with a clear suggestion that the Second Amendment is about collective rights, not individual liberty.[35] In a dissent from a ruling that invalidated part of the Violence Against Women Act, Souter added a lengthy footnote, at the end of which he declared that the Constitution "protected a range of specific individual rights against federal infringement, [but] did not, *with the possible exception of the Second Amendment*, offer any similarly specific protections to areas of state sovereignty" (italics added).

This battle of the footnotes presaged a far grander struggle to win Supreme Court sanction for the gradually ascendant individual rights view. In 2008, borne to our highest court by culture war, partisan struggle, and trends in legal thought, the Second Amendment was given new life.

Scalia takes no prisoners in legal argument. More than any of his colleagues, Scalia infuses his eloquent opinions with an unmistakable air of certainty and objectivity. He is right and lawful, and his opponents are wrong and occasionally dishonest—a view advanced with particular force in his scorching dissents. When the Court held that the Eighth Amendment ban on cruel and unusual punishment prevents execution of the intellectually disabled, Scalia charged that the opinion rested "upon nothing but the personal views" of the majority.[36] When the Court reaffirmed the pro-choice abortion holding of *Roe v. Wade* in 1992, Scalia opened his assault on the majority by remarking that "I must . . . respond to a few of the more outrageous arguments in today's opinion, which it is beyond human nature to leave unanswered."[37]

Scalia writes with such confidence partly because his chosen theory of interpretation, originalism, posits that judges act legitimately only when they rule in accordance with the Constitution's original public meaning. He knows exactly how to approach a new case: spend time in the archives, discover and respect what the text of the Constitution meant to the public that ratified it, and find the strongest available analogies to link past and present. Originalism, Scalia says, "establishes a historical criterion that is conceptually quite separate from the preferences of the judge himself."[38] Anything else risks illegitimacy.[39]

Objections to this view are legion. Some argue that it is undemocratic to let the dead hand of the past rule the present. Others say that people in the 1790s could not have "meant" anything with regard to unimaginable modern circumstances. Still other critics point out that there is immense subjectivity built into the process of "discovering" the supposed "fact" of original meaning and translating it to the present world through analogies. And most scholars doubt that originalism, faithfully applied, can justify race and sex equality doctrines—including that of *Brown v. Board of Education*—that have become central to our national self-understanding.[40]

Scalia is unimpressed by these arguments. He wields well-rehearsed responses to each objection and, after delivering them with practiced grace, adds with a sly wink that his critics lack any approach better than his.

As a sought-after star of the speaking circuit and an outspoken jurist who enjoys going toe-to-toe with liberals, Scalia is a cult hero to many lawyers. For long decades, however, his influence on the Court paled in comparison to that of Justices Kennedy and O'Connor, one or the other of whom usually provided the crucial fifth vote in closely divided cases (and limited how far the majority could go). Kennedy pictured the Court as the bold protector of an evolving vision of liberty, while O'Connor favored moderate rulings that stuck closer to contemporary national sentiment than to any particular constitutional method.[41] In decisions involving abortion, race and sex equality, and LGBT rights, Scalia let loose on what he saw as their lawless reasoning. He often accused those two justices of "activism," though his real objection concerned their methods and results rather than their muscular use of judicial power.

After enduring many years in a secondary role, Scalia beamed with new energy when Roberts and Alito arrived at the Court in 2005 and 2006, creating a more solidly conservative majority (although Kennedy's libertarian leanings sometimes pushed him leftward). Scalia's early optimism, however, was soon overshadowed by his frustration with the Chief's preference for narrow rulings, many of which limited and undermined disfavored precedents but didn't expressly overrule them.[42] By 2007, notwithstanding a string of notable conservative victories, Scalia publicly accused Roberts of "faux judicial restraint."[43]

Then, in 2008, the Chief gave Scalia one of the best opportunities of his judicial career: the majority opinion assignment in *District of Columbia v. Heller*. This would be the first time since 1939—and arguably the first time ever—that the Court authoritatively interpreted the Second Amendment. It would also be a rare chance to demonstrate the full power of an originalist analysis, backed by formidable scholarly work and unencumbered by decades of unoriginalist judicial precedent.

Scalia—long an avid hunter and gun owner—did not disappoint. His opinion devoted dozens of pages to a dissection of the Second Amendment. It drew on history and linguistics to interpret "well regulated Militia," "right of the people," and "keep and bear Arms." In a stunningly erudite display, Scalia appeared to range over every relevant source from the 1600s through the 1900s.

In critical part, Scalia concluded that "right of the people" unambiguously refers to an *individual* right enjoyed by the whole political community. Then, relying in part on the First and Fourth Amendments, which also address matters affected by evolving technology, he interpreted "Arms" to refer to any "instruments that constitute bearable arms, even those that were not in existence at the time of the founding." Finally, he addressed the original purpose of the Second Amendment. Acknowledging that its main purpose when enacted was to protect state militias capable of resisting federal tyranny, Scalia argued that the uselessness of handguns against a national government armed with "bombers and tanks" does not matter: "It may well be true today that a militia, to be as effective as militias in the 18th century, would require sophisticated arms that are highly unusual in society at large . . . but the fact that modern developments have limited the degree of fit between [the reference to a 'well regulated Militia'] and the protected right cannot change our interpretation of the right."

Scalia's opinion was promptly hailed by many in the popular press as a landmark, a tour de force of originalism, and a decisive victory for gun rights.[44] Four justices—Breyer, Stevens, Ginsburg, and Souter—dissented and charged the majority with grave error.

On close inspection, though, *Heller* is a much more complex and less strictly originalist ruling than it first seemed. Scalia took great pains to emphasize his opinion's modesty, noting that the Second Amendment right "is not unlimited." The right covers only weapons "typically possessed by law-abiding citizens for lawful purposes." It is designed to secure "self-defense" and is "not a right to keep and carry any weapon whatsoever in any manner whatsoever and for whatever purpose." Thus, it does not cover "the carrying of dangerous and unusual weapons."

Further, Scalia emphasized that "nothing in our opinion should be taken to cast doubt on longstanding prohibitions on the possession of firearms by felons and the mentally ill, or laws forbidding the carrying of firearms in sensitive places such as schools and government buildings, or laws imposing conditions and qualifications on the commercial sale of arms." This list of presumptively valid laws, he noted, is not exhaustive. Scalia did not explain how he selected these illustrations; nor did he link them to the Amendment's original history. Scalia also acknowledged "the problem of handgun violence in this country" and emphasized that "the Constitution leaves the District of Columbia a variety of tools for combating that problem, including some measures regulating handguns." In sum, though the Court refused to "pronounce the Second Amendment extinct," it also declined to disable effective gun regulation.

Because the Bill of Rights, by its own terms, limits only the federal government, the most obvious question left open by *Heller* was whether this new right also limited state and local governments. For almost a century, the Court has relied on a doctrine it calls "incorporation" to hold that certain rights limit states by virtue of the Fourteenth Amendment's command that no state shall "deprive any person of life, liberty, or property, without due process of law." Invoking what it describes as the "substantive" character of due process, the Court has looked to the Bill of Rights for guidance in deciding which rights are so "implicit in the concept of ordered liberty" or "deeply rooted in this Nation's history and tradition" that they should be "incorporated." Almost all the provisions of the Bill of Rights have been found to be so deeply rooted or fundamental that they must be enforceable against the states. Nonetheless, if the Court concluded that the right announced in *Heller* did not make the cut, then states and cities would be free to pass laws that would plainly violate the Second Amendment if passed by the federal government.

To no one's surprise, the Court applied its new right to the states in *McDonald v. Chicago*, decided in 2010. Reading *Heller* as a case that protects "a personal right to keep and bear arms for lawful purposes, most notably for self-defense within the home," Alito noted that "self-defense is a basic right, recognized by many legal systems from ancient times to the present day." "In *Heller*," he added, "we held that individual self-defense is 'the central component' of the Second Amendment right."

Had *Heller* identified the right to keep and bear arms with the original purpose of ensuring protection from tyrannical national government, *McDonald* might have come out differently. But that bridge had been crossed when *Heller* instead characterized the Second Amendment right as one of armed self-defense. Tracing the history of this right, Alito emphasized that after the Civil War, around the time the Fourteenth Amendment was ratified, the right to bear arms held particular importance because it afforded newly freed blacks an essential means of protection from hostile Southern militias.[45] Fusing nineteenth-century historical lineage to eighteenth-century original meaning, Alito held that this self-defense right governs the states. He emphasized, however, that "despite ... doomsday proclamations, incorporation does not imperil every law regulating firearms."

Alito rejected a battery of counterarguments, many focused on the supposed danger of a new gun right. Declining to treat firearms differently, he cited cases that confer rights on criminal defendants to support his rejoinder that "all of the constitutional provisions that impose restrictions on law enforcement and on the prosecution of crimes fall into the same category." Gun rights are dangerous, but so are many other rights, he reasoned. Danger may be a reason to allow the states some latitude in regulating firearms, but it isn't a reason to deny that these rights exist in the first place. Alito added that gun rights can also *prevent* violence and thereby protect "the rights of minorities and other residents of high-crime areas whose needs are not being met by elected public officials."

McDonald generated a cacophony of opinions. Stevens and Scalia battled over incorporation doctrine. They also fought over what the history demonstrated about the Amendment's original meaning. Breyer, joined by Ginsburg and Sotomayor, dissented from Alito's reasoning and challenged the Court's decision to transfer "regulatory authority over the private uses of firearms from democratically elected legislatures to courts." Thomas, who was characteristically willing to go his own way in pursuit of original meaning, argued that the Court should abandon its entire approach to incorporation. In its place, he urged the Court to invoke the Fourteenth Amendment's protection of the "Privileges or Immunities" of U.S. citizenship—a dramatic step freighted with potentially significant implications for privacy, marriage, and abortion rights (all of which are grounded, in part, on "substantive" due process). Thomas's argument is powerful and in many respects convincing on originalist grounds, but Scalia refused to join him.[46] In fact, Scalia mocked a lawyer who presented that position at oral argument by asking if he was "bucking for a place on some law school faculty." He bitingly added, "what you argue is the darling of the professoriate, for sure, but it's also contrary to 140 years of our jurisprudence."

Heller and *McDonald* marked the culmination of a decades-long struggle over constitutional method and meaning.[47] For good reason, *Heller* was hailed by Harvard Law Professor Cass Sunstein as "the most explicitly and self-consciously originalist opinion in the history of the Supreme Court."[48] Thanks to *Heller*, the individual rights view, with a central focus on self-defense, is now the law of our land. And it is fortified by originalist arguments that deem 1791 the decisive moment in legal time.[49]

Yet landmark Supreme Court decisions that create new rights are best understood as pivotal developments in larger stories. The tale of our post-*Heller* Second Amendment and its effect on national gun policy is still being written. Many of the most important decisions loom on the horizon. As Judge Wilkinson tartly remarked in a wide-ranging critique of *Heller*, "The decision to create a new blockbuster constitutional right can be compared to the decision to launch an invasion. The landmark decision is the easy part; the difficulty comes in the aftermath."[50]

There is a special wonder to *Heller*. Like astronomers privileged to witness the birth of a galaxy, we have been afforded the rarest of opportunities: a firsthand glimpse of the Court weaving text, history, and popular meaning into an opinion that breathes new but uncertain life into one of our oldest amendments. This case reveals the Supreme Court at the peak of its powers, grappling with first principles and the raw elements of law to forge a new right.

Wisely, the Court stepped with caution into this new minefield. In 2008, it struck down one of the most restrictive gun laws in America, but it left fuller elaboration of Second Amendment rights to a later day. In the interim, however, lower court judges—who must do more than delight in the Court's prudent wisdom—have found themselves in a tough spot. So have legislators committed to upholding the Constitution while passing gun laws. How, exactly, do we determine what the Second Amendment prohibits? In 2010, one judge captured the prevailing temper when he charged, with palpable frustration, that "*Heller* has left in its wake a morass of conflicting lower court opinions regarding the proper analysis to apply to challenged firearms regulations."[51]

Since 2010, the Court has relegated the task of elaborating a new body of constitutional law to lower courts, legislators, and scholars. Reading *Heller*'s tea leaves, these actors have broadly split between two sets of views. One approach, grounded in *Heller*'s rhetoric and its supposed originalism, calls for the blanket invalidation of laws that depart from the understanding of gun rights as of 1791. This view, however, misses *Heller*'s true message. The second approach, by contrast, more faithfully follows *Heller* by recognizing the need to temper strict adherence to history with an ongoing legislative and judicial role in shaping gun rights.[52]

Six years on, this debate about *Heller* continues. It is by no means academic. The heart of the disagreement concerns our ability to account for the danger of unregulated guns and evolving societal conditions in crafting Second Amendment law. And the Court's ultimate resolution of this debate may decide the fate of hundreds of gun laws, ranging from bans on assault weapons to licensing and safe storage requirements, and from background checks to prohibiting gun sales to minors.

At oral argument in *Heller*, Roberts articulated the historical view in a pointed question to the Solicitor General. Why isn't it enough, the Chief asked, "to determine the scope of the existing right that the amendment refers to, look at the various regulations that were available at the time . . . [and] determine how this restriction and the scope of this right looks in relation to those?" In other words, wouldn't it make more sense simply to ask whether a law fits within the scope of the Second Amendment as generally understood by the public in 1791?

As developed by many of its champions, the historical view would limit modern gun law to statutes with founding-era credentials.[53] If a statute emerged unscathed from this first look because it enjoyed clear historical support, it would fall beyond the scope of the Second Amendment and be rendered safe from further judicial review. If a law was a novelty, with no historical analogue, it could survive only if it did not infringe on gun rights as generally understood in the·1790s. If a law would have been understood as unconstitutional in the 1790s—or to lack support in text, history, and tradition, more broadly construed—it almost certainly fails again today.

This vision of gun rights proceeds from a full-bodied embrace of *Heller*'s originalist rhetoric. The logic is straightforward: in the 1790s, the framers struck a grand balance and made all the key decisions about which types of arms, people, and places get constitutional protection. It simply isn't our role to disturb their act of lawmaking. As *Heller* explains, "Constitutional rights are enshrined with the scope that they were understood to have when the people adopted them, whether or not future legislatures or (yes) even future judges think that scope too broad."

A purely historical approach may seem like a strange way to consider a question fraught with social peril and involving distinctly modern technology, but nobody ever accused lawyers of overreliance on practical sense. And, in all fairness, tradition-based analysis is a familiar legal tool. It plays a particularly important role in defining the First Amendment's protections for speech and religion, the Sixth Amendment right to confront one's accuser, and the Seventh Amendment right to jury trial in civil cases. In this vein, advocates of the historical view propose that judges faced with a ban on semiautomatic rifles head into the archives, look for similar laws or general statements about gun rights in the 1790s, and decide on the basis of their research whether to uphold the law. The scope of the Second Amendment right would be defined largely by history, and laws infringing rights within its scope would fall regardless of their social value.

That may all sound marvelously simple to figure out. It isn't. The practical problem is that "doing originalism" is always hard and sometimes impossible.[54] As Justice Robert Jackson confided in 1945, judges are not trained in history and are rarely "thorough or objective historians."[55] Figuring out what people who lived in the 1790s thought about specific kinds of gun regulations—let alone identifying a general "meaning" that we can apply to modern laws—is a daunting task, especially since Americans have always been divided over gun rights. As a federal court explained with obvious dissatisfaction in 2012, "What history demonstrates is that states often disagreed as to the scope of the right to bear arms ... Analogizing New York's licensing scheme (or any other gun regulation for that matter) to the array of statutes enacted or construed over one hundred years ago has its limits."[56]

Presented with the need to make complex judgments about history, judges risk crashing into what Breyer described in *McDonald* as the "reefs and shoals that lie in wait for those nonexpert judges who place virtually determinative weight upon historical considerations." The danger is that judges will gravitate toward versions of history that suit their personal beliefs about good versus bad policy, adopting a picture of the past that ultimately rests more on those beliefs than on a serious effort to reimagine the 1790s. Instead of engaging in a candid and well-informed debate about the benefits and dangers of gun rights, jurists may find themselves shadowboxing in archives and turning long-dead Americans into ventriloquist dummies.[57]

Scalia responds to these hazards by acknowledging that "historical analysis can be difficult," but he insists that originalism "is the *best means available* in an imperfect world." And in rare circumstances, he may be right. Yet *Heller* itself undermines Scalia's point. Stevens wrote a dissent that, like Scalia's opinion, is a marvel of historical craft, yet it reached precisely the opposite result. Their exchange, in which the left-leaning and right-leaning justices divided over meticulous historical accounts that just happened to match their predictable policy preferences, suggests the profound limits of supposedly originalist methods.[58]

More important, if we look past *Heller*'s insistence on its own use of originalism, we discover that it rests on more complex and intriguing foundations. Focusing instead on how *Heller* works—the sources it cites, its logic, the scope of the right it creates—we discover a ruling exquisitely attuned to the living constitutionalism that Scalia so vehemently disdains. Ironically, this feature is both the opinion's saving grace and its central lesson.

For starters, on careful examination, the sources cited in *Heller* betray its originalist rhetoric. As Yale Law Professor Reva Siegel has observed, the opinion is rife with "temporal oddities."[59] It purports to define gun rights through reference to the "epochal" moment of ratification in 1791, but it relies at key junctures on sources from the 1600s, the 1800s, and even the 1900s. Scalia firmly insists that these texts merely clarify public understanding as of 1791, but this claim has not persuaded many scholars. Indeed, an emerging academic consensus holds that *Heller* actually protects a gun right grounded in traditions stretching from the founding to the present, not just a single lawmaking moment in 1791.[60] If that is true, then the question of how we define relevant traditions—and the related question of why modern Americans are apparently denied the opportunity to start new traditions of our own—comes sharply into focus.

Heller's definition of "Arms" further disrupts an interpretation focused on the framers' original expectations of what laws the Second Amendment would allow. "Arms," the opinion states, are weapons "typically possessed by law-abiding citizens for lawful purposes," even if those weapons were unimaginable in 1791. This definition may be rooted in history, but its content could theoretically evolve to cover freeze rays, lightsabers, and laser blasters, assuming such weapons someday become popular tools for self-defense. If this seems far-fetched, consider a decision issued in 2012 in which a Michigan court relied on *Heller* to strike down a ban on stun guns.[61]

Given that Americans' understandings of "Arms" in 1791 were keyed to the relatively modest destructive capacity of handguns and muskets, should we unthinkingly transplant those beliefs to AK-47s and Tasers? Should we account for the greater lifesaving capacity of modern medicine in such analysis? It would be odd to keep all of Second Amendment doctrine anchored in 1791, even as the objects at the center of all those rules—"Arms"—now function in society in a way that is very different from the way they did back then. Evolving technology thus makes the Second Amendment a particularly strong candidate for evolving constitutional rules precisely because the Amendment's text refers directly to a concrete set of engineered objects. At the very least, we must recognize that abstract Second Amendment principles, even if held constant across time, will likely yield markedly different legal rules in different technological contexts.

Of course, lightsabers could become popular only if they weren't banned in the first place. This reveals another oddity in *Heller*'s reasoning. As Breyer observed in his dissent: "If tomorrow someone invents a particularly useful, highly dangerous self-defense weapon, Congress and the States had better ban it immediately, for once it becomes popular Congress will no longer possess the constitutional authority to do so." This sets in motion a bizarre arms race between innovators and regulators: the winner gets to define the level of constitutional protection afforded to each new technology of death. Once a weapon becomes popular enough to be deemed an "Arm," it is shielded by the Second Amendment forever. That one-way ratchet might secure an ever-growing list of protected firearms, unless regulators act quickly in response to new weaponry (or unless something can cease being an "Arm"). All this takes us far afield from originalism's domain.

To be sure, *Heller* does suggest an important exception to this rule: we are always free to ban weapons that are deemed "dangerous or unusual." Such determinations, though, are made in the present, not in 1791. They will undoubtedly reflect modern beliefs about the capacity and design features that set certain weapons apart. Once again, this is hardly the stuff of traditional originalism.

Perhaps the most striking evidence of the real methodology in *Heller* is the Court's list of "presumptively" valid regulations, which includes limits on possession by felons and the mentally ill. The first federal law to disqualify felons was passed in 1938, though it covered only a short list of felonies. The first federal law precluding the mentally ill from gun ownership dates to 1968. It is unclear how an exception for laws born in the twentieth century could possibly accord with *Heller*'s claim that Second Amendment rights were forever defined in 1791.[62] And if a "tradition" can date to the late 1930s or 1960s, the notion that modern legislatures are powerless to affect Second Amendment rights verges on the absurd. Relying on the logic of presumptively valid regulations, many courts have upheld laws that deny guns to perpetrators of domestic violence, a

misdemeanor of modern vintage. These courts speak of an "ongoing legislative role" in defining Second Amendment rights—and they all cite
Heller.[63]

Heller's exceptions pull it into the twenty-first century for another
reason: governments must be empowered to pass laws to enforce legitimate limits on gun ownership. Computerized background checks, for
instance, obviously lack direct historical analogues, but laws that permit
them may be the only practical way to keep guns away from felons and
the mentally ill. Under *Heller*, then, they should unquestionably be
deemed constitutional. This logic suggests that even a purely historical
definition of Second Amendment rights must allow considerable latitude in the design and implementation of permissible limitations on
gun rights. A useful analogy here is the right to vote: the Court has
repeatedly upheld voter identification schemes that burden voters,
explaining that they serve the vital end of protecting the integrity of our
electoral system.[64] This is yet another way in which *Heller* allows substantial room for modern ingenuity—and must do so, even when courts
insist on a purely historical approach.

Ultimately, a close look at *Heller* reveals an opinion that mixes
original meaning with broad national traditions and distinctly modern
understandings. As Yale Law Professor Jack Balkin noted just one day
after *Heller* was announced, "The Court changed existing law dramatically to adopt a new interpretation of the Second Amendment that is
actually fairly close to the center of public opinion."[65] We see this in *Heller*'s narrow compass, its unexplained list of presumptively valid regulations, and its embrace of rules that will change along with technology.
We also see it in *Heller*'s acknowledged protection of an individual right
that could never really serve the original purpose of thwarting a tyrannical government armed with tanks and drones.

This speaks to an important point. As Siegel explains, Scalia was not
standing "above the fray, disinterested, merely executing the commands
of Americans long deceased."[66] Rather, the *Heller* Court "itself [decided]
whether handgun bans are consistent with the best understanding of our
constitutional tradition." It made that decision "in the present" and in
response "to the beliefs and values of living Americans who identify with
the commitments and traditions of their forbears."

Held out as Scalia's originalist triumph and proof of originalism's "gravitational force,"[67] *Heller* was actually something far greater. Even as it demonstrated the stark limits of originalism, it showed the value of interpretation that fuses text, history, tradition, and evolving popular beliefs into a vision of the Constitution that can speak across generations.

Recognizing the deficiencies of a purely historical approach to gun rights after *Heller*, federal courts have uniformly adopted a more nuanced and defensible method of evaluating challenged gun regulations. It is therefore appropriate to call this the "consensus view."[68]

Following this approach, courts begin by asking whether a law burdens conduct within the scope of the Second Amendment, looking to both the 1790s and more recent traditions. After all, most laws—and even some gun regulations—don't implicate the Second Amendment. Gun laws that fit this description include some limits on concealed carrying of firearms in public and bans on the sale of guns to minors.[69] These laws fall wholly beyond the Amendment's reach, as the Constitution has *never* been understood to confer protection on such conduct.

If a law does fall within the Second Amendment's scope, courts demand that the government justify the burden its law imposes. The more serious the burden, and the closer it falls to the core of the Second Amendment right, the more convincingly the government must support its law. These justifications, based in social science, history, and common sense, look to a law's purpose and how well it actually achieves that purpose without gratuitously burdening gun rights. In other words, at this second step, courts balance a law's infringement on individual gun rights against its societal benefits.

These methods are familiar to most lawyers. In many other contexts, courts ratchet up their skepticism of a law to match its burden on a constitutional right. For example, states can regulate marriage and voting, but they trigger stricter review with laws that significantly burden these rights or pointlessly single them out for adverse treatment.[70] Abortions involving not-yet-viable fetuses can be regulated, but not at the expense of an "undue burden" on a woman's right to decide whether to continue her pregnancy.[71] And government can regulate private property without being forced to provide "just compensation" to the owner, but not if the regulation goes so far as to constitute a "taking" of that property by the government.[72]

In fact, a federal court in New York cited all of these examples while upholding a federal law that prohibits most people from obtaining a gun out of state and transporting it into their home state (with exceptions for licensed importers, manufacturers, dealers, and collectors).[73] In its opinion, the court noted that the federal law only trivially burdens gun rights but plays a big role in preventing circumvention of state laws that regulate local gun possession. That sort of balancing act is now par for the course in judicial opinions assessing gun laws.

One of the main flash points among federal courts is how to define the heavily protected core of the Second Amendment right—the zone in which judicial skepticism of regulation is highest. *Heller* makes clear that this core encompasses the possession of handguns by law-abiding adults in the home for self-defense. But it says little about what other kinds of regulations should be looked upon with particular distrust. Hard questions therefore arise when laws burden the right to armed self-defense in ways that fall between banning private handguns and banning military-grade rocket launchers.

In 2011, for example, a federal court reviewed a Chicago law that required one hour of firing-range training as a prerequisite to lawful gun ownership but also banned all firing ranges within the city.[74] Striking it down, the court explained that this law encroached "on the right to maintain proficiency in firearm use," which is critical to "meaningful exercise of the core right to possess firearms for self-defense." A few months later, a different federal court upheld the District of Columbia's ban on semi-automatic rifles and magazines with a capacity of more than ten rounds. It reasoned that these sorts of weapons—unlike handguns—are not "well-suited to or preferred for the purpose of self-defense or sport."[75] In both cases, courts determined how much the law before them burdened a core right to armed self-defense and then subjected it to a suitable level of scrutiny. This is the consensus view in action.

Courts are fiercely divided, however, on whether the "core" Second Amendment right extends to guns openly carried in public.[76] A federal court in New York has adopted a narrow view of gun rights outside the home, cautioning that "the state's ability to regulate firearms" is "qualitatively different in public than in the home."[77] A court in Denver took a similar view in a case holding that the Second Amendment is not implicated at all by laws banning concealed carrying of guns in public.[78]

Whereas the home has long enjoyed special constitutional protection from state surveillance and regulation, the public sphere lacks similar credentials. The traditions of regulating guns at home and out in public are also quite different. Judge Wilkinson has pointedly expressed this important post-*Heller* uncertainty: "There may or may not be a Second Amendment right in some places beyond the home, but we have no idea what those places are, what the criteria for selecting them should be, what sliding scales of scrutiny might apply to them, or any one of a number of other questions. . . . The whole matter strikes us as a vast *terra incognita* that courts should enter only upon necessity and only then by small degree."[79]

Disagreeing vehemently, Richard Posner, a federal judge in Chicago and a leading public intellectual, has assailed judicial skittishness about protecting Americans' rights to carry guns in public.[80] He observes that what Wilkinson described as a " 'vast *terra incognita*' has been opened to judicial exploration by *Heller* and *McDonald*." Posner adds that "a Chicagoan is a good deal more likely to be attacked on a sidewalk in a rough neighborhood than in his apartment on the 35th floor of the Park Tower" and that "a woman who is being stalked or has obtained a protective order against a violent ex-husband is more vulnerable to being attacked while walking to or from her home than when inside." As a result, he insists, it is "arbitrary" to leave gun owners unshielded out in public: "To confine the right to be armed to the home is to divorce the Second Amendment from the right of self-defense described in *Heller* and *McDonald*." After all, he writes in his inimitable style, these cases protect more than the "right to kill a houseguest who in a fit of aesthetic fury tries to slash your copy of Norman Rockwell's painting *Santa with Elves*."

These are more than abstract musings. Posner penned his arguments in an opinion invalidating an Illinois law that banned most people from carrying loaded guns in public (with exceptions for police officers, security personnel, hunters, and members of target shooting clubs). That decision forced Illinois to consider a legislative response and prompted controversy over the future of its gun regulations. Until the Court intervenes, this debate over the scope of Second Amendment rights in public is likely to remain among the most disputed open questions in constitutional law, one that is rife with implications for efforts to curb gun violence and judicial understandings of *Heller*.

In a wide range of cases since *Heller*, courts have worked hard to fashion law that is sensitive to history but also keyed to a rational balancing of society's strong interests in avoiding death and mayhem. By and large, they have succeeded. Within this calculus, the danger that a law seeks to eradicate is given central weight—along with a commonsense analysis, bolstered by empirical data, of whether the law actually achieves that goal without trampling too heavily on gun rights. While courts may not be experts on the policies implicated by gun violence, at least this form of analysis allows a forthright, rigorous, and (hopefully) rational dialogue about the role of constitutional limits.

Ultimately, the Court will likely be forced to choose between the historical view and the consensus view. As between these options, the consensus view is truer to *Heller*'s word and deed, and allows courts to respect our history and traditions without pretending that all the hard issues in gun rights were decided centuries ago. It embraces a delicate play of past and present, just as *Heller* did, and thus represents the kind of constitutional law that our society requires as it combats an epidemic of gun violence.

Recruiters from elite law firms enjoy posing the following question to aspiring attorneys: if you had to eliminate half of the amendments in the Constitution, would you eliminate the odd- or even-numbered rights? On impulse, many students immediately save the "odd" rights in order to preserve free speech, which virtually all Americans consider the backbone of our democracy. As the saying goes, there's a reason it's listed first! (For the record, it was actually listed *third* in the original set of twelve amendments proposed to the states, only ten of which were accepted and came to be known as the Bill of Rights.) The catch, so often overlooked, is that the First Amendment does not apply to the states on its own. Rather, it applies only by virtue of the Fourteenth Amendment, through the doctrine of incorporation, which was relied upon in *McDonald*. Sacrificing the even amendments, of course, nullifies that important detail. More than a few students have undoubtedly lost job offers after stumbling into such legal quicksand.

As this story suggests, the meaning and importance of a constitutional right can sometimes affect, and be dramatically affected by, other constitutional amendments. Which leads to a perhaps surprising question: does *Heller* matter?

More than once in the past decade, the Court has launched fireworks that seemed to fizzle on first impact. In 2005, for example, it dramatically concluded that the sentencing guidelines for federal judges must be advisory, not mandatory—but then, to drive home its point, the Court had to spend several years reversing a barrage of lower court opinions that came close to making the guidelines mandatory again.[81] In 2007, the Court upheld the Partial-Birth Abortion Act of 2003 and caused a panic in the pro-choice community; that sky has not yet fallen, although what the future will hold in this area is fraught with uncertainty.[82]

In a similar vein, for all the controversy over Second Amendment rights, state and federal courts have upheld almost every gun regulation challenged since *Heller* and *McDonald*. Unable to resist the pun, Adam Liptak of the *New York Times* suggested in 2009 that "*Heller* is firing blanks."[83] His article quoted a leading scholar who bitingly remarked that "the only real change from *Heller* is that gun owners have to pay higher legal fees to find out that they lose."[84] Are pundits of this persuasion right? Will *Heller* and *McDonald* fizzle?

No, they will not; tales of *Heller*'s early demise are greatly exaggerated. As we trace the decision's ripple effects, paying close attention to opportunities for Second Amendment lawmaking and the potential for interactions with other amendments, *Heller*'s implications for gun regulation loom large.

It's important to keep in mind that the gun cases are still freshly planted seeds. A measure of reluctance and modesty is to be expected from lower courts as they get a feel for this weighty new obligation and grow accustomed to Second Amendment analysis. It remains to be seen whether the Judiciary will ultimately become more assertive, especially if the Roberts Court revisits the field, emphatically strikes down another law or two, and urges a more protective approach to gun rights. Gun rights may also come to figure more prominently in future state and federal judicial selection, particularly under Republican administrations. If that happens, courts may shoot down a wider set of gun laws and impose tighter limits on legislatures.

Second Amendment doctrine, moreover, is likely to evolve as America grapples with new technologies—most notably, 3-D printers that allow owners to "print" functional firearms.[85] By mid-2013, these machines could already produce almost all the key components for an all-plastic assault rifle and appropriate ammunition. The federal government has sought to limit the spread of gun-printing software, but such efforts raise serious First Amendment concerns and may prove ineffective.[86] The government might try to monitor the use of such technology, but doing that in an effective manner could violate the First and Fourth Amendments. This leaves the question of what, if anything, the Second Amendment itself has to say about laws that prevent us from buying a printer, downloading software, and thereby manufacturing a handgun or assault rifle. Soon enough, this question may be more than an academic curiosity.

Innovation in gun laws may also push courts to forge new constitutional doctrine. One of the more intriguing examples of this point involves local mandates to purchase guns. Since 2000, communities in Colorado, Idaho, Georgia, Kansas, Utah, and Pennsylvania have passed laws encouraging or requiring all citizens to keep a firearm and ammunition in their homes.[87] Defenders of these laws have invoked as precedent laws from the late 1700s that compelled every able-bodied citizen to possess a usable firearm. As Duke Law Professor Joseph Blocher observes, however, *Heller*'s focus on individual self-defense may cut against these new laws: "A person who believes her home to be safer without a gun is attempting to protect herself from a risk of future violence, just like a person who chooses to keep a handgun on her bedside table. If self-defense is the 'core' of the Second Amendment, why should only one of these decisions be constitutionally protected? Shouldn't the interests giving rise to the affirmative right also protect a person's freedom not to exercise it?" Not every constitutional right protects its inverse, but some do: the right to freedom of speech, for example, protects a right *not* to say what one doesn't believe.[88] If these laws come under constitutional attack, courts may have to decide whether the right of individual self-protection recognized by *Heller* and *McDonald* safeguards decisions to keep potentially lethal firearms out of one's home and away from one's children.[89]

In the meantime, courts have reckoned with *Heller*'s ricochet into other areas of constitutional law. In 2008, for example, a New York federal judge concluded that a law requiring people released on bail to automatically surrender their firearms is invalid.[90] *Heller*, the judge ruled, requires an individualized determination "of the danger caused by the defendant and the efficacy of the proposed bail condition." In 2011, a federal court in Texas held that the right recognized in *Heller* does not extend to undocumented migrants.[91] This ruling touched on an oft-overlooked aspect of Scalia's opinion: its conclusion that when the Second Amendment refers to "the people," it means "members of the political community." The First and Fourth Amendments also refer to "the people," and the Court's leading prior opinion on the subject had defined "the people" as persons "who are part of a national community" or who have "substantial connections" to America.[92] By focusing on membership in the political community rather than on connections to the United States, *Heller* created tension in the law governing application of important constitutional rights to noncitizens.[93]

Several other examples of ricochet arise from the First Amendment field. Florida, for example, has invoked the Second Amendment to justify a law punishing doctors who ask their patients if they own guns and warn of hidden dangers. Doctors objected to this use of the Second Amendment to limit their First Amendment speech rights, and a trial judge agreed in 2012 that Florida had violated the First Amendment (a decision currently on appeal).[94] In a different context, while courts have denied challenges to "no guns in church" rules under the First and Second Amendments, several legislatures have invoked the Second Amendment to pass laws that protect a right to carry guns into places of worship. It remains unclear whether these laws might violate the rights of religious groups to congregate and pray without fear of guns; after all, rights of speech and prayer may be endangered by the chilling effect that some of us would experience in the presence of a semiautomatic.[95]

Another place to look for ricochet is adventurous claims that have failed but that mark paths for future gun-related litigation.[96] For example, a number of gun owners have argued that possession of a firearm, because it is now shielded by the Constitution, cannot constitute a valid basis for search and seizure under the Fourth Amendment.[97] Thus far, these claims have not succeeded, often because they have arisen from the carrying of guns in "sensitive" places, such as courts and parks. In one such case from Tennessee, a man walked through a state park in camouflage wielding an AK-47, prompting a passerby to spontaneously hold up his hands.[98] A park ranger disarmed and detained the man with the weapon to verify that the gun was allowed under state law. It was. When the gun owner sued, arguing that the ranger had no valid basis for this search and seizure, a federal court found no constitutional violation, partly because the law had been so unsettled after *Heller* that a reasonable officer would not have known whether the search was illegal. It is possible, perhaps even likely, that when Second Amendment rights stand on surer footing, some cases like this one may raise more substantial questions about grounds for searches and seizures.

Of course, constitutional law often matters as much in the realm of politics and the sphere of public debate as it does in courts of law. As Americans consider gun regulations, *Heller* may exert a different kind of influence: debates over public policy might be pushed closer toward debates focused mostly on rights. While rights have always played a major role in American discussion of guns, *Heller* and *McDonald* lent unprecedented credibility and the force of judicial legitimacy to claims for constitutional protection. This matters because, in American discourse, rights claims tend to trump ordinary politics. That is often desirable: by invoking rights, even unpopular minorities can lay claim to the shared foundations of our political order. On occasion, though, the results can be pernicious. As Harvard Law Professor Mary Ann Glendon writes, "A tendency to frame nearly every social controversy in terms of a clash of rights . . . impedes compromise, mutual understanding, and the discovery of common ground."[99] By directing attention away from the responsibilities we bear as citizens, and away from the public policy tool kit available to us as we address the complex causes of gun violence, a fixation on rights can interfere with democratic dialogue. What Glendon calls "rights talk" can thus be both a virtue and a vice.

Whatever its precise legal effect, *Heller* placed rights more firmly at the center of public and political debates over gun policy. Now groups like the NRA and Mayors Against Illegal Guns compete on legislative *and* constitutional terrain. Now the deaths of moviegoers watching *The Dark Knight Rises* in Aurora prompt Facebook and Twitter debates over constitutional law. In that respect, *Heller*'s influence is as mighty as it is subtle.

This leads to a more vital point about the links among the Second Amendment, the rest of the Constitution, and representative democracy. *Heller* and *McDonald* are landmark rulings, but they do not enjoy sole dominion over gun rights. The right to vote allows us to select the law-makers who pass regulations. The Equal Protection Clause ensures that gun ownership is not arbitrarily denied to disfavored groups. The division of state and federal power allows each state to forge its own gun rules and prevents the national government from commandeering state regulators to achieve its own goals. The Due Process Clause ensures that proper procedures are followed before anyone is denied a firearm on the basis of mental illness or some other supposedly disqualifying characteristic. The Fourth Amendment governs searches, seizures, and the use of force by police, and thereby protects gun owners against unauthorized surveillance. The conferral of power on the Senate to make its own rules allowed it to adopt the filibuster, which has proved to be an important force in shaping federal gun policy. In a game of constitutional "odds" and "evens," guns don't just fall under the "evens."

The First Amendment, in particular, has always played—and will always play—a central role in determining America's gun laws.[100] Although *Heller*'s interpretation of the Second Amendment takes certain options off the table, it leaves broad room for our democracy to debate and experiment with different forms of firearms regulation. The First Amendment, in turn, is vital in structuring the processes of deliberation and decision that define our democratic system.

There is a certain poetry to this dynamic. The core original purpose of the Second Amendment was to ensure that an armed citizenry could check a tyrannical government with the threat of revolution. This threat, in theory, would keep the federal government in line. Today, few seriously credit the idea that the option of armed resistance is essential to our democracy. In *Heller*, Scalia gave that argument the back of his hand, dismissing the notion that Americans enjoy a right to the sort of firepower that could resist tanks and rockets. Instead, we rely exclusively on the structure of democracy, the power of free speech, and our other liberties to maintain popular sovereignty. The First and Second Amendments are thus intertwined. The First Amendment secures the Second's original purpose, though with the power of the spoken word rather than the threat of gunfire. And it plays a central role in shaping the reality of gun rights for Americans, since the Second Amendment leaves to democracy the hardest questions about guns.

This potent interaction of the First and Second Amendments brings into even starker relief the potential importance of rulings like *Citizens United*, which pose hard questions about how money affects politicians, and *Brown v. Entertainment Merchants Association*, which limit efforts to combat a potential source of violent cultural norms.[101] More broadly, this perspective directs attention to widely condemned dysfunctions in our representative democracy—the causes of which extend far beyond the First Amendment into political culture, gerrymandered districts, filibuster rules, lobbying, and other such factors. As advocates and opponents of gun regulation have learned, the structure of democracy is often more important to their efforts than the Second Amendment.

At argument in *Heller*, Chief Justice Roberts looked askance at picking up "baggage" from the First Amendment and thrusting it upon the Second Amendment. When he said this, he meant that the Second Amendment didn't need an elaborate set of rules and complex standards of review; rather, we could just look to history and see what laws the Second Amendment was understood to allow. Whatever the merits of Roberts's point as a matter of doctrine, the simple fact is that the First and Second Amendments are inseparable. From that perspective, it could not be plainer that *Heller* will persist as a landmark opinion of the Roberts Court.

When policy debates are converted into constitutional cases, the implications are often far-reaching and surprising. Lawyers are well aware that "constitutionalizing" an issue is not a choice the Court makes lightly. It remains to be seen whether *Heller* will facilitate or hinder meaningful conversation about gun regulations; in the end, it will likely do both. But it is clear that *Heller* has already exerted—and will continue to exert—a profound influence on our life, law, and politics.

6

PRESIDENTIAL POWER:

HAIL TO THE CHIEF

Barack Obama couldn't hide his frustration.[1] In June 2009, he was in the middle of an important interview, but a fly kept buzzing around his head, derailing his train of thought. Even a president famed for his even keel could stand only so much. "Get out of here," he warned sternly. Then, suddenly, he became acutely focused. The interview forgotten, he tracked the fly like a targeting system for seven tense seconds before lashing out with deadly precision. He left the fly dead on the ground. Obviously pleased with himself, Obama turned back to the camera: "That was pretty impressive, wasn't it? I got the sucker."

Three years later, the public learned that Obama, with far greater stakes and the full power of the American military at his command, had reached out to kill many more times. Since assuming office in January 2009, Obama has aggressively prosecuted America's war against terrorism, relying heavily on a fleet of missile-equipped drones to kill suspected terrorists across the globe.[2] In May 2012, the *New York Times* revealed that Obama personally supervises the "grim debating society" that decides who is put on America's dreaded "kill list."[3] As the *Times* put it, Obama "[pores] over terrorist suspects' biographies on what one official calls the macabre 'baseball cards' of an unconventional war" and sometimes "has reserved to himself the final moral calculation."

Selecting targets only after extensive intelligence analysis, Obama and his advisers rely on an intricate system of checks and balances within the Executive Branch to decide who should live and who should die.[4] On occasion, the administration's targets have included U.S. citizens never proven guilty in a court of law. In Obama's view, the Executive's internal procedures were all the process those citizens were due under the Constitution.[5]

Such raw displays of presidential power inspire conflicted emotions. We want a strong, energetic leader to advance the national interest, but we fear that unchecked power is an invitation to tyranny. We laud efficiency, security, and order, even as we insist on accountability, privacy, and liberty. We yearn for justice, but we want safety. A pantheon of competing values converges on the design of that all-important office, the presidency. Since the earliest days of the Republic, Americans have agonized over how to calibrate the legal, political, and institutional pressures that define any president's ability to wield power.

John G. Roberts Jr. assumed stewardship of the Court at a pivotal moment in our history. After 9/11, George W. Bush declared a "war on terror" and laid claim to extraordinary powers.[6] Rather than collaborate with Congress and the Judiciary, Bush initially insisted in many contexts that his inherent power entitled him to proceed without involving either of the other two branches of government. Occasionally, especially in his first term, he made the stronger claim that the other branches had no power at all to limit him. Even when Bush did cooperate with the other branches, he adopted broad views of his unilateral authority. Advised by lawyers known for their bare-knuckled skepticism of limits on the Executive, Bush triggered fierce debate over the separation of powers.

By the time Roberts was confirmed in 2005, and continuously for the next three years, Bush was besieged. In particular, critics focused on the policies governing detention of "enemy combatants" in the military prison at Guantánamo Bay, the president's defense of interrogation tactics that many viewed as torture, and his approval of warrantless domestic surveillance of American citizens. Bush also drew censure for employing signing statements to express constitutional objections to new laws,[7] expanding the use of the "state secrets" privilege to block judicial review, and firing prosecutors who didn't toe the partisan line. Even though he ultimately backed away from some of his most controversial practices, Bush left in his wake a simmering debate over limits on presidential power.[8]

With the end of Bush's tenure, many of these concerns migrated sharply rightward. Obama took office amid promises of executive modesty and criticism of Bush, but as historians and political scientists have long observed, presidents are rarely inclined to return power of their own free will. While Obama does not favor overt Bush-style claims to unilateral constitutional power over national security affairs, he has adopted muscular views of his statutory and inherent authority. In 2011, for instance, he circumvented the apparent need for legislative approval of his bombing campaign in Libya—an obligation imposed by the War Powers Resolution—by insisting in the face of widespread public incredulity that the bombings did not qualify as "hostilities."[9]

Warnings of rampant abuse of presidential authority have recently become standard fare among conservatives and civil libertarians. These accusations are directed at Obama's lethal drone strikes against U.S. citizens, perpetuation of the seemingly endless detention regime at Guantánamo Bay, unilateral use of force in Libya, and qualified approval of the National Security Agency's domestic surveillance and data-mining programs. They also encompass key parts of Obama's domestic policy, such as his use of executive orders to limit gun acquisition, his refusal to defend the Defense of Marriage Act in court, his selective refusal to enforce immigration laws, and his suspension of key parts of the Affordable Care Act to facilitate its implementation.[10]

For the most part, these debates play out exclusively in politics and between the political branches—all in the shadow of the Constitution. Often, the precedents and constitutional interpretations in play come from a centuries-old dialogue between Congress and the President. Thanks to a matrix of rules that control when the Judiciary can involve itself in such affairs, questions about the separation of powers only rarely reach the Court.

When they do, the Court treads carefully. It has few duties more delicate than shaping the federal government's architecture of power. Its decisions can ripple out into hundreds of unforeseen contexts, affecting how Congress and the President address issues that aren't yet on anybody's radar. They also affect political and party dynamics; telling the President that he must seek approval from Congress has greater impact when Congress is controlled by the opposition party.[11] The justices know this well: most of them served as attorneys or advisers in the Executive Branch at some point during their careers, and all of them have lived in the capital long enough to appreciate that court orders are merely part of power's ebb and flow.

Generalizations about being "for" or "against" presidential power tend not to be especially helpful at the Court. No justice is uniformly of one mind about whether the President should have more or less power, especially because voting to limit the President often means voting to empower someone else—be it Congress, the Judiciary, one or more federal agencies, or the states. Views on separation of powers cases are thus attuned to the context in which they arise, respect for tradition, beliefs about the strengths and weaknesses of the other branches of government, and, at times, preferred policy outcomes. Justices regularly vote on both sides of the presidential power equation, a pattern that has persisted across the Bush and Obama administrations.

Since 2005, the Court has decided major cases involving detention at Guantánamo Bay, electronic surveillance, enforcement of immigration laws, and limits on the federal bureaucracy. These issues are not for the faint of heart: each stands at the center of a political firestorm. Viewed together, the Court's rulings offer a window into a Court divided. Nearly every case has been decided by a bare majority. In their opinions, the justices give no quarter when articulating opposed visions of the Constitution. Where some see protection of treasured rights, others see needless risks of disaster. Where some see bureaucracy run amok, others see workable government. The Roberts Court, like the rest of the nation, is at war with itself, caught between competing visions of the American presidency. As the Court navigates an uncertain path forward, it will play a vital role in shaping many of the most important issues of our time.

The President is Commander in Chief of the Armed Forces, not "Commander in Chief of the country, its industries and its inhabitants."[12] So remarked Justice Robert H. Jackson in his concurrence in *Youngstown Sheet & Tube Co. v. Sawyer*. Decided in 1952, *Youngstown* struck down an audacious presidential takeover of the nation's steel industry. Harry Truman had taken that extreme step after a breakdown in labor negotiations threatened to close the steel mills and interrupt the flow of heavy artillery to troops fighting in Korea.[13]

To Truman, who had witnessed Franklin D. Roosevelt's wide-ranging wartime action, it seemed obvious that he had acted lawfully—though he made clear to the Senate that "Congress can, if it wishes, reject the course of action I have followed in this matter." Some past presidential practices supported Truman's view; more important, the president knew he had the support of Chief Justice Fred Vinson, a close friend who had secretly assured Truman that his plan to seize the steel mills would pass muster. In 1949, Justice Tom Clark, during his tenure as Attorney General, had also counseled Truman that he enjoyed "exceedingly great" power to address emergencies. Even Jackson seemed likely to be sympathetic to Truman's point of view: in 1941, when Jackson was serving as Attorney General, he had articulated an expansive view of inherent presidential power to justify Roosevelt's seizure of the North American Aviation plant (thus avoiding a labor strike that threatened airplane manufacturing). In light of this apparent support on the Court, Truman had good reason to believe his decision would be legitimized.

But the President had miscalculated. By a vote of six to three, the Court quickly and decisively rejected Truman's claim of inherent power. With his approval rating in free fall, Truman ended his takeover. Vinson, true to his word, had dissented, but Clark voted with the majority. Truman never forgave Clark. "It isn't so much that he's a bad man," Truman is rumored to have said. "It's just that he's a dumb son of a bitch."[14]

Few cases testing the President's need for congressional authorization—or his ability to bluntly defy Congress—ever reach the Court. The system of checks and balances between Congress and the President usually produces a workable equilibrium without the need for judicial intervention; indeed, the political branches often prefer a fluid give-and-take to the rigidity of a court order. For its part, the Court, recognizing the perils of intervention in major interbranch disputes, has historically shied away from invitations to step into that minefield. But as Jackson explained in his concurring opinion in *Youngstown*, it is sometimes the Court's solemn duty to ensure that the President does not deprive people of basic rights, such as "life, liberty, or property," without affording them "due process of law" as required by the Fifth Amendment. Although Article II of the Constitution vests "the executive Power" in a single President, whom it charges with the duty to "take Care that the Laws be faithfully executed," that potentially sweeping executive authority "must be matched," Jackson reasoned in *Youngstown*, against "the Fifth Amendment." As Jackson explained, "One gives a governmental authority that reaches so far as there is law, the other gives a private right that authority shall go no farther. These signify about all there is of the principle that ours is a government of laws, not of men, and that we submit ourselves to rulers only if under rules."

Jackson's essay on the separation of powers, a marvel of the judicial craft, embodies an influential three-part theory. As Jackson put it, "presidential powers are not fixed but fluctuate depending upon their disjunction or conjunction with those of Congress." When the President acts pursuant to congressional authorization, "his authority is at its maximum, for it includes all that he possesses in his own right plus all that Congress can delegate." When the President takes action "incompatible with the expressed or implied will of Congress, his power is at its lowest ebb, for then he can rely only upon his own constitutional powers minus any constitutional powers of Congress over the matter." Finally, when Congress stands silent, the President acts in a "zone of twilight," where "any actual test of power is likely to depend on the imperatives of events and contemporary imponderables, rather than on abstract theories of law." Jackson saw *Youngstown* as a paradigmatic "lowest ebb" case: Congress had passed three different laws governing seizure of private property, and Truman had chosen a crude approach incompatible with all of them. Jackson therefore voted to end the seizure. Rather than define presidential power in a void, Jackson linked it to a living interbranch dialogue.

Interventions as dramatic as the Court's decision to turn back Truman's steel seizure do at least as much to educate the general public—and to shape the constitutional culture within which all power is ultimately exercised—as they do to tie the president's hands. This is particularly true when the president is deciding how best to defend the nation and its people in deploying America's military might abroad, with or without congressional approval. Still, understanding where the Court fits into this complex story of the separation of powers requires connecting a relatively small number of widely separated dots, because the tale of how our Constitution operates to shape the exercise of presidential powers is one told largely without the aid of a judicial narrative.[15] Both Congress and the President engage in an ongoing tug-of-war, each with at least one eye focused on what the Constitution's text, structure, and history seem to tell them about the President's authority and responsibility.[16]

On September 12, 2001, as towers of smoke drifted skyward in New York City, Washington, D.C., and Shanksville, Pennsylvania, all eyes turned to the White House. The nation, it seemed, was at war. The Constitution charged George W. Bush with the powers of the Commander in Chief, and he plainly intended to wield them. Two days later, Congress strengthened the president's hand by passing the Authorization for the Use of Military Force Act (AUMF), granting the nation's leader authority "to use all necessary and appropriate force" against those who had attacked our country or aided the attackers.

Since 9/11, America has invaded Afghanistan and Iraq; launched anti-terror operations and drone strikes in Pakistan, Yemen, and Somalia; massively expanded covert operations and surveillance; and established a detention regime centered on the naval base at Guantánamo Bay. Congress has mostly supported these undertakings, and Bush and Obama have both taken broad views of the power conferred by the AUMF and other national security laws.[17]

It was hardly foreordained that the Supreme Court would play a significant role in the effort to balance liberty against security in this brave new world. After all, the Court has generally yielded to the political branches in wartime. Although it struck down Truman's unilateral seizure of the steel mills in 1952, it upheld laws criminalizing seditious speech during World War I, summarily affirmed the execution of alleged saboteurs during World War II, and sidestepped legal attacks on the conduct of the Vietnam War. Over the past few decades, lower courts have refused to hear challenges to military action in El Salvador, Nicaragua, Grenada, Kosovo, Iraq, and Libya.[18] Judicial deference to the political branches is unsurprising: Congress and the President are politically accountable, explicitly entrusted by the Constitution with war powers, and far more knowledgeable about military operations and requirements.

The post-9/11 conflict, though, was unlike anything the United States had seen before. The nation was at war with amorphous enemies who had committed a mass atrocity on the American homeland. We had invaded Afghanistan and Iraq. The public openly debated torture, indefinite detention, and warrantless surveillance. The President and his advisers asserted inherent power under Article II of the Constitution to carry out parts of their national security agenda without—or even despite—Congress.

Bush's legal arguments might have caused less concern if there were territorial limits to this new kind of war, but after 9/11 the entire globe seemed like a potential battlefield. American security forces discovered Al Qaeda associates everywhere from the streets of Kabul to O'Hare Airport, in Chicago.[19] Nor did there appear to be any end in sight to a conflict that some have since warned may be a "Forever War."[20] Indeed, even though Obama has stated that "this war, like all wars, must end,"[21] it has already lasted more than a decade with no end in sight. These uncertainties of time and space disrupted faith that exceptional policies adopted for wartime would end when peace returned.[22]

As the President and his allies insisted that security must take priority over liberty, a wave of legal challenges rolled toward the Court. Many focused on Bush's military detention regime. In the years after 9/11, American and allied forces captured more than ten thousand individuals who were believed to be terrorists or their accomplices. Many were seized in Afghanistan, but others hailed from as far away as Bosnia, Gambia, and Yemen. Rather than deem them prisoners of war, afford them rights promised by the Geneva Conventions, or send them to federal court for trial, the military detained many suspected terrorists at bases such as the facility at Guantánamo Bay.

Relying on precedents authorizing the seizure of enemy soldiers on a battlefield for the duration of a war, and on cases limiting the reach of the Constitution beyond American territory, Bush's lawyers carefully designed a legal black hole for "enemy combatants."[23] Guantánamo, for instance, was almost entirely free of judicial and legislative oversight. At best, some detainees could challenge their indefinite detention before specially convened executive branch tribunals, though without ordinary rules of evidence and procedure. At worst, they were forced to languish in prison indefinitely, without lawyers, rights, or review. Assisted by a cadre of dedicated lawyers, some detainees filed suit.[24]

Inevitably, petitions for review reached the Court. Questions that once seemed abstract or hypothetical demanded an answer. What role, if any, would the Court and Constitution play in establishing the ground rules for twenty-first-century national security? Would the Court uphold Bush's actions or lay down some limits? Was the President constrained by the Constitution as enforced by the Court, or was he free to navigate this new world without checks and balances?

Ultimately, the Roberts Court chose to walk a delicate line. Intervening cautiously and strategically, it has refrained from asserting a bold vision of civil rights in wartime. It has declined to release any detainee, shied away from calls to limit military operations, refused to break through walls of state secrecy, and forged rules to shield the government from detention-related civil rights suits. But it has also refused to bow out altogether. Even while respecting the President's power as Commander in Chief, the Court has forced Bush and Obama to work with Congress and the Judiciary in creating a detention regime, and it might yet do the same for domestic surveillance and data-gathering programs. In that endeavor, it has repeatedly invoked the importance of involving all three branches in striking the balance between liberty and security.

The justices fired their first shots across the bow in 2004, the year before Roberts joined the Court.[25] At the time, Bush claimed near-exclusive presidential dominion over what he called the "war on terror." Faced with detainee lawsuits, Bush sent his emissaries to court with a clear message for the justices: you have no business here.

In a stroke of unfortunate timing for Bush's position, however, photos depicting vile and inhumane abuse of detainees at Abu Ghraib broke about seven hours after oral argument in one of the detainee cases, *Hamdi v. Rumsfeld*.[26] It's safe to assume these photos made an impression on the Court, not least because Justice Ginsburg had pressed a Bush administration lawyer that very day (in a different case) to identify a meaningful "check against torture" when the Executive acts in ways "unchecked by the Judiciary."[27]

Hamdi involved a U.S. citizen named Yaser Esam Hamdi, who had been captured while fighting in Afghanistan and detained in a South Carolina naval brig. The case forced the Court to decide whether a president could detain Americans and, if so, what sorts of procedures he had to follow. In cold and uncompromising prose, Justice Sandra Day O'Connor wrote for a plurality of four justices to reject Bush's most aggressive assertions of power. Citing *Youngstown*, she reaffirmed that "a state of war is not a blank check for the President when it comes to the rights of the Nation's citizens." Thus, "whatever power the United States Constitution envisions for the Executive in its exchanges with other nations or with enemy organizations in times of conflict, it most assuredly envisions a role for all three branches when individual liberties are at stake." She added, "History and common sense teach us that an unchecked system of detention carries the potential to become a means for oppression and abuse of others who do not present that sort of threat."

Ultimately, O'Connor's controlling opinion struck upon a middle ground. Bush could detain Hamdi because Congress had passed the AUMF—not, as his lawyers had urged, because Article II conferred that inherent power upon him as Commander in Chief. Further, when he exercised the authority conferred on him by Congress to seize United States citizens, Bush had to comply with the Due Process Clause and provide them a "meaningful opportunity to contest the factual basis for [their] detention before a neutral decisionmaker." Relying on procedure to protect rights, and on the combined power of Congress and the President to justify and circumscribe detention of U.S. citizens, *Hamdi* pushed back against Bush's effort to concentrate "war on terror" decision making in the Executive. Ultimately, only Justice Thomas fully accepted Bush's view. Every other justice voted against Bush—with Justices Scalia and Stevens, in rare alliance, insisting that Bush charge Hamdi with a federal crime or release him.

In *Rasul v. Bush*,[28] decided the same day as *Hamdi*, the Court rejected an assertion of total authority by Bush over Guantánamo. As Justice Breyer remarked at oral argument, "It seems rather contrary to an idea of a Constitution with three branches that the executive would be free to do whatever they want, whatever they want without a check." The Court, however, moved cautiously. It did not decide to release any detainee or set standards for detention. Nor did it decide whether the Constitution required judicial review. Rather, it held only that a federal statute authorized judicial review of detention at the naval base. Still, as Harvard Law Professor Jack Goldsmith has observed, *Rasul* "marked the first time in American history that enemy soldiers held outside the United States during wartime could force the executive branch to explain and defend their detention before a court."[29]

Hamdi and *Rasul* together constituted a devastating rebuke to the Bush administration. In response, Bush set up Combatant Status Review Tribunals (CSRTs) and Administrative Review Boards to provide for ongoing review of detentions within the Executive Branch. Partly motivated by the Court, Congress also took a more active role. *Rasul* relied on an Act of Congress, but what Congress gives, Congress can take away. In

2005, with bipartisan support, it passed the Detainee Treatment Act (DTA). The DTA stripped courts of ordinary jurisdiction over suits by detainees at Guantánamo. At the same time, it bolstered the procedural rights afforded to detainees in CSRTs and provided for limited judicial review of CSRT rulings, changes that ultimately led the Executive to release several hundred detainees.[30]

The Court took up these matters again in 2006. This time, Salim Ahmed Hamdan, Osama bin Laden's chauffeur, brought suit to challenge a military tribunal convened to try him for violating the laws of war. In *Hamdan v. Rumsfeld*,[31] the Court ruled that, under existing statutory law, Bush could not create such tribunals without approval from Congress. The Court also held that some of the Geneva Conventions' protections of human rights applied to the war with Al Qaeda—a position that Bush had rejected, and that imposed new legal limits on American military and intelligence programs.

Hamdan was a narrow ruling.[32] It afforded Congress room to legislatively grant Bush the power to create tribunals, an invitation Congress accepted when it passed the Military Commissions Act of 2006 (MCA). Although the MCA conferred stronger procedural protections than did the President's tribunals, it was a big win for Bush: it established a military commission system and confirmed with unmistakable clarity that the courts should keep away.[33] But it was also a win for the Court: *Hamdi* and *Hamdan* had triggered the system of checks and balances, forcing Bush into a dialogue with Congress and the public about America's evolving regime of indefinite detention.[34]

That dialogue, though, led the political branches to speak with a single voice in telling the Court to stop hearing Guantánamo cases. Never before had the Court overruled both Congress and the President in wartime. As challenges to the detention regime piled up and Guantánamo cast a pall of illegitimacy across America's global standing, a once unthinkable question echoed around the Capitol: would the Court claim supreme power to remake America's architecture of indefinite detention?

"Habeas corpus" is a Latin phrase meaning "may you have the body." For centuries, prisoners have relied on this arcane legal device as their last line of defense against tyrannical imprisonment.[35] By filing a petition for a writ of habeas corpus, a prisoner asks a judge to send a message to the jailer: *Come to court and explain yourself. Who is your prisoner, and what is your legal basis for imprisoning him?*

In 2001, Lakhdar Boumediene lived with his family in Bosnia, where he directed an office that provided humanitarian aid to children.[36] On October 19, 2001, he was seized by Bosnian intelligence at America's request on suspicion of plotting to blow up the U.S. embassy in Sarajevo. On January 20, 2002, he was taken to Guantánamo, where he spent the next seven years, three months, three weeks, and four days of his life. Bush was so proud of this seizure that he referred to it explicitly in his 2002 State of the Union Address. Recounting his experience at Guantánamo, Boumediene later described brutal interrogation techniques and twice-daily force-feeding after he undertook a two-year hunger strike. Asserting his innocence, Boumediene petitioned for review in the American courts. He kept up his legal fight even after Congress passed the MCA, which purported to bar judicial review.

The Court initially refused to hear *Boumediene v. Bush,* with Souter, Ginsburg, and Breyer dissenting. Stevens and Kennedy held back, probably because Stevens worried about how Kennedy would vote. In a last-ditch effort to sway the Court, Boumediene's legal team submitted a statement by Lieutenant Colonel Stephen Abraham, an officer in the U.S. Army Reserve. Abraham portrayed the CSRTs as kangaroo courts in which no detainee could obtain a fair hearing. Only the Judiciary, Boumediene argued, could adequately protect detainees' rights. On the last day of its 2006 term, the Court announced that it would hear the case, a decision requiring five votes. By granting Boumediene's plea, the Roberts Court had tipped its hand.[37]

Even so, Boumediene faced an uphill fight. He argued that the MCA, by stripping courts of the power to hear his suit, violated the Constitution. Specifically, he said the law violated the Suspension Clause, which provides that "The Privilege of the Writ of Habeas Corpus shall not be suspended, unless when in Cases of Rebellion or Invasion the public Safety may require it."[38] To win, he first had to persuade the Court to sidestep precedent suggesting that foreigners held outside the United States have no right to judicial review of their detention. Guantánamo Bay, after all, is technically located in Cuba, even though the United States exercises total sovereign control of the base by virtue of a treaty dating back to 1934. Boumediene also needed to persuade the Court to find a violation of the Suspension Clause and to overrule a military provision passed jointly in wartime by Congress and the President—steps the Court had never previously taken.

On June 12, 2008, though, the Court gave Boumediene what he had long sought: a chance to prove his innocence and the hope of eventual freedom.[39] Writing for five justices, Kennedy composed a magnum opus on fundamental constitutional principle.[40]

Boumediene reflected Kennedy's deep fascination with the relationship between individual liberty and constitutional structure. Surveying centuries of English history, a tale rife with royal tyranny, Kennedy recalled that "the Framers [knew] that pendular swings to and away from individual liberty were endemic to undivided, uncontrolled power." Their "inherent distrust of government was the driving force behind the constitutional plan that allocated powers among three independent branches." As Kennedy explained, "This design serves not only to make Government accountable but also to secure individual liberty."

The writ of habeas corpus, Kennedy added, is an "essential mechanism in the separation-of-powers scheme." The framers therefore stitched habeas corpus into the very fabric of the Constitution, ensuring that "the Judiciary will have a time-tested device, the writ, to maintain the delicate balance of governance that is itself the surest safeguard of liberty." It is through judicial review of detention, after all, that courts discharge their duty of holding Congress and the President to account when faced with charges of tyranny. In spelling out the system of checks and balances, Kennedy reveled in the genius of requiring interbranch dialogue, and he placed characteristic emphasis on the importance of an independent, dynamic judiciary. With these principles in play, it's no surprise that Kennedy was disturbed by the prospect of an indefinite detention regime devoid of judicial involvement. He saw the political branches constructing a new separation of powers—one without courts and thus less capable of safeguarding freedom—and fiercely objected.

This concern drove Kennedy's entire opinion. Concluding that the Constitution's guarantee of habeas corpus applied in Guantánamo, he noted that the base "is under the complete and total control of our Government." Indeed, Kennedy added, "in every practical sense, Guantánamo is not abroad." It would therefore be dangerous, he warned, to let formalities of sovereignty control legal analysis: "The necessary implication of the argument is that by surrendering formal sovereignty over [foreign territory] to a third party, while at the same time entering into a lease that grants total control over the territory back to the United States, it would be possible for the political branches to govern without legal constraint."

Faced with the threat of a judicial black hole, Kennedy rejected the "striking anomaly" of "a regime in which Congress and the President, not this Court, say 'what the law is.'" Forcefully, he declared, "Our basic charter cannot be contracted away like this." Solicitude for the judicial role and its unique protections also led Kennedy to reject the argument that executive review of detainee status under the MCA was an adequate substitute for writs of habeas corpus.

Kennedy summarized his opinion by preaching the virtues of interbranch collaboration. Security, he wrote, requires sophisticated intelligence and a powerful military, but it also subsists "in fidelity to freedom's first principles." "Chief among these," he instructed, "are freedom from arbitrary and unlawful restraint and the personal liberty that is secured by adherence to the separation of powers." Kennedy also argued that judicial involvement would ultimately benefit the President: "The exercise of those powers is vindicated when confirmed by the Judicial Branch." In 2008, this argument carried special force: America's detention regime was besieged at home and abroad with charges of illegitimacy that judicial review could help refute.

Looking forward, Kennedy called on the political branches to "engage in a genuine debate about how best to preserve constitutional values while protecting the Nation from terrorism." Out of respect for that process, he then left open the vital question of how vigorously courts should examine the President's justifications for detention. Kennedy warned, though, that if the political branches failed in their duty, the Court might be forced to define "the outer boundaries of war powers."

Kennedy concluded his opinion by celebrating the judicial role and the rule of law: "The laws and Constitution are designed to survive, and remain in force, in extraordinary times. Liberty and security can be reconciled; and in our system they are reconciled within the framework of the law. The Framers decided that habeas corpus, a right of first importance, must be a part of that framework, a part of that law."

Summoning a fury rare even by his lights, Scalia dissented and blasted Kennedy for intruding into military affairs. This "devastating" opinion, he prophesied, "will make the war harder on us . . . [and] almost certainty cause more Americans to be killed." After all, he asked, "What competence does the Court have to second-guess the judgment of Congress and the President on such a point? None whatever. But the Court blunders in nonetheless. Henceforth, as today's opinion makes unnervingly clear, how to handle enemy prisoners in this war will ultimately lie with the branch that knows least about the national security concerns that the subject entails." Scalia concluded ominously: "The Nation will live to regret what the Court has done today."

The Chief Justice signed Scalia's dissent, but he wrote a separate dissent more in tune with his pragmatic proclivities. "Today," he announced, "the Court strikes down as inadequate the most generous set of procedural protections ever afforded aliens detained by this country as enemy combatants." Moreover, the majority's ruling rejected a "review system designed by the people's representatives" only to replace it with "a set of shapeless procedures to be defined by federal courts at some future date." Doubtful that courts would craft more detainee-friendly review procedures, Roberts saw a "distinct possibility that [the Court's] 'habeas' remedy will, when all is said and done, end up looking a great deal like" the very procedures Kennedy had decisively rejected.

Boumediene rocked the legal universe. The outcome was hardly a bolt from the blue, not after *Hamdi, Rasul,* and *Hamdan*. But the sheer enormity of the Court's unprecedented intervention—and its suggestion of more to come—dazzled observers. Kennedy's opinion was promptly hailed by civil rights advocates as a "great victory."[41] Some even dared to dream that *Boumediene* would launch the Court into a bold new era of "war on terror" lawmaking. The Court, they insisted, had finally made clear its willingness to fundamentally realign the balance of liberty and security. Now the President would be forced to defend his detention regime in federal court, a crucible that some of his critics were sure would liberate many detainees. Lakhdar Boumediene himself was freed on May 15, 2009, after Judge Richard J. Leon ordered the government to release him and successfully implored it not to appeal.[42] Lawyers on all sides of the detention system held their breath, waiting to see what this new law of habeas corpus would become—and if the Court would return to the field.

Hope for a new dawn was quickly dashed. In *Boumediene*'s aftermath, trial court judges in D.C. scrutinized the basis for detentions and found quite a few of them wanting. But the D.C. Circuit Court of Appeals soon issued a string of opinions taking a very narrow view of *Boumediene*.[43] Since 2008, its decisions in detainee habeas corpus cases have tilted the playing field overwhelmingly in the government's favor.[44] Frustrated, one judge bitterly noted that "*Boumediene* called for a meaningful review, habeas review, and what's happened in the circuit has been to first, to take the capital letter off the word 'meaningful,' and then . . . take the letters 'ful' off the end of 'meaningful,' and then to sort of deprive it of meaning."[45]

By 2011, several conservatives on the D.C. Circuit had publicly declared war on *Boumediene* and accused the Court of making a terrible mistake. Judge Janice Rogers Brown excoriated "*Boumediene*'s airy suppositions."[46] Judge A. Raymond Randolph delivered a public speech titled "The Guantanamo Mess," in which he likened the justices to characters in *The Great Gatsby*, "careless people, [who] smashed things up . . . and let other people clean up the mess they had made."[47] And Judge Laurence Silberman openly castigated the Court for its refusal to hear appeals from any ruling on Guantánamo detention, caustically remarking that "taking a case might obligate it to assume direct responsibility for the consequences of *Boumediene*."[48]

Understandably, the combination of the Court's continued silence and these lower court rulings have led to charges that *Boumediene* didn't matter much after all.[49] Indeed, measured against its most civil libertarian potential, *Boumediene* proved to be a disappointment. But charges of irrelevance, just like original claims of unqualified victory, miss the mark.

In truth, for better or worse, *Boumediene* was never mainly about freeing detainees held at Guantánamo. The Court seems content to leave most such decisions to the political branches. As Scalia drove home in his outraged dissent, the Court is inexpert in these matters and reluctant to set aside judgments shared by Congress and the President. Further, if freeing detainees held on questionable bases were its principal concern, the Court would likely have reviewed and reversed a post-*Boumediene* D.C. Circuit detainee case to make its intentions clear.

Instead, *Boumediene* was meant to vindicate the separation of powers in wartime. Faced with a plea by the political branches to abdicate the field, Kennedy saw a threat to liberty—not only (or even especially) the liberties of Guantánamo detainees but those of all Americans. In his view, some engagement with the Judiciary is essential to keep government in line and in touch with rule of law values. This is why Kennedy strongly emphasized "the delicate balance of governance that is itself the surest safeguard of liberty." *Boumediene* guaranteed that all three branches would remain involved, to at least some degree, in America's evolving detention regime. As Kennedy intended, it thus helped legitimize that system—which appeared lawless in the absence of judicial involvement— even as it left the President and Congress with broad control over detention at Guantánamo and other detention facilities around the world.

In some respects, *Boumediene* was therefore a deeply conservative ruling in its ultimate purpose. It lent the imprimatur of judicial respectability and elaborate procedure to America's detention regime without asking very much of the political branches or bringing a strong civil libertarian voice to the table. From that perspective, *Boumediene* sanctioned the status quo without forcing much (or any) change, thereby validating the Executive's national security policies and opening the door to future rulings that create equally anemic judicial protections of individual liberty.

There is great force to this view, but it misses out on some of *Boumediene*'s systemic effects. Most important, *Boumediene* sent a forceful rule of law message at a time when Americans were deeply divided over the continued relevance of traditional legal restraints on power. It therefore reminded the public of America's fundamental values and burnished the country's image in the eyes of a global community whose support is vital to success in anti-terrorism efforts. Further, *Boumediene* and the line of rulings that preceded it led to more intense debate within the political branches, which have released hundreds of detainees over the past decade without direct judicial intervention. In fact, less than 4 percent of all detainee releases through 2010 resulted from judicial order, though in some cases the threat of judicial review may have played a role.[50] By forcing the Executive to defend its detention decisions in open court, even before as friendly an audience as the D.C. Circuit, the Court also pressured military lawyers to more carefully scrutinize their own practices and detention criteria.

Boumediene's implications for the rule of law, moreover, extend into many other contexts. As Professor Goldsmith has observed, by empowering federal courts to hear detainee lawsuits, the Court triggered a judicial lawmaking project with broad national security implications. In deciding detainee cases, judges have interpreted the AUMF, the laws of war, and other important statutes that govern American military operations. The Executive, in turn, is constrained and guided by these judicial rulings as it undertakes such operations throughout the world.

Laws may not fall silent at the sound of gunfire, but courts certainly step more carefully. *Hamdi*, *Rasul*, *Hamdan*, and *Boumediene* represent the effort of a bare majority of the Roberts Court, often over heated dissents, to strike a balance suitable to the needs of our time. To many, these cases either go too far in deferring to the political branches or don't go nearly far enough. Nonetheless, they represent historically unparalleled efforts by our highest court to uphold a particular and respectable vision of America's separation of powers in wartime. As Breyer has written, "Rather than leaving a future executive administration free to act as it wishes . . . the Court left four cases for study by future presidential advisors." These cases, he has emphasized, "make clear that a president must take account of the Constitution, as interpreted independently by the Court." It is uncertain if and when the Court will return to this remarkable project, but the detainee cases will undoubtedly constitute one of the Roberts Court's most important legacies.

Boumediene set forth a cautiously bold vision of the judicial role in wartime. In retrospect, however, that case denotes the high-water mark of the Roberts Court's willingness to intervene in national security affairs.[51] As it has turned aside subsequent detainee appeals, the Court has taken a narrow view of its appropriate role in assessing other post-9/11 policies. Many lower courts are of the same mind. As a result, the legality of such controversial policies as enhanced interrogation, drone strikes, and the rendition of terrorist suspects to foreign nations has never been finally settled. Invoking a battery of rules created to respect the separation of powers and give judges ways to avoid unwanted (or untimely) confrontations, courts have repeatedly denied private plaintiffs and civil rights groups a judicial forum in which to advance constitutional objections.

Weighty questions of liberty, security, privacy, and power have therefore been left almost entirely to the political branches.

The Judiciary has long recognized that its power to "say what the law is," in words taken from a famous early Supreme Court opinion,[52] creates a risk of usurping functions properly reserved to Congress and the President. Such overreaching could produce damaging backlash and inflict great harm on the nation; courts, after all, lack the democratic accountability, expertise, and access to information vital to effective governance. Respect for its own institutional limits and legitimacy has thus led the Judiciary to adopt doctrines that tell it when *not* to decide constitutional issues.[53] Use of these doctrines often raises hard questions about the line between judicial modesty and abdication.

Generally speaking, courts refuse to decide "political questions" entrusted by the Constitution to another branch of government. In 2010, for example, a federal court invoked this doctrine to dismiss a lawsuit brought by Nasser Al-Aulaqi, who claimed that Obama had violated the constitutional rights of his son—Anwar Al-Aulaqi—by designating Anwar for targeted killing as a terrorist.[54] "Decision-making in the realm of military and foreign affairs is textually committed to the political branches," the opinion explained, and "courts are functionally ill-equipped to make the types of complex policy judgments that would be required to adjudicate the merits of plaintiff's claims."

Courts also recognize a "state secrets privilege," which provides that in exceptional circumstances judges must dismiss a case entirely in order to protect state secrets whose disclosure would compromise national security. In 2010, the Ninth Circuit Court of Appeals addressed a case in which the plaintiffs alleged that the CIA used a secret rendition program to transfer suspected terrorists to Egypt, Morocco, and Afghanistan, where they were detained and tortured for information at America's behest.[55] Acknowledging that it faced a "painful conflict between human rights and national security," the court upheld invocation of state secrets and refused even to hear the case.

One of the most significant limits on the Judiciary flows from Article III of the Constitution, which specifies that the "judicial power shall extend" only to "cases" and "controversies." Judges are not free to roam about the landscape, answering questions in the abstract. Rather, they can decide constitutional issues only when presented with a concrete

dispute between parties. This limit, the Court has observed, is "fundamental to the judiciary's proper role in our system of government."[56]

"Standing" is a key element of the "case" or "controversy" requirement. To prove standing—and thus to obtain judicial review—a plaintiff
must meet three criteria: he or she must have suffered (or must imminently face) a "concrete injury," the injury must be traceable to the alleged
illegal action, and the court must be able to redress the injury. The standing doctrine's demand of concrete injury prevents citizens from suing
just because they are offended that the government is not adhering to
their view of the law, or because their taxes are being used to fund what
they regard as illegal activity. It therefore ensures that plaintiffs are motivated to prosecute their cases and that judges decide legal questions only
in the context of real-world problems they are called upon to resolve as
forums of last resort.

As Congressman Dennis Kucinich learned in 2011, standing looms as
an insurmountable hurdle to judicial review of many executive actions.
Relying on both the Constitution and a federal statute to support his claim,
Kucinich filed a suit alleging that Obama had acted illegally in bombing
Libya without legislative approval. A federal judge swiftly dismissed the
case for lack of standing, finding that the congressman had not been sufficiently injured by Obama's actions to challenge them in court.[57]

The Roberts Court's most important foray into standing doctrine
and the war on terrorism occurred in 2013, when it decided *Clapper v.
Amnesty International USA*.[58] Like many other cases still winding their
way through courts across America, *Clapper* involved a challenge to the
federal government's vast post-9/11 expansion of its electronic surveillance programs—specifically, to amendments made to the 1978 Foreign
Intelligence Surveillance Act (FISA).

Those amendments resulted from intense public debate, sparked
mainly by a revelation in 2005 that the Bush administration had carried
out a massive, secret program of warrantless wiretapping.[59] Although
the program's details remain shrouded in mystery, the government has
acknowledged that it allowed the interception of any international communication when one party was located abroad and suspected of affiliat-
ing with Al Qaeda, even if the other party was an American based in the
United States. Following years of dispute over Bush's claim to unilateral
power, and after it became clear that America's evolving surveillance

regime posed questions calling for legislation, Congress passed the FISA Amendments Act in 2008.

The Act conferred sweeping new power on the federal government. It allowed the Attorney General and the Director of National Intelligence—with easily obtained approval from the Foreign Intelligence Surveillance Court—to authorize electronic eavesdropping for up to one year of foreigners reasonably believed to be located outside the United States. This surveillance did not require any showing that the object of the eavesdropping was likely to be involved in any wrongful activity, and it could reach all of the target's communications. The Act did not limit the collection of communications by Americans, so long as the surveillance program was intended to target the foreigners with whom they communicated. As a consequence, the Act allowed surveillance that could easily result in the collection of extensive international communication between targets and United States citizens.

The *Clapper* plaintiffs were journalists, lawyers, and human rights researchers who frequently communicated with foreign clients and sources likely to be targets of surveillance. They alleged two kinds of injury: their electronic communications had likely been intercepted, and their "reasonable fear" of surveillance had forced them to alter their conduct to protect confidentiality. On this basis, they claimed standing to challenge the Act.

Split along ideological lines, the Court showed them the door. Writing for the right-leaning majority, Justice Alito reasoned that a mere risk of exposure to surveillance was too speculative an injury to create standing. In his view, the plaintiffs relied on a "highly attenuated chain of possibilities" but lacked "any evidence that their communications have been monitored." Nor did subjective fear of surveillance, Alito added, constitute a sufficient injury by itself. Absent proof that surveillance was "certainly impending," the plaintiffs could not invoke the jurisdiction of the federal courts to challenge the Act.

In a dissent for the more liberal justices, Breyer criticized Alito's high bar to standing. The plaintiffs, he argued, faced a harm "as likely to take place as are most future events that commonsense inference and ordinary knowledge of human nature tell us will happen." After all, the plaintiffs were engaged in communication with people whom the Act was passed to target, the government had the means and motive to spy on them, and recent history showed that the government had actually eavesdropped on conversations of this sort. To Breyer, *Clapper* was an easy case: "We need only assume that the Government is doing its job (to find out about, and combat, terrorism) in order to conclude that there is a high probability that the Government will intercept at least some electronic communication to which at least some of the plaintiffs are parties." This harm, Breyer concluded, was not "speculative."

Although general beliefs about what it means to be "injured" certainly affected how the justices voted, *Clapper* was ultimately a case about this Court's reluctance, at least so far, to subject America's electronic surveillance regime to judicial review. Alito's opinion painstakingly described all the safeguards in place within the Executive to protect against abuse, strongly hinting that they did quite enough to keep the Executive in check. Invoking the importance of judicial modesty, Alito added that "we have often found a lack of standing in cases in which the Judiciary has been requested to review actions of the political branches in the fields of intelligence gathering and foreign affairs."

By requiring the plaintiffs to prove that they were being spied on under a law whose operation is itself a tightly guarded secret, Alito devised a Catch-22 plainly meant to afford the political branches some breathing room in their intelligence efforts—at least for the time being. The majority might have been worried about the consequences of allowing inexpert courts to pry open these delicate matters in public view, especially when the political branches had already begun reevaluating their policies. Since *Clapper*, of course, that public and political debate has only intensified. The Court may also have hesitated before committing to the creation of new constitutional law to govern foreign electronic surveillance. After all, for long decades, the legal boundaries of such programs have been established mainly by Congress and the Executive, not the Court. The justices therefore lacked both expertise and a well-developed body of precedent to guide their hand. Fully aware that the issue would inevitably return, the majority may have preferred to buy some time—particularly given that the Court is busily creating new and potentially instructive privacy precedents addressing cell phones, text messages, and GPS tracking. In that vein, its decision also ensured that questions about electronic surveillance would percolate in the lower courts and legal academy for a few more years, hopefully yielding greater insight into the doctrinal and policy issues that the Court will eventually need to consider.

These benefits, though, came at a notable price: for at least a few years, the vast surveillance regime at issue in *Clapper* would operate largely beyond the reach of meaningful judicial review. The pressing need for a delicate interbranch balance at the heart of *Boumediene*, it seems, did not sway a majority in *Clapper*.

Still, greater judicial engagement is inevitable. Dozens of new lawsuits, informed by recent National Security Agency disclosures and documents leaked by former NSA contractor Edward Snowden, have been filed. Lower courts have begun to weigh in and have already split in their legal conclusions. It is likely that the Roberts Court will soon confront cases in which even *Clapper*'s high bar for standing is unquestionably cleared. When that time comes, this Court will come face-to-face with the profoundly difficult questions deferred in *Clapper*. Soon enough, the Act will stand or fall.

Each week, the *Washington Post* bestows upon someone the doubtful honor of having had the "Worst Week in Washington." Its regular recipients include the president, senators, cabinet members, and scandal-plagued bureaucrats. On Thursday, June 28, 2012, the prize went to Justice Scalia.[60]

That week marked the end of a bruising term for Scalia. Over his dissents, the Court had bolstered defendants' rights to counsel in plea bargaining and had taken a broad view of how many crack cocaine offenders could benefit from a law reducing mandatory prison terms.[61] After reportedly holding a bare majority, Scalia and his allies had ultimately met with defeat in their effort to strike down the Affordable Care Act.[62] He had also been driven to join Alito's dissent in a decision overturning the Stolen Valor Act, which criminalized lying about the receipt of military honors.[63] In all, Scalia wrote ten dissents that term, leaving him tied with Breyer as chief dissenter.

Arizona v. United States, announced just three days before the Court revealed that it had upheld the ACA, dealt Scalia yet another defeat on an important structural question. Kennedy, joined by Roberts, Ginsburg, Breyer, and Sotomayor, invalidated most of Arizona's controversial immigration statute SB 1070.[64] (Kagan was recused.) Invoking the Constitution's

Supremacy Clause, which provides that federal law shall be the "supreme Law of the Land," the Court concluded that parts of SB 1070 intruded upon a field occupied by federal law or stood as obstacles to its purpose. These sections of SB 1070 were therefore "preempted" and could not stand.

Scalia dissented. Anticipating the tenor of his assault on the Chief's ruling upholding the ACA, Scalia charged that Arizonans "feel themselves under siege by large numbers of illegal immigrants who invade their property, strain their social services, and even place their lives in jeopardy." Yet the federal government, he observed, "does not want to enforce the immigration law as written, and leaves the States' borders unprotected against immigrants whom those laws would exclude." If Arizona could not secure its territory in the face of such glaringly ineffective federal enforcement, Scalia wrote, "we should cease referring to it as a sovereign state." Scalia's strong defense of states' rights was firmly in line with his prior jurisprudence, and his colorful description of what he perceived to be the Court's profound mistake befitted his reputation as a passionate, engaging, and combative rhetorician.

The Supreme Court commentariat, though, was scandalized by the dissent Scalia read from the bench.[65] In a highly unusual turn, he assaulted an executive order that bore no direct legal relationship to the case before the Court: "After this case was argued and while it was under consideration, the Secretary of Homeland Security announced a program exempting from immigration enforcement some 1.4 million illegal immigrants. . . . The President has said that the new program is 'the right thing to do' in light of Congress' failure to pass the administration's proposed revision of the immigration laws. Perhaps it is, though Arizona may not think so. But to say as the Court does, that Arizona contradicts federal law by enforcing applications of federal immigration law that the President declines to enforce boggles the mind."

Why, in a case about whether Arizona had stepped too far into federal turf, was Scalia picking a fight with Obama? On its face, *Arizona* looked like a battle over the balance of state and federal power, not one about the scope of Obama's authority or his wisdom in exercising it.

Indeed, Arizona's main argument was that SB 1070 harmonized with federal law. Two of its provisions made it an offense not to comply with federal immigration law. A third allowed police to arrest, without a warrant, anyone they believed might have committed a deportable offense under federal law. A final provision required state police to make a "reasonable attempt . . . to determine the immigration status" of any person they stopped or arrested when "reasonable suspicion exists that the person is an alien and is unlawfully presented in the United States." (This last section was the only one to survive *Arizona*, but it has since been attacked on the ground that it creates racial discrimination.) In Arizona's view, SB 1070 simply added the weight of state resources to enforcement of federal law and thereby furthered the will of Congress. Arizona was eager to help shoulder this burden, it explained, because unregulated border traffic results in an "epidemic of crime, safety risks, serious property damage, and environmental problems."

The Obama administration, however, rejected Arizona's offer. As Solicitor General Donald Verrilli told the Court, "Congress vested the Executive Branch with the authority and the discretion to make sensitive judgments with respect to aliens, balancing the numerous considerations involved: national security, law enforcement, foreign policy, humanitarian considerations, and the rights of law-abiding citizens and aliens." He added that, under federal law, "the Executive Branch has considerable statutory discretion to decide who may enter and who must leave . . . and when an alien is subject to removal, what considerations might justify allowing her to remain at liberty temporarily, or even to remain in the country permanently." In contrast, Verrilli warned, by focusing single-mindedly on maximum enforcement and mandating that police take action against aliens, Arizona had impermissibly engineered what SB 1070 openly described as a nondiscretionary policy of "attrition through enforcement."

This is where *Arizona* became a case about presidential power. The critical issue before the Court was whether Congress's goals would be frustrated if the President lost his discretion in enforcing the immigration laws. Despite its superficial consistency with federal statutes, would SB 1070 fall because it violated the President's prerogative to decide how vigorously to enforce them? Had Congress meant to make nearly unlimited presidential discretion the law of the land? Like few cases before it, *Arizona* set up a dramatic conflict among the President, the states, and Congress over interaction between the states and the federal government.[66] This clash was all the more important because Congress had repeatedly failed to pass immigration reform. If the Court prohibited states from stepping into that void, presidential policy would control the field.

In *Arizona*, the Court encountered an aspect of presidential power—the power *not* to enforce laws to their fullest extent—that has rocketed to public prominence under Obama.[67] His administration has limited enforcement of anti-drug laws in states where marijuana is legal; avoided seeking mandatory minimums for low-level, nonviolent drug offenders; delayed enforcement of key provisions of the ACA that govern insurers and employers; and decided not to deport undocumented migrants who entered the United States before age sixteen, have lived here for at least five years, and meet other requirements. (It was this last policy that drew Scalia's ire in *Arizona*.)

In op-eds and scholarly works, conservatives have charged Obama with lawlessness, decrying his aggressive use of presidential discretion to pursue liberal policies.[68] To be sure, Obama has been unusually explicit in his embrace of non-enforcement powers, and he has used them in new and aggressive ways. These questions, though, cut across both sides of the partisan aisle: for decades, liberals have sounded alarms about under-enforcement by Republican administrations of laws governing consumer safety, the environment, and a range of business practices.

Presidential decisions not to enforce laws that regulate private conduct justifiably inspire strong feelings.[69] (Decisions not to enforce laws that regulate the Executive itself are a whole different beast.) In some cases, this discretion is unavoidable: the reach of federal law vastly exceeds available enforcement resources. As a result, the President must establish priorities, some of which will inevitably reflect his beliefs about what kind of enforcement makes the world better or suits his political goals. Further, the President may sometimes conclude that he best fulfills a law's letter and spirit by not enforcing it. As Judge Brett Kavanaugh of the D.C. Circuit has observed, "One of the great unilateral powers a President possesses under the Constitution . . . is the power to protect individual liberty by essentially under-enforcing federal statutes regulating private behavior."[70] Congress, moreover, often intentionally delegates broad discretion to the Executive when instructing it to promulgate and enforce regulations. This makes sense: Congress may prefer to entrust the Executive Branch with the task of producing and implementing complex regulation. It may also wish to pass the political buck.

As Zachary Price warns, however, "by permitting presidents to read laws, both old and new, out of the code, unrestricted enforcement discretion could provide presidents with a sort of second veto, an authority to make law on the ground without asking Congress to revise the law on the books."[71] In extreme cases, the President might destabilize the separation of powers by wielding essentially legislative authority. There may be particular reason to fear this exercise of executive power when Congress is paralyzed, as presidents deprived of substantial legislative achievements feel pressure to use enforcement discretion to orchestrate high-profile victories. Obama, for example, decided to stop deporting certain undocumented migrants who arrived in America as children only after Congress failed to enact that policy in the DREAM Act.

In sum, it would be undesirable and, indeed, impossible to require maximum enforcement of every federal law but dangerous to allow presidents simply to ignore any law they dislike. For the most part, delicate questions about how much a president must enforce particular laws are left to the political process. Out of respect for their own role in the separation of powers, and given the absence of a body of constitutional law on the subject, courts virtually never conclude that the Executive must be ordered to enforce a law. The main exception consists of statutes that expressly dictate or prohibit executive action.

Nonetheless, non-enforcement loomed over *Arizona*. The Court could not control Obama's immigration policy, but its ruling would decide whether states with a view different from his could readjust the enforcement balance. As a result, although *Arizona* technically hinged on a careful parsing of statutory text to determine whether Congress actually meant to provide the President with sole enforcement discretion, the justices turned to fundamental beliefs about presidential power and the role of the states.

In Scalia's view, *Arizona* posed a stark question: "Are the sovereign States at the mercy of the Federal Executive's refusal to enforce the Nation's immigration laws?" As he saw the case, *Arizona* stripped away "a defining characteristic of sovereignty: the power to exclude from the sovereign's territory people who have no right to be there." Worse, according to Scalia, it did so by manufacturing a conflict between federal law and SB 1070, which "applies only to aliens who neither possess a privilege to be present under federal law nor have been removed pursuant to the Federal Government's inherent authority." In a separate dissent, Alito echoed Scalia's concerns, warning that the Court afforded "the Executive unprecedented power to invalidate state laws that do not meet with its approval, even if the state laws are otherwise consistent with federal statutes." This result, Alito cautioned, "is fundamentally at odds with our federal system."

Writing for the majority, Kennedy took a very different view of *Arizona*. Noting that federal law is shot through with "broad discretion exercised by immigration officials," he dwelled on the virtues of such executive power, which "embraces immediate human concerns." As Kennedy remarked, "Unauthorized workers trying to support their families likely pose less danger than alien smugglers or aliens who commit a serious crime." To Kennedy, federal law's grant of discretion to account for these equities conflicted squarely with SB 1070's pedal-to-the-metal vision of state troopers laying down the law. Kennedy also worried that Arizona's policy would come into conflict with the President's constitutional power over foreign affairs: deportations can infuriate allies and cause retaliation against Americans abroad. As Kennedy emphasized, the Constitution entrusts foreign affairs to one president, not fifty states.

Arizona revealed deep schisms between Scalia and Kennedy. Scalia saw a state overwhelmed by undocumented migrants and the burdens they impose, a president using his discretion to make that problem worse, and a national legislature incapable of actually legislating. He could not limit Obama's considerable discretion in telling federal agents when and where to enforce the immigration laws, but Scalia could read federal law to permit Arizonans to protect their sovereign borders.

Kennedy, while acknowledging Arizona's concerns, firmly disagreed with Scalia. To him, there was no unbridgeable gap between the genius of federalism and allowance of presidential discretion to achieve humanitarian and foreign policy goals. His opinion celebrated "the stories, talents, and lasting contributions of those who crossed oceans and deserts to come here." Relating the tale of "a dozen immigrants" who "stood before the tattered flag that inspired Francis Scott Key to write the National Anthem" and "took the oath to become American citizens," Kennedy remarked that they "now share a common destiny." But even as he confirmed federal authority—which in this case mainly belonged to the Executive—Kennedy offered an important reminder. "With power," he wrote, "comes responsibility, and the sound exercise of national power over immigration depends on the Nation's meeting its responsibility to base its laws on a political will informed by searching, thoughtful, rational civic discourse."

The Executive Branch has thus scored some major victories in the Roberts Court. But although the President of the United States is one of the most powerful figures on earth, our government is too big, complex, and fast-moving for a mere mortal to call every shot, even a mortal imbued by Article II with "the executive Power." The endless network of laws and regulations that govern the country are well beyond the ken of raw presidential authority. The President therefore sits atop a vast bureaucratic edifice, comprising hundreds of agencies and thousands of offices.

Because the federal bureaucracy wields so much power, a question naturally arises: who will check and balance it?[72] Some may find it comforting that squads of experts are watching over us, nudging our decisions, and regulating critical industries. Justice Breyer, for one, is famously enthusiastic about the promise of expertise: "Without delegation to experts, an inexpert public, possessing the will, would lack the way."[73] But others look skeptically on the notion that experts are particularly good at making decisions that often involve political or value-laden judgments. They doubt the legitimacy of delegating so much power to bureaucrats and see in unaccountable government agencies a creeping threat to liberty.

Over the past few decades, these anxieties have prompted many leading conservative thinkers to call for greater presidential control over federal agencies.[74] One might suppose that presidents already enjoy plenty of authority over their own branch, and sometimes they do, but lines of control are complex and unstable. As Bill Clinton joked, "Being president is like running a cemetery: you've got a lot of people under you and nobody's listening."[75] Presidents, after all, have a lot of competition for control over agency policy. Congress and the Judiciary each have tools of influence, regulated and affected parties heavily lobby regulators, and agency staffs often have their own agendas. This contest plays out in many ways: the President hires and fires officials, the Senate refuses to confirm nominees, Congress curbs agency powers or cuts their funding, and courts strike down agency action as arbitrary and capricious.

The justices are exquisitely sensitive to this struggle for power. They live and breathe it. As professors, Scalia, Breyer, and Kagan specialized in administrative law. Ginsburg, Thomas, Roberts, and Scalia all served on the D.C. Circuit, which decides many appeals from agency action. And the Court's docket is loaded with high-profile challenges to federal regulations, requiring every justice to develop serious expertise.

In 2010, Roberts and Breyer clashed over presidential control of agencies in a case called *Free Enterprise Fund v. PCAOB*.[76] Their opinions swept broadly and provide a revealing glimpse into how each justice views our constitutional design.

After the Enron and WorldCom accounting scandals, Congress passed the Sarbanes-Oxley Act to tighten the standards governing all U.S. public company boards and accounting firms. This Act created the Public Company Accounting Oversight Board—the PCAOB, a.k.a. Peekaboo—to regulate the accounting industry, investigate registered firms, and sanction lawbreakers. The five members of the PCAOB were appointed by the SEC and could be removed by the SEC only "for good cause." In turn, SEC commissioners—by custom, not by statutory language—could be removed by the President only due to "inefficiency, neglect of duty, or malfeasance in office."

In *PCAOB*, the Court had to decide whether this dual insulation, which meant that the President could never directly remove a member of the PCAOB, even for good cause, violated the separation of powers. Emotions ran high over this seemingly obscure question because the President's firing power has long been treated as one of the most important sources of his ability to control the bureaucracy. Split five to four, the Court struck down the PCAOB good-cause removal provision.

Writing for the Court and quoting Article II, Roberts grounded his opinion in the importance of formal control: "The President cannot 'take Care that the Laws be faithfully executed' if he cannot oversee the faithfulness of the officers who execute them. . . . Neither the President, nor anyone directly responsible to him, nor even an officer whose conduct he may review only for good cause, has full control over the [PCAOB]." Invoking the image of a Russian nesting doll, he explained that "the officers of such an agency—safely encased with a Matryoshka doll of tenure protections—would be immune from Presidential oversight, even as they exercised power in the people's name." He added, "The diffusion of power carries with it diffusion of accountability."

Laying bare his motivating concern, Roberts expressed deep unease with the modern administrative state: "Where, in all this, is the role for oversight by an elected President? . . . One can have a government that functions without being ruled by functionaries, and a government that benefits from expertise without being ruled by experts. Our Constitution was adopted to enable the people to govern themselves, through their elected leaders. The growth of the Executive Branch, which now wields vast power and touches almost every aspect of daily life, heightens the concern that it may slip from the Executive's control, and thus from that of the people."

In the end, Roberts saw *PCAOB* as a case about liberty. Only if agencies are held to account, he warned, can we thwart creeping bureaucratic tyranny. Thus, "the Constitution that makes the President accountable to the people for executing the laws also gives him the power to do so," including the ability to fire agency officials. To Roberts, the Constitution's structure simply requires that the President enjoy certain formal authority—in this case, the power to fire without an intermediary.

PCAOB was not a one-off ruling. The Chief's concern about unsupervised bureaucrats runs deep. It dates back at least as far as the 1980s. In his formative years as a young lawyer, Roberts worked at the White House Counsel's Office and in the Department of Justice during the Reagan administration. Eager to advance the deregulatory agenda Reagan had been elected to pursue, many administration attorneys were infuriated by the need to engage in trench warfare with their own agencies, which were staffed mainly by liberals hostile to Reagan's program. This insubordination led more than a few of Reagan's attorneys to believe that the Constitution's design prohibits any such rogue fourth branch of government and that presidential power over agencies is the best antidote to a dearth of democratic accountability.[77] Working in the Reagan administration, Roberts generally pushed a broad view of executive authority.[78] He then spent a decade practicing law in Washington, where he developed a reputation as a skilled advocate for reduced government regulation.[79] As the *New York Times* noted in a review of the Chief's brief tenure as a judge on the D.C. Circuit, from 2003 to 2005, Roberts had an "eye for the absurd and an impatience with bureaucracy."[80]

That perspective has been unwavering. In 2013, for example, Roberts wrote a dissent in which he pushed for a rule that would give the Judiciary a lot more power to review and reverse agency action. His opinion looked skeptically on our "headless fourth branch of government" and quoted Harry Truman's biting remark: "I thought I was the president, but when it comes to these bureaucrats, I can't do a damn thing."[81]

In that dissent, Roberts also reiterated his concern about the inadequacy of checks and balances by the political branches: "The citizen confronting thousands of pages of regulations—promulgated by an agency directed by Congress to regulate, say, 'in the public interest'—can perhaps be excused for thinking that it is the agency really doing the legislating. And with hundreds of federal agencies poking into every nook and cranny of daily life, that citizen might also understandably question whether Presidential oversight—a critical part of the Constitutional plan—is always an effective safeguard against agency overreaching." With characteristically dry humor, Roberts observed, "It would be a bit much to describe the result as 'the very definition of tyranny,' but the danger posed by the growing power of the administrative state cannot be dismissed."

PCAOB reflects the Chief's skepticism of politically unaccountable bureaucrats. It also displays a wariness of pragmatic arguments that purport to justify new institutional arrangements that do not conform to the Constitution's formal separation of powers. Roberts has long voiced this concern. As he tartly observed in the 1980s when Congressman Elliott Levitas proposed a conference on power sharing between the political branches: "There already has, of course, been a 'Conference on Power Sharing' to determine 'the manner of power sharing and accountability within the federal government.' It took place in Philadelphia's Constitution Hall in 1787, and someone should tell Levitas about it and the 'report' it issued."[82]

The key question, of course, is what *PCAOB* portends for the future.[83] The ruling says much about Roberts's views of the separation of powers, and thus suggests the direction in which he may try to take the Court. But will it change much on the ground? The Chief's opinion was typically cautious. Even as the Court fired this warning shot, it rejected broader challenges to the design of the PCAOB. Some commentators suggested that this victory was little more than "symbolic." They saw it as ironic that the Court, in the name of enhancing presidential power, had done little more than give a different agency with its own powerful constituency—the SEC—even greater control over the PCAOB. As former Solicitor General Paul Clement remarked, "I cannot quite decide whether it is an important separation-of-powers decision that portends a major doctrinal shift in the court's approach to separation-of-powers issues or a nothing-burger that does not provide any meaningful relief even to the parties that challenged the law."[84]

Breyer entertained few doubts about *PCAOB*'s importance. The greatest ally of government agencies, Breyer spent much of his pre-judicial career advising the Senate Judiciary Committee, writing influential articles on the administrative state, and serving on the U.S. Sentencing Commission. Breyer starts with the premise that our Constitution creates, as he puts it, a "workable democracy—a democratic process capable of acting for the public good," and he believes that it is the Court's obligation to make democracy work.[85] In separation of powers cases, he cares about function over form: in light of our politics and the need for checks and balances, he asks, does the arrangement make sense?

The Chief's opinion in *PCAOB* represented everything Breyer opposes in constitutional law, so Breyer pushed back, hard. "The statute does not significantly interfere with the President's 'executive Power,'" he wrote. "It violates no separation-of-powers principle. And the Court's contrary holding threatens to disrupt severely the fair and efficient administration of the laws."

Describing the reach of federal law, Breyer emphasized that, "given the nature of the Government's work, it is not surprising that administrative units come in many different shapes and sizes." Because of this diversity, he reasoned, the Constitution recognizes "the various ways presidential power operates." Such a pragmatic approach doesn't treat presidential power to fire as the sine qua non of control over agencies. Instead, it acknowledges that, "as human beings have known ever since Ulysses tied himself to the mast so as safely to hear the Sirens' song, sometimes it is necessary to disable oneself in order to achieve a broader objective." By freeing bureaucrats from political control, Breyer reasoned, we can enhance their legitimacy and credibility as technocrats and neutral arbiters.

Rejecting the view that power is "always susceptible to the equations of elementary arithmetic," Breyer articulated a different approach. "A rule that takes power from a President's friends and allies may weaken him," Breyer wrote, while "a rule that takes power from the President's opponents may strengthen him." As Kagan explained to her colleagues at argument, "removal is just a tool," and the ultimate constitutional question is the level of presidential control over agencies. Pointing to the overwhelming support for Sarbanes-Oxley in Congress and Obama's support for the PCAOB, Breyer noted that the political branches didn't seem to find this arrangement worrisome. Nor should they, he added, since in the real world no president has ever "actually sought to exercise" removal power "by testing the scope of a 'for cause' provision." To drive home his point, Breyer then offered a detailed account of why, as a practical matter, the "double-layer" limit on removal would never actually impede a president from exercising sufficient control over the PCAOB.

Concluding an opinion that perfectly embodied his pragmatic approach to the separation of powers, Breyer warned against the Chief's determined focus on structural formalities. "In my view the Court's decision is wrong—very wrong. . . . It will create an obstacle, indeed pose a serious threat, to the proper functioning of that workable Government that the Constitution seeks to create."

Despite the brilliance of Breyer's argument, no one can predict whether *PCAOB* will ultimately make much difference in how government actually works. The ruling's importance lies in the mood of distrust it expresses more than in the way it rearranges authority. As Breyer's dissent demonstrated, it isn't the formal statutory terms governing the removal of bureaucrats that determine how either they or the President will operate. Despite the name we give their discipline, the best political scientists know that politics is more art than science. They understand that the dynamics of power are too subtle to be cabined by the geometry of an organization chart or mapped by the vectors in a flow diagram. For that reason, among many others, the Court's decisions about the separation of powers are often more important for what they teach than for what they do. What Justice Louis D. Brandeis once said of government as a whole is true of the Court as well: it is "the potent, the omnipresent teacher. For good or ill, it teaches the whole people by its example."[86]

7

PRIVACY:

WHAT HAVE YOU GOT TO HIDE?

"Nine scorpions in a bottle."[1]

This classic description of the Court in the mid-twentieth century—borrowed by a recent biographer[2]—is singularly apt. As America spun from crisis to crisis in the years after World War II, its highest court stood fractured by bitter personal rivalries, ideological conflict, and political maneuvering. In 1953, when Chief Justice Fred Vinson died halfway through stalled deliberations in *Brown v. Board of Education*, leaving open a seat soon filled by Earl Warren, Justice Felix Frankfurter confided that Vinson's passing was "the first solid piece of evidence I've ever had that there really is a God."[3] Thrown together by the politics of appointments, the midcentury justices seethed and struggled inside the Marble Palace. Scorpions, indeed.

Ours is an age of comparative harmony. Justice Kagan won immediate goodwill on the Court by acquiring a frozen yogurt machine, and she now jokes that she will forever be remembered as "the frozen yogurt justice."[4] When Justice Alito first arrived, Justice Breyer arranged a celebratory dinner and invited a special guest from Alito's hometown baseball team.[5] "He opened the door," Alito recalls, "and the Phillie Phanatic came in and gave me a big hug. And it was great." Justice Ginsburg, soft-spoken and steely, is famously close with brash and wisecracking Justice Scalia—a friendship grounded in their love of opera and shared sense of humor. As Ginsburg fondly admits, Scalia "is one of the few people in the world who can make me laugh."[6]

Still, the Roberts Court isn't all flowers and hugs. The justices may be friendly, but they are also fierce and competitive participants in a struggle to define the Constitution. Each was carefully chosen by a president who sought a gladiator to champion particular ideals, whether through sheer force of intellect or the subtler arts of persuasion. Collegiality and compromise enjoy an important role on the Court, but it is ultimately a limited one. A shifting matrix of alliances, betrayals, and bitter defeats quickly teaches new arrivals that no vote can ever be taken for granted. Although ours is not an age of scorpions, the Court is still rife with intrigue and power struggles.

That drama unfolds awkwardly in a semitransparent institution. The image of scorpions in a bottle evokes both painful claustrophobia and an intrusive public eye, and in this way the metaphor applies to every era of the Court. In our Internet age more than ever, though, the justices carefully calibrate how much information they willingly reveal to outsiders. Some of these safeguards reflect principles of fairness: it wouldn't do to permit anyone to profit politically or financially by obtaining advance notice of how cases will be decided. Other policies protect the integrity of the Court's deliberative process: if the first round of tentative votes were announced, or if all deliberations were thrown open to the public, the justices might feel less willing to speak freely or change their minds. Still other privacy rules are meant to protect the Court's reputation and the justices' personal lives.

Nowhere are these concerns more pronounced than in the debate about whether to allow cameras in the courtroom. Despite vehement criticism by journalists and legislators, most justices firmly oppose televising oral arguments.[7] Aware that recordings could be manipulated or distorted, some of them see little benefit to cameras—and great potential for mischief. Justice Sotomayor has warned that "very few [viewers] understand what the process is, which is to play devil's advocate,"[8] and Scalia has bluntly insisted that "it will misinform the public . . . to have our proceedings televised."[9] Ever protective of judicial integrity, Justice Kennedy has explained why he views cameras as dangerous: "Our dynamic works. The discussions that the justices have with the attorneys during oral arguments is a splendid dynamic. If you introduce cameras, it is human nature for me to suspect that one of my colleagues is saying something for a soundbite. Please don't introduce that insidious dynamic into what is now a collegial court."[10] Kennedy added that the Court's policy sends a considered message about its role: "We teach, by having no cameras, that we are different. We are judged by what we write. We are judged over a much longer term. We're not judged by what we say."

Cameras also cause the justices to worry about privacy in their personal lives. Justice Thomas, for example, has cautioned that "regular appearances on TV would mean significant changes in the way my colleagues conduct their lives."[11] Referring to his bruising confirmation fight, he elaborated, "My anonymity is already gone, [and] it's already affected the way I conduct my own life. But for some of my colleagues, they've not yet lost that anonymity."

The Court's formal policies make up only part of the justices' choices about how to go about their lives outside their sanctum. During the summer recess, Thomas likes to tour the nation with his family in a forty-foot customized RV, camping out at Walmarts and stopping to watch NASCAR races. Scalia mixes old-fashioned hunting trips with an active and battle-ready presence on the national lecture circuit. Breyer and Scalia have both published popular works of legal theory, while Sotomayor and Thomas have offered intensely personal accounts of their remarkable life stories.[12] Ginsburg has recently taken a star turn, describing her experience as a woman on the Court and speaking out publicly against "one of the most activist courts in history."[13] Alito, in contrast, tends to favor intimate events sponsored by law schools and conservative groups.[14] As every member of the Court knows well, there are many kinds of privacy, ranging from anonymity at the supermarket to shielding one's childhood traumas from public awareness. The justices vary widely in striking the public-private balance that works for them as individuals.

Sometimes, however, a justice is forced roughly into open view. Confirmation hearings involve merciless investigation of every aspect of a nominee's life, from temperament to sexual orientation. Near the end of many presidencies, politically motivated calls for one justice or another to resign prompt invasive questioning into justices' health and future plans. Unpopular judicial decisions can trigger public denunciations, ranging from mild editorials to burnings in effigy. In 2006, after Justice David Souter joined an opinion upholding a government confiscation of private property, radical conservatives forced a vote in Weare, New Hampshire, on whether to seize Souter's beloved farmhouse.[15] Their efforts to forcibly convert his home into what they dubbed the "Lost Liberty Hotel" failed, but they brought the prying eye of the media into Souter's private life. Baseless calls for Thomas and Kagan to recuse themselves in the *Health Care Case* triggered inquiries into Kagan's e-mail correspondence at the Department of Justice and political activities by Thomas's wife.[16]

If privacy at the Court can be elusive, the same is increasingly true for many Americans. We live in the era of the PATRIOT Act; sweeping electronic surveillance by the National Security Agency; the collection of massive amounts of consumer information by such companies as Google, Amazon, and Facebook; GPS tracking, data mining, spy satellites, thermal sensors, and drones; and smartphones, navigators, and household appliances that chart our every movement. Privacy is not what it used to be. At times, it seems like a casualty of technology.

The Roberts Court has only just begun to mark the outlines of what the Constitution will (or will not) say about twenty-first-century privacy. In cases involving DNA databases, drug-sniffing dogs, GPS tracking of cars, and text messages, it has adopted a cautious approach to our brave new world. Aware that privacy's older paradigms need to be updated or replaced, the Court has rendered narrow rulings on broad issues, buying time to reflect before it directly confronts the big questions.

True to form, Scalia has sought a rebirth of originalist approaches to privacy law; at nearly every turn, though, he has been opposed by Alito, who has focused on evolving societal expectations and the role the other branches of government should play in policing the police. Sotomayor, willing to reconsider foundational precedents and more open to an active judicial role, has emerged as an eloquent champion of privacy's importance. Kagan and Kennedy, in contrast, have preferred to acknowledge the demands of modernity while avoiding firm commitments to particular reforms. All of the justices, though, have made clear their intense interest in these still-evolving debates. As Kagan observed in 2013, privacy issues are "a growth industry for the court."[17]

At the Roberts Court, the Constitution's uncertain role in protecting our privacy is up for grabs. And as the justices struggle inside their bottle to craft law adequate to the needs of this era, our national values hang in the balance.

———

The Fourth Amendment protects "the right of the people to be secure in their persons, houses, papers, and effects" against "unreasonable searches and seizures." Atop this slender reed, the Court has built an enormously complex system of rules designed to protect certain kinds of privacy from unjustified government invasion.[18] Many of these rules are of recent vintage: only in the twentieth century did the Court embrace a broad vision of the Fourth Amendment. This ongoing project remains bedeviled by hard questions about what privacy means, how it stacks up against competing values, and what role courts should play in protecting it.

Privacy takes many forms.[19] Among other things, it consists of secrecy and solitude, but it also transcends them. It covers control over our bodies, reputations, and personal information. It ebbs and flows in different settings, waxing in our homes and waning in public. It varies wildly from culture to culture, and across history and social groups within cultures. Its meaning can change with evolving social expectations, even as the kinds of privacy we experience shape the views we come to hold. Despite its shifting shape, five aspects of the right to privacy provide crucial context to the Roberts Court's central Fourth Amendment rulings.

First and foremost, the right to privacy is a social right. It isn't only about secrecy, which involves the complete refusal to share something with others. Privacy also encompasses decisions about what to share, whom to share it with, and when and how to share it. This sort of selective control over personal information is profoundly important: just imagine if your coworkers knew everything about you that your parents know, or if your credit card company shared your files with a first date. Even in an age of indiscriminate sharing on social media sites such as Facebook, each of us tries to maintain informational boundaries that only certain other people can cross. Trusting someone with our innermost thoughts, feelings, and experiences is the surest foundation for establishing and defining relationships—ranging from our most casual acquaintances to our deepest love. The right to limit the group of people entrusted with our personal information is therefore directly related to the right to flourish in society.

Second, the right to privacy includes the right to establish our own identity, to emphasize the accomplishments and attributes we care most about. Are you a gay NBA star or an NBA star who happens to be gay? Or someone who doesn't tell anyone about his sexuality? The basketball player Jason Collins explained his own dilemma in an open letter published in *Sports Illustrated*: "I'm a 34-year-old NBA center. I'm black. And I'm gay. . . . I wish I wasn't the kid in the classroom raising his hand and saying, 'I'm different.' If I had my way, someone else would have already done this. Nobody has, which is why I'm raising my hand."[20] What we tell others—and how and when and why we do so—is intimately related to how we think about ourselves. The creation of our own identities is impossible without a measure of privacy. Often, we make self-discoveries only at the moment we vocalize them. The right to shape our identity is thus nothing less than the right to control the course of our lives.

The right to privacy encompasses, third, the right to leave our past behind and experiment with different futures. We have all made mistakes, from a hastily written e-mail to youthful indiscretions to substance abuse. As Alexander Solzhenitsyn once wrote, "Everyone is guilty of something or has something to conceal. All one has to do is look hard enough to find what it is."[21] Privacy lets us escape the suffocating weight of these missteps, to reinvent ourselves and be judged as the people we are, not the individuals we once were. Alexander Pope thought that "to err is human; to forgive, divine,"[22] but respect for privacy is itself a form of societal forgiveness that shouldn't depend on divine intervention. It is also a principle on which any open society depends. When our every move is recorded and cataloged, innovation and experimentation suffer; behavior turns toward the mainstream and conformity seems the safest path. The knowledge that our past will not haunt us forever is liberating. It helps unleash the whimsical, radical, and generative energies essential to democratic culture and economic innovation.

Fourth, the right to privacy is the guardian of many other rights. The religious need it to pursue their faith. Political activists need it to hone their arguments and plan their protests. Academics need privacy to bounce wild ideas off students, and businesses need it to test new products. We all need privacy to figure out what we care about, what upsets us, and what turns us on. The Court recognized this deep connection in 1969 when it held that the possession of obscenity in the privacy of one's home is protected as a facet of broader personal freedoms.[23] "Our whole constitutional heritage," Justice Thurgood Marshall wrote, "rebels at the thought of giving government the power to control men's minds." Life under constant surveillance is incompatible with full enjoyment of our liberties.

Finally, the right to privacy is a requirement of democracy. When none of us can be certain what the state knows about us or how it might use that information, the relationship between the governed and the government is fundamentally altered. The state's unlimited access to whatever information it wishes to obtain about each citizen can create a profound power imbalance and feeling of vulnerability. As Justice Robert Jackson once wrote of searches and seizures, "Among deprivations of rights, none is so effective in cowing a population, crushing the spirit of the individual and putting terror in every heart."[24] This is especially true when the state develops the ability to combine many small pieces of data into a full picture of our lives. Even if we trust the state not to abuse the information and search only for true threats, the risk that our vast intelligence bureaucracy will make an egregious error is unavoidable. Entirely innocent personal information can be abused, leaked, distorted, and put to mischievous use in unpredictable ways. Without protection of privacy, democratic life could suffer a dangerous chill.

As the Roberts Court knows, privacy is vital but delicate. Every major technological breakthrough of the twentieth century prompted warnings of privacy's demise. Offering a measure of perspective, Deborah Nelson has remarked, "Privacy, it seems, is not merely dead. It is dying over and over again."[25] Yet it is no exaggeration to say that privacy is now threatened as never before. We are studied by government, political campaigns, universities, and retailers. We share detailed information with sites like Twitter, Facebook, Tumblr, Google, and OkCupid. Our smartphones and Kindles create records of our habits. Drones, closed-circuit cameras, and thermal sensors reveal what was once hidden. Analysts create ever more powerful tools for discovering useful patterns in seemingly isolated fragments of information. The world imagined by George Orwell in *1984* seems more and more possible: "Always the eyes watching you. . . . Asleep or awake, working or eating, indoors or out of doors, in the bath or in bed—no escape. Nothing was your own except the few cubic centimetres inside your skull."[26]

New technologies also mean that our personal information is of interest to a large number of actors who have many ways of obtaining it. As the *New York Times* reported in 2012, "Almost every major retailer, from grocery chains to investment banks to the U.S. Postal Service, has a 'predictive analytics' department devoted to understanding not just consumers' shopping habits but also their personal habits, so as to more efficiently market to them."[27] The national retailer Target, for example, has reportedly assigned many of its shoppers an individual code, which it uses to track age, marital status, hometown, estimated salary, favorite websites, and job history. Through information traders, Target also has access to data about ethnicity, magazine preferences, favorite coffee brands, political leanings, and charitable giving—all of which allows the company to identify and appeal to key demographics, such as new parents, by sending timely special offers. Each of us now receives a level of personal surveillance that, in decades past, was reserved for national figures like the justices.

But the right to privacy cannot be considered in a vacuum, because it is in constant competition with other values.[28] A free flow of data supports entrepreneurship, creativity, and innovation. Limiting others' ability to share our information may infringe on their free speech rights and their control over intellectual property. Expanded surveillance has enhanced local and national security, as terrible crimes are often planned behind closed doors or a veil of anonymity. Facebook's privacy settings offer limited protection, but it is now easier than ever before to develop, maintain, and rekindle relationships all over the world. Access to information about us allows retailers and politicians to target their messages more effectively, scholars to better understand society, and government to more capably provide social services. By voluntarily sharing personal data with companies from eBay to Apple, we obtain personalization and convenience. While informational privacy doesn't always come at the cost of security, efficiency, or convenience, that trade-off has become a fixture of American life.

In that dynamic, individuals are not always, or even often, the key players. Though it's up to us whether to "like" posts on Facebook or confess secrets on Twitter, we have no choice but to leave a revealing trail of information—about where we go, whom we see, what we say, and how we spend our money. Each of us is regularly matched to medical, cell phone, bank, insurance, Social Security, and tax records. Benjamin Franklin once remarked that "three can keep a secret, if two of them are dead,"[29] but now even a single person must struggle to retain privacy.

Indeed, in the modern world, privacy rarely exists by default.[30] Instead, privacy is the product of myriad choices made by individuals, businesses, and governments about how to organize access to information. If you give the clerk at Old Navy your phone number, who else gets it? Will Google resist government requests for your e-mail records? Can the police use the GPS in your iPhone to track your movements? Decisions about these kinds of issues are governed by an overlapping network of rules that include corporate privacy policies, state and federal laws and regulations, and "new governance" schemes in which private businesses partner with governments to share information. Especially in the corporate and national security fields, many of these privacy rules are themselves secret—though, as the National Security Agency learned in 2013, few programs remain hidden forever.[31] Even when secret, the rules governing privacy rarely aim to provide either total confidentiality or unlimited access. Rather, they specify what requirements must be met to invade certain aspects of our privacy, how information can be used, and whether to permit transparency and accountability. To see this balancing act at work, just check the privacy policy on your next online purchase—if you can manage to read the fine print and fathom its meaning.

Courts play a limited, but important, role in protecting our right to privacy from the government. For instance, when Congress, the states, or other regulators haven't imposed specific limits, the police are restricted mainly by the Fourth Amendment. Since there are only a handful of statutes and regulations that protect our privacy, and since many of them are badly out of date, the first issue about questionable police conduct is often whether it constituted a "search" or "seizure."[32] If so, the Fourth Amendment is triggered and the officers' conduct must be "reasonable."

Reasonableness, often described as the touchstone of the Fourth Amendment, is determined by an intricate series of context-sensitive rules. These doctrines govern what level of police suspicion justifies a particular type of search, when a judicially approved warrant is required, when a type of search is deemed unreasonable regardless of the specific circumstances, how searches must be executed, and a lot more. Failure to comply with these rules is risky: any evidence discovered during a search later determined to be unreasonable may be subject to suppression in court, and in some cases the officers may be vulnerable to a civil rights suit. The Fourth Amendment thus keeps the government and its agents accountable and imposes boundaries on searches that might otherwise allow the police to indiscriminately rummage through people's lives.

But the Fourth Amendment shields only certain kinds of privacy from invasion by particular actors. It doesn't affect the conduct of private businesses, gossipy friends, or even most government practices. As a result, for all their power, judges will never be privacy's savior. Still, the Court's rulings are profoundly important. They express our values and fears, shape social expectations, and sometimes impose robust limits on the government's most far-reaching surveillance activities. At a time when the government's partial secrecy about intelligence programs prevents voters from holding their leaders fully accountable, the Court's pronouncements on the Fourth Amendment are understood as binding even in the darkest caverns of the National Security Agency. Accordingly, the lines the Court draws matter to every one of us—especially since the Roberts Court is in the middle of a foundation-shaking reappraisal of those principles.

Charles Katz liked to gamble. In the 1960s, he made a business of it, with clients in Los Angeles, Miami, and Boston. When he placed bets for them over the phone, though, he violated a federal statute criminalizing interstate wagering by wire. To evade detection, he made most of his calls from a public phone booth. This trick did not succeed. The FBI eventually caught on and attached an electronic listening and recording device to the outside of a booth Katz favored. The federal agents didn't have a warrant, but precedent at the time strongly suggested that they didn't need one. Relying on taped conversations, federal prosecutors successfully convicted Katz. On appeal to the Court, Katz argued that the FBI had violated his Fourth Amendment rights in eavesdropping on his private conversations.

From the outset, it was clear to at least some of the justices that *Katz v. United States* afforded a vehicle to reverse one of the Court's greatest mistakes: *Olmstead v. United States*.[33] Decided in 1928, *Olmstead* held that wiretapping a phone is not a "search" within the meaning of the Fourth Amendment. It reasoned that the Constitution's protections of privacy are limited solely to invasions of personal property. Searches that trigger the Fourth Amendment, therefore, must be of "material things—

the person, the house, his papers, or his effects." A wiretap, the Court argued in *Olmstead*, involves "no entry of the houses or offices of the defendants." Instead, evidence is "secured by the use of the sense of hearing and that only." Under this logic, which pegged privacy protections to property rights, police were free to tap every phone line in America without obtaining a warrant and without even a reasonable basis for suspecting wrongdoing.

Olmstead was wrong the day it was decided, a fact memorialized in one of the Court's greatest dissents. Justice Louis Brandeis warned against a narrow focus on property, explaining that "clauses guaranteeing to the individual protection against specific abuses of power, must have a similar capacity of adaptation to a changing world." Refusing to treat wiretaps as a search made no sense where "discovery and invention have made it possible for the government, by means far more effective than stretching upon the rack, to obtain disclosure in court of what is whispered in the closet."

Writing with the force of prophesy, Brandeis declared that the right to privacy must be conceived in grander terms: "The makers of our Constitution undertook to secure conditions favorable to the pursuit of happiness. They recognized the significance of man's spiritual nature, of his feelings and of his intellect. They knew that only a part of the pain, pleasure and satisfactions of life are to be found in material things. They sought to protect Americans in their beliefs, their thoughts, their emotions and their sensations. They conferred, as against the government, the right to be let alone—the most comprehensive of rights and the right most valued by civilized men. To protect that right, every unjustifiable intrusion by the government upon the privacy of the individual, whatever the means employed, must be deemed a violation of the Fourth Amendment."

Brandeis also dismissed the wiretappers' apparently noble goals: "Experience should teach us to be most on our guard to protect liberty when the government's purposes are beneficent. . . . The greatest dangers to liberty lurk in insidious encroachment by men of zeal, well-meaning but without understanding."

When *Katz* reached the Court in 1967, principles announced in *Olmstead* framed the debate. Katz urged the justices to treat the phone booth as a "constitutionally protected place," subject to all the property-based protections of a house. Placement of the recording device, on that theory, was something akin to a trespass by the government—and thus an action that required a warrant under *Olmstead*.

The Court initially split four to four and seemed resigned to affirming the lower court ruling without any opinion. But after weeks of debate in chambers, a coalition of seven justices voted to overrule *Olmstead* and broadly extend Fourth Amendment coverage. Writing for the majority, Justice Potter Stewart laid down a new rule: "The Fourth Amendment protects people, not places. What a person knowingly exposes to the public, even in his own home or office, is not a subject of Fourth Amendment protection. But what he seeks to preserve as private, even in an area accessible to the public, may be constitutionally protected."

Stewart rejected *Olmstead*'s insistence that the Constitution guards privacy only in certain places, or where we have property rights. Instead, he invoked our expectations of privacy: "The Government stresses the fact that the telephone booth from which the petitioner made his calls was constructed partly of glass. . . . But what he sought to exclude when he entered the booth was not the intruding eye—it was the uninvited ear. . . . One who occupies [a phone booth], shuts the door behind him, and pays the toll that permits him to place a call is surely entitled to assume that the words he utters into the mouthpiece will not be broadcast to the world." In an influential concurrence, Justice John Marshall Harlan framed a two-part test: the Fourth Amendment is triggered when a person has an actual expectation of privacy and society is prepared to view that expectation of privacy as reasonable.

Implicitly linking the First and Fourth Amendments, Stewart added, "To read the Constitution more narrowly is to ignore the vital role that the public telephone has come to play in private communication." Because universal access to unmonitored communication in the 1960s turned mainly on use of public phones, he reasoned, the Constitution must protect privacy in places like phone booths. *Katz* thus recognized that an interplay of changing social norms, technologies, and police needs would shape privacy law.[34]

Katz attracted widespread support because it outlined a fragile middle ground: when individuals expect privacy and society is prepared to view that expectation as reasonable, government intrusions constitute a "search" for Fourth Amendment purposes. Liberals were satisfied that government would not be granted unlimited authority to spy on all its citizens. Conservatives felt confident that the police could continue to investigate crimes effectively. And both groups understood that *Katz* provided a framework for the security-versus-privacy debate without prematurely resolving many of its thorniest issues.

In 1979, faced with one of the most important post-*Katz* questions, the Court dealt a significant blow to the Fourth Amendment's privacy protections. In *Smith v. Maryland*, it held that the installation of a "pen register," which records all numbers dialed from a specific telephone, does not constitute a "search."[35] The Court emphasized that the defendant had every reason to believe that the telephone company knew what numbers he dialed—and thus had no "reasonable expectation of privacy" with respect to that information.

Smith has become central to what is now called the "third-party doctrine," which holds that we typically lose any reasonable expectation of privacy regarding information that we have provided to someone else. Given that our bank, Internet, credit card, cell phone, and GPS records are all available to third parties—many of them private businesses—this doctrine, applied broadly, could devastate modern privacy. And it rests on the counterintuitive theory that, by allowing *particular* third parties to see our information, we lose any expectation of privacy vis-à-vis the government—even though privacy often involves selective disclosure, not pure secrecy. We might want to let American Express or Yahoo know things for particular purposes, but we don't necessarily want that information to get into the hands of Uncle Sam, especially because the government can then freely combine information from many other private actors.[36]

Dissenting in *Smith*, Stewart lambasted the majority for its broad reading of third-party doctrine. He also disagreed with the Court's assertion that the numbers dialed from a private phone, unlike the conversation itself, are without "content." As he explained, "Most private telephone subscribers may have their own numbers listed in a publicly distributed directory, but I doubt there are any who would be happy to have broadcast to the world a list of the local or long distance numbers they have called. This is not because such a list might in some sense be incriminating, but because it easily could reveal the identities of the persons and the places called, and thus reveal the most intimate details of a person's life." This argument has particular modern currency because of debates over the National Security Agency's reliance on *Smith* to justify surveillance of "metadata," which is incisively defined by *Slate*'s Dahlia Lithwick and Georgetown's Steve Vladeck as "the details of when, where, and how we used the Internet—not what we actually read or wrote."[37] However meaningless a single bit of information may seem, metadata can be assembled into an illuminating picture of our lives.[38]

Katz and *Smith* thrust the Court into debates about the uncertain architecture of Fourth Amendment doctrine: what it would protect and how it would respond to changing technology. Since then, a succession of justices has struggled to hammer out rules that apply *Katz* and *Smith* to rapidly evolving circumstances. Over the past few years, the Roberts Court has stepped cautiously into that breach.

At argument, it isn't usually an auspicious sign when a justice describes something bad and asks the government, "Are you saying you can do that to me?" Deputy Solicitor General Michael Dreeben may therefore have felt a pang of foreboding while arguing *United States v. Jones*, a 2012 case about the government's power to attach GPS trackers to cars.[39] Striking to the heart of the matter, Chief Justice Roberts asked, "You think there would also not be a search if you put a GPS device on all of our cars, monitored our movements for a month? You think you're entitled to do that under your theory?" Taken aback, Dreeben asked, "The justices of this Court?" "Yes," Roberts bluntly replied, as nervous laughter filled the courtroom. Driving his point home, the Chief said, "So your answer is yes, you could tomorrow decide that you put a GPS on every one of our cars, follow us for a month; no problem under the Constitution?" Dreeben couldn't deny it.

The government lost in *Jones* by a vote of nine to zero, though the Court split over why the Constitution required that result. The government lost again, one year later, in *Florida v. Jardines*, another major privacy case, this one about when the use of a drug-sniffing dog counts as a search. In *Jardines*, though, the vote was five to four.[40] Both cases fractured the Court in unusual ways, revealing deep divisions about the Fourth Amendment's future. In both cases, Scalia wrote the majority and Alito wrote an opinion disagreeing with Scalia's logic. Also in both, one of

Obama's appointees wrote separately: in *Jones*, Sotomayor proposed far-reaching changes; in *Jardines*, Kagan wrote to limit Scalia's originalist opinion and propose common ground between him and Alito.

Jones was set in motion in 2005, when Antoine Jones, the owner of a nightclub in Washington, D.C., came under suspicion of drug trafficking. Although they lacked a valid warrant, federal agents installed a GPS tracker on the undercarriage of his Jeep. They then spent twenty-eight days tracking the Jeep's every move, including Jones's visit to a cocaine stash house later found to contain ninety-seven kilograms of cocaine, $850,000 in cash, and one kilogram of cocaine base. Relying in part on the GPS data, a jury convicted Jones and a judge sentenced him to life in prison without the possibility of parole.

Jardines followed from an unverified tip to the Miami-Dade Police Department that Joelis Jardines was growing marijuana in his house. Police surveilled the house but could not see anything, so they sent a trained drug-sniffing dog to investigate. As Kagan recounted in her concurrence, "Officers came to Joelis Jardines' door with a super-sensitive instrument, which they deployed to detect things inside that they could not perceive unassisted. The equipment they used was animal, not mineral." That dog, she added, "was not your neighbor's pet, come to your porch on a leisurely stroll . . . [he was] to the poodle down the street as high-powered binoculars are to a piece of plain glass." Franky, the police dog, immediately picked up the scent of marijuana, ran to sniff the home's front door, and then sat down to signal that he smelled drugs. Based on this identification, the police obtained a search warrant that led to the discovery of live marijuana plants. Jardines was charged with drug trafficking. He filed a motion to suppress the evidence, arguing that it had been illegally obtained.

Scalia saw both cases in terms of the link between privacy and property, writing opinions that sounded a lot like *Olmstead*, although he claimed conformity with *Katz*. In *Jones*, joined by Roberts, Kennedy, Thomas, and Sotomayor, Scalia deemed the police conduct a search because the government had placed a GPS tracker on the Jeep. As he explained, "The Government physically occupied private property for the purpose of obtaining information," and "we have no doubt that such a physical intrusion would have been considered a 'search' within the meaning of the Fourth Amendment when it was adopted." In *Jardines*, joined by Thomas, Ginsburg, Sotomayor, and Kagan, Scalia reasoned that the police physically entered a "constitutionally protected area" when they approached the front porch of the house. He added that the police had gathered information by engaging in "conduct not explicitly or implicitly permitted by the homeowner." Whereas few would doubt that police are free to walk up to a front porch, "an invitation to engage in canine forensic investigation assuredly does not inhere in the very act of hanging a knocker."

To Scalia, the attachment of a GPS tracker in *Jones* was a search because it involved a trespass; the conduct in *Jardines* was a search because it exceeded the implied license to enter property for limited purposes. In neither case did Scalia ask the typical post-*Katz* question: did the government's conduct violate reasonable expectations of privacy and thereby constitute a search subject to Fourth Amendment limits? Instead, he looked mainly to centuries-old rules governing property rights.

This was hardly surprising, because Scalia is, first and foremost, a lover of clear rules, tradition, and original understanding. The *Katz* test, which offers a vague and evolving standard for defining Fourth Amendment rights, offends his legal sensibilities. As he noted at argument in *Jones*, "I think that [*Katz*] was wrong. I don't think that was the original meaning of the Fourth Amendment." Conceding that "it's been around for so long, we are not going to overrule that," Scalia has nonetheless made clear his determination to ensure, at the very least, that *Katz* doesn't end up depriving us of privacy rights promised by the framers. It is not difficult to imagine how that might happen: given the intrusive new technologies now available to both business and government, our reasonable expectations of privacy could drop below a baseline that would have been taken for granted in the 1790s.

As usual, Scalia didn't trust judges to keep a steady eye on their compass while searching for clear lines in the shifting sands of modernity. Without a firm rule—such as the one he offers in *Jones*—how are we to know when around-the-clock GPS tracking has gone too far? And what if, by frequently tracking people this way, the police bring about the expectation that we are never really alone? In Scalia's view, the Constitution imposes limits on the government apart from what the public expects or even desires: "We must assure preservation of that degree of privacy against government that existed when the Fourth Amendment was adopted." *Katz* may add to our privacy rights, Scalia declared, but it may not subtract. An originalism-based approach keyed to physical intrusions on protected areas always provides a constitutional minimum.[41]

In a separate concurrence joined by Ginsburg, Breyer, and Kagan, Alito echoed Scalia's doubts about *Katz*: "The *Katz* test rests on the assumption that this hypothetical reasonable person has a well-developed and stable set of privacy expectations. But technology can change those expectations." Citing articles entitled "The End of Privacy" and "Everything About You Is Being Tracked—Get Over It," Alito conceded that *Katz* can cause privacy rights to vary either up or down, as technology evolves.

Alito's agreement with Scalia, however, extended no further. Alito especially objected to Scalia's reliance on history to save privacy's future. In general, he views Scalia's originalism as quaint and blind to modern developments. (Scalia, in turn, views Alito's preference for a cautious balancing of constitutional values and technological trends to be dangerously uncertain and insensitive to the preservation of our rights.) Thus, in *Jones*, Alito's Burkean instincts rebelled at Scalia's suggestion that there is nothing new under the sun. As Alito put it, whereas Scalia insisted on deciding *Jones* "based on 18th-century tort law," he preferred to "apply the Fourth Amendment's prohibition of unreasonable searches and seizures to a 21st-century surveillance technique." Alito took obvious delight in mocking Scalia's equation of GPS tracking with obsolete police practices: "Is it possible to imagine a case in which a constable secreted himself somewhere in a coach and remained there for a period of time in order to monitor the movements of the coach's owner?" Alito wryly added, "The Court suggests that something like this might have occurred in 1791, but this would have required either a gigantic coach, a very tiny constable, or both—not to mention a constable with incredible fortitude and patience."

Alito also warned that Scalia's property-based approach had little to say about instances of GPS tracking that involve remote activation of built-in GPS systems. This is particularly problematic in light of the third-party doctrine: rather than conducting any kind of physical search, the police could simply call up our phone or car companies to obtain our tracking data from them. Scalia's rule in *Jones* may set a useful floor on some police conduct, but in most cases it probably won't accomplish much.

Rejecting Scalia's property-based approach, Alito argued that the Court should have decided *Jones* on reasonable expectation of privacy grounds. As he freely admitted, this was no easy task. That is why, he explained, it would have been better for Congress to create statutory limits on surveillance: "A legislative body is well situated to gauge changing public attitudes, to draw detailed lines, and to balance privacy and public safety in a comprehensive way." Indeed, given "dramatic technological change," Alito suggested that "the best solution to privacy concerns may be legislative." But in 2012, Congress had not passed such privacy legislation, and Alito had to address the constitutional issue.

In his view, the police had crossed a line: while we don't usually have an expectation of privacy in our public movements, "the use of longer term GPS monitoring in investigations of most offenses impinges on expectations of privacy." For minor offenses like drug trafficking, he reasoned, "society's expectation has been that law enforcement agents and others would not—and indeed, in the main, simply could not—secretly monitor and catalogue every single movement of an individual's car for a very long period." With this statement, Alito embraced a version of what has become known as "mosaic theory"—the notion that, even if individual acts of surveillance, considered independently, do not constitute a search, a cumulative pattern of such acts might trigger the Fourth Amendment.[42] As natural as this may sound, it is a marked departure from prior cases, which have focused on discrete acts of surveillance rather than the whole symphony of government conduct.[43]

Alito suggested in *Jones* that GPS tracking may call for a probing reevaluation of Fourth Amendment rules about the government's freedom to follow our public movements. He is not alone. As Chief Judge Alex Kozinski of the Ninth Circuit Court of Appeals observed in 2010, "A small law enforcement team can deploy a dozen, a hundred, a thousand such devices and keep track of their various movements by computer, with far less effort than was previously needed to follow a single vehicle. . . . There's no hiding from the all-seeing network of GPS satellites that hover overhead, which never sleep, never blink, never get confused and never lose attention."[44] These tools trouble some judges not only because they are readily available, but also because they are uniquely revealing. The New York State Court of Appeals thus warned in 2009, "Disclosed in the data retrieved ... [will be trips] to the psychiatrist, the plastic surgeon, the abortion clinic, the AIDS treatment center, the strip club, the criminal defense attorney, the by-the-hour motel, the union meeting, the mosque, synagogue or church, the gay bar and on and on."[45] This technology thus yields a full picture of our lives. As Breyer remarked at oral argument in *Jones*, if "there is nothing to prevent the police or the government from monitoring 24 hours a day the public movement of every citizen of the United States ... you suddenly produce what sounds like 1984." Kozinski put it even more bluntly—and personally: "There is something creepy and un-American about such clandestine and under-handed behavior. To those of us who have lived under a totalitarian regime, there is an eerie feeling of déjà vu."

Mosaic theory approaches to the Fourth Amendment, however, are hard to put into practice.[46] When does the sum total of a surveillance program become a search? Does the amount of surveillance constituting a search vary with the seriousness of the crime being investigated? When police conduct a search under the framework of this theory, do they need a warrant, or will some lesser showing of suspicion suffice? More broadly, how can the police be expected to protect the public adequately when they are guided by such vague rules?

In *Jones*, Alito dodged the thorny issues of formulating a clear judicial approach to the burgeoning threat of comprehensive GPS tracking. The government's four-week, warrantless surveillance of Antoine Jones, he concluded, "surely crossed" the line and, for Fourth Amendment purposes, constituted a search. Alito was content to mark that boundary and reserve for the future "more difficult questions."

Jones evidenced Alito's taste for a slow and cautious approach that links constitutional law to our society's shifting expectations and values. His opinion dotes on the details of new technology, portraying them with a mix of awe and worry. Alito does not seem perturbed, in general, by weaker privacy protections; he dissented in *Jardines*, seeing no search in the police deploying Franky to sniff for drugs. But he cares deeply about the Court's institutional role in managing our transition toward a world in which privacy looks very different. And he is willing to undertake the daunting task of altering Fourth Amendment law—slowly and carefully—to keep it in step with the times.

While Alito dissented in *Jardines*, Scalia's majority divided against itself. In a separate writing joined by Ginsburg and Sotomayor, Kagan distanced herself from Scalia's property-based majority opinion. As she explained, "The Court today treats this case under a property rubric; I write separately to note that I could just as happily have decided it by looking to Jardines' privacy interests. A decision along those lines would have looked . . . well, much like this one." She added, "It is not surprising that in a case involving a search of a home, property concepts and privacy concepts should so align." After all, "the sentiment 'my home is my own,' while originating in property law, now also denotes a common understanding—extending even beyond that law's formal protections— about an especially private sphere."

Kagan rarely writes separately and does so only with clear goals in mind. In *Jardines*, it's likely that she wanted to ensure that Scalia's rekindling of originalism and property analysis in *Jones* and *Jardines* would not jeopardize *Katz*. When the Court issues enough opinions that purport to remain faithful to one way of doing things but actually do something else, there is always a risk that someone will come along and say, "Well, the logic of our recent rulings really does mean that we must adopt a different rule." Plainly concerned that Scalia might try to pull off such a coup d'état, dethroning *Katz* and its emphasis on evolving, reasonable expectations, Kagan strategically deprived him of a proper majority for his *Olmstead*-style reasoning. At the same time, she proposed some common ground for Scalia and Alito in a moment of doctrinal fracture, thus suggesting a possible path toward reconciliation in future privacy cases.

Whereas Kagan concurred in *Jardines* to build common ground, Sotomayor concurred in *Jones* to chart a bold new frontier. Although she provided Scalia with a fifth vote for his majority, she also wrote her most adventuresome opinion yet as a member of the Roberts Court. GPS monitoring, she emphasized, is uniquely dangerous: it "generates a precise, comprehensive record of a person's public movements that reflects a wealth of detail about her familial, political, professional, religious, and sexual associations." She went on to observe that GPS data are searchable, cheap, and surreptitious, and thus "evades the ordinary checks that constrain abusive law enforcement practices." Rejecting a narrow view of privacy, she embraced a rich picture of privacy's essential role in our lives, including its importance to "associational and expressive freedoms" and its effect on "the relationship between citizen and government."

In a bold move, Sotomayor suggested that the Court take all this into account as part of its *Katz* analysis. "I would ask," she elaborated, "whether people reasonably expect that their movements will be recorded and aggregated in a manner that enables the Government to ascertain, more or less at will, their political and religious beliefs, sexual habits, and so on." She added, "I would also consider the appropriateness of entrusting to the Executive, in the absence of any oversight from a coordinate branch, a tool so amenable to misuse, especially in light of the Fourth Amendment's goal to curb arbitrary exercises of police power . . . and prevent a too permeating police surveillance."

Finally, Sotomayor called for reconsideration of the third-party doctrine: "This approach is ill suited to the digital age, in which people reveal a great deal of information about themselves to third parties in the course of carrying out mundane tasks. . . . I would not assume that all information voluntarily disclosed to some member of the public for a limited purpose is, for that reason alone, disentitled to Fourth Amendment protection." In words that seem especially salient in light of recent revelations about government spying, she expressed doubt that "people would accept without complaint the warrantless disclosure to the Government of a list of every Web site they had visited in the last week, or month, or year."

This remarkable opinion plants the seeds of a very different and far more privacy-protective approach to the Fourth Amendment. Sotomayor does more than express abstract fears; she offers thoughtful justifications for judicial intervention. In the world as she imagines it, the warrant requirement—and thus the courts—would play a far greater role in overseeing and legitimizing government efforts to obtain and store our private information, whether for immediate analysis or for later inspection.

Jones and *Jardines* reveal a Court openly dissatisfied with the status quo. No justice even pretended that precedent afforded direct or workable answers to the complex questions prompted by these two cases, and Scalia, Alito, and Sotomayor offered very different ideas about how best to respond. When the Roberts Court does choose a path forward, its rulings will undoubtedly redefine the contours of our relationship with the government and the meaning of American privacy.

It could have been an episode from the television show *Cold Case*. In 2003, a man broke into a woman's home in Maryland and raped her. The police could not identify him, but they obtained and preserved a DNA sample from the crime, then entered that sample into the Combined DNA Index System (CODIS), which connects DNA laboratories throughout the nation. Six years later, Alonzo King was arrested for assault after a witness identified him as the man who had menaced a group of people with a shotgun. Pursuant to Maryland law governing arrests for serious offenses, police used a cotton swab of King's cheek to obtain a DNA sample. Four months later, after a private vendor tested it, police learned that King's DNA matched the sample from the 2003 rape. King was convicted of rape and sentenced to life in prison. On appeal, he argued that the cheek swab was an unconstitutional search.

Maryland v. King, decided in 2013, forced the Court to address what limits, if any, the Constitution imposes on the creation of a national DNA database.[47] Rarely have the stakes of a privacy case been higher. The stuff of fantasy and nightmares, a national genetic repository would centralize in government hands a staggering amount of information. Calling for a vast expansion of DNA collection, Cyrus Vance, the Manhattan District Attorney, has celebrated its unparalleled potential to "identify the guilty, exonerate the innocent, bring justice to crime victims and prevent additional crimes from occurring."[48] Others take a less sanguine view. In 2004, Judge Stephen Reinhardt of the Ninth Circuit Court of Appeals reminded us of "all of the dangers inherent in allowing the government to collect and store information about its citizens in a centralized place."[49] Recalling the Palmer raids in 1920, the roundup and internment of Japanese-Americans during World War II, J. Edgar Hoover's use of FBI surveillance to terrorize civil rights leaders, and the midcentury witch hunt of suspected Communists, he concluded that "even governments with benign intentions have proven unable to regulate or use wisely vast stores of information they collect regarding their citizens." More than any technology before it, DNA sampling brings into stark relief the frightening difficulty of striking a balance between liberty and security, privacy and order.

Of course, the Court does not deal with technologies in the abstract. *King* addressed Maryland's scheme, which required officers to perform a cheek swab to obtain DNA from all people arrested for serious offenses. In the course of briefing and argument, however, the Court encountered many related issues: Can states require that all citizens submit DNA samples or only certain people, such as those arrested for particularly serious crimes? Must the government destroy DNA samples after entering them into CODIS and, if not, what other uses may it make of that stored DNA? Do privacy interests require the deletion of genetic records if an arrestee is released?

Faced with all these issues, the Court walked a path unlike the one it followed in *Jones*. Rather than meditate broadly about the future of the Constitution, it offered an opinion that, at first glance, seems steadfastly narrow.

Kennedy, joined by Roberts, Thomas, Breyer, and Alito, held in *King* that using a cotton swab to collect King's DNA did not violate his Fourth Amendment rights. The fundamental issue Kennedy addressed is whether the police must obtain a warrant based on individualized suspicion before collecting DNA or whether a general practice of swabbing all people arrested on suspicion of committing a serious crime is permissible. Fully aware that a warrant requirement could defeat widespread, involuntary collection of DNA, Kennedy held that Maryland did not need a warrant. He reasoned that, even though warrants based on individualized suspicion of wrongdoing are typically required when police undertake searches to solve crimes, the police do not need a warrant when they search for other reasons. These "special needs" searches include the warrantless scans we have all experienced at airports. When police search for reasons other than solving a crime, the Fourth Amendment requires only that the law enforcement interests at stake outweigh the individual privacy interests invaded.

The first question, then, was why Maryland collected DNA. Kennedy answered by exalting Maryland's interest in "identification," defined as "the need for law enforcement officers in a safe and accurate way to process and identify the persons and possessions they must take into custody." This interest, he maintained, drove the whole Maryland program, not an interest in solving crimes. Kennedy also emphasized that arrestees have diminished expectations of privacy and that Maryland police have little discretion in deciding when to collect DNA—factors that he linked to other "special needs" cases. Thus, Kennedy held, Maryland did not need any warrants. It just needed to win the balance of competing interests.

Starting with law enforcement's side of the equation, Kennedy highlighted the importance of identifying arrestees. This interest, he explained, includes information about an arrestee's "past conduct" and "criminal history." Armed with such knowledge, "police can ensure that they have the proper person under arrest and that they have made the necessary arrangements for his custody." He added, "Just as important, they can also prevent suspicion against or prosecution of the innocent." (This Court's concern for innocence, however, has its limits; in 2009, Kennedy joined a conservative majority to hold that inmates have no right to testing of DNA that may prove their innocence.[50]) Kennedy clinched his argument with an analogy to fingerprinting: both technologies facilitate identification, and "the additional intrusion upon the arrestee's privacy [in taking DNA] beyond that associated with fingerprinting is not significant."

Kennedy described King's privacy interests as comparatively meager. A cheek swab is a "minimal" intrusion, he argued, especially for arrestees with reduced privacy rights. Turning to the DNA sample, he emphasized that the CODIS genetic loci "come from non-coding parts of the DNA that do not reveal the genetic traits of the arrestee" and that the DNA is not tested in any other way. Finally, he approvingly noted that Maryland law protects against the collection of DNA for reasons other than identification.

Carefully weighing these law enforcement and individual privacy interests, Kennedy concluded that "DNA identification of arrestees is a reasonable search that can be considered part of a routine booking procedure."

In a scathing dissent joined by Ginsburg, Sotomayor, and Kagan, Scalia tore into Kennedy's central premise: "The Court's assertion that DNA is being taken, not to solve crimes, but to identify those in the State's custody, taxes the credulity of the credulous." In Scalia's view, Maryland's unmistakable goal in collecting DNA samples was to solve

crimes, and it is a bedrock principle that "the Fourth Amendment forbids searching a person for evidence of a crime when there is no basis for
believing the person is guilty of the crime or is in possession of incriminating evidence." The Court should therefore never have engaged in a
general "reasonableness" analysis. Instead, he exclaimed, it should have
insisted that Maryland support its crime-solving searches with individual warrants, each supported by probable cause sufficient to justify a
DNA test.

Scalia challenged Kennedy on several fronts. First, he took issue with
Kennedy's capacious definition of Maryland's interest in "identification."
To Scalia, Kennedy had demolished the line between investigating
unsolved crimes and "the normal sense" of identification, which "would
identify the author of *Introduction to the Principles of Morals and Legislation* as Jeremy Bentham." Second, Scalia pointed out that the DNA
sample wasn't actually used to identify King. Indeed, it took Maryland
four months to process the DNA sample, partly because state law barred
DNA testing until after King was arraigned. "Does the Court," Scalia
artfully wondered, "really believe that Maryland did not know whom it
was arraigning?" In truth, Scalia observed, "if anything was 'identified'
at the moment that the DNA database returned a match, it was not
King—his identity was already known. . . . Rather, what the [match]
'identified' was the previously-taken sample from the earlier crime. That
sample was genuinely mysterious to Maryland." It was thus absurd, Scalia concluded, to think that the real goal was the arrestee's identification.
Nor was Scalia impressed by Kennedy's fingerprint analogy; DNA, he
observed, takes far longer than fingerprints to analyze. For now, and
likely for at least the near future, DNA cannot seriously be described as a
quick identification tool.

To Scalia, Kennedy's majority used a wholly disingenuous description of Maryland's program to short-circuit the Fourth Amendment, all
in service of cracking more cases. In his view, *King* boiled down to a
choice the framers made long ago: "Solving unsolved crimes . . . occupies
a lower place in the American pantheon of noble objectives than the protection of our people from suspicionless law-enforcement searches."
Recalling the dark history of royal abuses that gave rise to the warrant
requirement, Scalia marked his "doubt that the proud men who wrote
the charter of our liberties would have been so eager to open their mouths

to royal inspection." In closing, he wrote, "I therefore dissent and hope that today's incursion upon the Fourth Amendment . . . will some day be repudiated."

At one level, for all of Scalia's fireworks, *King* was a narrow case. The Court decided that Maryland's program was about identification, not fighting crime. It then balanced the competing values at issue and reached a result that would be subject to change as the uses of DNA evolved. Read this way, *King* deals mainly with how to describe the goal of one DNA collection program in relation to familiar Fourth Amendment law and in the midst of rapid technological change.[51]

This reading accords with Kennedy's stated reluctance to issue broad pronouncements on privacy rights. In a recent case about searches of public employee text message records, he advised caution: "The judiciary risks error by elaborating too fully on the Fourth Amendment implications of emerging technology before its role in society has become clear."[52] Noting that the roles of cell phones and text messaging in American society are still in flux, Kennedy added, "Prudence counsels caution before the facts in [this] case are used to establish far-reaching premises that define the existence, and extent, of privacy expectations enjoyed by employees when using employer-provided communication devices." A similar concern may have shaped his decision not to offer wide-ranging commentary on DNA databases in *King*.

Nonetheless, *King* is a landmark opinion. In its first case addressing a DNA database, the Court upheld the program and did not even suggest that Maryland's law presented a close question. It thereby set an encouraging constitutional mood, signaling to lower courts and policy makers that the Constitution will not stand broadly in the way of DNA collection. Because constitutional law may previously have chilled innovation and cast a pall of illegitimacy over DNA programs, *King* likely will boost the recent trend favoring rapid expansion of CODIS. This trend has already led more than half the states to collect DNA from some arrestees.[53] To those who fear such databases, viewing in them the terrors of Big Brother, *King* is a disaster. But to those who see a potentially remarkable boost in the fight against crime, *King* is—as Alito suggested at oral argument—"perhaps the most important criminal procedure case that [the] Court has heard in decades."

King is so important partly because the majority's insistence that the

Maryland program is really all about identification is hard to accept. Surely it was not by coincidence that Maryland's lawyer opened her argument at the Court by stating, "Since 2009, when Maryland began to collect DNA samples from arrestees charged with violent crimes and burglary, there have been 225 matches, 75 prosecutions and 42 convictions." (Scalia promptly jabbed back, "Well, that's really good. I'll bet you if you conducted a lot of unreasonable searches and seizures, you'd get more convictions, too.") Kennedy dealt with Maryland's openly expressed concern with solving crimes by shoehorning it into the "identification" interest; he reasoned that a suspect's past criminal acts are part of his "identity." This controversial move will make it very difficult in the future to separate a state's interest in identification from its interest in solving crimes—and will thus bar judges from imposing the limits on police officers embodied in a warrant requirement.

Even *King*'s seeming narrowness is actually a powerful statement in its own right. Kennedy barely acknowledged the concerns of those who deem DNA collection a threat to liberty. His opinion said little about what it means under the Constitution to permit vast, state-operated DNA databases in our democratic society. Nor did it address worries that lawmakers may not fairly balance privacy and security when they build massive DNA databases with samples taken mainly from arrestees, a group that is disproportionately poor, undereducated, and black.[54] If anything, the majority was unreservedly enthusiastic about the promise of this new technology, despite the warnings by Orwell, Kafka, and Huxley that lace so much writing about DNA databases. Scalia, in contrast, charged the majority with permitting a "genetic panopticon"—another reference to Jeremy Bentham, who described a prison in which a single guard could see any inmate at any time, leaving each to wonder when he was being watched.

Scalia's charge has some force. No doubt intentionally, Kennedy made little effort to cabin the scope of his ruling. He said almost nothing about the Fourth Amendment requiring privacy safeguards, such as eventual expungement of DNA records, as a condition of permitting DNA databases. He narrowly described the privacy interests at stake, declining to acknowledge the risk of government abuse as a weighty concern. He set aside the fact that the noncoding loci taken for CODIS are sometimes used to match family members. And, most important, he did not explicitly limit his ruling to people arrested on suspicion of serious offenses, a point evidenced most clearly by his analogy of DNA collection to ordinary fingerprinting.

This last point led Scalia to issue a warning: "As an entirely predictable consequence of today's decision, your DNA can be taken and entered into a national DNA database if you are ever arrested, rightly or wrongly, and for whatever reason." He is likely correct. It may even come to pass that *King* will be invoked to justify DNA sampling of nonarrestees thought to have reduced expectations of privacy. Indeed, *King* could ultimately be but a brief stop along the road to DNA sampling of the entire population. Some people would deplore that development, but others would welcome it—either on crime-prevention grounds or because a database to which all Americans are subject is far more likely to generate meaningful political safeguards against abuse than is a database to which we consign only the powerless. The majority in *King* does not seem perturbed by the thought of a universal database—unlike in *Jones*, where Roberts imagined his own car being tracked and reacted with alarm. Although interpreting the sounds of silence in a judicial opinion is a treacherous task, *King*'s narrowness is obviously a considered message.

King will also alter the constitutional landscape in even subtler ways. In 2004, almost a decade before *King*, Chief Judge Kozinski described the slippery slope toward which rulings like *King* impel us: "When further expansions of CODIS are proposed, information from the database will have been credited with solving hundreds or thousands of crimes, and we will have become inured to the idea that the government is entitled to hold large databases of DNA fingerprints. . . . A highly expansive opinion . . . , one that draws no hard lines and revels in the boon that new technology will provide to law enforcement, is an engraved invitation to future expansion. And when that inevitable expansion comes, we will look to the regime we approved today as the new baseline and say, this too must be OK because it's just one small step beyond the last thing we approved. . . . By then the line—never very clear to begin with—will have shifted. The fishbowl will look like home."[55] Fourth Amendment law protects privacy, but it also shapes what we think privacy means. In ways large and small, *King* orients us toward a future in which the Constitution says little about DNA databases.

Kennedy's is not the last word, however. DNA databases remain subject to vigorous political debate. Privacy advocates warn of the potential for abuse and error, adding that it is anomalous for a democratic society to let the government store intimate information about our genome in secret warehouses and vast computer networks.[56] Database enthusiasts retort that the state can protect against misuse, and that the unparalleled crime-solving and crime-preventing potential of this new tool demands that we deploy it.[57] As battles over fundamental principles rage, practical disputes over the specific policies governing DNA collection and storage occupy legislators, police officers, and courts.[58] Those issues extend beyond deciding whose DNA we will take, where we will store it, what uses we will make of it, and how we will guard it against hackers and abusive bureaucrats. They reach out to encompass the whole criminal justice system, since racial disparities in arrest rates, failure to collect crime-scene DNA, and backlogged crime labs all threaten the integrity of DNA databases.[59] The future may bend toward expansive use of DNA, but American society still faces questions about making privacy real in that genetic panopticon.

King proves the wisdom of Chief Judge Kozinski's admonition that "new technologies test the judicial conscience."[60] A precarious five-justice majority has opened the door to a new world of involuntary DNA collection, offering an opinion whose silence speaks volumes. Right or wrong, *King* will change the landscape of American privacy—even as it offers an invitation to democratic debate over the rules that govern these databases of human life.

In the wee hours of a Southern California morning in September 2007, Mission Control at NASA's Jet Propulsion Laboratory (JPL) waited nervously as the team prepared for liftoff of the *Dawn* spacecraft at Cape Canaveral Air Force Station. It was a thrilling moment. A year before, NASA had canceled the mission for budget reasons, only to reauthorize it months later, at which point weather problems delayed liftoff several times. Finally, at about seven A.M. eastern standard time, *Dawn* began its years-long trip to reach what NASA called the "uncharted and distant worlds Vesta and Ceres," two asteroids that may well reveal secrets about our solar system's original formation.[61]

Earlier that same year, the people at NASA had other secrets on their minds. As a response to 9/11, the White House had ordered all federal agencies to conduct background checks on contract employees. Agencies like NASA had long required their direct hires to undergo complete background investigations, but NASA hadn't extended that rule to contract workers. Now, at the Jet Propulsion Laboratory—a NASA facility staffed entirely with contract employees and operated by the California Institute of Technology—workers came face-to-face with intensive government investigations.

Although most of the paperwork was routine, some of the questions the forms asked were probing. One asked employees to disclose any illegal drug use in the past year. Another form was sent to the employees' references and to previous landlords; it asked about "any adverse information" concerning "violations of the law," "financial integrity," "abuse of alcohol and/or drugs," or "mental or emotional stability." All responses to these forms were subject to the Privacy Act, which imposes limits on the government's retention, use, and disclosure of personal information.

A group of scientists, engineers, and administrative personnel filed suit, arguing that the Constitution required the government to conduct its background checks with a more discerning eye. They did not assert that NASA had no business asking them anything at all; rather, they maintained that the government needed to show sufficiently compelling reason to pose such personal inquiries in its background investigations. But because questionnaires don't count as searches under the Fourth Amendment, the employees had to look elsewhere in the Constitution for privacy protections.

They ultimately invoked an unwritten "right to informational privacy." In two cases decided in the 1970s, the Court referred to a constitutional "interest in avoiding disclosure of personal matters."[62] Since then, most federal appellate courts have recognized that the Constitution limits the acquisition and disclosure of sensitive personal information by the government. They have reasoned that this right applies when people legitimately expect privacy—and that the government, in such cases, must show a compelling reason to violate those expectations and demonstrate its adoption of adequate safeguards against abuse. These informational privacy cases have arisen in a wide range of contexts, from the disclosure of an individual's HIV status in public records, to mandatory disclosure of personal financial records by state senators, to the disclosure of nude photos of an assault victim taken by police, to state regulations requiring abortion clinics to disclose unredacted copies of all patient records.[63] The NASA plaintiffs asked the Court to hold that their comprehensive background checks violated this right.

When *NASA v. Nelson* reached the Roberts Court in 2011, every justice voted to reject the employees' claim.[64] Writing for the majority, Alito explicitly assumed, without finally deciding, that an informational privacy right exists. But he then concluded that, under any understanding of the right, the employees could not show that it had been violated. The government, he explained, "has a strong interest in conducting basic background checks into the contract employees minding the store at JPL." Courts must "keep those interests in mind when asked to go line-by-line through the Government's employment forms." And to Alito, the questions about drugs made perfect sense: "Like any employer, the Government is entitled to have its projects staffed by reliable, law-abiding persons who will efficiently and effectively discharge their duties." The presence of protections against disclosure of this information to the public only made it clearer that the employees must lose.

It would be easy to infer from the Court's unanimity that this was an easy case. But the employees had prevailed below: a unanimous three-judge panel saw merit in their claim.[65] Addressing NASA's request for "any adverse information" about JPL employees, Judge Kimberly Wardlaw of the Ninth Circuit Court of Appeals had concluded that there was no basis for this intrusive inquiry: "It is difficult to see how the vague solicitation of derogatory information concerning the applicant's 'general behavior or conduct' and 'other matters' could be narrowly tailored to meet *any* legitimate need, much less the specific interests that [NASA has] offered to justify the new requirement."

NASA was a hard case because laws requiring the disclosure of sensitive personal information as a condition of government employment pose a risk of constitutional injury. Both the Ninth Circuit and the Roberts Court displayed admirable sensitivity to that danger, even though they disagreed over whether NASA had crossed the constitutional line and whether to formally recognize a right to informational privacy.

In an opinion concurring only in the result, Scalia, joined by Thomas, tore into Alito's analysis. Scalia thought *NASA* was an easy case because, in his view, the "right to informational privacy" simply doesn't exist. "Like many other desirable things not included in the Constitution," Scalia wrote, " 'informational privacy' seems like a good idea—wherefore the People have enacted laws at the federal level and in the states restricting the government's collection and use of information." But, he continued, "it is up to the People to enact those laws, to shape them, and, when they think it appropriate, to repeal them." Nearly always hostile to the recognition of rights not specifically listed in the Constitution, Scalia asserted that the employees sought to "invent a constitutional right out of whole cloth." It was "farcical," he added, to contend that "a right deeply rooted in our history and tradition bars the Government from ensuring that the Hubble Telescope is not used by recovering drug addicts."

Scalia took particular issue with Alito's "never-say-never" approach, which avoided any final judgment on the existence of a right to informational privacy. He argued that the Court thereby "gets to pontificate upon a matter that is none of its business: the appropriate balance between security and privacy." Scalia maintained that this made no sense: "The Court decides that the Government did not violate the right to informational privacy without deciding whether there is a right to informational privacy, and without even describing what hypothetical standard should be used to assess whether the hypothetical right has been violated." Finally, Scalia warned, Alito's opinion opened the door to confusing and absurd claims without providing the lower courts with any real guidance. "Thirty-three years have passed since the Court first suggested that the right may, or may not, exist," Scalia protested. "It is past time for the Court to abandon this Alfred Hitchcock line of our jurisprudence."

Alito left most of Scalia's assault unanswered, though he did include an aggressive footnote listing other cases in which Scalia had assumed the existence of a right without finally deciding the question. If Alito had wanted to press the point, though, he could have advanced plenty of good arguments. Notwithstanding Scalia's disdain, a right to informational privacy has deep roots in the Constitution's text. It is often described by federal courts as a fundamental liberty interest protected under the Due Process Clause, just like the rights to abortion and same-sex intimacy.[66] Viewed in this light, it can be conceptualized as part of our evolving traditions of liberty and respect for human dignity. It is also rightly understood as a product of the pattern formed by other amendments: the First, which safeguards expression and conscience; the Third, which keeps troops out of our homes; the Fourth, which watches over reasonable expectations of privacy; the Fifth, which thwarts self-incrimination; and the Ninth, which tells us that the Bill of Rights isn't the final accounting of American freedom.[67]

In its parts and in sum, the Constitution may well guard a right to informational privacy. Even if it does, though, we can expect that statutes and regulations will usually strike an adequate balance between privacy and competing values. Only in special cases might the courts need to step in and impose constitutional limits. *NASA* wisely left room for the Court to breathe new life into this dimension of the Constitution, recognizing that the demands of our information era may call upon it to revisit the subject again.

"As nightfall does not come at once, neither does oppression. In both instances, there is a twilight when everything remains seemingly unchanged. And it is in such twilight that we all must be most aware of change in the air—however slight—lest we become unwitting victims of the darkness."[68] Justice William Douglas served on the Court from 1939 to 1975 and had more than a passing familiarity with threats to liberty. He knew that values like privacy are not lost suddenly; they wither and weaken over time, buffeted by changed politics and culture until we forget why they once seemed so vital. By the time they fall, it's easy to pronounce their loss inevitable or desirable.

Our experiences of privacy shape our beliefs about where we should expect it and why we should value it. Those experiences, in turn, are defined as much by government and corporate action as by our own choices. In that great struggle for privacy's soul, the Roberts Court will never have the final word. Its decisions are nonetheless of great moment. By deciding when the government may intrude upon our privacy, the Court crafts law that helps define the relationship between governed and government. By reminding us of the core values at stake in debates over privacy, the Court calls upon our better angels and steers our social dialogue toward shared principles. By stepping gingerly into a fast-changing world, the Court allows room for democracy to function and affords itself time to think carefully before reinterpreting the Constitution.

Justice Oliver Wendell Holmes Jr. was known to quip, "If my fellow citizens want to go to Hell I will help them. It's my job."[69] Fair enough. Courts can't save a nation from itself. The Roberts Court, though, doesn't have the luxury of nihilism. It must create new constitutional law to deal with the new technologies that make possible such marvels as GPS tracking, DNA swabs, and text messages. And as it does so, it tinkers with the deep architecture of privacy that shapes our lives in countless and often mysterious ways.

8

RIGHTS FOR SALE:
DISCOUNTING THE CONSTITUTION

Question: "What do you have when a lawyer is buried up to his neck in sand?" Answer: "Not enough sand."

Question: "Why won't sharks attack lawyers?" Answer: "Professional courtesy."

Lawyer jokes, some of them at least half funny, have a long and distinguished history. Clarence Darrow, a champion of civil liberties who famously defended evolution at the Scopes Monkey Trial, cracked that "the trouble with law is lawyers."[1] Justice Oliver Wendell Holmes Jr. solemnly advised that "lawyers spend a great deal of their time shoveling smoke."[2] Even the framers appreciated this brand of humor. Frustrated with Congress, Thomas Jefferson asked, "How can it be otherwise in a body to which the people send one hundred and fifty lawyers, whose trade it is to question everything, yield nothing & talk by the hour?"[3] More succinctly, and with his typically savage wit, Ben Franklin once exclaimed, "God works wonders now & then; Behold a Lawyer, an honest Man!"[4]

These sentiments are understandable. Lawyers are trained to cause verbose, drawn-out, and expensive havoc. Their weapons of choice, procedure and paperwork, often inspire dread. With such power comes great responsibility, a lesson that seems lost on too many attorneys.

When the state violates our rights, though, the Constitution does not magically spring to life, leap from the shelves, and register a protest. We usually look to lawyers to play that role. This is where the profession achieves many of its noblest ideals. The government, after all, can be a terrifying opponent. When it refuses to pay Social Security benefits, orders police to stop and frisk certain kinds of people, accuses our loved ones of heinous crimes, or imposes absurd rules on how we conduct business, we call our lawyers. And once we hire attorneys to represent us, we rightly expect independence from the government and zealous advocacy for our cause.[5]

Just imagine, then, how you would feel if, after being wrongfully denied essential welfare benefits, you went to court one day and watched your publicly appointed lawyer respond to the judge's questions this way:

JUDGE: I asked you a question, counsel. You're testing my patience. I asked whether the U.S. Constitution protects your client from being treated like this.

LAWYER: Your Honor, I apologize, but I just can't answer. You see, I work for a legal aid organization that receives funding from the federal government, and—

JUDGE: Hold on just a minute. I didn't ask who pays you. I asked whether the State violated your client's rights in refusing to pay welfare benefits.

LAWYER: All I can say is "no comment."

JUDGE: What kind of answer is that? Your client, sitting right there, looks pretty unhappy with it. And I can understand why!

LAWYER: Your Honor, I realize this is unusual, but federal law prohibits me from addressing the constitutionality of *any* welfare law. I simply cannot make that argument on my client's behalf, even if it might decide the case in her favor.

JUDGE: How can that possibly be true?

LAWYER: Well, I work for an organization that provides legal aid to the poor. We receive some of our funding from Congress. In exchange for that funding, Congress said that we can't challenge the constitutionality of any welfare laws in court. We can argue that those laws aren't being interpreted properly or are being misapplied, but we can't say they violate the Constitution.

JUDGE: But, counsel, how should I decide this case if you're waiving your best argument? Besides, how can Congress limit what you can say in a court of law? Doesn't that violate your freedom of speech and your First

Amendment right to petition the government for a redress of griev-
ances?

LAWYER: Well, I'm not a First Amendment lawyer . . .

JUDGE: In that case, you'd better get one. And just one more question,
counsel. Why on earth did your organization agree to abide by that
funding condition?

LAWYER: (*Shrugs.*) We needed the money.

It requires little imagination to see how, as a client, you'd be appalled
by this display. In exchange for your use of a public lawyer, you've for-
feited a critical means of challenging an unconstitutional law. Nor would
your lawyer feel great: bought off by the federal government, he was
forced to stand silent on a fundamental point of law—effectively selling
his own First Amendment rights to speak and petition the government.
The judge would be furious, too, since she was deprived of argument on
the decisive issue in the case. Finally, because just about all welfare recipients need to use publicly funded counsel, the same unconstitutional law
could be applied to thousands of people, all of them incapable of obtaining a lawyer with permission to challenge it in court.

The whole thing just feels *dirty.* There's something terribly wrong with
the government breaking out its huge checkbook and buying the ability to
violate our rights. Although we understand that our rights aren't absolute,
surely there is some kind of constitutional limit to this power. Right?

To borrow a favorite Hollywood trope, the courtroom exchange we've
just described is "based on a true story." In October 2000, a scene just
like it weighed on the minds of several justices as they heard argument in
Legal Services Corporation v. Velazquez.[6] A fifty-six-year-old grandmother
from the Bronx had challenged the termination of her welfare benefits,
relying on a public attorney. In 1996, however, Congress had added a condition to its partial funding of legal aid groups: recipients of federal lar-
gesse could not challenge any welfare law on constitutional grounds.

The Court ruled by a five-to-four vote that this condition violated
the First Amendment. Writing for the majority, Justice Kennedy focused
on one of his principal concerns: judicial independence. "By seeking to

prohibit the analysis of certain legal issues," he reasoned, "the enactment under review prohibits speech and expression upon which courts must depend for the proper exercise of the judicial power." Kennedy saw *Velazquez* mainly as a case about separation of powers; he therefore emphasized that "Congress cannot wrest the law from the Constitution" and threaten a "severe impairment of the judicial function." Kennedy also highlighted a threat to the "unfettered interchange of ideas." If Congress could insulate its laws from attack by barring public lawyers from certain "vital theories," a chill might fall across our legal discourse.

Ultimately, Kennedy emphasized not the plight of poor people like Carmen Velazquez but the majestic role of the Judiciary. As a result, the Court had little reason to offer broader commentary on the legitimacy of government offers for Americans to give up their rights. But that issue is neither new nor insignificant. To the contrary, bribes (in this sense of the word) are a pervasive fixture of modern governance. The Court, meanwhile, has been far from consistent in deciding when and why tempting you to sell your rights violates your rights. The recent record of cases dealing with this problem vividly illustrates the multitude and diversity of these transactions. Several have been struck down, others upheld, and many are still in limbo.

In 1988, for example, regulations promulgated by the Department of Health and Human Services offered family-planning funds to organizations that would guarantee that no one working at any of their federally funded clinics would say a word about abortion to any of the clinic's patients. (These regulations were upheld in 1991.)[7] In other contexts, Congress has used tax relief as its currency of choice. For instance, churches don't have to pay taxes on their income—but in exchange for this exemption, religious leaders may not endorse political candidates from the pulpit. (The legality of this restriction has never been settled in court.)[8] Of course, not all state inducements involve cash. In fact, the most common form of such quid pro quo deals is probably the criminal plea bargain: plead guilty and give up your constitutional right to a trial, says a prosecutor, and in exchange we'll offer you a shorter prison sentence. (The arrangement has repeatedly been upheld.)[9]

Government-sponsored bribes also affect the relationship between levels of government. They explain, for example, why the minimum drinking age in all fifty states is the same: in 1984, Congress threatened to withhold a small percentage of federal highway funding from any state that didn't raise its drinking age to twenty-one. Cash-strapped and disinclined to fight, every state acquiesced. (This law was upheld in 1987.)[10]

The Court's rulings throughout this storied tradition of government bribery have veered from aggressive skepticism of such bribes to tolerant deference. Yet the Court has consistently been clear about one principle. As Chief Justice Roberts recently reaffirmed, "If a party objects to a condition on the receipt of federal funding," that party's first line of defense "is to decline the funds."[11] In other words, your best protection against government bribery is to "just say no." But consider this fair warning: as long as you've got rights, you've got rights for sale.

One cold winter morning in 1942, a teacher at a tiny four-room schoolhouse in the West Virginia countryside noticed that Marie and Gathie Barnette were not reciting the Pledge of Allegiance along with their classmates. In the early 1970s, a New Hampshire resident named George Maynard cut off part of his license plate, thereby removing "or Die" from the state motto, "Live Free or Die." Nearly four decades later, in the early 2000s, a coalition of groups devoted to fighting HIV and AIDS faced a difficult choice: accept millions of federal dollars and take an anti-prostitution stance, or decline the money to ensure the efficacy of programs meant to protect sex workers.

At first glance, these stories have little in common. But as Mark Twain dryly remarked, although history doesn't repeat itself, it occasionally rhymes.[12] Each of these stories ended up at the Court. And each, in its own way, presented the justices with a chance to vindicate an important principle: the Constitution limits government's power to pressure us into expressing messages with which we disagree, whether as a condition of giving us a free public education, a license to drive, or many other benefits. Sounding the latest note in this historical progression, the Roberts Court has recently confirmed that Congress should sometimes be prevented from using our desire for federal benefits as leverage to get us to sacrifice our rights.

The story of the two silent Barnette girls began in 1892, an age of unprecedented immigration, social radicalism, and economic inequality.[13] Determined to reaffirm patriotism and unity in this era of unrest,

Francis Bellamy wrote a "Pledge of Allegience" in August 1892 at the behest of a widely known children's magazine, the *Youth's Companion*.[14] A few months later, President Benjamin Harrison issued a proclamation declaring October 12 a national holiday—Columbus Day—to be celebrated with a flag-salute ceremony and this new pledge: "I pledge allegiance to my flag and the Republic for which it stands, one nation indivisible, with liberty and justice for all." Compulsory flag salutes in public education soon followed. New York added the requirement in 1898, one day after America declared war on Spain, and by 1935 forty states had enacted laws requiring patriotic exercises in public schools. The patriotic fervor that led to mandatory pledges reached a fever pitch during World War II.

The Barnette girls were Jehovah's Witnesses and, like many of their coreligionists, believed that pledging allegiance to a flag was tantamount to worshipping a graven image. Although the Barnettes felt a duty to obey school policy, they were more compelled by a fear of mortal sin, and they refused to recite the pledge. The school rewarded this sincere display of religious faith with expulsion—at least until the girls changed their minds. The girls filed suit to defend religious liberty.

In 1942, their case may have seemed like a lost cause. Just two years earlier, the Court had issued an eight-to-one ruling affirming compulsory flag salutes in schools.[15] Dubbed the "Fall of France" opinion, and delivered as America raced to arm itself against the Axis powers, that decision wrapped itself in the American flag and demands of wartime unity. In his blazing majority opinion, Justice Felix Frankfurter proclaimed, "A society which is dedicated to the preservation of these ultimate values of civilization may in self-protection utilize the educational process for inculcating those almost unconscious feelings which bind men together in a comprehending loyalty, whatever may be their lesser differences and difficulties." Shortly after it was published, though, this opinion had gone wobbly, partly because many of the justices who had joined it were horrified to see it trigger a vicious backlash against Jehovah's Witnesses. In a rare turn of events, particularly for an all-but-unanimous opinion on so solemn a subject, several justices publicly signaled regret—and eagerness to reconsider the question.[16]

When the Barnettes' case reached the Court in 1943, Justice Robert Jackson, joined by five other justices, called a stop to the deeply un-American assault on their liberty.[17] Fashioning an opinion that still echoes across the decades, Jackson warned that pressuring Americans into loyalty oaths was wrong and dangerous: "Those who begin coercive elimination of dissent soon find themselves exterminating dissenters. Compulsory unification of opinion achieves only the unanimity of the graveyard." Born of religious freedom, *West Virginia State Board of Education v. Barnette* spoke broadly of free speech and thought.

Like the Barnettes, George Maynard was a Jehovah's Witness. The philosophical New Hampshire resident believed that life was too sacred to sacrifice in defense of freedom; while he wished to live free, he would not die for the cause. As he told a court, "I believe my 'government'— Jehovah's Kingdom—offers everlasting life. It would be contrary to that belief to give up my life for the state, even if it meant living in bondage." As a matter of earthbound political philosophy, Maynard also believed "that life is more precious than freedom."

New Hampshire took a different view. Echoing Patrick Henry's famous battle cry from the American Revolution—"Give me liberty or give me death"—it began stamping "Live Free or Die" on its license plates in 1969, another period of cultural upheaval. But the state's famously libertarian spirit apparently did not extend to those who tempered liberty with other values. In 1974 and again in 1975, New Hampshire sentenced Maynard to jail and ordered him to pay fines after he removed the words "or Die" from his plate. His crime? Illegal failure to display the state motto.

The Court struck down Maynard's conviction in *Wooley v. Maynard*, citing *Barnette* to show that the First Amendment guards "both the right to speak freely and the right to refrain from speaking at all."[18] As Chief Justice Warren Burger reasoned: "Here, as in *Barnette*, we are faced with a state measure which forces an individual, as part of his daily life . . . to be an instrument for fostering public adherence to an ideological point of view he finds unacceptable. In doing so, the State invades the sphere of intellect and spirit which it is the purpose of the First Amendment . . . to reserve from all official control."

In 2003, the state invaded the sphere of intellect and spirit in a different way. After an intense lobbying campaign by George W. Bush, Congress passed the United States Leadership Against HIV/AIDS, Tuberculosis, and Malaria Act. The Leadership Act authorized $15 billion over its first five years (expanded in 2008 to $48 billion over another five years) to roll back the "unprecedented path of death and devastation" caused by HIV/

AIDS. The Act constituted the largest effort in history by any single country to fight HIV/AIDS and honored America's global responsibilities.

This commitment, though, came with two catches: no money from the Act could be "used to promote or advocate the legalization or practice of prostitution or sex trafficking," and no funds could be used by any group "that does not have a policy explicitly opposing prostitution and sex trafficking." In effect, the second condition offered a bribe: we'll give you unprecedented financial support to fight the spread of HIV/AIDS, but in exchange you must publicly subscribe to a policy opposing prostitution. Health groups bristled at the second requirement, insisting that effective HIV prevention often depends on earning the trust of commercial sex workers, not branding them with a scarlet letter. The anti-prostitution clause also posed a worrisome threat of censorship at private conferences focused on HIV/AIDS prevention.

In a petition to Bush in 2005, more than one hundred organizations, including many associated with the rights of women, protested the anti-prostitution pledge on policy and First Amendment grounds. That same year, several of those groups filed a constitutional challenge to the anti-prostitution clause. Their case bore the name *Agency for International Development v. Alliance for Open Society International* ("*AID*").[19] When *AID* reached the Court, Chief Justice Roberts composed a landmark opinion holding in the organizations' favor.

Justice Scalia, joined by Justice Thomas, vehemently disagreed with the Chief Justice. In his view, *AID* was a simple case: the First Amendment had nothing to do with the matter. The government is entitled to its own views on prostitution, and it has the right to enlist allies in its cause by offering grants. That is especially so, he noted, where conditions on the receipt of money speak to core features of a program, like an anti-prostitution stance in the context of HIV/AIDS prevention. If Congress cannot require groups it supports to toe the party line, then federal funds earmarked for HIV/AIDS programming might be spent by a recipient on prostitution-tolerant projects. As a result, Congress would effectively have funded efforts at ideological loggerheads with its own agenda. In Scalia's words: "Money is fungible. The economic reality is that when

NGOs can conduct their AIDS work on the Government's dime, they can expend greater resources on policies that undercut the Leadership Act."

Scalia buttressed his dissent by pointing out that the government had not actually forced anybody to speak. Public health groups could just decline the money. As a result, "like King Cnut's commanding of the tides, here the Government's 'requiring' and 'demanding' have no coercive effect." Scalia was almost certainly right about the absence of direct coercion: the Act created a new funding source, one upon which no organizations were already dependent and that they were free to reject.

In his powerful majority opinion, Roberts disagreed with Scalia's view of how the First Amendment applies to government bribes. He began with the premise that "freedom of speech prohibits the government from telling people what they must say," then turned straight to the crucial question: "Whether the Government may nonetheless impose that requirement as a condition on the receipt of federal funds."

Acknowledging that, "as a general matter, if a party objects to a condition on the receipt of federal funding, its recourse is to decline the funds," Roberts rejected Scalia's premise that *only* coercive offers are constitutionally suspicious. After explaining that coercion has never been deemed the sine qua non of illegitimate government bribery, the Chief surveyed precedents and strung together a more persuasive thread: Congress may impose some conditions on noncoercive offers of money, but it may do so only if those conditions affect just the use of the government funds in question, not the use of a recipient's private money. Congress could therefore require that taxpayers' funds not be spent on prostitution-tolerant programs, but it could not order grant recipients to abstain from drawing down their private accounts to speak favorably about prostitution. Yet that is exactly what the Act required: any organization accepting federal funds under the Act would be required to oppose prostitution in *all* of its activities.

Turning to Scalia's point that "money is fungible," the Chief retorted that this familiar argument "assumes that federal funding will simply supplant private funding, rather than pay for new programs or expand existing ones." A group newly flush with government cash, however, will not necessarily shift resources toward the types of programs of which the government disapproves. Rather, it might direct all the public funding to new programs, holding the allocation for existing initiatives constant, or it might substantially increase its expenditures on government-favored work, shifting capital away from programs the government dislikes. These are hardly remote possibilities, so if the federal government wanted to maintain the Act's conditions, it would have to provide the Court with persuasive evidence substantiating its concerns. This makes good sense: if the government wants to limit First Amendment rights, it needs to demonstrate actual harm.

But the Chief wasn't finished. At the core of his majority opinion, building directly upon ideas first espoused by Jackson in *Barnette*, Roberts offered a more fundamental critique of the dangers of state-sponsored bribes that would lead Americans to renounce their First Amendment rights.

The Act, Roberts explained, "goes beyond preventing recipients from using private funds in a way that would undermine the federal program. It requires them to pledge allegiance to the Government's policy of eradicating prostitution. As to that, we cannot improve upon what Justice Jackson wrote for the Court 70 years ago: 'If there is any fixed star in our constitutional constellation, it is that no official, high or petty, can prescribe what shall be orthodox in politics, nationalism, religion, or other matters of opinion or force citizens to confess by word or act their faith therein.' "[20] The Chief must have relished making this connection. He is a devoted Robert Jackson fan—perhaps an admiration passed down to Roberts from his mentor, Chief Justice William Rehnquist, who had clerked for Jackson.[21]

Scalia, though, was underwhelmed by what he described as this "head-fake" argument. In his view, the Court "pussyfoot[ed] around the lack of coercion" and cited Jackson's soaring oratory in *Barnette* "only to distract attention from the elephant in the room: that the Government is not forcing *anyone* to say *anything.*" But Scalia's swipe at the Chief's opinion missed the mark. Roberts's reliance on *Barnette* ran deep, vindicating the values Jackson had unearthed and honoring them with an even more sensitive and thoughtful application.

An understanding of the Chief's reasoning requires a close look at the aftermath of *Barnette* and *Maynard*. Although the Court overturned the punishments inflicted on the plaintiffs, it did not rule that routine recitation of the Pledge of Allegiance in schools must end, nor that New Hampshire could no longer emblazon "Live Free or Die" on its license plates. Rather, the Court held only that the government must give dissenters like the Barnette family and Mr. Maynard a chance to opt out of that state-sponsored speech.

In so doing, the Court struck upon a problematic middle ground—one that it had deliberately avoided in cases about official religious prayers in public schools by forbidding such prayers altogether rather than just affirming a right to opt out.[22] Any child seeking to take advantage of the right recognized in *Barnette* would have to single herself out, likely inviting ostracism if not outright bullying by her peers. And by vindicating a right to refuse license plates bearing the state's slogan while permitting the state to keep distributing plates carrying that slogan, the Court forced those most offended by the state's ideology to come out of the closet. Unable to just blend in as law-abiding citizens whose views nobody could guess from their license plates, those displaying the state's "Live Free or Die" slogan would be marked as accepting the sentiment it expressed, while those replacing it would be marked as having affirmatively rejected that sentiment.[23] Not every dissenter wants to be a poster child for a cause. The privacy and free spirit of such dissenters may deserve constitutional protection.

In truth, coercion can take many forms. By forcing dissenters to choose between publicly identifying themselves as such or lying about their beliefs, the right to opt out of the Pledge of Allegiance perpetuated a different kind of coercion. So, too, did the right to opt out of the HIV/AIDS anti-prostitution compact by turning down the government's offer of money. Organizations opposed to the anti-prostitution policy were left by Congress with just three lawful choices: (1) accept the money and lie by expressing the government's position; (2) accept the money and convey the convoluted message that they had agreed to oppose prostitution only to get the money, not because they believed that prostitution was necessarily objectionable (which might be deemed legally insufficient or at least hypocritical); or (3) reject the money, in which case, given its significance, they would probably have to explain that choice to the public and their overseers. And if they did choose to decline so much funding, that choice would likely convey the impression that their opposition to the policy was somewhere between impassioned and fanatical. In short, Congress's conditional HIV/AIDS funding offer coerced most recipients into becoming liars, hypocrites, or zealots.

In comparing these dissenting public health organizations to the vulnerable schoolchildren of another era, Roberts evinced sympathy for the no-win predicament Congress had forced upon them. His opinion in *AID* suggested why federally sponsored bribes can infringe upon valid desires to keep private views private—desires that sometimes reflect important constitutional rights to free thought and conscience.

The Chief may not have realized the scope of his triumph. "We cannot improve," he said, "upon what Justice Jackson wrote for the Court 70 years ago." But he could, and he did.

In October 2007, Elena Kagan stood with characteristic poise before the cadets of the United States Military Academy at West Point. At the time, she was the Dean of Harvard Law School. Never one for indirection or euphemism, Kagan addressed a then-controversial issue head-on: "I have been grieved in recent years to find your world and mine, the U.S. military and U.S. law schools, at odds indeed, facing each other in court [on] the military's don't-ask-don't-tell policy. Law schools, including mine, believe that employment opportunities should extend to all students, regardless of their race or sex or sexual orientation. And I personally believe that the exclusion of gays and lesbians from the military is both unjust and unwise."[24]

The court encounter to which Kagan referred was *Rumsfeld v. FAIR*, a case that reached the Supreme Court in 2005 and produced one of Roberts's first rulings as Chief Justice.[25] FAIR, the Forum for Academic and Institutional Rights, was a united faction of law schools that sued the U.S. Defense Department to challenge the Solomon Amendment. The Amendment was a federal law requiring universities to give military job recruiters the same access to their law school campuses that the schools provided to other employers or to stop accepting federal money.

This harsh choice was designed to end a protest that some law schools had carried out since the late 1970s. In 1978, New York University's law school had decided to ban access to its career services office to any employer, public or private, that discriminated against gay students in hiring. A number of other law schools had followed suit, and by 1990, the Association of American Law Schools had adopted NYU's policy.[26]

The military, meanwhile, enforced a blatantly discriminatory hiring policy against gays and lesbians. Before 1993, the institution had flatly prohibited gay soldiers from joining. Then, in 1993, Bill Clinton ushered in "don't ask, don't tell," a supposed compromise—since repealed—that wrought little improvement.[27] If anything, by banning only "out" gay soldiers from military service, "don't ask, don't tell" may have made things worse: in pressuring soldiers to remain closeted and live a lie, it achieved both prejudice and censorship. It was therefore abhorrent not only to principles of equality but also to the First Amendment.[28]

The law schools' blanket nondiscrimination policy required them to bar the military from interviewing students through their official hiring processes. This was not an absolute ban (at Harvard, for example, the student veterans' association organized interviews); rather, it was mostly a symbolic protest.

The Solomon Amendment, like other federal laws that attach strings to government funding, did not directly mandate that law schools facilitate military interviews. Instead, the law declared that federal funding to programs throughout entire university systems would be conditional upon law schools voluntarily opening their doors to military recruiters. Because medical schools and scientific research institutions depended heavily on this funding, it quickly became clear that if the Amendment was constitutional, the law schools' protest would be unsustainable.

In a striking rebuff to the legal academy, the Court unanimously upheld the Amendment. It did so, moreover, on grounds that reached beyond the Amendment's funding conditions. Writing for the Court, Roberts concluded that, even if Congress had coerced all law schools into making a military exception to their nondiscrimination policies, it would not have violated the First Amendment. By this reasoning, Congress could have directly mandated—even under threat of fines or imprisonment—that law schools open their career-center doors to military recruiters.

According to the Chief, the Amendment neither forced law schools to express any particular message nor prevented them from expressing their opposition to "don't ask, don't tell." Schools could simply say, "We oppose 'don't ask, don't tell,' even though our university took the money." No school officials had to endorse or otherwise vocalize the message that gays and lesbians were unfit for military service.

But the limits the Court had previously imposed on government attempts to coerce individuals into broadcasting its message were not confined to compelled endorsement as such. In *Maynard*, for example, George

Maynard was never forced to speak, even in the narrow sense discussed by Roberts. He never had to utter the words "Live Free or Die"; nor did he even have to display the message in such a way that anyone would attribute the motto to Maynard himself. After all, everybody in New Hampshire knew that the state, not Maynard, printed "Live Free or Die" on his license plate and required him to keep the motto there. And Maynard was free to post a sign in his window expressing his real view. Nonetheless, the Court in those prior cases held that the government had gone too far in forcing a dissenter either to give up driving or to play a personal role in helping the state promulgate a message he found repugnant.

Under *Maynard*, it would have been patently unconstitutional for Congress to force the nation's law schools to post flyers in campus hallways reading, "The United States Military: *Gays and Lesbians Can't Apply*." But was the Amendment's impact on law schools truly distinguishable? Like George Maynard, law schools deeply opposed a government message and yet were conscripted to assist the government in communicating it. Their only other option was to get out of the business of teaching law, just as Maynard's only other option was to stop driving.

Though the government publicized "don't ask, don't tell" in a number of ways, military recruiting was part and parcel of its message of gay inferiority. Military recruiters would discuss the policy if asked, as they often were by gay students who signed up for recruiting sessions as a form of protest. The recruiters didn't have to say anything to get that point across. Indeed, their very presence on campus was enough to express a potent message: *We're here to recruit, and we're here to recruit straight people.* Requiring law schools to host that message under the auspices of their official recruiting platforms forced the schools to facilitate its promulgation in a deeply intimate way. This burden on liberty was arguably every bit as objectionable as requiring Maynard to host a state motto on his car.

In ruling against FAIR, the Court reasoned as follows: because Congress could have exercised its authority to "raise and support Armies" to force *all* schools to let the military recruit on their campuses, surely they must also be able to do so as part of a financial package. Though it may seem compelling, this logic is not bulletproof. The fact that schools remained theoretically free to opt out made things *worse* in an important sense, just as the conditional funding requirement foisted upon public health organizations by Bush's HIV/AIDS program did. It turned the schools' messages into a hypocritical, convoluted mess: "We've taken the money, but (please, believe us!) our doing so doesn't mean we support 'don't ask, don't tell'; it's just that the situation is really complicated." The schools were coerced into confronting a Catch-22.

FAIR also involved a different and more subtle sort of constitutional injury: the Solomon Amendment forced law schools to put a price on their condemnation of "don't ask, don't tell." By compelling law schools to shift their message from "We oppose 'don't ask, don't tell,' period" to "We oppose it, but not so much that we'd risk losing our millions," Congress shifted the schools' message from one of idealism to one of realism. The Amendment did not simply compel the institutions to reveal a private dollar amount that would end their protest; it forced the institutions to change their entire way of thinking about the military's policy.

Because idealism sparks change and instills political courage, the Constitution should not readily countenance its suffocation. Roberts, however, reached the opposite conclusion: the challenge to the Amendment, he argued, "is simply not the same as forcing a student to pledge allegiance, or forcing a Jehovah's Witness to display the motto 'Live Free or Die,' and it trivializes the freedom protected in *Barnette* and *Maynard* to suggest that it is."

FAIR undeniably presented a tough question. But it was the Court, not the plaintiffs, that diminished those earlier cases by subscribing to a narrow reading of the values they espoused. It would take seven more years before the Chief would do the two classic cases honor—and show a touch of idealism himself—by invoking Justice Jackson's poetry to strike down the anti-prostitution pledge in *AID*.

Sonia Sotomayor represented the people of the County of New York from 1979 to 1984. Serving as a prosecutor in the New York County District Attorney's Office, the future justice endured brutal hours and faced moral challenges that few Americans ever encounter. She observed firsthand the devastating impact of a murder on a victim's surviving spouse, the depravity of those who trade in child pornography, and the pressure to bring cases to trial even with flimsy evidence. As a prosecutor on the front lines, she saw the criminal justice system in all its splendor and all its tragedy.[29]

In her best-selling memoir, Sotomayor makes plain that she never lost faith in the legal system's potential to do justice. Responding to critics who argue that the system suffers from intractable racial biases, she writes, "Knowing that the poor and minorities are disproportionately the victims of crimes, I'm loath to view the adversarial process of the law as class warfare by another name." Regarding her commitment to serving as a prosecutor, she explains, "If the system is broken, my inclination is to fix it rather than to fight it. I have faith in the process of the law, and if it is carried out fairly, I can live with the results, whatever they may be."[30] Sotomayor mixes noble ideals with a strong dose of realism, a practical bent, and a firm commitment to justice, all of which have served her well on the Court.

Since her arrival in 2009, Sotomayor has emerged as the Court's most creative and pragmatic thinker about reforming our criminal justice system. As a consequence, she has joined the ranks of another former prosecutor whose yearning for fairness led him to call for a new age of reform: Chief Justice Earl Warren.

Warren led a very liberal Court throughout the 1950s and '60s, enshrining into law many of the rights of the accused that we know so well today.[31] Sotomayor's effort to forge a set of rights adapted to twenty-first-century realities, however, has met a more hostile audience among her colleagues. She wrote alone in a case about warrantless GPS tracking to argue that we may need to fundamentally rethink privacy rights.[32] She faced down a furious dissent when she held that police must take a suspect's status as a child into account when deciding whether to read him his rights.[33] She stood alone in dissent when she argued that eyewitness identification testimony should be excluded from criminal trials if it was obtained under suggestive circumstances and poses a substantial likelihood of misidentification.[34] More recently, she was joined only by Breyer when she dissented from the Court's refusal to hear a chilling death penalty appeal from Alabama: the defendant had been sentenced to death by an elected judge after the jury voted eight to four to spare his life. To no avail, Sotomayor called on the Court to reconsider such judicial overrides, pointing out that Alabama judges stand nearly alone in their willingness to disregard juries and that evidence suggests that they are heavily influenced by morbid electoral politics.[35]

On occasion, though, the Roberts Court has embraced Sotomayor's appreciation of the need to change with the times. In 2012, one of those occasions produced an important exception to this Court's prevailing trend of turning aside calls to mandate greater fairness in our criminal justice system. Surprisingly, perhaps, this case involved the most pervasive of all government bribes: the plea bargain.

On March 25, 2003, Anthony Cooper tried to shoot Kali Mundy in the head but missed. He was later arrested and charged by Michigan authorities with assault with intent to murder. The prosecutor decided to offer a deal: plead guilty and I'll dramatically reduce the potential sentence. Cooper, if convicted after a trial, faced the possibility of fifteen to thirty years in prison; the prosecutor offered Cooper four to seven years for giving up his right to a trial (and all the other rights that come with it).

So far, this story is entirely routine.[36] The criminal justice system dispenses with the vast majority of criminal prosecutions through plea deals rather than full trials. Over 95 percent of criminal cases now end with plea bargains, meaning that one of our most treasured constitutional rights—the right to a jury trial—plays only a bit part in today's criminal law. Many plea deals include waivers of the right to appeal, preventing review of even close questions. Instead, we place a lot of trust in prosecutors and criminal defense lawyers to operate a shadow market of plea negotiations, where evidence, the law, personal relationships, politics, the burden of a trial, and many other factors shape dispositions.

That trust failed Anthony Cooper. His lawyer told him not to take a deal, asserting that the prosecution could not prove assault with intent to murder because Cooper had hit only his intended victim's abdomen, hip, and buttock—even though he had clearly aimed right at her head. Following his lawyer's preposterous advice, Cooper rejected the deal, went to trial, lost, and received a fifteen-to-thirty-year mandatory minimum term of imprisonment. Cooper then challenged his sentence, arguing that his right to the effective assistance of counsel had been violated by the incompetent legal advice he'd received during plea negotiations. The Supreme Court ruled in his favor.[37]

Writing the principal dissent in *Lafler v. Cooper*, Scalia argued that Cooper's claim was ridiculous. Cooper had received a full trial—what Scalia called "the 24-karat test of fairness"—and was sentenced to precisely the number of years the law required. No defendant has a right to a plea deal, so what could Cooper legitimately complain about?

For years, Scalia would have been in the majority.[38] Like many government attempts to bribe Americans to surrender their rights, the plea bargain has long been considered more than a little unseemly. As Scalia put it, "In the United States, we have plea bargaining a-plenty, but . . . it has been regarded as a necessary evil." He added, "We accept plea bargaining because many believe that without it our long and expensive process of criminal trial could not sustain the burden imposed on it, and our system of criminal justice would grind to a halt."

Until recently, this attitude had mostly led judges to steer clear of plea bargaining.[39] Only grudgingly did courts note its vital role in the day-to-day administration of American criminal justice—and they did little to ensure that the Constitution's fundamental values of fairness were safeguarded in those life-altering transactions. Adhering to this view in *Lafler*, Scalia derisively rejected what he called a "sporting-chance theory of criminal law, in which the State functions like a conscientious casino-operator, giving each player a fair chance to beat the house, that is, to serve less time than the law says he deserves."

As Sotomayor remarked at oral argument, however, "sometimes one's experience has to be challenged." And in a surprise to most observers, in *Lafler* the Court charted a new path. Writing for the majority, Justice Kennedy reasoned that we don't necessarily have to think of the plea bargain as a coercive or otherwise suspicious bribe to abandon constitutional rights. Instead, he elaborated, it can be treated as a substitution of one type of right (a fair plea-bargaining process) for another (a fair trial). Prosecutors don't have to offer plea bargains, but once they do, defendants are entitled to adequate representation in the ensuing negotiations.[40] Kennedy thus recognized "the reality that criminal justice today is for the most part a system of pleas, not a system of trials." He added, "The right to adequate assistance of counsel cannot be defined or enforced without taking account of the central role plea bargaining plays in securing convictions and determining sentences."

Kennedy's opinion, joined by the four left-leaning justices, reveals an admirable aspiration. By looking beyond the basic trial rights written into the Constitution more than two centuries ago, the Court can at least try to recognize rights in the contexts necessary to bring the entire criminal system closer to the ideal of justice. Even if courts cannot directly oversee prosecutors or monitor the course of negotiations, they can at least safeguard fair procedures by insisting that both parties are well represented in plea talks. In Cooper's case, this meant recognizing that he had a right to receive better advice from his attorney about whether to accept the plea deal.

Much more will be required if this approach to criminal justice is to have a meaningful impact. Because the Roberts Court has generally been loath to expand defendants' rights, it's difficult to be optimistic. But *Lafler* reveals a powerful impulse to ensure that the Constitution remains relevant to the contemporary world of negotiated criminal justice.

The deal became known as the Cornhusker Kickback.[41] It was December 2009; for weeks, Senate Majority Leader Harry Reid and other Senate leaders had been trying to woo the last vote to push Barack Obama's bill to reform the nation's health care system across the finish line. The holdout was Senator Ben Nelson, a conservative Nebraska Democrat. Throughout the debate over health care reform, Nelson had questioned the wisdom of expanding Medicaid as part of the administration's effort to deliver health coverage to most uninsured Americans.

Medicaid, signed into law alongside Medicare by Lyndon B. Johnson in 1965, is a cooperative state and federal program that provides health care to millions of poor Americans. The program mainly covers children from very poor families, poor pregnant women, and disabled people. Contrary to myth, it has never provided health insurance to all, or even most, Americans in poverty. When Medicaid was passed, federal law set minimum coverage criteria, and states were given considerable leeway when deciding how much or how little to expand the group of poor citizens eligible for coverage. When the Affordable Care Act (ACA) was passed, Democrats wanted to add an entirely new coverage requirement: all state Medicaid programs must cover *every* nonelderly person whose earnings didn't exceed 133 percent of the federal poverty level. Of the roughly 32 million uninsured Americans who stood to gain health coverage under the ACA, about half would receive it through this Medicaid expansion.[42]

What kept Senator Nelson up at night was how the states would afford this mandate. Since its inception, Medicaid has been funded by a combination of federal and state contributions. Prior to the ACA's passage, Congress picked up roughly half to three-quarters of the tab, leaving states to come up with the rest. Nelson had served as Governor of Nebraska and knew how hard it was for states to cover existing Medicaid programs—much less an expanded regime. Indeed, even before the Great Recession punctured state budgets, states had faced ballooning health care costs that had led many to slash Medicaid benefits and stretch their remaining funds. Recalling his time in the governor's mansion, Nelson dubbed Medicaid the "Pac-Man who ate the state budget."[43]

To assuage concerns, the ACA's authors decided to federally fund 100 percent of the cost of the expansion for the first few years and about 90 percent thereafter. Relative to the traditional funding scheme, this seemed like a great deal, but Nelson still wasn't persuaded. Even a small share of the burden in financing this massive Medicaid expansion, he felt, could be enough to push state budgets to the brink. And what if the Feds reneged on their promise? As the Senate vote on the bill drew near, Nelson demanded that states be given a right to opt out of the Medicaid expansion.

Unwilling to countenance the prospect of states breaking away and creating gaps in the ACA's expansion of coverage, Reid made Nelson an irresistible offer: if Nelson voted for the ACA, the federal government would permanently fund the *entire* cost of Nebraska's Medicaid expansion. Nelson took the deal and the Senate passed the bill.

It wasn't long, however, before everyone discovered the special break Nelson had wrangled. Conservatives seized on the so-called Cornhusker Kickback and made it a poster child for the entire law, which they said (with some accuracy) had been written for months behind closed doors to dodge public scrutiny. Unable to quell this firestorm, Nelson joined in calls for all states to receive the same deal. As negotiations played out on the final bill, Democratic leaders cut out the Cornhusker Kickback and upped the federal contribution to the Medicaid expansion for all fifty states. But that was only the sweet half of the deal. The bitter half, familiar from preexisting law, was that states would lose *all* federal Medicaid funding if they refused to expand their Medicaid programs.

After the ACA was signed into law, twenty-six states challenged the constitutionality of its Medicaid expansion. They argued that it crossed a line between permissible pressure to expand Medicaid and impermissible coercion, giving states no genuine choice. The states did not object to taking federal money. But even in the face of what looked like a good deal, they still wanted the prerogative to respond, "No, thanks." They didn't think they could do so, however, unless the Court struck down the federal government's power to strip away all Medicaid funds from any state that declined the ACA's new Medicaid offer. Nelson's initial demand in Senate negotiations had been transformed into constitutional supplication.

It also turned out to be constitutional prophecy. With all eyes on the individual mandate, the ACA's challengers quietly scored one of the most important victories for states' rights—and against federal coercion—in American history. As part of its 2012 ruling, the Court struck down the federal government's threat to withdraw all Medicaid funding from any state refusing to transform its Medicaid program into the broader program contemplated by the ACA. In that holding, Roberts was joined not only by his four right-leaning colleagues but also by Breyer and Kagan. The seven-to-two Medicaid ruling delivered precisely what Nelson originally desired: the right for states to keep their preexisting Medicaid funding even if they decided not to take part in the expansion.[44] Many observers were surprised. To be sure, the Court had hinted in the past that threats by Congress to strip vital funding from states if they refused to administer federal policies might at some point become too intimidating to pass muster. But it had never actually ruled that a federal spending program was unconstitutionally coercive.

In the ACA's Medicaid expansion, though, the Court had finally encountered a federal threat it deemed worthy of such condemnation. "Medicaid spending," Roberts noted, "accounts for over 20 percent of the average State's total budget, with federal funds covering 50 to 83 percent of those costs." By threatening the "loss of over 10 percent of a State's overall budget," he added, Congress had engaged in "economic dragooning that leaves the States with no real option." The Chief deemed "the size of the new financial burden" to be "irrelevant in analyzing whether the State has been coerced into accepting" it. For Roberts, " 'Your money or your life' is a coercive proposition, whether you have a single dollar in your pocket or $500."

The Chief thus treated each state's preexisting Medicaid funding from the Federal Treasury much like that state's own money—essentially like an entitlement. No such view would have been plausible if Congress were starting from scratch and Medicaid hadn't existed at all before 2010. But over the decades since Medicaid's passage, the states had come to depend heavily on that federal funding stream. As a result, in Roberts's memorable words, "the financial 'inducement' Congress has chosen is much more than 'relatively mild encouragement'—it is a gun to the head."

This opinion left open many questions about how to determine when Congress has gone too far. It did not set a percentage of state budgets as a threshold, nor did it explain how to deal with cases where one state faces a huge threat while another faces no threat at all. Roberts was content to leave those questions to the future: "It is enough for today that wherever that line may be, this statute is surely beyond it. Congress may not simply conscript state [agencies] into the national bureaucratic army, and that is what it is attempting to do with the Medicaid expansion."

Whereas the Court's recent cases involving bribery of individuals have not involved blunt coercion to accept a government offer, that is precisely what Roberts said the ACA did to the states. Though it may seem odd to think of the states in this way, the Court regularly speaks of their "dignity," their "rights," and the need to "respect" them. This makes some sense: if the federal government could use its various powers to commandeer, coerce, and ride roughshod over the states, our constitutional design would be thwarted. Although Congress can cajole and play hardball, there must be limits on how it treats the states.[45]

The Chief's view did not stand unchallenged. In dissent, Ginsburg, joined by Sotomayor, vigorously disagreed that the federal government had crossed any constitutional line. Ginsburg's lengthy, passionate duel with Roberts constituted a master class in constitutional argument.

To Ginsburg, it was hogwash to equate the Medicaid expansion's imposition on the states with "your money or your life." The states, she argued, had signed up for a program called Medicaid. And they had done so *voluntarily* at a time when Congress, in the Medicaid statute itself, expressly reserved the "right to alter, amend, or repeal" portions of Medicaid. It was silly to cry foul when the states had signed up forewarned of potential changes on which all Medicaid funding was conditioned.

The Chief had anticipated this rejoinder. True, he conceded, the states had once voluntarily agreed to something called Medicaid, but Ginsburg's argument lacked a limiting principle. Congress couldn't add just *anything* to the Medicaid statute, call it part of Medicaid, and then force the states to abide by it. For instance, Congress couldn't require states to move their capitals under threat of losing existing Medicaid funds. A line had to be drawn somewhere. For Roberts, it was crossed if Congress added policies to Medicaid that did not fall foreseeably within the bounds of the original program. He characterized the original program as one "designed to cover medical services for four particular categories of the needy: the disabled, the blind, the elderly, and needy families with dependent children." The ACA's Medicaid expansion, by contrast, was something else entirely: "an element of a comprehensive national plan to provide universal health insurance coverage."

A powerful point, but Ginsburg wasn't going down without one last shot. She agreed for the sake of argument that there must be some limit on Congress's prerogative to redefine a previously enacted federal program. Here, however, Congress hadn't come close to that limit. The Court's majority, she thought, characterized Medicaid's purposes far too narrowly. It was not merely a program designed to provide coverage to just four groups; it was a program designed to provide health coverage to the poor. From this perspective, states could have predicted that Congress would someday take Medicaid in the ACA's direction. The passage of Medicaid, after all, was the start of a dream that promised a better future in which America took care of its poorest citizens. To Ginsburg, it was dishonest to pretend that this vision wasn't part of Medicaid's enactment from the start and, in so doing, to dash the hopes that so many Americans had sustained for so long.

Knowing he had the votes to win, Roberts declined to respond to this argument. But he had strong responses ready to hand. Even if states that had voluntarily signed up for Medicaid could have predicted that Congress might one day expand the program to all of the country's poorest residents, they had signed up decades ago. Surely, Roberts might have argued, a decision made long ago couldn't keep a state locked in the trunk of a federal program forever, thus forcing it to be driven down whatever road Congress decides to take today.

Roberts's landmark ruling on the Medicaid issue was the first of its kind. The doctrine that it sketches is plainly meant for truly exceptional circumstances. Out of respect for Congress's broad and long-recognized authority to nudge (and even shove) states with financial inducements, the Court is likely to invoke this logic again only in the most extreme cases of federal coercion. Otherwise, the Court might radically destabilize the vast policy architecture of state-federal cooperation, significant parts of which involve state use of and dependence on federal funds.[46]

Indeed, the Medicaid ruling itself has already triggered a cascade of unanticipated legal, political, and practical consequences, some of which have impeded effective implementation of other parts of the ACA.

Yet for all these uncertainties, the Chief delivered a clear and resounding message: Congress may not use its enormous bank account or its power over state-federal programs to coerce the surrender of constitutional rights.

No matter how strongly a justice feels about a constitutional issue, there sometimes comes a point when he or she faces a difficult dilemma: when to give up. When is it time to stop dissenting, to recognize that the Court has fully embraced a turn in the law and there's no going back?[47] That question presented itself to the left-leaning justices when they confronted the Medicaid expansion issue.

There is precedent for drawing out a fight. Battling the death penalty, Justices Thurgood Marshall and William Brennan never gave up.[48] The Court struck it down in 1972 but then reinstated it—with an elaborate set of new rules—in 1976.[49] Marshall and Brennan valiantly kept dissenting, insisting in every capital case to reach the Court that "the death penalty is in all circumstances cruel and unusual punishment forbidden" by the Eighth Amendment.[50] Justice Harry Blackmun adopted a similar posture in 1994 when he wrote, "From this day forward, I no longer shall tinker with the machinery of death."[51] The issue was too important and their disagreement with the death penalty too deep to call an end to their protest of an institution that had become all too peculiar.[52]

When the Court released its decision on the ACA, however, it soon became clear that a dam built to hold back the flood of a federalism revolution—one long prophesied by conservative jurists—had cracked. In joining the Chief to strike down the Medicaid expansion, Breyer and Kagan embraced a core precept of states' rights that the Court had first announced in the 1990s: Congress may not compel state governments to implement Congress's policies.[53] If Congress wants something done, it has to do it by itself, empower the Executive, or nudge states into cooperating without coercing them. When the Court first announced these principles, Breyer vigorously dissented. At the time, he argued that in other federalist democracies with strong state governments (Germany, for example), national mandates actually signify respect, not contempt, for states' rights. Such mandates, Breyer explained, entrust state governments with the solemn responsibility of implementing essential national policies.[54]

Somewhere along the line, however, Breyer apparently decided to stop dissenting from a core tenet of the states' rights view. Kagan, still new to the Court, joined him. Why? One theory casts the duo as guileful agents in a cunning plot to give Roberts at least one victory in exchange for his vote to uphold the individual mandate. Another posits that the two either embraced some conservative beliefs about state autonomy or determined that they just did not feel strongly enough to forever dissent.

Neither explanation is entirely satisfying. Roberts already had five votes to invalidate the Medicaid expansion; he didn't need their support. Besides, it's hard to imagine that Breyer and Kagan voted against their respective consciences as part of some elaborate trade. Nor can it be said that the Chief's argument was so irrefutable that it *must* have won over Breyer and Kagan, neither of whom has ever displayed particular sympathy for states' rights. After all, although Ginsburg did not land a knockout blow, her opinion makes excellent points. In particular, Roberts's equation of a threat to withdraw all Medicaid funds with a gun to the head was open to some doubt: in 2009, the respected Heritage Foundation had urged states to reject Medicaid funding,[55] and in late 2010 a group of legislators in Texas had seriously considered that option.

Although it is likely that Kagan and Breyer went along with Roberts because they were genuinely persuaded that the Medicaid expansion resulted in coercion, more than just that one consideration may have influenced their conclusion. Indeed, there is another explanation for their votes that is too often overlooked—and it goes to the heart of why we maintain limits on federal power to buy off our rights.

When government becomes too comfortable with bribing Americans to give up constitutional rights, a culture is bred in which government no longer respects those rights in the first place. In turn, as "We the People" grow accustomed to government disrespecting our rights, our own disrespect may not lag far behind. Americans' experience with the Constitution may gradually become one in which rights are perceived as mere commodities to be discounted and bargained away, and not as fundamental guarantors of life, liberty, and the pursuit of happiness. This is a dangerous path for us to follow, and it justifies a strong stand.

Brennan, the liberal icon who never stopped trying to rid America of the death penalty, understood the gravity of this threat. In the 1987 case *South Dakota v. Dole*, the Court upheld Congress's effort to push states into raising the minimum drinking age to twenty-one by threatening to withhold a small portion of federal highway funding from states that didn't roll over.[56] Brennan was the only liberal dissenter. He voted to strike down the law even though *Dole* apparently involved only a question of states' rights, for which he had little patience. But Brennan was, above all, a constitutional architect, a justice who focused on basic questions of legal design. At that level, he saw little distinction between threats to the states and threats to individuals: bribery that threatened one constitutional restriction posed a threat to all constitutional restrictions. In his view, the federal government sought to bribe its way past the Twenty-first Amendment—which, by repealing Prohibition, guaranteed that states retain absolute authority over internal regulation of alcohol consumption. Brennan would not abide such maneuvers.

Breyer and Kagan followed in Brennan's footsteps with their votes on the ACA's Medicaid expansion. With national attention focused squarely on the Court, they must have understood that this case presented the rare opportunity to send a strong message to Congress and state legislatures: if you're tempted to pressure states *or* individual Americans to relinquish constitutional rights, proceed with caution. The era of playing unlimited games with coercion is over.

Roberts probably didn't expect to cause a stir with a few off-the-cuff remarks in 2011 about how he finds the writings of law professors all but useless. "Pick up a copy of any law review that you see," he explained, "and the first article is likely to be, you know, the influence of Immanuel Kant on evidentiary approaches in 18th century Bulgaria, or something, which I'm sure was of great interest to the academic that wrote it, but isn't of much help to the bar."[57] For most readers, this comment probably triggers bemusement or indifference. From the lofty standpoint of the ivory tower, however, Roberts may as well have confided that the Court had plans to tar and feather the next law professor who dared to argue a case.

Roberts's opinion aside, academics have often provided keen insights into the constitutional issues addressed by the Court.[58] Oddly, however, the use of government bribes to discourage Americans from standing their constitutional ground has attracted only a small measure of scholarly attention.[59] The Roberts Court's weighty interventions suggest the need for deeper examination of this doctrine.

Three principles offer helpful clarity. They do not solve every question, but they can frame a discussion.

The first principle is that constitutional rights are rarely absolutes. Even when everyone agrees that a law obstructs constitutionally protected activities or intrudes on the states, courts typically allow the law to stand if the government has sufficient reason for its action and the imposition is no greater than necessary in light of that reason. What is true of ordinary limits on constitutional rights should also be true of government attempts to bribe people (or states) to give up their rights: when the government has a compelling reason to bribe, it should be allowed to do so if the bribe is open, aboveboard, and goes no further than necessary to achieve the government's objective.

Examples of this point are legion. The federal government imposes conditions on the grant or continued receipt of benefits all the time, and the vast majority of these conditions are plainly legitimate. Thus, plea bargains in which the defendant is adequately counseled by his lawyer pose no serious constitutional question. Nor would the creation of a new Medicaid statute—Medicaid 2.0—that covers everyone living below the poverty line and gives each state a choice about whether to opt in. The National Institutes of Health are free to condition research grants on publication of any results, and Congress can deny HIV/AIDS funding to groups that use its funding to promote messages it rejects. In sum, government enjoys broad power to offer deals in which we trade rights for other benefits, and in most cases we have no option but to make a choice. This is occasionally unfair, but in many cases it allows for a creative and workable government.

The second principle is that sometimes bribes that might otherwise be acceptable turn into coercive threats. Warning lights ought to flash when a government proposal becomes, in words that Marlon Brando's Vito Corleone immortalized, "an offer you can't refuse."

For instance, many universities have long received over half their budgets for scientific research from the federal government. Imagine that tomorrow, Congress "offers" to continue providing all this funding provided the universities agree not to publish anything about climate change. Because entire programs have come to rely on federal funds, many universities would have no real choice but to go along with the new restriction; in effect, this coercive "offer" is equivalent to a command. Carrying this tactic to an extreme, Congress might as well make it a criminal offense for any university president to allow a faculty member to publish a paper on climate change. In both cases, university officials would be all but forced to comply, and both actions clearly violate the First Amendment's freedom of speech.

The final principle is that the government must be held to a higher standard than private individuals and organizations, even when it makes an offer that gives potential recipients the freedom to say, "No, thanks."

This precept rests on several considerations. The most important is that, typically, only the government is bound to follow the Constitution. Whereas the president can potentially violate your First Amendment rights, neither your father nor your neighbor can do so. Thus, it would be perfectly constitutional (if morally questionable) for a mother to bribe her child not to become a Tea Party activist or an Occupy Wall Street leader by buying him a car. It would also be constitutional for a private individual to pay a politician openly to put a certain policy in place. Such private bribery might well violate certain statutes, but it wouldn't violate anything in the Constitution. When Congress acts this way, though, we face much harder questions.

Simply put, the Constitution is designed as the ultimate constraint on government. When the state acts, its behavior raises a fundamentally different set of legal questions, because the state is a creature of the Constitution—and because the state has deep pockets that it alone can replenish through the coercive power of taxation. Moreover, for both theoretical and practical reasons, we expect government to protect our rights, not undermine them. If we allow the state to act like a huge corporation that is prone to buying its way out of brushes with the law, the state might begin by bribing its way out of constitutional limits and later start resisting and disrespecting those limits altogether.

It's also important to remember that the systemic consequences of government bribes are different from those of private bribes. Even if individuals or state governments voluntarily choose to give up some of their rights in exchange for federal prizes, constitutional rights do more than just protect individuals or states. The First Amendment's protection of free speech, for example, serves as a bulwark against government attempts to rig the universe of ideas readily available to the public. It is both an individual right and a structural guarantor of democratic society. If the government persuades you to sell *your* free speech rights, you affect all of *our* free speech rights, because your friends, coworkers, and Twitter followers benefit (in theory, anyway) from hearing what you have to say about politics, culture, or science.

Put another way, even when government uses carrots rather than sticks, it can distort the distribution of information and ideas in society in ways private donors generally cannot do. For instance, if a state passes a law giving veterans a special break on their property taxes only if they refrain from voicing anti-war views, it can bring about a world in which it looks like many vets are pro-war when that's not the case at all. The Court accordingly held precisely that sort of bribe unconstitutional in 1958.[60]

Bribes directed at states can have similarly insidious effects. Constitutional protections of federalism exist not only to protect states against federal coercion but also to safeguard a system in which states act as "laboratories of democracy," free to experiment with different approaches to public policy. If Congress were free without limit to bribe states to amend their laws, each state's self-interest might lead it to accept the offer. But then, suddenly, we could be left with a system in which Congress, rather than state legislatures, sets a uniform policy on an issue traditionally reserved to individual states. As a result, just a single legislature—rather than fifty individual legislatures—would end up brainstorming about how to solve the problem at hand.

Failure to follow any of these principles could do profound damage to our constitutional democracy. Fortunately, a majority of the Roberts Court has begun to approach the knotty problem of government bribery more thoughtfully, offering new insights on its vices and reaffirming limits on its practice. Although considerable uncertainty remains, this sensitivity looks like it could emerge as a defining feature of the Roberts Court—enabling it to safeguard liberty more effectively from the many threats and offers that can imperil our rights.

9

MAKING RIGHTS REAL:

ACCESS TO JUSTICE

Nearly fifty thousand fans held their breath as St. Louis Cardinals center fielder Jon Jay hit a hard ground ball toward second base. Game 3 of the 2013 World Series was tied 4–4 in the bottom of the ninth inning, with one out and Cardinals runners on second and third base. The series was tied 1–1. It was the sort of game Little League players everywhere dreamed of.

Boston Red Sox second baseman Dustin Pedroia made a terrific stop and threw home to catcher Jarrod Saltalamacchia, who tagged out Yadier Molina as he slid home from third. Two outs. Saltalamacchia then looked up and saw Allen Craig barreling toward third. Saltalamacchia threw to diving Red Sox third baseman Will Middlebrooks but missed. As the ball rolled down the left field foul line, Craig raced for home plate. Middlebrooks was still on the ground, recovering from his dive, and his legs tangled with Craig's. After stumbling briefly, Craig ran toward home. A throw from left fielder Daniel Nava arrived moments ahead of Craig, whom Saltalamacchia tagged out. Three outs. Extra innings. Or was it?

It was not. Citing a Major League Baseball rule governing "obstruction," which occurs when a fielder not in the process of fielding the ball "impedes the progress of any runner," third-base umpire Jim Joyce awarded Craig the game-winning run.[1]

Joyce later claimed the call was an easy one: "Unfortunately for Middlebrooks, he was right there, and there was contact. [Craig] could not advance to home plate naturally."[2] Whether or not Joyce made the correct call—an issue commentators hotly disputed—he was wrong on one point: the call was anything but simple. It involved a complex judgment about the counterfactual question of whether Craig would have scored if not for the obstruction. Unsurprisingly, Joyce's ruling triggered familiar debates over the role umpires play in baseball. In the view of some critics, it seems unsporting and unfair for umpires to make these sorts of judgment calls, transforming games from a clash of athletes into a lottery wheel of subjective and unpredictable technicalities.

In 2005, at his confirmation hearings, John G. Roberts Jr. tapped into that sentiment to frame a judicial philosophy: "Judges are like umpires. Umpires don't make the rules, they apply them. The role of an umpire and a judge is critical. They make sure everybody plays by the rules." Like the best and most modest umpires, Roberts promised, he'd apply the law fairly. "I will remember that it's my job to call balls and strikes," he explained, "and not to pitch or bat."[3]

Senate Republicans swooned at Roberts's all-American analogy. John Cornyn of Texas warmly responded, "You were quite eloquent in saying that you wanted to be an umpire."[4] Sam Brownback of Kansas agreed, describing as "very apt" the nominee's point about "the courts and baseball."[5] The Senate seemed eager to confirm Roberts to preside over both the Supreme Court and Major League Baseball. These great institutions have competed for talent before: former President William H. Taft was passed over for the job of Commissioner of Baseball in 1920, before being confirmed as Chief Justice in 1921.[6]

The "Umpire Moment" of Roberts's confirmation hearing looms large in many critical assessments of his Court.[7] Typically, it is presented by the Chief's detractors as his great vow of neutrality and then followed by a blistering charge of bias and betrayal. In the view of many commentators, the Roberts Court is pro-business and anti-consumer,[8] hostile to civil rights claims,[9] and unsympathetic to criminal defendants.[10] These trends in the Court's rulings, critics usually add, reflect an activist departure from the neutrality Roberts so earnestly promised. Vague suggestions of sinister motives occasionally lurk about the edges of these allegations, hints that this Court is influenced by sympathy for big business and disdain for the very rights and regulations it is charged with enforcing.

These critiques are only partly right. In its nearly decade-old existence, the Roberts Court has issued a string of opinions that, by and large, favor businesses over consumers, law enforcement officers over civil rights plaintiffs, and the government over criminal defendants. The "winners" and "losers" in these fields are not hard to discern; nobody has seriously suggested that civil rights plaintiffs are faring well these days. Although the Court may not have moved as quickly toward the right as some conservatives hoped after Roberts and Alito were confirmed, no one can deny that the trend is a significant one. Notably, the left-leaning justices have joined quite a few of these "conservative" rulings; on these issues, they don't always lean terribly far to the left.[11]

The explanation for these trends, though, is not a story of "neutrality" versus "activism." Rather, it is a tale that mixes competing beliefs about what the law requires with a fundamental disagreement about the role of courts and litigation in American life. In the mid-twentieth century, moved by a desire to protect groups it saw as powerless, the Court threw open courthouse doors and created new law to combat widespread inequalities and injustices.[12] In stark contrast, the Roberts Court's temperament reflects the deregulatory and cynical tenor of our age. Most of the justices look skeptically on the use of litigation to regulate big business, on the efficacy and value of civil rights lawsuits, and on efforts to deter police misconduct through court-enforced constitutional law. They also seem to doubt the legitimacy and social benefits of some of the regulations and constitutional rights that give rise to many of these suits. Whereas the midcentury Court saw itself as a protector of the powerless and was willing to vastly expand its authority to achieve its vision of justice, the Roberts Court is mostly uninterested in that role. Overall, it is far more sensitive to the substantial burdens of litigation than to the potential benefits of lawsuits.

As a result, this Court has sounded a general retreat, narrowing and shutting down many of the doctrines and procedural devices through which plaintiffs invoke the courts to vindicate their rights. In a series of important, low-profile rulings, it has dealt critical legal rules a death of a thousand cuts—leaving many of our rights intact but making them effectively impossible to enforce in any court. The consequence in many fields of law has been a sharp trend toward deregulation, leaving businesses and government freer to act without the checks and balances— and burdens and frustrations—of judicial oversight.

One of the defining features of the Roberts Court is thus its reimagining of the judicial role in far narrower terms. Whether damned or praised, this dawning era of an anti-court Court promises to forever reshape the role of the Judiciary in "establishing justice."

For all the criticism it has received, Roberts's use of the umpire metaphor at his confirmation hearings was a stroke of public relations genius. Hitching his wagon to a beloved national pastime, Roberts connected with viewers and legislators alike at a gut level that abstract legal theory could never reach.

Baseball has played a revered role in life at the Court for several decades. Justice Potter Stewart, for example, used to keep a small TV set in his chambers so that he could carefully track the Cincinnati Reds. Aware of his boss's priorities, a clerk sent a mid-argument note for Stewart into the courtroom during the 1973 Mets-Reds play-offs; it read, "Kranepool flies to right. [Vice President Spiro] Agnew resigns."[13] Justice Harry Blackmun shared Stewart's love of the game. Inspired by a baseball antitrust case, Blackmun generated furious negotiations in the early 1970s by creating a selective list of eighty-eight players "that have sparked the diamond and its environs and that have provided tinder for recaptured thrills." Wrangling over whom to include on Blackmun's list produced more heat than did the legal reasoning in the case.[14]

That love of baseball persists. In 2013, after Justice Sotomayor presided over a reenactment of the argument in Blackmun's case, the diehard Yankees fan confided that she would have demanded Joe DiMaggio's inclusion.[15] This was no surprise: raised in the Bronx, Sotomayor won national fame in 1994 as "the judge who saved baseball" by breaking a strike.[16] In 2009 she threw the first pitch at a Yankees–Red Sox game— and Yankees Manager Joe Girardi recalls saying, "We'll be calling you next week with a contract." (Sotomayor reportedly replied that she'd "stick to her day job."[17]) Sotomayor's passion is matched only by that of Justice Alito, who has reportedly transformed his desk at the Court into a shrine to the Philadelphia Phillies.[18] Justice Breyer's adoration of the sport, in turn, shone through when he peppered lawyers in a football antitrust case with detailed questions about the Red Sox. "I know baseball better," he slyly explained.[19]

Thus, when Roberts described himself as an umpire, he did more than sound fair and modest. He talked the talk of a baseball-loving justice.

Yet the umpire metaphor—and Roberts's claim that he would enforce rules, not make them—may have engendered unrealistic expectations. While judges and umpires both strive toward basic values of fairness and impartiality, we learn more about the two jobs by contrasting them than we do by noting their similarities.

On the one hand, umpires enjoy more discretion than meets the eye. For example, they decide when weather conditions are "unsuitable" for play and rule on whether a pitch was made with the "obvious intent to catch a batter off balance." Not to mention, of course, the all-important strike zone, described by one umpire as "a living, breathing document."[20] In these ways, umpires must exercise judgment—though a kind of judgment that can (and should) operate without any favoritism for particular players or teams, and without a broader agenda for the rules of Major League Baseball or the role of umpires.

On the other hand, while umpires mostly *enforce* rules and make judgment calls on the margins, judges *create* constitutional law. As Judge Richard Posner writes, "No serious person thinks that the rules that judges in our system apply . . . are given to them the way the rules of baseball are given to umpires."[21] Rather, to a judge deciding a truly close case, "there are no balls or strikes until he calls them. . . . His activity is creation rather than discovery." In recognizing rights to armed self-defense and freedom from warrantless GPS surveillance, for example, the Court forged new law.

Further, judges—unlike umpires—regularly disagree over what the rule for a particular case should be and what principles should determine those rules. That is the very nature of constitutional interpretation. These disputes are important because judges wield a tool denied to umpires: invalidation. If judges deem a law unconstitutional, perhaps because it is "unreasonable" or "shocks the conscience," the law falls. While umpires fill minor gaps in the rules of baseball, judges enjoy the far greater power to fashion and refashion the basic terms of our legal system.[22]

This is increasingly true of the Court's role in interpreting some of our most important commercial and anti-discrimination statutes. These laws often leave lots of room for judicial interpretation. In theory, if the courts get it wrong, Congress can pass a new law to correct their error. And in rare cases, this actually happens. Motivated by a call to arms from Justice Ginsburg, for example, Congress passed the Lilly Ledbetter Fair Pay Act in 2009 to reverse a five-to-four ruling by Alito that cut back on pay discrimination claims filed by women. Congress, however, rarely manages such course corrections these days. As Rick Hasen, a professor at the University of California, Irvine School of Law, showed in a study of cases from 2001 to 2012, "the number of Congressional overrides has fallen off a cliff."[23] Political dysfunction and partisanship, he notes, bear much of the blame. With respect to defining statutory law, then, the Court plays an increasingly prominent and unchallenged role.

This is not to say that every legal question requires some profound act of value-inflected judgment. The vast majority of cases, in fact, are too clear-cut to make it as far as the Supreme Court. In 2013, for example, 375,870 cases were filed in federal district courts; 56,475 appeals were lodged in the federal circuit courts; and 7,509 petitions for review of state and federal court rulings were submitted to the justices.[24] Yet in its term from October 2012 to June 2013, the Court issued a mere 78 opinions, turning aside all other petitions. By well-established custom, it left to the lower courts cases that called for mere umpiring, granting only cases involving particularly important and divisive issues of federal law. As a result, nearly all the matters the Court considered defied easy resolution under settled principles of legal interpretation.

Many of the cases that the Court did agree to hear, moreover, mattered for reasons other than their legal bottom line. As Justice Kennedy has recognized, "By our opinions, we teach."[25] The lessons the justices offer affect how Americans give life to constitutional values. When Roberts warns against being ruled by "functionaries" and Kennedy affirms the "dignity" of same-sex marriage, they do more than call balls and strikes. They help us navigate the Constitution. They affect political debate, increase the salience of selected issues, and influence which ideas are taken seriously. They urge us to think hard about our current practices and fundamental beliefs.[26] The justices know this. As Chief Justice Earl Warren wrote decades ago, "Our judges are not monks or scientists, but participants in the living stream of our national life."[27]

Against this complex reality, comparing judges to umpires can convey the mistaken impression that judges do not make value-laden

choices. In many cases that the Court agrees to review, the simple truth is
that totally "neutral" positions do not exist. As Justice Kagan told the Senate Judiciary Committee during her confirmation hearing, "The metaphor
might suggest to some people that law is a kind of robotic enterprise . . .
that we just sort of stand there and, you know, we go 'ball' and 'strike'
and everything is clear-cut and that there is no judgment in the process.
And I do think that that is not right, and it is especially not right at the
Supreme Court level, where the hardest cases go."[28]

In other words, the Court is nothing like a computer, spitting out
disinterested free speech and gun rights rulings based on an algorithm
known only to the nine justices. Nor is it, as Jeffrey Toobin has rightly
explained, "an honor society for smart people."[29] The Court is an institution of government, charged with creating law that matches the evolving
experiences of a diverse nation with shared, timeless principles. "Correct" answers to privacy and equality cases aren't hovering out in the
ether, awaiting their discoverer. Instead, they are forged from precedent,
principle, history, and the interactions of nine men and women.

It would therefore be strange for a justice to be "impartial" or "neutral" in the sense of being utterly open-minded on all legal issues. As
Scalia observed in 2002, "It is virtually impossible to find a judge who
does not have preconceptions about the law."[30] He added, "Indeed, proof
that a Justice's mind at the time he joined the Court was a complete
tabula rasa in the area of constitutional adjudication would be evidence
of lack of qualification, not lack of bias."

In that respect, Supreme Court justices inevitably have agendas:
beliefs about what the law is, what it should be, and how to move it that
way. These high politics of law are entirely appropriate. Breyer celebrates
pragmatic rulings that make democracy work. The former prosecutors,
Alito and Sotomayor, share deep interests in privacy and criminal justice, though they approach those fields with different sympathies. Scalia
advances pointed views on nearly every subject, from speech to abortion
to gun rights. Ginsburg carries the banner for women's rights and exults
in the mysteries of civil procedure, while Thomas recasts whole fields
of law in originalist terms. Kennedy works hard to safeguard a particular vision of human liberty, and Roberts sets forth bold statements of
principle in cases about racial equality. Kagan remains something of a

question mark, though her plainspoken opinions reveal a strong com-monsensical streak.

These agendas encompass beliefs about what the law should say and beliefs about the role of courts in getting the law to mean what it says. Often, those beliefs are intertwined. For example, constitutional rights, regula-tions that can be enforced in court by private plaintiffs, and procedures that make it easier to sue tend to give judges greater influence. When the justices are skeptical of the underlying rights, doubtful of litigation, or concerned about overly broad uses of judicial power, they might understandably deem it appropriate to alter the legal framework in favor of a lesser judi-cial role. In so doing, they achieve many goals at once in their decades-long struggle over the Court's high politics.

Perhaps the most common charge leveled against the Roberts Court is that it is pro-business.[31] Assessing the Court's rulings in a wide range of legal fields, many critics allege that the justices have displayed an unmis-takable sympathy for "big business"—and a comparative disdain for reg-ulation designed to protect fair markets. Articles with titles like "Supreme Court, Inc." and "Business Reigns Supreme" now dot the journalistic landscape.[32]

There is some empirical support for this view. A study published in 2013 concluded that Roberts, Scalia, Kennedy, Thomas, and Alito are among the five most business-friendly justices since 1946, and that Alito and Roberts rank first and second, respectively.[33] The same study noted that, since joining the Court, Alito and Roberts have pulled their right-leaning colleagues to more pro-business positions. As a result, it con-cluded, the Roberts Court has been friendlier to business than any Court since World War II. These results echoed a *New York Times* report from 2010, which found that "the percentage of business cases on the Supreme Court docket has grown in the Roberts years, as has the percentage of cases won by business interests."[34]

The business cases covered by these studies arose from many con-texts. They involved antitrust statutes meant to prevent unlawful monop-olies, securities rules aimed at ensuring market integrity, product liability doctrines, anti-discrimination statutes, intellectual property protections, and a battery of other laws. In sum, they touched on a broad panoply of the nation's economic regulations. And across these varied domains, the studies found, this Court has shown a sustained sympathy for the interests of big businesses—at least as litigated against consumers, regulators, and smaller businesses.

The United States Chamber of Commerce is widely thought to have played a role in this development, a perception that it has occasionally encouraged.[35] Carter Phillips, a leading business attorney, thus remarked in 2007 that "except for the Solicitor General representing the United States, no single entity has more influence on what cases the Supreme Court decides and how it decides them than the [Chamber]."[36] Writing for *SCOTUSblog* in 2013, Adam Chandler confirmed that, from 2009 to 2012, the Chamber had filed more petitions asking the Court to hear a case than any other private entity (54) and had the second-highest success rate with its requests (32 percent).[37]

A heated battle over the Roberts Court's true sympathies rages in the shadow of these studies.[38] Some scholars dispute the categorization of particular decisions as "pro-business." They observe that winning three minor cases can matter a lot less than winning a single major case, and they emphasize that the ultimate consequences of "wins" and "losses" at the Court often look very different from what the initial scorecard might suggest. Each side points to cases that seemed close but went the other way. One side insists that the Court is being activist; the other side insists that the Court is rightly reversing a lot of mistaken rulings. And hanging over all this wrangling is a dispute over whether "pro-business" rulings might actually be beneficial to groups like consumers, shareholders, and small business owners. That dispute, in turn, often reduces to a familiar back-and-forth over whether economic regulations are generally good or bad for the public.

These arguments can quickly get very messy, and it is virtually impossible to wade through them to arrive at an iron-clad conclusion about whether the Roberts Court is indeed "pro-business" in its interpretation of economic regulations. The path is blocked by subjective judgments about the nature and effects of the Court's decisions, how "easy" certain cases were as a matter of law, and the relative importance of various rulings. Further, in many of these cases the Court addressed only a small part of broader regulatory schemes, control of which is ultimately reserved to Congress and federal agencies. As a consequence, the Court may be influenced by what it perceives to be signals from the other branches of government; at the very least, the effects and importance of its rulings can be understood only in relation to actions taken by those branches.

On a review of the available data and a close reading of the Roberts Court's opinions, however, two conclusions stand up to scrutiny: this Court is unusually interested in business affairs, and a majority of its justices are receptive to legal arguments that tend toward deregulation. As Kagan explained to an audience at the Aspen Ideas Festival in 2013, "It's not like the Chamber of Commerce appears in Court and you vote, I like the Chamber of Commerce or I don't. . . . But I do think that in a number of cases with respect to a number of areas of law, there is a majority of the Court that has a set of legal views that provide some significant relief from both federal and state regulation to businesses."[39]

Kagan did not mention any specific areas of law, but she may well have had in mind the arcane realm of procedure. However we evaluate the Court's approach to the statutes and doctrines that govern our economy, its dramatic rewriting of the procedural rules that structure litigation is unmistakably favorable to big businesses.

"When a chess player looks at the board," Arthur Koestler once wrote, "he does not see a static mosaic, a 'still life.'"[40] Rather, he sees "a magnetic field of forces, charged with energy—as Faraday saw the stresses surrounding magnets and currents as curves in space; or as Van Gogh saw vortices in the skies of Provence." Each piece radiates possibility. Every move ripples out, shuffling the deck of possible futures. This is why chess masters must possess a talent for grand strategy, which necessarily includes the ability to visualize an expanding field of uncertain events and chart a flexible path toward victory.

Now imagine a game of chess where, every other move, a player is entitled to move a piece *and* to modify the rules that govern any piece. He knows, or can guess, how that new rule will affect the ongoing game. Such is life at the Court. When the justices shape law, they form plans within plans.[41]

Some of the rules that attract the justices' attention have nothing to do with rights to bear arms or get an abortion; instead, they control a litigant's path through the justice system. One might think that someone who believes his rights have been violated can always go to court and obtain a remedy, but in practice that is only sometimes true. Lawyers must navigate a tangled web of procedural rules before they can reach the holy grail of damages for illegal conduct or an order preventing the conduct from recurring. The justices engage in some of their subtlest intrigues while shaping those rules.

Though procedural doctrines may seem obscure, they provide an essential means of balancing values like fairness, efficiency, and justice.[42] By tinkering with procedure, the Court can discourage people from filing suits, make it both more essential and more difficult to afford a lawyer, and stack the deck in favor of defendants by constructing obstacles to the discovery of relevant evidence. Indeed, a single, well-aimed procedural bullet can knock down dozens of legal claims when all those claims turn on the same procedural rule. Because America relies heavily on private plaintiffs to enforce many of its economic regulations, the practical result of pro-defendant procedures is often a form of deregulation—a result congenial to many business interests.

The Roberts Court has displayed a keen interest in procedural rules, issuing a string of opinions that make it harder to bring and maintain many kinds of claims. Several of its most significant lines of cases have focused on limiting suits by consumers and employees. The result has been a substantial diminution in the role of courts as places in which to enforce statutory limits on corporate behavior. The underlying rights remain standing, but they have been deprived of most of the legal force they once accrued through the threat of litigation.

That project has found its purest expression in a devastating assault on class actions. The class action mechanism allows representative plaintiffs to bring suit on behalf of much larger groups whose members have all been injured in the same way. This kind of lawsuit is often essential when each person's potential damages are so low that it would make no sense for anyone to file an individual case (or for any lawyer to get involved). Often, the availability of a class action determines whether a company alleged to have violated the law will ever be forced to defend the legality of its conduct in court.

For that reason, class actions have long played an important role in providing relief to those without the means or motive to combat corporate abuses by themselves. As New York University Law Professor Arthur Miller notes, they have also become part of a "satellite regulatory system."[43] By empowering private individuals, he explains, the class action "augments and sometimes serves as a substitute for the work of official government agencies that typically are under resourced, captured by the industries they are expected to regulate, or ossified by internal regulation." In the 1990s, battles over asbestos and tobacco proved the power of class actions. Today, they remain valuable tools in the ongoing fight against discrimination, consumer fraud, deadly drugs and products, the creation of illegal monopolies, and efforts to cheat the financial markets. This is especially true when regulators aren't up to the challenge.

But class actions also present the troubling possibility of different kinds of unfairness. Consumers with particularly strong claims may lose out when tossed into a massive class. The plaintiffs' lawyers who control many class actions may seek to advantage themselves at the expense of class members. Defendants, faced with the threat of drawn-out, expensive class litigation, may feel compelled to settle even weak claims just to avoid the steep costs, unwanted disclosures, and inevitable risks associated with fighting a class. And the public, which supposedly benefits when big companies are deterred from engaging in wrongdoing, may end up suffering the consequences of a haphazard and wasteful method of ensuring that businesses play by the rules.

Faced with this difficult balance, the Roberts Court has come down squarely in favor of sharply limiting the circumstances under which plaintiffs can band together into classes. To the justices who are already skeptical of economic regulation in general, the potential benefits of class litigation seem thin when compared to its presumed burdens on lawful corporate activity. The Court has reflected that sentiment by issuing a string of opinions—all decided five-to-four and all authored by Scalia— that have the obvious purpose of destroying most consumer and employment class actions.

One of the most important of these cases is *AT&T Mobility LLC v. Concepcion*, which was filed by Liza and Vincent Concepcion against AT&T in 2006.[44] AT&T had advertised that anyone who signed up for its services could get a free phone. Relying on this deal, the Concepcions paid $149.99 and got a free Nokia phone. But AT&T hadn't mentioned that it was obliged by state law in California to charge $30.22 in sales taxes for this "free" phone. The Concepcions asserted that they hadn't learned of this additional charge until after signing AT&T's contract and alleged that this hidden fee had violated consumer protection laws.

The Concepcions filed a class action suit for false advertising and fraud. AT&T responded by invoking the fine print of the Concepcions' contract, which said that all such disputes must be handled one by one and in private arbitration. Lower courts disagreed with AT&T, noting that California law prohibited any contract in which a consumer waived the right to proceed by class action—including contracts that waived the right to seek class arbitration. This policy reflected California's belief that class actions are key to consumer protection, as well as its awareness that consumers rarely read the small print of contracts before signing away their rights. The Concepcions argued that the AT&T contract's ban on class arbitration violated this rule of California law and that they were therefore free to bring a regular class action in federal court.

At oral argument, Scalia unabashedly favored the Concepcions. So it came as a surprise to many when he wrote an opinion ruling for AT&T. His opinion captured two related trends in how the Roberts Court has dramatically limited consumer litigation: hostility to class actions and strong support for private arbitration.

Even though Scalia is famously skeptical of efforts to interpret statutes by divining their purpose, he took an expansive view of the purpose of the Federal Arbitration Act (FAA) in *Concepcion*. The FAA dates to 1925 and tells courts to honor contracts that provide for private arbitration. But it also lets courts invalidate those agreements under general principles of contract law, much like California's general ban on class action waivers. On its face, the California rule thus seemed to be compatible with the FAA. The Concepcions argued that there was no need to deem it preempted—in other words, overridden—by virtue of a conflict with the purposes of federal law.

Scalia disagreed. His opinion interpreted the FAA as a shield against *any* state rule that might discourage companies from requiring arbitration of claims arising from consumer contracts. To Scalia, the whole point of private arbitration as a streamlined alternative to public litigation would be undermined if companies had to allow burdensome class procedures within it. Driving home the point, his opinion dwelled on many potential disadvantages of class actions: "The switch from bilateral to class arbitration sacrifices the principal advantage of arbitration—its informality—and makes the process slower, more costly, and more likely to generate procedural morass than final judgment." The fact that California's rule didn't target arbitration as such made no difference to Scalia. On his reading of the FAA, California's policy conflicted with the federal law because it had the effect of making mandatory arbitration clauses less attractive to businesses.

Although Scalia pushed it further than any other recent case, *Concepcion*'s pro-arbitration tenor would have seemed unpredictable only to an observer attaching too much significance to his remarks at oral argument. The Roberts Court has issued a string of rulings that make it virtually impossible to escape arbitration agreements.[45] Taking the cue, companies and employers are rapidly adding arbitration clauses to many of the contracts we sign without thinking about it, clauses just like the one AT&T used to boot the Concepcions out of court.

The result has been a rapid expansion of private arbitration as a parallel justice system that has supplanted a role once occupied almost entirely by state and federal courts.[46] With each passing day, public courts more permanently disappear as a real option for many Americans in their dealings with big business—when we seek employment, buy phones, sign up for nursing homes, or open bank accounts. Arbitration can be fair and efficient, but it can also strongly favor business. The proceedings are secret, arbitrators aren't always bound by the law, there is no jury or right to appeal, and companies sometimes pick their own arbitration firms. Documents that could force changes in corporate governance if disclosed in open court are kept in the dark. Plaintiffs can also have a harder time finding lawyers, as the potential recovery in private arbitration is often much lower than in courts. Not surprisingly, then, the merits of arbitration as a replacement for courts remains disputed. But the Roberts Court has declined to wade into that debate and has repeatedly instructed courts to bow out in the face of arbitration agreements (except in rare cases of manifest injustice in arbitration proceedings).

In its undisguised hostility to class procedures and with its emphatic vote of confidence for private arbitration, *Concepcion* was a pro-business opinion. It is big business, after all, that stands to benefit most substantially from a decline of class litigation and that firmly favors arbitration agreements. As Harvard Law Professor Mark Tushnet writes, rulings like *Concepcion* "don't actually deny that the plaintiffs were screwed by big business. They simply make it impossible for plaintiffs to bring cases that would impose liability on businesses for their violations of the law."[47] Nor can it be said that *Concepcion* was compelled by precedent. At best, it was a difficult case; in the view of many scholars, it reflected a policy-driven desire to deregulate by reshaping the ground rules of civil litigation.

Concepcion is just the tip of an ever-growing iceberg of procedural rulings that deregulate by functionally immunizing big businesses from suit, even in the face of clear wrongdoing. Another case—*American Express v. Italian Colors Restaurant*—further illustrates the general trend.[48]

In the early 2000s, a restaurant owner claimed that American Express had illegally abused its monopoly position in the market to compel rates 30 percent higher than those charged by competing cards, thus harming consumers and small businesses. American Express, however, had allegedly used that same monopoly power to force the restaurant owner to sign a contract mandating arbitration and waiving many procedural rights, including class action. The restaurant couldn't afford to sue American Express by itself, since it would cost several million dollars to hire an economics expert capable of proving a violation of the antitrust laws, and the potential damages from victory amounted to less than $40,000. As a result, even if it were true that American Express had illegally used its monopoly power to impose higher rates, it could never be held accountable through private litigation, despite the fact that federal law recognized a private right to sue for antitrust violations in circumstances just like this one.

Before *Italian Colors*, the Court had created an exception to its pro-arbitration doctrine when necessary to allow "effective vindication" of legal rights. If ever a case seemed to call for application of that rule, this was it. Joined by the other right-leaning justices, though, Scalia ruled for American Express. His opinion marginalized the effective vindication precedents, reiterated the familiar reasons to disapprove of class actions, and said virtually nothing about the vast gap it created in antitrust regulation. As in *Concepcion*, Scalia pushed hard on existing law to reach this result. In an outraged and largely unanswered dissent, Kagan warned

that "the monopolist gets to use its monopoly power to insist on a contract effectively depriving its victims of all legal recourse." She added,
"And here is the nutshell version of today's opinion, admirably flaunted
rather than camouflaged: Too darn bad."

Like *Concepcion*, *Italian Colors* safeguarded big businesses from private suits that could enforce economic regulations designed to protect
consumers and small businesses. Although Scalia insisted that the FAA
required this result, Kagan made a powerful point in response: "What
the FAA prefers to litigation is arbitration, not *de facto* immunity." *Italian Colors* laid bare a profound difference of opinion concerning the role
of litigation—and thus the role of courts—in affording a means by which
to hold big businesses to account when they may have acted illegally.

On occasion, the Roberts Court has taken a more direct approach to
knocking out class actions. In 2011, for instance, it broke apart a proposed class action in which 1.5 million women argued that Wal-Mart
had engaged in systematic pay discrimination.[49] The plaintiffs explained
that Wal-Mart had violated their rights by maintaining a corporate culture that implicitly encouraged and accepted discriminatory decisions
by store managers throughout the country. Although the Court unanimously refused to certify the case as a class action, Scalia wrote a separate opinion for the five right-leaning justices in which he made it much
harder for plaintiffs ever to show that they have enough in common to
form a class. Specifically, he took aim at circumstances in which an institution like a school, prison, or employer has one (legal) practice on the
books and another (illegal) practice on the ground. In those situations,
he warned, plaintiffs need to demonstrate that they have suffered from
more than just abuses of mid-level discretion; rather, they must prove
that they have suffered violations arising from a common source. Scalia's
opinion has already been invoked by corporations across the country to
decertify classes challenging practices that involved even trace elements
of managerial discretion. When that happens, lawsuits often come to a
crashing halt, leaving companies largely free of litigation-based enforcement of regulation.[50]

To the extent that its high politics align with the interests of big business, the Roberts Court reveals this impulse principally through its procedural decisions. Arbitration and class actions are only part of this
story, which also encompasses rulings on the standard for dismissing

cases as "implausible" before parties are allowed to engage in discovery,[51] limits on the liability of companies for actions outside the United States,[52] and restrictions on where companies can be sued for allegedly unlawful conduct.[53]

Because they operate across many areas of law simultaneously—affecting private enforcement of nearly every type of economic regulation—these procedural rulings are enormously powerful. A crude favoritism for big business, though, is not what drives them. In most cases, they flow from a desire to ensure a particular view of fairness in litigation, limit the role of courts, and reduce the role of lawsuits as a regulatory tool. The majority seems especially skeptical of the whole concept of representative litigation, in which plaintiffs sue on behalf of larger groups, and clearly favors the traditional model of one-on-one litigation between two parties—even when disparities of bargaining power or resources make a one-on-one alignment infeasible for most potential plaintiffs. Fused to its respect for formal contracts and its warm attitude toward cheaper, informal modes of dispute resolution, this hostility to facilitating representative litigation has also shaped the Court's arbitration rulings in cases like *Concepcion* and *Italian Colors*.

The justices who render these rulings do not think of themselves as intentionally favoring big business over "the little guy"; to the contrary, they see themselves as creating reasonable rules that are likely to benefit both big business and the rest of society. Still, it cannot be denied that such procedural decisions reflect a deregulatory mood that makes it easy for the right-leaning majority to discount the potential burden of their rulings on the broader American public.

The left-leaning justices, in contrast, see victims of corporate wrongdoing denied any remedy, possessed of a right without any way to enforce it. They see an invitation to further corporate abuses in the absence of an enforcement mechanism for vital regulations. And they see a majority aggressively creating new law to keep people out of court who, for decades, would unquestionably have made it in.

This deep split in the Roberts Court, rooted in incompatible views of economic regulation and access to judicial justice, is fast transforming American legal practice. As a private system of arbitration becomes dominant and class actions face a mortal threat, the role of courts as places in which to hold businesses accountable for violating the law has diminished. This trend, however, is not at all unique to the context of big business. Elsewhere in the law, the Roberts Court is determinedly proving that it is, in effect, an anti-court Court.

In the recorded annals of human experience, no city has generated more controversy than Jerusalem. Distilling its story, Benjamin Disraeli once remarked that "the view of Jerusalem is the history of the world; it is more, it is the history of earth and of heaven."[54] One small part of that tale came before the Court in 2011, and in a somewhat unusual turn, Roberts took the opportunity to offer a vivid defense of the role courts play in proclaiming the law.[55]

In 2002, Congress had ordained that, upon request, the Secretary of State must list Israel as the "place of birth" on the passports of Americans born in Jerusalem. The Executive, however, refused all such requests, citing its power to conduct foreign affairs and its policy of not taking a position on Jerusalem's political status. Menachem Binyamin Zivotofsky was born in Jerusalem on October 17, 2002; when the Secretary of State refused to issue a passport listing Israel as his place of birth, Zivotofsky's mother filed suit. She argued that the Secretary had illegally ignored Congress. A lower court, however, dismissed her suit on the ground that it was powerless to decide this "political question."[56] In its view, Jerusalem's status was entrusted by the Constitution to the political branches. Congress and the President had to sort it out without judicial intervention.

Writing for a near-unanimous Court, Roberts rejected this limit on judicial power. His opinion drew an important distinction: it is one thing for the Judiciary itself to decide that Congress infringed on the Executive by imposing this passport rule but quite another for the Judiciary to let the President make that decision unilaterally. While the Constitution entrusts the President with foreign affairs powers, Roberts wrote, "there is, of course, no exclusive commitment to the Executive of the power to determine the constitutionality of a statute." Invoking a famous case from 1803, Roberts explained that "at least since *Marbury v. Madison*, we have recognized that when an Act of Congress is alleged to conflict with the Constitution, it is emphatically the province and duty of the judicial department to say what the law is."

This ringing proclamation of judicial power to state the law, though powerful, stands in poignant tension with this Court's approach to most civil rights lawsuits. Since 2005, the Roberts Court has issued a string of decisions that make it much harder to hold the government accountable in court when it violates the Constitution. As in the business context, the Court has focused on technical rules, deploying legal stealth missiles that leave rights standing while destroying their efficacy.

One of the Court's subtlest tools is the removal of remedies for violations of civil rights.[57] Remedies, of course, are of ancient lineage in our tradition. When he wrote *Marbury* in 1803, Chief Justice John Marshall did more than just declare that it is the Judiciary's role "to say what the law is."[58] He added that the laws are expected to furnish a "remedy for the violation of a vested legal right." As Marshall realized, rights mean little if their violation goes uncorrected and unpunished.

The judicial role in interpreting and implementing the Constitution is therefore married to a role in crafting remedial schemes. In most civil rights suits, the Court looks to 42 U.S.C. § 1983, a federal statute that authorizes courts to award money damages and injunctive relief to victims of misconduct by state or local officials. By offering remedies, the law compensates victims of abuse, aims to deter illegal behavior, and sends a message to the public and politicians that rights must be honored. When the law denies a remedy for even persistent and egregious violations, it risks sending the startling and dangerous signal that violating people's rights isn't all that big a deal.

A majority of the Roberts Court, while recognizing these concerns, has nonetheless made it significantly harder to prevail on civil rights claims, even when the plaintiff undoubtedly suffered a violation of her rights. In that undertaking, it has continued and accelerated a decades-old trend. The Court has been moved mainly by a conviction that courts should be wary of second-guessing most ground-level government decisions. Its opinions suggest a general willingness to trust the other branches of government, the states, and the political process to keep public officials in line most of the time. Emphasizing that it would be absurd to expect all police officers to follow every intricate detail of judge-made constitutional law, the Court has issued decisions affording the police shields from suit when they did not act with clear malevolence or gross incompetence. The Court has also shown skepticism that civil

rights suits deter enough misconduct to justify the steep financial burden that they impose on municipalities (and, thus, on taxpayers). In general, a majority of the Roberts Court seems to doubt the value and
legitimacy of many civil rights suits and favors legal rules that keep most
of them out of court. The result is a shrinking judicial role in enforcing
the Constitution and protecting our liberties.

Connick v. Thompson exemplifies the point.[59] On January 17, 1985,
John Thompson was charged with murder. Because of his conviction in
an earlier armed robbery trial, Thompson decided not to testify at his
murder trial, since any testimony would open the door to evidence of
his robbery conviction. This was no accident: the prosecutors had tried
Thompson for the robbery first in order to disable him at the murder
trial. The prosecutors then successfully sought death at the murder trial,
arguing that only the ultimate penalty would suffice for someone serving
a near-life sentence for robbery. Thompson was consigned to death row.

Mere weeks before Thompson's scheduled execution date in 1999, his
private investigator stumbled upon proof that prosecutors had concealed
key evidence in the robbery trial. This material included an eyewitness
identification that described a man who looked totally unlike Thompson, blood tests from the scene that didn't match Thompson's blood type,
and a recorded conversation in which the key police informant sought a
$15,000 reward from the victim's family. Apprised of the new evidence,
Louisiana courts stayed Thompson's execution and vacated his convictions. It soon came to light that five different New Orleans prosecutors
had played a role in keeping this terrible secret, even though the Constitution requires prosecutors to disclose evidence tending to prove a defendant's innocence. The New Orleans District Attorney abandoned the
armed robbery charge but retried Thompson for the 1985 murder. Freed
of the robbery conviction, Thompson testified in his own defense and
presented previously concealed evidence. A jury acquitted him after less
than thirty-five minutes of deliberation.

Thompson then sued Harry Connick Sr., the New Orleans District
Attorney (and the famous singer's father), for failing to train his prosecutors in their legal duties. That failure, he contended, could predictably
result in tragedies like his own. A jury of his peers agreed and awarded
Thompson $14 million for violations of his civil rights: $1 million for
each year unjustly spent in jail.

In 2011, over a potent dissent by Ginsburg and her left-leaning colleagues, the Court stripped Thompson of all damages. Writing for the
majority, Justice Thomas argued that Connick had been entitled to
assume that his prosecutors were trained in law school, so Thompson
couldn't show that Connick had acted with the requisite "deliberate
indifference" to his rights. Along the way, Thomas articulated a legal
standard that will make it nearly impossible to hold municipalities liable
for failing to train prosecutors. That aspect of his ruling lined up with
other cases that render prosecutorial misconduct in all of its troubling
manifestations almost completely immune from judicial supervision.[60]

Ultimately, the Roberts Court listened to Thompson's tale and heard
a story about the need to shield cities from lawsuits. In many respects,
this is characteristic of how the Court treats civil rights cases. The majority sympathized with Connick and officials like him, showing comparatively little concern for Thompson or other potential victims. It warned
about judicial overreaching, plainly worried that allowing liability for
"failure to train" could result in sweeping judicial mandates of required
staff programming. Federal law, Thomas emphasized, "does not provide
plaintiffs or courts carte blanche to micromanage local governments
throughout the United States." In another common Roberts Court move,
Thomas pointed to other institutions and explained that they were adequately equipped to ensure that law enforcement complied with the Constitution. Specifically, he argued that law schools and legal ethics exams
afford enough legal training to allow head prosecutors to trust their staffs
without a judicial overseer.

In a wide-ranging concurrence, Scalia argued that there may have
been no constitutional violation at all in *Connick*. As he saw the matter,
the legal rules governing prosecutorial disclosure duties were still unsettled on important issues in the mid-1980s. Indeed, he added, the Court
still has not required prosecutors to "respect a right to untested evidence," such as the blood evidence that exculpated Thompson.

This separate writing reflected two more standard Roberts Court
themes. First, it hinted that ongoing uncertainty in the law made it unfair
to hold police and prosecutors liable.[61] This concern has dominated the
Court's recent civil rights rulings, many of which hold that only violations of crystal-clear law are actionable—a high bar to meet, given that
constitutional law is often open to at least some dispute.[62] Moreover, in

these rulings conferring immunity on the police, the Roberts Court rarely takes the opportunity to clarify the relevant constitutional law—thus leaving key questions open and ensuring that future abuses of the same sort will also result in police immunity.[63] Second, Scalia's concurrence suggested his narrow view of the underlying civil right to disclosure of potentially exculpatory evidence. Many of the surviving rights involving the police and prosecutors are products of a far more liberal era, in the 1960s and '70s, and while this Court has generally declined to erase them, it has taken many opportunities to limit them. In doing so, the Court has hinted that those rights lack firm constitutional support and give judges too much power to intrude upon affairs properly reserved to other parts of government. In *Connick*, Scalia made clear that he would look with great skepticism on arguments for expanded disclosure duties.

Ultimately, fearful that a ruling for Thompson would launch an endless cascade of frivolous and valueless suits, each a drain on public funds and each a request for judges to dominate local government, the Court preferred to shut its door.

Dissenting, Ginsburg blasted Thomas's factual argument. In the decade before Thompson's trial, she pointed out, Louisiana courts had reversed four convictions from Connick's office for failure to turn over evidence. That sent a clear signal about the quality of his prosecutors' training and put Connick on unmistakable notice about the pressing threat of yet another violation if he failed to act. Ginsburg added that, as the head of an office staffed mostly by young prosecutors, many of whom had attended law schools where criminal procedure was not even a required course, Connick was directly responsible for ensuring that his staff received adequate training. Marking his failure to do so, Ginsburg concluded that Connick "had created a tinderbox in Orleans Parish in which [constitutional] violations were nigh inevitable." In that respect, she maintained, his "deliberate indifference" to the civil rights of people like Thompson could not have been more apparent. As Ginsburg pictured it, *Connick* arose not from the deliberate bad acts of a few evil prosecutors, but rather from a culture of disregard for civil rights and disinterest in adequate training that imperiled every man, woman, and child in New Orleans.[64]

Critics on the left echoed Ginsburg's outrage. Writing in *Slate*, Dahlia Lithwick described Thomas's opinion as "a master class in human apathy."[65]

It displays, she wrote, absolutely no sympathy for Thompson. The opinion's rhetoric and reasoning are indeed spare and pitiless: Thomas glosses over Thompson's near-death encounter and highlights the tough circumstances Connick confronted. From a Court that votes each year to remove limits on capital punishment, there is no twinge of concern about error. Scalia once defended the death penalty by saying that if an innocent were ever executed, his "name would be shouted from the rooftops."[66] Yet faced with a case where the plaintiff was saved by sheer good luck, his critics noted, Scalia wrote separately only to suggest that Thompson's rights *might not* have been violated by the prosecutors' lies.

Ginsburg's dissent rested on foundations very different from Thomas's majority opinion. From its point of view, the majority had abdicated the judicial duty to remedy and prevent the sorts of abuses that may someday cost an innocent man his life. The courts cannot closely govern prosecutors, of course, but they can use remedies to compensate victims and send a message when our public advocates break the law so egregiously. After all, high-profile judicial rebukes can deter misconduct and trigger a political debate that ripples out and ultimately reshapes official policy. Especially in cities with strained budgets, like New Orleans, big damages awards can also generate immense pressure on law enforcement to follow constitutional rules. By punishing civil rights violations, courts can thus trigger other safeguards against abuse.[67]

Connick, however, is part of a clear arc in the Roberts Court's jurisprudence toward conferring near-total immunity on prosecutors and police. Skeptical of calls to review their conduct in civil rights suits, the Court has fortified older barriers to judicial remedy and erected several of its own. The result is a different and lesser judicial role in providing victims of public abuse with a forum in which to obtain relief and recognition—and a great vote of confidence in public officials to abide by the law even without the threat of liability under federal civil rights statutes. Ginsburg's dissent in *Connick* lodged a powerful protest. To the majority, though, this result is justified by its fear of judges riding roughshod over local governments, its doubt that civil rights litigation does all that much good, and, on occasion, its skeptical view of the very constitutional rights that give rise to civil rights suits in the first place.

Sirens blaring, police cars appear from everywhere in a darkened alley-way. The night splits into shards of flashing red and blue light. Panicked, a hooded suspect breaks into a mad dash and leaps a fence with aston-ishing agility. Impressive, but futile: two officers, guns drawn and eyes bloodshot with anticipation, knock the suspect to the ground and bru-tally cuff him. Desperate for answers, they get right to business: *Tell us where you hid the body!* When the suspect spits out a snarky retort, the cops knock his head into the ground and ask how he'd manage with a pair of broken legs. Terrified, he visibly deflates and confesses to a grue-some murder. Case closed, right? No: since it's only twenty-two minutes into the fast-paced episode of *Law & Order* or *NYPD Blue*, we know there's a catch.

On these facts, the twist is clear: the officers never read the suspect his rights as required by *Miranda v. Arizona*.[68] They never told him he had the right to remain silent, that anything he said could and would be used against him in a court of law, that he had the right to an attorney, and that he had the right to have the state pay for an appointed attorney if he couldn't afford one. Even if they had Mirandized him, their use of force to compel a confession constituted a distinct violation of the sus-pect's rights. As a result, the confession isn't admissible as evidence. After a dramatic showdown in court we can expect another twenty minutes of struggle to find damning proof.

The threat that evidence will be suppressed plays a critical role in cre-ating captivating TV drama. On many police procedurals, though the cops are (mostly) well-intentioned, their hatred of bad guys, the thrill of the chase, and a passion for justice often cloud their good judgment. So they skate on thin ice, bending the rules to ransack an apartment or rough up a suspect under interrogation. The main limit on the officers' zeal, it seems, is fear that the evidence they collect may be tossed out of court. That's the big gun to their head, giving them pause and forcing them to comply with maddening rules. In the heat of the moment, it's often easy for us, as viewers, to sympathize with their frustration—though we might feel differently if we were one of the many suspects they mistakenly suspected and roughed up before catching the real wrong-doer.

This makes for great television—not just suppression of evidence but the many other rules that create dramatic courtroom clashes. Much of this law is based on the Fourth Amendment, which protects against unreasonable searches and seizures, and the Fifth Amendment, which guards against coerced self-incrimination. If those rules faded away, writers for shows like *The Closer* would lose one of their best plot devices. But that would not be the only price. In this field, art imitates life. The officers who patrol our streets are moved to obey the law, at least in part, by stiff court-enforced penalties for failure to do so. If courts were to abandon that role, police might act differently when it matters most.

That, however, is where the Roberts Court is heading.[69] In recent years, it has continued a long project of narrowing constitutional limits on police and prosecutors. On its watch, the law of criminal procedure has grown ever more deferential to law enforcement—more willing to accept claims that, if officers violated the law, they did so in good faith and therefore the evidence they turned up should not be suppressed. This trend reflects the same skepticism of using constitutional law to regulate police that has animated this Court's approach to civil rights issues. The Roberts Court views the costs as too high, the benefits as too doubtful, and the legitimacy of such judicial supervision as questionable. Better, in its view, to leave these matters to politics and police profession-alism. In that respect, this Court's criminal procedure rulings are part of its broader deregulatory agenda—though here, as in the civil rights context, it is deregulating the other branches of government and the states.

In *Herring v. United States*, a 2009 decision, the justices' profound differences of opinion about when to suppress evidence came to a head.[70] The facts are straightforward: Bennie Herring was well known to law enforcement in Coffee County, Alabama. So when Herring stopped at the Sheriff's Department to retrieve something from his impounded truck, Investigator Mark Anderson asked the County Clerk to check for any outstanding arrest warrants. None turned up, so Anderson had the clerk get in touch with her counterpart in neighboring Dale County. When that clerk reported an active warrant, Anderson placed Herring under arrest. While searching Herring after arresting him, Anderson found drugs in Herring's pocket and an unlawful gun in his truck.

The case took a complicated turn, though, when it was discovered that the Dale County Clerk had been wrong. There was no active warrant; it had been recalled five months earlier, but through an oversight it had never been removed from the County database. Faced with federal crim-

inal charges, Herring argued that the drugs and gun had to be suppressed because his arrest and the subsequent search were obviously
illegal.

Suppression is a dramatic but controversial remedy.[71] Nothing in the
Fourth Amendment's text expressly requires suppression of unlawfully
obtained evidence; the Amendment is silent on remedies for illegal
searches and seizures. Judges fashioned the suppression remedy in the
mid-twentieth century to give the Fourth Amendment force—to make
its rights real.[72] In theory, we might instead rely on civil rights actions
against officers, criminal prosecutions, or police department discipline
to punish and deter misconduct. And we do rely on all of these tools, to a
greater or lesser extent. Suppression, however, remains the gold standard, a double-edged sword that cuts us but that we still wield because it
gives life to the Fourth Amendment's limits on police conduct. As Justice
William Brennan argued in 1984, we must sometimes allow suspects to
go free because suppressing illegally obtained evidence "is the 'price' our
society pays for enjoying the freedom and privacy safeguarded by the
Fourth Amendment."[73] Nonetheless, judges are bitterly divided over when
the strong medicine of suppression is warranted.

Writing for the Court in *Herring*, Roberts agreed that Bennie Herring's rights had been violated but refused to grant a suppression remedy.
In his view, Anderson had done nothing wrong and Dale County had
merely (and perhaps forgivably) failed to update its computer system.
Such clerical error didn't call for suppression, Roberts reasoned, because
that penalty "has always been our last resort, not our first impulse." Roberts's opinion highlighted suppression's "costly toll upon truth-seeking
and law enforcement objectives" and recited Justice Benjamin Cardozo's
famous warning that criminals should not automatically "go free because
the constable has blundered." Roberts argued that these costs are justified
only when suppression will effectively deter Fourth Amendment violations in the future.

This logic channeled an article by Judge Henry Friendly, a legal giant
for whom Roberts clerked fresh out of Harvard Law School in 1979. In
Friendly's influential view, "the sole reason for exclusion is that experience has demonstrated this to be the only effective method for deterring
the police from violating the Constitution."[74] In other words, suppression is all about regulating police conduct, and its success in this regard

is the sole test of its value. As Friendly explained, "It does not seem consistent with the objective of deterrence that the maximum penalty of exclusion should be enforced for an error of judgment by a policeman, necessarily formed on the spot and without a set of the *United States Reports* in his hand . . . The object of deterrence would be sufficiently achieved if the police were denied the fruit of activity intentionally or flagrantly illegal." Thus, Friendly concluded, to the extent courts doubt that suppressing evidence is an effective way of influencing the police— who are, of course, influenced by a wide range of considerations in deciding when to search and seize—they should shy away from suppression.

In *Herring*, Roberts followed Friendly and viewed the psychology of police incentives narrowly. He held that to trigger suppression, "police misconduct must be sufficiently deliberate that exclusion can meaningfully deter it, and sufficiently culpable that such deterrence is worth the price paid by the justice system." Even when police violate the Fourth Amendment, then, suppression isn't allowed unless the police demonstrably acted with gross negligence, recklessness, or deliberate bad faith. In other words, suppression is about punishing egregiously bad cops, not protecting individual rights generally by pushing police to zealously respect every minute detail of Fourth Amendment doctrine. Applying this rule, the Chief concluded that Dale County's negligence in failing to keep its computer system updated didn't justify suppression of Herring's drugs and firearm.

Ginsburg struck back in a dissent joined by Justices Stevens, Souter, and Breyer. Writing with gusto, she challenged Roberts's view of the Fourth Amendment and his approach to Bennie Herring's situation. Starting with fundamentals, Ginsburg rejected a purely deterrence-based account of suppression. Instead, she invoked what she called a "more majestic conception of the Fourth Amendment." Suppression deters, she argued, but it also "enables the judiciary to avoid the taint of partnership in official lawlessness." It thereby "assures the people—all potential victims of unlawful government conduct—that the government would not profit from its lawless behavior." In contrast to the Chief's focus on whether courts can effectively regulate police, Ginsburg highlighted judicial integrity and broader public respect for civil rights.

Ginsburg also took issue with the Chief's logic as applied to the case before him. Why, she asked, can't suppression deter simple mistakes?

And why isn't it worth the price? In other areas of law, we often impose penalties for negligence to encourage greater care. If you make a mistake and injure a neighbor, you typically pay for those injuries; this rule is both fair and designed to encourage careful conduct. By the same token, she argued, if police departments aren't punished for their mistakes, they may lack sufficient incentive to train their staffs and check for error. This is especially true for high-maintenance databases, which, Ginsburg wrote, "form the nervous system of contemporary criminal justice opera-tions." Indeed, "inaccuracies in expensive, interconnected collections of electronic information raise grave concerns for individual liberty." In her dissent, Ginsburg argued that suppression is justified because it protects liberty against incompetence, not just intentional wrongdoing.

In *Herring*, as in many civil rights cases, the Roberts Court acknowl-edged a rights violation but refused to provide any remedy. The Chief's opinion took a starkly limited view of the role courts should play in cre-ating incentives for police to follow the law. The cost of excluding evi-dence, he maintained, isn't worth the price—especially when officers do not knowingly or intentionally violate a suspect's rights. Ginsburg's dis-sent offered a totally different view of the basis for suppression and a broader account of how the threat of suppression can be used to regulate law enforcement. As in so many other areas of law, a majority of the Roberts Court instructed the courts to adopt a more minimal role in American life, leaving day-to-day enforcement of constitutional values in searches and seizures largely to the police and the public.

Whereas *Herring* revealed skepticism of the remedy for a rights viola-tion, this Court's Fifth Amendment rulings have pointed to even deeper skepticism of some well-known constitutional rights—including the var-ious rights specified in the famous *Miranda* warning. *Berghuis v. Thomp-kins*, decided in June 2010, is a perfect example.[75]

On February 22, 2001, Van Chester Thompkins was interrogated by officers who suspected him of a strip mall shooting. He was locked in a small room, placed on a hard chair, and questioned for three straight hours, even after he refused to sign a form waiving his right to remain silent. For nearly the entire interrogation, Thompkins sat silently. He spoke only twice, to complain about the chair and decline a peppermint.

But that changed after two hours and forty-five minutes. As the Court recounted in its opinion: "[Officer] Helgert asked Thompkins, 'Do you believe in God?' Thompkins made eye contact with Helgert and said 'Yes,' as his eyes 'welled up with tears.' Helgert asked, 'Do you pray to God?' Thompkins said 'Yes.' Helgert asked, 'Do you pray to God to forgive you for shooting that boy down?' Thompkins answered 'Yes' and looked away. Thompkins refused to make a written confession." Over his vehement objection, the prosecution used these answers at trial. Thompkins was convicted of murder.

The Roberts Court's right-leaning majority is, for the most part, critical of the vast expansion of criminal defendants' rights that took place in the mid-twentieth century. It is sensitive to all the ways in which those rights tie the hands of the police and sometimes result in wrongdoers getting off on "technicalities." It worries about judicial overreaching and sees relatively little benefit in maintaining such an intricate network of rules to govern law enforcement. Moreover, it tends to doubt that all those rules are really required by the Constitution; if it had been sitting in the 1960s and '70s and had been asked whether to impose many of them, this Court would likely have declined.

Fifth Amendment rights are no exception to this view; in fact, Scalia and Thomas both voted in 2000 to overturn *Miranda* entirely.[76] As a consequence, the Roberts Court is sometimes uncompromising in imposing stringent requirements for invoking and benefiting from *Miranda*: if a suspect wants to rely on *Miranda*'s formidable protections, is it really too much to ask that he say so at the time and then stick to his guns if pushed by the police?

Or so the Court reasoned in *Berghuis v. Thompkins*: in a five-to-four opinion for the right-leaning justices, Kennedy found no *Miranda* violation. He first held that a suspect can invoke his right to silence—and thereby cut off questioning—only by doing so "unambiguously." Since Thompkins "did not *say* he wanted to remain silent," he hadn't invoked his *Miranda* rights, so the police were free to continue the interrogation. Kennedy then held that, as a separate matter, Thompkins had impliedly waived his right to remain silent by answering Helgert's questions. Kennedy reasoned that Thompkins had been read his rights, understood them, and then freely chose to speak.

In her first major dissent as a justice, and in a forecast of her emerging role as a champion of defendants' rights, Sotomayor criticized the Court for "turn[ing] *Miranda* upside down." Whatever the rule might be as to other rights, she underscored the irony of requiring anyone to speak—and to do so unambiguously—in order to invoke a supposed right to remain silent. As she explained, "advising a suspect that he has a 'right to remain silent' is unlikely to convey that he must speak (and must do so in some particular fashion) to ensure the right will be protected." In addition, she wrote, the harsh rule of *Berghuis* is totally unnecessary. If a suspect's invocation of his legal right to silence is at all unclear, police can (and should) ask simple follow-up questions.

Sotomayor then returned to the original basis for *Miranda*: the Constitution does not allow confessions obtained through coercion, and courts presume that custodial interrogations are inherently coercive. The warnings are designed to dispel that air of coercion—which can overbear free will—by ensuring that suspects know their rights. As a result, she explained, courts presume against waiver of the *Miranda* rights and demand proof that waiver *really* occurred: if a suspect's self-incriminating statements while in custody could be taken as proof in themselves that he freely chose to waive his rights, *Miranda* doctrine would be at war with its own premises. Further, Sotomayor argued, it could hardly be said that Thompkins had freely decided to give up his right to silence by remaining almost completely silent for just under three hours and then offering three one-word answers to Helgert's questions about God. This was precisely the sort of coercive atmosphere that *Miranda* targets.

In sum, Sotomayor warned that *Berghuis* may eviscerate *Miranda* by inviting "police to question a suspect at length—notwithstanding his persistent refusal to answer questions—in the hope of eventually obtaining a single inculpatory response which will suffice to prove waiver of rights." She also sounded a more fundamental note of alarm about a breakdown in *Miranda*'s deepest constitutional foundations.

It would be hard to fault Sotomayor's practical and doctrinal logic, and the majority made little attempt to do so. But there was a simple reason the majority and the dissent were ships passing in the night: the dissent fully embraced a precedent that the majority regarded as dubious from the start. The prospect of allowing police to conduct their interrogations freer of *Miranda*—and of the judicial effort to regulate the police that it represents—was welcomed by most of the Roberts Court.

———

In this age of an anti-court Court, it is more important than ever to recall that judges don't have a monopoly on justice. When they retreat from the field or stand silent, we look elsewhere: to the democratic process, social movements, arbitration, our communities and families, consumer report websites, and other means of ensuring that everyone comply with the law. Indeed, the Constitution presumes that democracy, not litigation, is how we're supposed to resolve many disputes.

Yet sometimes courts truly are the last, best hope for justice. And sometimes the Constitution or an Act of Congress *does* tell us that we have a legal right enforceable in court, even against the most powerful opponents. One of the defining features of the Roberts Court has been its extremely narrow view of the circumstances in which that is so—and its willingness to leave plaintiffs and criminal defendants to whatever justice they can find beyond its doors.

Nor is this Court's trajectory the only force contributing to a substantial diminution of access to judicial justice in twenty-first-century America. Even when courts are open for business, a very different threat looms: the inability of indigent (and even sometimes middle-class) Americans to afford to hire lawyers.[77] In criminal cases, it is an outrage that we have yet to fulfill the half-century-old promise of the Court's 1963 ruling in *Gideon v. Wainwright*, which held that the Constitution requires the provision of competent defense counsel to all criminal defendants, even those who cannot afford to hire one on their own.[78] In civil cases, which can involve equally momentous stakes, the situation is also dire. As Attorney General Eric Holder remarked in April 2013, "Estimates suggest that more than 80 percent of civil legal needs faced by low-income individuals currently go unmet."[79] These failures, Holder added, range across "matters involving the care and custody of minor children and dependent adults, to questions of personal finance, housing, employment, and even public safety." At deportation, eviction, asylum, and custody proceedings, the most vulnerable among us are rarely represented by lawyers, who can provide valuable counsel at these life-altering moments. As Stanford Law Professor Deborah Rhode has summarized, "We tolerate a system in which money often matters more than merit, and equal protection principles are routinely subverted in practice."[80]

The availability of justice in courts of law is also under threat from the Executive Branch, which has invoked its constitutional power to conceal weighty surveillance and national security matters from the Judiciary.[81] It has been aided in this effort by deferential judicial opinions. As a consequence, some of the fundamental legal issues of our times are being debated and decided without any judicial input or oversight. The Obama administration, for instance, has publicly taken the view that it can use drones to kill U.S. citizens abroad when the Executive uses sufficient internal process to deem them an imminently dangerous threat.[82] Whatever the merits of this position as a matter of law, it is also a statement about the role of courts in a key national security issue.

A different sort of challenge has emerged within the Court itself: the justices are deciding to hear fewer and fewer cases.[83] Whereas the Court heard 100 to 150 cases per year just a few decades ago, nowadays it hears around 75 a year. As a result, the Court may play a reduced role in guiding the development and enforcement of the law. It has also allowed terrible injustices to stand uncorrected—in many cases over strong dissents by Sotomayor, who has challenged her colleagues' willingness to ignore death sentences marred by racist overtones, death sentences where the defense lawyer failed to present any mitigation evidence, and cruel and unusual punishments inflicted on an inmate just because he refused to take his HIV medication.[84]

One thing is clear: the role of courts in dispensing justice is changing at a rapid clip, and the Roberts Court is playing a central role in engineering that transformation. As the American public loses faith in its institutions of government, the Court remains our most trusted civilian branch. But its approval ratings have dropped steeply in recent years and seem likely to keep falling, at least for the near term.[85] In time, perhaps the Court can rise above the disenchantment with government that is our generation's lot. Much will depend on the Court's vision of its role—and of the role of courts in general—in American life.

On May 4, 2010, the Supreme Court's great bronze doors slammed shut with haunting finality. Henceforth, visitors would be relegated to an entirely unremarkable side entrance. Security concerns, the Court ominously explained. Not worth it, responded Breyer and Ginsburg in what they styled a dissent: "This Court's main entrance and front steps are not only a means to, but also a metaphor for, access to the Court itself."[86]

No longer do the humble and the mighty enter the Court's inner sanctum beneath a marble promise of "EQUAL JUSTICE UNDER LAW." Protests will still rock and rage on those forty-four classical steps, which have witnessed the thunder of abortion rallies and the silence of caskets. Visitors can still admire the glorious architecture. But even if the security arguments for closing the front doors were compelling, our nation lost something wonderful and precious on that spring day in 2010. At the same time, we acquired a perfect metaphor for one of this Court's most remarkable projects: transforming the judicial role in establishing justice under the Constitution.

EPILOGUE:

THE COURT AND THE CONSTITUTION

The Supreme Court is part of the world it helps create. No major case is truly over when it's over. The winners and losers may go home, but the reverberations from the Court's decision continue, generating new controversies that will return to a Court that has itself been changed by the altered legal and cultural landscape.[1]

No one can doubt that great cases like *Brown v. Board of Education* have this kind of boomerang effect. That's true partly because interpreting and implementing the principles and requirements such cases lay down often prove harder than anticipated.[2] Thus, six decades on we are still grappling in a wide range of contexts with the challenge of enforcing *Brown*'s desegregation mandate.[3] That project is all the more daunting because even today, the nation—and, unsurprisingly, its highest court—remains divided over what *Brown*'s mandate really means and, more fundamentally, what the Constitution's promise of "equal protection of the laws" requires.[4]

So, too, with the *Health Care Case* and *Citizens United* and the Roberts Court's decisions about gun rights, GPS surveillance, and presidential detentions at Guantánamo. Once those cases were decided, the world would never be quite the same again. But just *how* it was changed remains deeply uncertain, so the paths ahead lead to many possible futures all at once.

In his great novel *Absalom, Absalom*, William Faulkner found the perfect metaphor for the uncertain effects of this kind of reverberation.

Maybe nothing ever happens once and is finished. Maybe happen is never once but like ripples maybe on water after the pebble sinks, the ripples moving on, spreading, the pool attached by a narrow umbilical water-cord to the next pool which the first pool feeds.[5]

Sometimes the justices surprise even themselves. It is in the nature of the Court's limited power that the forces unleashed, amplified, or redirected by its interventions are not wholly within its control. That is part of the uncertainty of the justice the Court is fated to dispense. It may carefully craft a decision about firearms, affirmative action, or marriage equality with the intention of leaving important questions unresolved. And it may hope that the nation and the lower courts will take time to debate the issues it has left up in the air, creating needed breathing space before the Court must intervene again. Yet the justices may find that the ripples caused by their decision expose unforeseen problems or return more quickly than expected, in altered form. Even painstakingly narrow rulings can generate unintended social and political consequences; what began as a ripple can rapidly become a towering wave that crashes against shores the Court carefully constructed. By the same token, broad rulings meant to sweep across the nation and inspire widespread change sometimes barely budge a firmly entrenched status quo.

Well aware of this danger, the justices cannot avoid wondering whether some of their more adventuresome decisions might ultimately hurt the very people whose rights they mean to vindicate.[6] Many believe that the pro-choice ruling in *Roe v. Wade* had exactly this effect, unleashing a backlash that persists through the present day and keeps abortion rights under siege.[7] Yet judicial decisions occasionally have just the opposite effect, by legitimizing and opening the public mind to experiences and shared values that undercut prior opposition. Recent gay and lesbian rights rulings will likely fall into this category, as the image of devoted same-sex couples taking their marriage vows before close friends and family influences public attitudes.[8] Since the Court makes new law in many contested domains of American life, even the justices cannot know with any great certainty how the opinions they fashion will shape the future of the Republic.

As we complete this book, in early 2014, the Roberts Court is well into its current term, and it's already clear that the Court is once again taking on a number of high-profile and controversial issues.

After a federal judge in Utah held that the Constitution requires marriage equality, relying on the Court's recent opinion striking down part of the Defense of Marriage Act, the Court temporarily halted same-sex marriage in Utah while an expedited appeal unfolds in the lower courts.[9] Stepping into another social minefield, the Court is also considering how to reconcile abortion rights with free speech rights in a Massachusetts case about buffer zones around abortion clinics.[10] In that case, the Court may reconsider a precedent involving a similar law from Colorado that it upheld fourteen years ago, a precedent that generated long-term consequences of its own.[11] Other cases challenging legislative efforts to limit access to abortion—often by regulating doctors and the drugs they can use—are already piling up in petitions for Supreme Court review.[12] And the Court is poised to decide a pair of contentious cases about church and state: one about official prayer at town meetings,[13] the other brought by corporations whose owners object on religious grounds to the Affordable Care Act's requirement that contraception be covered by employer-provided health insurance.[14]

Questions of constitutional structure also loom large on this year's docket. The Court will address a contentious debate over the President's power under the Recess Appointments Clause to temporarily appoint officials without Senate approval during brief breaks in the congressional session.[15] The Court may also address fundamental limits on the federal government's ability to expand its power over domestic affairs by entering into treaties with foreign nations.[16]

The Court's slate of cases thus continues to fill up with the most pressing and conflicted issues of our time. Questions about how the Court will resolve the controversies that reach it, what considerations will influence its decisions, what effects it expects those decisions to have, and how well those expectations will match what actually ensues—all of these uncertainties remain a constant in the unfolding story of the Court and the Constitution. It could hardly be otherwise. The decisions the Court will render, and the effects those decisions might have, are beyond precise calibration and exact prediction.

In one of his memorable radio addresses to the British people, a speech broadcast in October 1939, Winston Churchill famously described Russia as "a riddle, wrapped in a mystery, inside an enigma."[17] Although the lens through which we have chosen to view the Roberts Court is hardly a crystal ball, it is not entirely clouded, either. Despite the virtually impenetrable wall of silence with which our highest court surrounds its internal deliberations, the Court is not the Kremlin. Much can be learned by paying close attention to what the nine justices reveal through what they say and write—and through what they conspicuously do *not* say.

Some of the justices write books, give interviews, and make speeches, and these informal pronouncements are worth considering when attempting to understand the Court and its rulings. The justices also cast votes, which can be mined for all sorts of interesting patterns, connections, and predictions. But alone among the institutions of our government, the Court operates under a deeply felt obligation to explain its decisions in fully public written opinions. Whatever the secret deliberations that gave them birth, these official opinions become essential parts of our national history. Opinions written for a majority of the Court change the law and, thus, the country by their very publication. Concurring and dissenting opinions typically have no such instantly operative effect. Still, they are usefully plumbed for clues to the future by lower courts, politicians, and the public. They can also influence that future by offering a theory or protest that carries the day years later or becomes a landmark around which the losing parties rally.[18]

We have often observed in these pages that much is revealed by what the justices' opinions obscure and that much can be learned from what they *avoid* saying: the sounds of silence sometimes speak most loudly of all. The opinions also take part in a centuries-old dialogue, an understanding of which illuminates much that would remain hidden if they were viewed only with an eye to present concerns. In each of the constitutional domains we have explored, the justices' published opinions offer critical insights into the values and higher politics propelling the fiercely independent men and women who serve for life on this enormously powerful body.

By analyzing those opinions rigorously, we have aimed to dispel some of the uncertainty that surrounds the Roberts Court. Reading the Court's remarkable decisions in cases involving health care, voting rights, and detainees, we have attempted to explain why some of the justices deeply believe that robust judicial enforcement of the Constitution's structural provisions is central to protecting personal freedom. In the same way, we have sought to shed light on why justices sometimes draw radically different conclusions from the same body of evidence in cases about race, guns, and campaign spending. We have also explored why justices of a similar ideological bent can nonetheless disagree about the weight that original understanding, history, and practical concerns should receive in interpreting the Constitution.

By looking closely at the justices' opinions in cases involving threats to privacy and the use of federal funds to buy off rights, we have tried to explain the unexpected ways in which right-leaning justices diverge dramatically from one another. Similarly, we have endeavored to take the mystery out of the way in which unusual alliances emerge among justices commonly understood to be at very different points on the ideological spectrum. As Stanford Law Professor Pam Karlan has observed, "Strange bedfellows on the bench are a source and a sign of the Constitution's flexibility."[19]

Dissecting the logic of opinions with care, and attending to how each of the nine justices views the Court and the Constitution, helps narrow the range of what seem like possible futures. That is so, however, only if we refuse to stereotype the justices and if we explore their opinions with an open and welcoming mind. The recurring disagreements between otherwise like-minded justices about privacy, free speech, and "rights for sale" should leave no doubt that it is often counterproductive to reduce the justices' views to political caricature. Although some see those disagreements as exceptions that prove the rule, their persistence can provide a basis for cautious optimism: the process by which the nine justices reach their decisions is not foreordained by the policy views and political backgrounds the justices bring with them to their lifetime positions. Those factors are relevant and can be influential, but they are hardly the whole story or even its most important part.

In case after case, the Court's decisions are shaped mainly by the justices' deep beliefs about the architecture and design of the constitutional system itself, the way its parts fit together to make a working whole.

What matters to each of the justices is how the Constitution defines values of liberty, equality, and dignity, and how it fuses them to historic precepts of state-federal relations and the separation of powers. What counts is how the justices perceive their vital role in our democratic society as they grapple with the realities of the past and then deal with the uncertainties posed by technological change, cultural transformation, and evolving societal expectations.

The Court is engaged in a dialogue not just with itself and its future incarnations but also with the lower courts, the other branches of our federal government, the sovereign states, and the American people. Stanford Professor of Literature Robert Pogue Harrison reminds us that "conversation is as essential to learning as it is to the life of the republic, for republicanism, as the civic humanists understood it, is all about a plurality of voices making themselves heard in an open forum."[20]

What emerges from an attempt to pursue these conversations through the stories of the Roberts Court and its encounters with American life is not a blueprint or a road map; nor is it a polemic praising or damning this Court's rulings. What emerges instead is greater insight into what the Roberts Court is doing, where it is going, and how it is moving—at times haltingly and uncertainly—along the moral arc of history, the long arc that bends toward justice.

NOTES

PROLOGUE

1. This quote is attributed to Mencken in many sources, such as David Hillson and Ruth Murray-Webster, *Understanding and Managing Risk Attitude*, 2nd ed. (Burlington, Vt.: Gower Publishing Company, 2007), 153. It appears, though, that the original quote is slightly different: "There is always an easy solution to every human problem—neat, plausible, and wrong." See H. L. Mencken, "The Divine Afflatus," reprinted in H. L. Mencken, *A Mencken Chrestomathy: His Own Selection of His Choicest Writings* (New York: Vintage Books, 1982), 443.
2. For a superb introduction to the Supreme Court, see Linda Greenhouse, *The U.S. Supreme Court: A Very Short Introduction* (New York: Oxford University Press, 2012).
3. In recent years, several scholars and journalists have produced excellent works on the Roberts Court. See Mark Tushnet, *In the Balance: Law and Politics on the Roberts Court* (New York: W. W. Norton, 2013); Marcia Coyle, *The Roberts Court: The Struggle for the Constitution* (New York: Simon & Schuster, 2013); and Jeffrey Toobin, *The Oath: The Obama White House and the Supreme Court* (New York: Random House, 2012).
4. *Boumediene v. Bush*, 553 U.S. 723 (2008).
5. *District of Columbia v. Heller*, 554 U.S. 570 (2008).
6. *Citizens United v. Federal Election Commission*, 558 U.S. 310 (2010).
7. *National Federation of Independent Business v. Sebelius*, 132 S Ct. 2566 (2012).
8. *Arizona v. United States*, 132 S. Ct. 2492 (2012).
9. *United States v. Jones*, 132 S. Ct. 945 (2012).
10. *Shelby County v. Holder*, 133 S. Ct. 2612 (2013).
11. *United States v. Windsor*, 133 S. Ct. 2675 (2013).
12. *Hamdi v. Rumsfeld*, 542 U.S. 507, 536 (2004) (O'Connor, J.).
13. *League of United Latin Am. Citizens v. Perry*, 548 U.S. 399, 511 (2006) (Roberts, C.J., concurring in part, concurring in the judgment in part, and dissenting in part).

14. Michael Howard and Peter Paret, ed. and trans., *Carl von Clausewitz: On War* (Princeton, N.J.: Princeton University Press, 1989).

15. To be sure, philosophers would point out that model building in the natural sciences is far more complex than a simple search for perfection. See Roman Frigg and Stephan Hartmann, "*Models in Science*," *Stanford Encyclopedia of Philosophy* (Fall 2012), http://plato.stanford.edu/archives/fall2012/entries/models-science/.

16. Joe E. Decker, "Letter to the Editor: Teddy Roosevelt's Metaphor," *New York Times*, March 9, 1986.

17. For an engaging—though controversial—work on different approaches to explaining judicial behavior, see Richard A. Posner, *How Judges Think* (Cambridge, Mass.: Harvard University Press, 2008).

18. Justice David H. Souter, "Harvard University's 359th Commencement Address," *Harvard Law Review* 124 (2010): 435.

19. Ibid., 433.

20. See Charles Fried, "On Judgment," *Lewis & Clark Law Review* 15 (2011): 1025.

21. See Phillip Bobbitt, *Constitutional Fate: Theory of the Constitution* (New York: Oxford University Press, 1982). There is, of course, a rich and diverse scholarly literature on constitutional interpretation.

22. See, generally, Stephen G. Breyer, *Making Our Democracy Work: A Judge's View* (New York: Knopf, 2010). For a wonderful historical survey of how the Court has influenced and been influenced by these concerns, see Barry Friedman, *The Will of the People: How Public Opinion Has Influenced the Supreme Court and Shaped the Meaning of the Constitution* (New York: Farrar, Straus and Giroux, 2009).

23. Jack Balkin, "High Politics and Judicial Decisionmaking," *Balkanization*, May 4, 2003, http://balkin.blogspot.com/2003/05/high-politics-and-judicial.html.

24. Adam J. White, "Book Review: *In the Balance*, by Mark Tushnet" *Wall Street Journal*, October 6, 2013.

25. Oliver Wendell Holmes Jr., "Law and the Court," in *Collected Legal Papers* (1920; repr., Clark, N.J.: The Lawbook Exchange, 2006), 292.

26. For an excellent account of the politics of this nomination, see Jan Crawford Greenburg, *Supreme Conflict: The Inside Story of the Struggle for Control of the United States Supreme Court* (New York: The Penguin Group, 2007).

27. The leading biography of Justice Scalia is Joan Biskupic, *American Original: The Life and Constitution of Supreme Court Justice Antonin Scalia* (New York: Farrar, Straus and Giroux, 2010).

28. Adam Liptak, "A Taxonomy of Supreme Court Humor," *New York Times*, January 24, 2011.

29. Clarence Thomas has written a powerful autobiography that illuminates his background: Clarence Thomas, *My Grandfather's Son: A Memoir* (New York: Harper-Collins, 2007).

30. *Nomination of Judge Clarence Thomas to Be Associate Justice of the Supreme Court of the United States: Hearing Before the Senate Committee on the Judiciary,* Part IV of IV, 102nd Cong. 157–58 (1991).

31. Erin Fuchs, "Why Clarence Thomas Still Hasn't Asked a Question in Seven Years,"

Business Insider, February 27, 2013, http://www.businessinsider.com/why-clarence
-thomas-doesnt-ask-questions-2013-2.

32. See Breyer, *Making Our Democracy Work*.
33. Stephen Breyer, *Active Liberty: Interpreting Our Democratic Constitution* (New York: Knopf, 2005).
34. Sonia Sotomayor, *My Beloved World* (New York: Knopf, 2013).
35. Emma G. Fitzsimmons, "Sotomayor to Lead Countdown to New Year in Times Square," *New York Times*, December 29, 2013.
36. Jodi Kantor, "On Book-Tour Circuit, Sotomayor Sees a New Niche for a Justice," *New York Times*, February 3, 2010.
37. Kainaz Amaria, "As a Latina, Sonia Sotomayor Says, 'You Have to Work Harder,'" NPR, January 13, 2004, http://www.npr.org/2014/01/13/262067546/as-a-latina-sonia-sotomayor-says-you-have-to-work-harder.
38. The leading biographies of Anthony Kennedy are Helen J. Knowles, *The Tie Goes to Freedom: Justice Anthony M. Kennedy on Liberty* (New York: Rowman & Littlefield, 2009); and Frank J. Colucci, *Justice Kennedy's Jurisprudence: The Full and Necessary Meaning of Liberty* (Lawrence: University Press of Kansas, 2009).
39. See, e.g., *Gonzales v. Carhart*, 550 U.S. 124, 169 (2007) (Ginsburg, J., dissenting); *Ledbetter v. Goodyear Tire & Rubber Co., Inc.*, 550 U.S. 618, 643 (2007) (Ginsburg, J., dissenting); *United States v. Virginia*, 518 U.S. 515 (1996).
40. Jan Crawford, "Alito Emerges as Supreme Court Rock Star," CBS News, October 6, 2010, http://www.cbsnews.com/news/alito-emerges-as-supreme-court-rock-star/.
41. Todd Ruger, "Alito Defends 'Citizens' in Speech to Federalist Society," *Blog of the Legal Times*, November 6, 2012, http://legaltimes.typepad.com/blt/2012/11/alito-defends-citizens-in-speech-to-federalist-society.html.
42. *Pleasant Grove v. Summum*, 129 S. Ct. 1125 (2009).

1: EQUALITY

1. Jennifer Steinhauer, "House Reading of the Constitution Is Not Without Issues," *New York Times*, January 6, 2011.
2. Daniel Okrent, *Last Call: The Rise and Fall of Prohibition* (New York: Scribner, 2010).
3. Omar Khayyám, *The Rubaiyat*, Stanza 71.
4. On this theme more generally, see Jack M. Balkin, *Constitutional Redemption: Political Faith in an Unjust World* (Cambridge, Mass.: Harvard University Press, 2011).
5. *West Virginia State Board of Education v. Barnette*, 319 U.S. 624 (1943).
6. See Laurence H. Tribe, "America's Constitutional Narrative," *Daedalus* (Winter 2012), 18.
7. Quoted in Conal Furay and Michael Salevouris, *The Methods and Skills of History: A Practical Guide* (New York: Wiley-Blackwell, 1988), xvi.
8. See, e.g., Khalil Gibran Muhammad, *The Condemnation of Blackness: Race, Crime, and the Making of Modern Urban America* (Cambridge, Mass.: Harvard University Press, 2011); Michelle Alexander, *The New Jim Crow: Mass Incarceration in the Age of Colorblindness* (New York: New Press, 2010); Glenn C. Loury, *The Anatomy of Racial Inequality* (Cambridge, Mass.: Harvard University Press, 2003); and Dinesh

D'Souza, *The End of Racism: Principles for a Multiracial Society* (New York: Free Press, 1996).

9. "King's Dream Remains an Elusive Goal; Many Americans See Racial Disparities," Pew Research, August 22, 2013, http://www.pewsocialtrends.org/2013/08/22/kings -dream-remains-an-elusive-goal-many-americans-see-racial-disparities/.

10. Remarks by the President on Trayvon Martin, White House (July 19, 2013).

11. William Faulkner, *Requiem for a Nun* (New York: Vintage, 2011), 73.

12. *Regents of Univ. of Cal. v. Bakke*, 438 U.S. 265, 407 (1978) (separate opinion of Blackmun, J.).

13. Oral argument in *Schuette v. Coalition to Defend Affirmative Action*, No. 12-682.

14. For a thoughtful essay on Kennedy's approach to race in several cases, see Heather K. Gerken, "Justice Kennedy and the Domains of Equal Protection," *Harvard Law Review* 104 (2007): 121.

15. Jess Bravin, "Justice Kennedy Speaks Out on Gay Marriage, Shutdown," *Wall Street Journal*, October 10, 2013.

16. Lydia Saad, "In U.S., 52% Back Law to Legalize Gay Marriage in 50 States," Gallup Politics, July 29, 2013, http://www.gallup.com/poll/163730/back-law-legalize-gay -marriage-states.aspx.

17. See 133 S. Ct. 1136 (2013) (Sotomayor, J., respecting the denial of the petition for writ of certiorari).

18. "Transcript of Obama Speech," *Politico*, March 18, 2008, http://www.politico.com /news/stories/0308/9100.html.

19. See, e.g., Michael J. Klarman, *Unfinished Business: Racial Equality in American History* (New York: Oxford University Press, 2007).

20. See Charles L. Ogletree Jr., *All Deliberate Speed* (New York: W. W. Norton, 2004); James E. Ryan, "The Supreme Court and Voluntary Integration," *Harvard Law Review* 121 (2007): 139–42; and Richard Kluger, *Simple Justice* (New York: Knopf, 1976).

21. See Martha Minow, "'A Proper Objective': Constitutional Commitment and Educational Opportunity After *Bolling v. Sharpe* and *Parents Involved in Community Schools*," *Howard Law Journal* 55 (2012): 575, 576–89; and Wendy Parker, "The Future of School Desegregation," *Northwestern University Law Review* 94 (2000): 1157, 1162–78.

22. Gary Orfield and Chungmei Lee, "Historic Reversals, Accelerating Resegregation, and the Need for New Integration Strategies," Civil Rights Project, UCLA (2007).

23. See 551 U.S. 701 (2007).

24. Linda Greenhouse, "A Tale of Two Justices," *Green* Bag 11, 2nd ser. (Autumn 2007): 37, 44.

25. *League of United Latin Am. Citizens v. Perry*, 548 U.S. 399, 511 (2006) (Roberts, C.J., concurring in part, concurring in the judgment in part, and dissenting in part).

26. A vast literature debates whether the Constitution is "color-blind." See, e.g., Christopher W. Schmidt, "*Brown* and the Colorblind Constitution," *Cornell Law Review* 94 (2008): 203; Ian Haney López, "'A Nation of Minorities': Race, Ethnicity, and Reactionary Colorblindnes," *Stanford Law Review* 59 (2007): 985; J. Harvie Wilkinson III, "The Seattle and Louisville School Cases: There Is No Other Way," *Harvard*

Law Review 121 (2007): 158; and Reva B. Siegel, "Equality Talk: Antisubordination and Anticlassification Values in Constitutional Struggles Over *Brown*," *Harvard Law Review* 117 (2004): 1470.

27. Clarence Thomas, *My Grandfather's Son: A Memoir* (New York: HarperCollins, 2007), 78.

28. Ibid., 79.

29. Pamela Karlan, "What Can *Brown*® Do for You?: Neutral Principles and the Struggle over the Constitution," *Duke Law Journal* 58 (2009): 1049, 1052.

30. See, e.g., Jack Balkin, *Living Originalism* (Cambridge, Mass.: The Belknap Press of Harvard University Press, 2011), 234–35; Cass Sunstein, *Radicals in Robes* (New York: Basic Books, 2005), 131–50; Jed Rubenfeld, "Affirmative Action," *Yale Law Journal* 107 (1997): 427; and Eric Schnapper, "Affirmative Action and the Legislative History of the Fourteenth Amendment," *Virginia Law Review* 71 (1985): 753. But see Michael Rappaport, "Originalism and the Colorblind Constitution," *Notre Dame Law Review* 89 (2013): 71.

31. For excellent analyses, see James E. Ryan, "The Supreme Court and Voluntary Integration," *Harvard Law Review* 121 (2007): 131; and Erica Frankenberg and Chinh Q. Le, "The Post–*Parents Involved* Challenge: Confronting Extralegal Obstacles to Integration," *Ohio State Law Journal* 69 (2008): 1015.

32. Adam Liptak, "The Same Words, but Differing Views," *New York Times*, June 29, 2007.

33. 539 U.S. 306 (2003).

34. See 133 S. Ct. 2411.

35. See, e.g., Will Baude, "Where's *Fisher*," *Prawfsblog*, June 7, 2013, http://prawfsblawg .blogs.com/prawfsblawg/2013/06/wheres-fisher.html.

36. Thomas, *My Grandfather's Son*, 74–75.

37. Ibid., 75-76.

38. Ibid., 252.

39. Ariane de Vogue, "'Silent' Justice Outspoken on Affirmative Action," ABC News, September 30, 2007, http://abcnews.go.com/TheLaw/story?id=3667079&page=1.

40. Charlie Savage, "Videos Shed New Light on Sotomayor's Position," *New York Times*, June 10, 2009.

41. Sonia Sotomayor, *My Beloved World* (New York: Knopf, 2013), 191.

42. Ibid., 192.

43. "Sotomayor on Role Affirmative Action Played in Her Life," CBS News, January 11, 2013, http://www.cbsnews.com/news/sotomayor-on-role-affirmative-action-played -in-her-life/.

44. Sotomayor, *My Beloved World*, 145.

45. David D. Kirkpatrick, "'85 Document Opens Window to Alito Views," *New York Times*, November 15, 2005.

46. Emily Bazelon, "The Place of Women on the Court," *New York Times*, July 7, 2009.

47. Ibid.

48. *Adarand Constructors, Inc. v. Mineta*, 534 U.S. 103 (1995) (concurring).

49. *Gratz v. Bollinger*, 539 U.S. 244, 298 (2003) (Ginsburg, J., dissenting).

50. See, generally, Randall Kennedy, *For Discrimination: Race, Affirmative Action, and the Law* (New York: Pantheon, 2013); Richard D. Kahlenberg, "A Better Affirmative

...e Universities That Created an Alternative to Racial Preferences,"
...oundation Report (October 2012); Richard Sander and Stuart Taylor
...atch: How Affirmative Action Hurts Students It's Intended to Help, and
...Universities Won't Admit It (New York: Basic Books, 2012); Richard D.
...enberg, The Remedy: Class, Race, and Affirmative Action (New York: Basic
...oks, 1996); Kimberley Jenkins Robinson, "The Constitutional Future of Race-
...eutral Efforts to Achieve Diversity and Avoid Racial Isolation in Elementary and
Secondary Schools," Boston College Law Review 50 (2009): 277; and Jesse Rothstein
and Albert H. Yoon, "Affirmative Action in Law School Admissions: What Do
Racial Preferences Do?," University of Chicago Law Review 75 (2008): 649.

51. Richard Kahlenberg, "The Class-Based Future of Affirmative Action," American
Prospect, June 25, 2013.

52. Sherrilyn A. Ifill, "Race vs. Class: The False Dichotomy," New York Times, June 14,
2013.

53. See Deirdre M. Bowen, "Meeting Across the River: Why Affirmative Action Needs
Race and Class Diversity," Denver University Law Review 88 (2011): 751; Paul Brest
and Miranda Oshige, "Affirmative Action for Whom?," Stanford Law Review 47
(1995): 855; and Reginald T. Shuford, "Why Affirmative Action Remains Essential
in the Age of Obama," Campbell Law Review 31 (2009): 503.

54. There is a vast literature on this subject. See, e.g., Brian K. Landsberg, Free at Last
to Vote: The Alabama Origins of the 1965 Voting Rights Act (Lawrence: University
Press of Kansas, 2007); Taylor Branch, At Canaan's Edge: America in the King Years,
1965–68 (New York: Simon & Schuster, 2006); Michael Klarman, From Jim Crow to
Civil Rights: The Supreme Court and the Struggle for Racial Equality (New York:
Oxford University Press, 2004); David J. Garrow, Protest at Selma: Martin Luther
King, Jr., and the Voting Rights Act of 1965 (New Haven, Conn.: Yale University
Press, 1978); and Steven F. Lawson, Black Ballots: Voting Rights in the South, 1944–
1969 (New York: Columbia University Press, 1976).

55. Lyndon B. Johnson, "Special Message to the Congress: The American Promise,"
Transcript of the Johnson Address on Voting Rights to Joint Session of Congress,
New York Times, March 15, 1964, http://www.nytimes.com/books/98/04/12
/specials/johnson-rightsadd.html.

56. See, e.g., Chandler Davidson and Bernard Grofman, eds., Quiet Revolution in the
South: The Impact of the Voting Rights Act, 1965–1990 (Princeton, N.J.: Princeton
University Press, 1994).

57. Chandler Davidson, "The Voting Rights Act: A Brief History," in Controversies in
Minority Voting, ed. B. Grofman and C. Davidson (Washington, D.C.: The Brookings Institution, 1992), 7, 21.

58. South Carolina v. Katzenbach, 383 U.S. 301 (1966).

59. City of Boerne v. Flores, 521 U.S. 507 (1997).

60. See Voting Rights Act: Section 5 Preclearance and Standards: Hearings Before the
Subcomm. on the Constitution of the H. Comm. on the Judiciary, 109th Cong. 96-
181 (2005).

61. See, e.g., Richard L. Hasen, "Congressional Power to Renew the Preclearance Provisions of the Voting Rights Act After Tennessee v. Lane," Ohio State Law Journal 66

(2005): 177; Samuel Issacharoff, "Is Section 5 of the Voting Rights Act a Victim of Its Own Success?," *Columbia Law Review* 104 (2004): 1710; Michael J. Pitts, "Section 5 of the Voting Rights Act: A Once and Future Remedy?," *Denver University Law Review* 81 (2003): 225; Victor Andres Rodriguez, "Section 5 of the Voting Rights Act of 1965 After *Boerne*: The Beginning of the End of Preclearance?," *California Law Review* 91 (2003): 769; Paul Winke, "Why the Preclearance and Bailout Provisions of the Voting Rights Act Are Still a Constitutionally Proportional Remedy," *New York University Review of Law and Social Change* 28 (2003): 69; and Pamela S. Karlan, "Two Section Twos and Two Section Fives: Voting Rights and Remedies After *Flores*," *William & Mary Law Review* 39 (1998): 725.

62. See Rick Hasen, "How Would a Justice Roberts Vote on the Constitutionality of a Reauthorized Section 5?," *Election Law Blog*, August 15, 2005, http://electionlaw blog.org/archives/003863.html.

63. *Nw. Austin Mun. Util. Dist. No. 1 v. Holder,* 557 U.S. 193 (2009).

64. 133 S. Ct. 2612 (2013).

65. "LDF Lawyer the Sole Black Lawyer to Argue in Supreme Court This Year," LDF, May 12, 2013, http://www.naacpldf.org/news/ldf-lawyer-sole-black-lawyer-argue -supreme-court-year.

66. For a superb work on modern barriers to voting rights, see Richard L. Hasen, *The Voting Wars: From Florida 2000 to the Next Election Meltdown* (New Haven, Conn.: Yale University Press, 2012).

67. The following paragraphs are informed by several articles about the Lovings. See Kate Sheppard, "'The Loving Story': How an Interracial Couple Changed the Nation," *Mother Jones*, February 13, 2012; Douglas Martin, "Mildred Loving, Who Battled Ban on Mixed-Race Marriage, Dies at 68," *New York Times*, May 6, 2008; "*Loving v. Virginia:* The Case over Interracial Marriage," ACLU.org, https://www .aclu.org/racial-justice/loving-v-virginia-case-over-interracial-marriage; and "The Crime of Being Married," *Life*, March 18, 1966.

68. Robert A. Pratt, "Crossing the Color Line: A Historical Assessment and Personal Narrative of *Loving v. Virginia*," *Howard Law Journal* 41 (1998): 229, 237.

69. The next several paragraphs are based on a remarkable profile of Edith Windsor by Ariel Levy, "The Perfect Wife," *New Yorker*, September 30, 2013, and on an article about her marriage to Thea Spyer: Adam Gabbatt, "Edith Windsor and Thea Spyer: 'A Love Affair That Just Kept On and On and On,'" *Guardian*, June 26, 2013. It also draws on the brief Windsor filed in her Supreme Court case.

70. "Edith Windsor Statement on Supreme Court Steps: Full Text," *Guardian*, March 27, 2013.

71. Jill Hamburg Coplan, "When a Woman Loves a Woman," *NYU Alumni Magazine* (Fall 2011).

72. Michael Klarman, *From Jim Crow to Civil Rights* (New York: Oxford University Press, 2004), 321–22.

73. See Justin Driver, "The Consensus Constitution," *Texas Law Review* 89 (2011): 755, 823–25.

74. 388 U.S. 1 (1967). Three years earlier, in *McLaughlin v. Florida*, 379 U.S. 184 (1964), the Court had unanimously struck down Florida's law making it a crime for

two unmarried people of opposite sex to cohabit if one was black and the other white.

75. The next several paragraphs are informed by Michael Klarman, *From the Closet to the Altar: Courts, Backlash, and the Struggle for Same-Sex Marriage* (New York: Oxford University Press, 2013); Linda Hirshman, *Victory: The Triumphant Gay Revolution* (New York: Harper, 2012); Margot Canaday, *The Straight State: Sexuality and Citizenship in Twentieth-Century America* (Princeton, N.J.: Princeton University Press, 2009); and George Chauncey, *Why Marriage? The History Shaping Today's Debate over Gay Equality* (New York: Basic Books, 2009).

76. On the politics of disgust in gay and lesbian rights struggles, see generally Martha C. Nussbaum, *From Disgust to Humanity: Sexual Orientation and Constitutional Law* (New York: Oxford University Press, 2010).

77. See 478 U.S. 186 (1986). One of us (Larry Tribe) argued the case against Georgia's law at the Supreme Court in *Bowers* and had earlier argued *Board of Education v. National Gay Task Force*, 470 U.S. 903 (1985) (affirming, four to four, a lower court decision that struck down a school board's ban on gay rights advocacy by public school teachers).

78. 517 U.S. 620 (1996). Larry Tribe submitted an amicus brief proposing the rationale ultimately adopted by the Court in *Romer*.

79. 539 U.S. 558 (2003). A leading work on *Bowers* and *Lawrence* is David A. J. Richards, *The Sodomy Cases: Bowers v. Hardwick and Lawrence v. Texas* (Lawrence: University of Kansas Press, 2009). For a superb overview of the history of sodomy laws in the United States, see William N. Eskridge Jr., *Dishonorable Passions: Sodomy Laws in America 1861–2003* (New York: Viking, 2008).

80. See Laurence H. Tribe and Joshua Matz, "The Constitutional Inevitability of Same-Sex Marriage," *Maryland Law Review* 71 (2012): 471. For an engaging overview of some of the most important same-sex marriage litigation, see Adam Liptak, *To Have and Uphold: The Supreme Court and the Battle for Same-Sex Marriage* (New York: New York Times/Byliner, 2013).

81. A massive literature addresses the role of courts in debates over same-sex marriage rights. See, e.g., Klarman, *From the Closet to the Alter*; Gerald N. Rosenberg, *The Hollow Hope: Can Courts Bring About Social Change?* (Chicago: University of Chicago Press, 2008), 339–419; Tribe and Matz, "The Constitutional Inevitability of Same-Sex Marriage"; William N. Eskridge Jr. and John Ferejohn, "Constitutional Horticulture: Deliberation-Respecting Judicial Review," *Texas Law Review* 87 (2009): 1273; Martha C. Nussbaum, "A Right to Marry?: Same-Sex Marriage and Constitutional Law," *Dissent* (Summer 2009): 43; and Richard A. Posner, "Should There Be Homosexual Marriage? And If So, Who Should Decide?," *Michigan Law Review* 95 (1997): 1578.

82. For a canonical statement of this view, see Alexander M. Bickel, *The Least Dangerous Branch: The Supreme Court at the Bar of Politics* (New York: Bobbs-Merrill Co., 1962).

83. *Goodridge v. Dep't of Pub. Health*, 798 N.E. 2d 941, 954–55 (Mass. 2003). One of us (Larry Tribe) submitted an amicus brief in *Goodridge* on behalf of dozens of law professors and law school deans, urging the Court to reach the decision it did.

84. Klarman, *From the Closet to the Altar*, 89–142.

85. Ibid., 48–74.

86. See *Hollingsworth v. Perry*, 133 S. Ct. 2652 (2013).

87. See 133 S. Ct. 2675 (2013).

88. For a critical view of the Department of Justice's "duty to defend," see Neil Devins and Saikrishna Prakash, "The Indefensible Duty to Defend," *Columbia Law Review* 112 (2012): 507.

89. John C. Jeffries Jr., *Justice Lewis F. Powell, Jr.: A Biography* (New York: Scribner, 1994), 521. It was Powell's seat on the Court that Kennedy was eventually selected to fill, after Reagan's nomination of Judge Robert Bork was rejected by the Senate in 1987. Three years after retiring from the Court, Powell announced that the only vote he had cast as a justice that he had come to regard as mistaken was his vote in *Bowers* (p. 530).

90. Joan Biskupic, "Will Acceptance of Gays by High Court Influence Rulings?," Reuters, September 9, 2012, http://www.reuters.com/article/2012/09/09/us-usa-court -gay-rights-idUSBRE88808M20120909.

91. Robert Barnes, "High Court Reflects Diversity of Modern Marriage," *Washington Post*, http://www.washingtonpost.com/politics/high-court-reflects-diversity-of-mod ern-marriage/2013/03/17/123cbaec-8b2c-11e2-b63f-f53fb9f2fcb4_story.html.

92. Some scholars have argued that *Windsor* is principally a federalism opinion. See, e.g., Ernest A. Young and Erin C. Blondel, "Federalism, Liberty, and Equality in *United States v. Windsor*," *CATO Supreme Court Review* (2013): 117.

93. The Judicial Branch derives its power from Article III, which extends only to certain "Cases" and "Controversies."

94. See, e.g., *Kitchen v. Herbert* (D. Utah, December 20, 2013), which struck down Utah's ban on same-sex marriages on the authority of *Windsor*.

95. Ariel Levy, "How Edith Windsor Learned She Won," *New Yorker*, June 26, 2013.

96. See Bravin, "Justice Kennedy Speaks Out on Gay Marriage, Shutdown."

2: HEALTH CARE

1. "Obama Claims Broccoli Is His Favorite Food," Reuters, July 9, 2013, http://www .reuters.com/article/2013/07/09/us-usa-obama-broccoli-idUSBRE96819X 20130709.

2. Maureen Dowd, "'I'm President,' So No More Broccoli!," *New York Times*, March 23, 1990.

3. James Gerstenzang and Thomas H. Maugh II, "Choking on Pretzel, Bush Faints Briefly," *Los Angeles Times*, January 14, 2002.

4. "New Reason-Rupe Poll: Americans Think Health Care and Broccoli Mandates Are Unconstitutional," *Reason*, March 26, 2012, www.reason.com/poll/2012/03/26 /reason-rupe-health-care-mandate-poll.

5. Adam Liptak, "Kagan Reminds Senators: Legislation Is Your Job," *New York Times*, July 1, 2010.

6. Robert Mankoff, "I Say It's Government-Mandated Broccoli, and I Say the Hell with It," *New Yorker*, April 9, 2012.

7. For a lively and illuminating tour through the evolution of arguments against the ACA, as developed by a group of scholarly bloggers who played an instrumental role in the challenge, see Randy E. Barnett et al., *A Conspiracy Against Obamacare: The Volokh Conspiracy and the Health Care Case* (New York: Palgrave Macmillan, 2013).

8. *NFIB v. Sebelius*, 132 S. Ct. 2566 (2012). For a wide-ranging scholarly discussion of the ruling, see Nathaniel Persily, Gillian E. Metzger, and Trevor W. Morrison, eds., *The Health Care Case: The Supreme Court's Decision and Its Implications* (New York: Oxford University Press, 2013). For engaging and comprehensive accounts of the litigation and maneuvering at the Court, see Josh Blackman, *Unprecedented: The Constitutional Challenge to Obamacare* (New York: Public Affairs, 2013); and Jeffrey Toobin, *The Oath: The Obama White House and the Supreme Court* (New York: Doubleday, 2012), 263–93.

9. See, e.g., Mark Tushnet, *In the Balance: Law and Politics on the Roberts Court* (New York: W. W. Norton, 2013), 20–43; Toobin, *The Oath*, 291–96; Jonathan Chait, "John Roberts Saves Us All," *New York Magazine*, June 28, 2012; Michael Dorf, "Obamacare Upheld Thanks to CJ Roberts: I'm Back to Thirty Percent," *Dorf on Law*, June 28, 2012, www.dorfonlaw.org/2012/06/obamacare-upheld-thanks-to-cj-roberts.html; and David L. Franklin, "Why Did Roberts Do It? To Save the Court," *Slate*, June 28, 2012, www.slate.com/articles/news_and_politics/jurisprudence/2012/06/john_roberts_broke_with_conservatives_to_preserve_the_supreme_court_s_legitimacy.single.html.

10. See generally Donald A. Barr, *Introduction to U.S. Health Policy: The Organization, Financing, and Delivery of Health Care in America* (Baltimore: Johns Hopkins University Press, 2011); Theda Skocpol, *Boomerang: Health Care Reform and the Turn Against the Government* (New York: W. W. Norton, 1997); Paul Starr, *Remedy and Reaction: The Peculiar American Struggle over Health Care Reform* (New Haven, Conn.: Yale University Press, 2003); and Beatrix Hoffman, "Health Care Reform and Social Movements in the United States," *American Journal of Public Health* 93 (2003): 75.

11. Theodore Roosevelt, "A Confession of Faith," speech before the 1912 Progressive Party national convention, August 6, 1912, available at www.theodore-roosevelt.com/images/research/speeches/trarmageddon.pdf.

12. See G. John Ikenberry and Theda Skocpol, "Expanding Social Benefits: The Role of Social Security," *Political Science Quarterly* 102 (1987): 389, 397.

13. Truman also made history as the first person ever to enroll as a Medicare recipient. See Robert Dallek, *Flawed Giant: Lyndon Johnson and His Times, 1961–1973* (New York: Oxford University Press, 1998), 209.

14. See Stephen Pearlstein, "Kennedy Saw Health-Care Reform Fail in the '70s," *Washington Post*, August 28, 2009.

15. Bill Clinton, *My Life* (New York: Knopf, 2004), 620–21; and Hillary Clinton, *Living History* (New York: Simon & Schuster, 2003), 248.

16. See, e.g., Stuart M. Butler, "Why Conservatives Need a National Health Plan," Heritage Foundation, March 22, 1993, available at www.heritage.org/research/lecture/why-conservatives-need-a-national-health-plan.

17. "Obama Flip-Flops on Requiring People to Buy Health Care," *Politifact*, July 20, 2009, www.politifact.com/truth-o-meter/statements/2009/jul/20/barack-obama/obama-flip-flops-requiring-people-buy-health-care/.

18. Ryan Lizza, "The Mandate Memo: How Obama Changed His Mind," *New Yorker*, March 26, 2012, www.newyorker.com/online/blogs/newsdesk/2012/03/the-man date-memo-how-obama-changed-his-mind.html.

19. See, e.g., Michael Cooper, "G.O.P. Senate Victory Stuns Democrats," *New York Times*, January 19, 2010.

20. See, e.g., Lawrence R. Jacobs and Theda Skocpol, *Health Care Reform and American Politics: What Everyone Needs to Know* (New York: Oxford University Press, 2010); and John E. McDonough, *Inside National Health Reform* (Berkeley: University of California Press, 2012).

21. For academic discussions of this phenomenon, see, e.g., Henry J. Aaron, "Systemic Reform of Health Care Delivery and Payment," Brookings, December 2010, www .brookings.edu/research/articles/2010/12/health-reform-aaron; Matthew Buettgens et al., "Why the Individual Mandate Matters: Timely Analysis of Immediate Health Policy Issues," Urban Institute, December 2010, www.urban.org/uploadedpdf /412280-individual-mandate-matters.pdf; and David M. Cutler and Richard J. Zeckhauser, "Adverse Selection in Health Insurance," *Frontiers in Health Policy Research* 1 (1998): 1.

22. This account of Obama's reaction to the *Health Care Case* is based on several sources, including Glenn Thrush, "Barack Obama Fooled on Supreme Court Ruling by CNN, Fox News," *Politico*, June 28, 2012, http://www.politico.com/news /stories/0612/77974.html; and Ed Henry, "Obama Learned of the Health Care Ruling Just Like the Rest of the Public," Fox News, June 28, 2012, http://www .foxnews.com/politics/2012/06/28/obama-learned-health-care-ruling-just-like -rest-public/.

23. Marcia Coyle, *The Roberts Court: The Struggle for the Constitution* (New York: Simon & Schuster, 2013), 1–2.

24. On this silence at the Court, see Jack Goldsmith, "Temple of Silence," *New Republic*, June 23, 2012. On pre-announcement leaks in the *Health Care Case*, see Blackman, *Unprecedented*, 227–33.

25. See, e.g., Charles Fried, "Health Care Law's Enemies Have No Ally in Constitution," *Boston Globe*, May 21, 2010, A13; and "Over 100 Law Professors Agree on Affordable Care Act's Constitutionality," *American Progress*, http://www.ameri canprogress.org/issues/2011/01/pdf/law_professors_ACA.pdf. One of this book's authors initially shared the general view. See Laurence H. Tribe, "On Health Care, Justice Will Prevail," *New York Times*, February 8, 2011, A27; and Laurence Tribe, "Congress Can Compel Action Due to Public Necessity," *Boston Globe*, April 3, 2001, A11.

26. Eric Zimmermann, "Pelosi to Reporter: 'Are You Serious?,'" *Hill*, October 23, 2009, http://thehill.com/blogs/blog-briefing-room/news/64547-pelosi-to-reporter-are -you-serious.

27. Linda Greenhouse, "Never Before," Opinionator, *New York Times*, March 21, 2012, http://opinionator.blogs.nytimes.com/2012/03/21/never-before/.

28. "Toobin: Mandate in Grave Trouble," *CNN Newsroom*, CNN television, broadcast March 27, 2012, available at http://www.cnn.com/video/?/video/crime/2012/03/27 /nr-toobin-mandate.cnn#/video/crime/2012/03/27/nr-toobin-mandate.cnn.

29. See, e.g., George F. Will, "Liberals Put the Squeeze to Justice Roberts," *Washington Post,* May 25, 2012; Jeffrey Rosen, "Are Liberals Trying to Intimidate John Roberts?," *New Republic,* May 28, 2012; and Mark Tushnet, "Lobbying the Supreme Court Update," *Balkinization,* May 23, 2012, http://balkin.blogspot.com/2012/05/lobbying-supreme-court-update.html.

30. Brett Logiurato, "Intrade Is Going Absolutely Nuts Ahead of the Obamacare Decision," *Business Insider,* June 28, 2012, http://www.businessinsider.com/obamacare-intrade-odds-supreme-court-decision-constitutional-2012-6.

31. For *SCOTUSblog*'s report on how Ruemmler received the news at the White House that day, see http://www.scotusblog.com/2012/07/were-getting-wildly-differing-assessments/. Full disclosure: one of us (Joshua Matz) wrote for *SCOTUSblog* at the time.

32. See Sabrina Tavernise and Robert Gebeloff, "Millions of Poor Are Left Uncovered by Health Law," *New York Times,* October 3, 2013, A1; and Sabrina Tavernise, "Cuts in Hospital Subsidies Threaten Safety-Net Care," *New York Times,* November 9, 2013, A1.

33. Justin Sink, "Justice Roberts Jokes About Vacationing on an 'Impregnable Island Fortress,'" *Hill,* June 29, 2012, http://thehill.com/blogs/blog-briefing-room/news/235707-roberts-jokes-about-vacationing-on-a-impregnable-island-fortress.

34. Vikram David Amar and Akhil Reed Amar, "Chief Justice Roberts Reaches for Greatness," *Los Angeles Times,* July 1, 2012; David Von Drehle, "Roberts Rules: What the Health Care Decision Means for the Country," *Time,* June 29, 2012; Ezra Klein, "The Political Genius of John Roberts," *Washington Post,* June 28, 2012, http://www.washingtonpost.com/blogs/wonkblog/wp/2012/06/28/the-political-genius-of-john-roberts/; Jeffrey Rosen, "Welcome to the Roberts Court: How the Chief Justice Used Obamacare to Reveal His True Identity," *New Republic,* June 29, 2012, http://www.newrepublic.com/blog/plank/104493/welcome-the-roberts-court-who-the-chief-justice-was-all-along; and Chelsea Schilling, "America Has a Brand-New Benedict Arnold," *WND,* December 26, 2012.

35. Jeffrey Toobin, "To Your Health," *New Yorker,* July 9, 2012, http://www.newyorker.com/talk/comment/2012/07/09/120709taco_talk_toobin; Josh Gerstein, "Liberals Fear the John Roberts Rebound," *Politico,* July 3, 2012, http://www.politico.com/news/stories/0712/78084.html; and Greg Stohr, "Roberts Faces Shot at Republican Redemption in Race Cases," *Bloomberg Businessweek,* July 5, 2012, http://www.businessweek.com/news/2012-07-05/roberts-faces-shot-at-republican-redemption-in-race-cases.

36. See, e.g., Randy Barnett, "We Lost on Health Care. But the Constitution Won," *Washington Post,* June 29, 2012; and James B. Stewart, "In Obama's Victory, a Loss for Congress," *New York Times,* June 30, 2012, B1.

37. Pamela S. Karlan, "The Supreme Court, 2011 Term—Foreword: Democracy and Disdain," *Harvard Law Review* 126 (2012): 1, 47.

38. See Blackman, *Unprecedented,* 183–84 (noting that only Larry Tribe had made a point of highlighting this signal in several nationally televised appearances immediately after the argument, having previously predicted publicly that Roberts would uphold the law on the basis of congressional taxing power).

39. Jan Crawford, "Roberts Switched Views to Uphold Health Care Law," CBS News, July 1, 2012, http://www.cbsnews.com/8301-3460_162-57464549/roberts-switched-views-to-uphold-health-care-law.

40. For a powerful critique of this "great substantive and independent power" argument, see Michael C. Dorf, "What Really Happened in the Affordable Care Act Case," *Texas Law Review* 92 (2013): 133.

41. Roberts was quoting from *Panhandle Oil Co. v. Mississippi ex rel. Knox*, 277 U.S. 218, 223 (1928) (Holmes, J., dissenting).

42. See Laurence H. Tribe, "Respecting Dissent: Justice Ginsburg's Critique of the Troubling Invocation of Appearance," *Harvard Law Review* 127 (2013): 478.

43. *Vance v. Ball State University*, 133 S. Ct. 2434, 2466 (2013) (Ginsburg, J., dissenting); *Ledbetter v. Goodyear Tire & Rubber Co.*, 550 U.S. 618, 661 (2007) (Ginsburg, J., dissenting).

44. Adam Liptak, "Court Is 'One of Most Activist,' Ginsburg Says, Vowing to Stay," *New York Times*, August 25, 2013, A1; and Jeffrey Toobin, "Heavyweight," *New Yorker*, March 11, 2013, 38.

45. Amy Leigh Campbell, *Raising the Bar: Ruth Bader Ginsburg and the ACLU Women's Rights Project* (Bloomington, Ind.: Xlibris, 2003).

46. Ariane de Vogue, "Justice Ginsburg: 'As Long As I Can Do the Job Full Steam, I Will,'" *ABC News* (October 7, 2013), http://abcnews.go.com/blogs/politics/2013/10/justice-ginsburg-as-long-as-i-can-do-the-job-full-steam-i-will/.

47. See the excellent discussion in Michael Dorf, "Fear of a Vegetarian State—and Other Reflections on the Obamacare Decision," *Dorf on Law*, June 28, 2012, www.dorfonlaw.org/2012/06/fear-of-vegetarian-state-and-other.html. (Dorf notes that "we vegans aim to convert, not coerce.")

48. 358 U.S. 1 (1958).

49. Martha Minow, "The Supreme Court 2011 Term—Comment: Affordable Convergence: 'Reasonable Interpretation' and the Affordable Care Act," *Harvard Law Review* 126 (2012): 133.

50. Pamela Karlan, "No Respite for Liberals," *New York Times*, June 30, 2012.

51. Gillian E. Metzger, "The Supreme Court 2011 Term—Comment: To Tax, to Spend, to Regulate," *Harvard Law Review* 126 (2012): 85–86.

52. *Sky-Seven v. Holder*, 661 F.3d 1, 53 (D.C. Cir. 2011) (Kavanaugh, J., dissenting as to jurisdiction).

53. Yet another possible explanation is proposed in Tushnet, *In the Balance*, 32–33. Tushnet suggests that the Reagan-era Department of Justice (an important influence on Chief Justice Roberts early in his career) focused heavily on convincing the Court to impose stricter limits on Congress's power under the Commerce Clause, while the taxing power attracted little attention. Thus, Roberts had little history, and hence little baggage, when it came to the taxing power.

54. Abraham Lincoln, "Address at a Sanitary Fair," April 18, 1864, quoted by Eugene Volokh, "We All Declare for Liberty; but in Using the Same Word We Do Not All Mean the Same Thing," *The Volokh Conspiracy*, January 9, 2014, http://www.volokh.com/2014/01/09/declare-liberty-using-word-mean-thing/.

55. Other scholars have also emphasized that the *Health Care Case* turned mainly on

competing visions of American freedom. See, e.g., Andrew Koppelman, *The Tough Luck Constitution and the Assault on Health Care Reform* (New York: Oxford University Press, 2013).

56. Randy E. Barnett, Lecture, "Commandeering the People: Why the Individual Health Insurance Mandate Is Unconstitutional," *New York University Journal of Law and Liberty* 5 (2010): 581, 605.

57. For an overview of the rise of libertarianism in twentieth-century America, see Angus Burgin, *The Great Persuasion: Reinventing Free Markets Since the Depression* (Cambridge, Mass.: Harvard University Press, 2012). Particularly influential libertarian texts include Freidrich A. Hayek, *The Constitution of Liberty* (Chicago: University of Chicago Press, 1960), Milton Friedman, *Capitalism and Freedom* (Chicago: University of Chicago Press, 1962), and Robert Nozick, *Anarchy, State, and Utopia* (New York: Basic Books, 1974).

58. See Michael J. Sandel, *Justice: What's the Right Thing to Do?* (New York: Farrar, Straus and Giroux, 2009) 58–74. Of course, libertarianism takes many forms and this summary cannot do justice to all of them.

59. Alexander Hamilton, "The Federalist No. 33" (Clinton Rossiter, ed., 2003). For an argument that the Commerce Clause portion of the ACA case represents an example of a majority of the Court adopting libertarian reasoning, see Koppelman, *The Tough Luck Constitution*.

60. The Court upheld various portions of the Social Security Act in several cases decided in 1937. See *Steward Mach. Co. v. Davis*, 301 U.S. 548 (1937); *Helvering v. Davis*, 301 U.S. 619 (1937); and *Carmichael v. S. Coal & Coke Co.*, 301 U.S. 495 (1937). It likewise upheld the public accommodations portions of the Civil Rights Act of 1964 in *Heart of Atlanta Motel Inc. v. United States*, 379 U.S. 241 (1964), and *Katzenbach v. McClung*, 379 U.S. 294 (1964).

61. For a good introduction, see Eric Foner, *The Story of American Freedom* (New York: W. W. Norton, 1998), 139–62.

62. Ibid., 153.

63. Ibid., 195–218.

64. See, generally, Cass R. Sunstein, *The Second Bill of Rights: FDR's Unfinished Revolution—And Why We Need It More Than Ever* (New York: Basic Books, 2004).

65. Blackman, *Unprecedented*, 211.

66. Jack M. Balkin, "The Court Affirms the Social Contract," in *The Health Care Case*.

67. As Oliver Wendell Holmes famously observed, "A Constitution is not intended to embody a particular economic theory." *Lochner v. New York*, 198 U.S. 45, 75 (1905) (Holmes, J., dissenting). Nonetheless, the relationship between the Constitution, the framers, and political economics continues to be controversial. For some recent explorations of this issue that are largely critical of Justice Holmes's remark, see the contributions to the Thirtieth Annual Federalist Society National Student Symposium on Law and Public Policy: Capitalism, Markets, and the Constitution, *Harvard Journal of Law and Public Policy* 35 (2012): 1. See also James W. Ely, *The Guardian of Every Other Right: A Constitutional History of Property Rights* (New York: Oxford University Press, 2007) 26–58; and Harry N. Scheiber, "Economic

Liberty and the Constitution," *Essays in the History of Liberty: The Seaver Lectures* (San Marino, Calif.: Henry E. Huntington Library, 1989).

68. See, generally, Akhil Reed Amar, *America's Unwritten Constitution: The Precedents and Principles We Live By* (New York: Basic Books, 2013); and Laurence H. Tribe, *The Invisible Constitution* (New York: Oxford University Press, 2008).

69. *Lawrence v. Texas*, 539 U.S. 558 (2003) (sodomy); *Griswold v. Connecticut*, 381 U.S. 479 (1965) (contraception); *Roe v. Wade*, 410 U.S. 113 (1973) (abortion); *Loving v. Virginia*, 388 U.S. 1 (1967) (interracial marriage); *Pierce v. Soc'y of Sisters*, 268 U.S. 510 (1925) (private schools).

70. See Benjamin F. Wright, *The Growth of American Constitutional Law* (Boston: Houghton Mifflin, 1942), 154 (counting 184 Supreme Court cases from the *Lochner* era in which state laws were invalidated on the grounds that they abridged economic liberty in violation of what scholars called "substantive due process"); and Howard Gillman, *The Constitution Besieged: The Rise and Demise of Lochner Era Police Powers Jurisprudence* (Durham, N.C.: Duke University Press, 1993).

71. But see David E. Bernstein, *Rehabilitating Lochner: Defending Individual Rights against Progressive Reform* (Chicago: University of Chicago Press, 2011). The era is named for the case of *Lochner v. New York*, 198 U.S. 45 (1905), which struck down a state law limiting the hours that bakers could work.

72. *Adkins v. Children's Hospital*, 261 U.S. 525 (1923).

73. See, generally, Jeff Shesol, *Supreme Power: Franklin Roosevelt vs. the Supreme Court* (New York: W. W. Norton, 2010).

74. See *West Coast Hotel* Co. *v. Parrish*, 300 U.S. 379 (1937), which upheld state minimum-wage laws against a due process challenge.

75. Thomas came close to this view in *McDonald v. Chicago*, 561 U.S. 3025 (2010), when he argued that the Court should overrule more than a century of precedent and protect unenumerated rights under the Privileges or Immunities Clause of the Fourteenth Amendment. This holding would likely lead the Court to consider whether various economic liberties qualify as "privileges" or "immunities" of American citizenship under an originalist approach, and could embroil the Court in economic affairs that it has left mostly untouched since the 1930s. See, e.g., "Incorporation of the Right to Keep and Bear Arms," *Harvard Law Review* 124 (2010): 229–39.

76. On the subject of economic and civil rights in constitutional law, see Laurence H. Tribe, *American Constitutional Law* (New York: Foundation Press, 1988), 581–82, 1335–37, 1625–87. See also Jack M. Balkin, *Constitutional Redemption: Political Faith in an Unjust World* (Cambridge, Mass.: Harvard University Press, 2011), 119–225; Sunstein, *Second Bill of Rights*; James A. Dorn and Henry G. Manne, eds., *Economic Liberties and the Judiciary* (Fairfax, Va.: George Mason University Press, 1997); Goodwin Liu, "Rethinking Constitutional Welfare Rights," *Stanford Law Review* 61 (2008): 203; Richard A. Epstein, "The Indivisibility of Liberty Under the Bill of Rights," *Harvard Journal of Law and Public Policy* 15 (1992): 35; Mark Graber, "The Clintonification of American Law: Abortion, Welfare, and Liberal Constitutional Theory," *Ohio State Law Journal* 58 (1997): 731; and Richard A. Posner,

"The Constitution as an Economic Document," *George Washington Law Review*, 56 (1987): 4.

77. See *Cruzan v. Dir., Mo. Dep't of Health*, 497 U.S. 261, 278–79, 287–88 (1990), which acknowledged long-recognized constitutionally protected liberty interests in bodily integrity and assumed that they include the right to refuse lifesaving medical treatment.

78. See Michael Stokes Paulsen, "The Power to Destroy," *Public Discourse*, August 8, 2012, http://www.thepublicdiscourse.com/2012/08/6096/.

79. See, e.g., *Garcia v. San Antonio Metropolitan Transit Authority*, 469 U.S. 528, 551–52 (1985) and *United States v. Lopez*, 514, 549, 580, 583 (1995) (Kennedy, J., concurring).

80. See *Bond v. United States*, 131 S. Ct. 2355 (2011).

81. Letter from James Madison to Thomas Jefferson, October 17, 1788, in *Selected Writings of James Madison*, edited by Ralph Ketcham (2006), 158, 159.

82. For contrasting perspectives on the relationship between constitutional structure and individual liberties, compare Geoffrey P. Miller, "Liberty and Constitutional Architecture: The Rights-Structure Paradigm," *Harvard Journal of Law and Public Policy* 16 (1993): 87; and Michael W. McConnell, "Contract Rights and Property Rights: A Case Study in the Relationship Between Individual Liberties and Constitutional Structure," *California Law Review* 76 (1988): 267, with Akhil Reed Amar, "Of Sovereignty and Federalism," *Yale Law Journal* 96 (1987): 1425; and "The Bill of Rights as a Constitution," *Yale Law Journal* 100 (1991): 1131. For recent discussions of constitutional design with implications for the relationship between structure and rights, see Bradford R. Clark, "Separation of Powers as a Safeguard of Federalism," *Texas Law Review* 79 (2001): 1321; and Daryl Levinson, "Empire-Building Government in Constitutional Law," *Harvard Law Review* 118 (2005): 915.

83. Hamilton, "The Federalist No. 84," 515 (C. Rossiter, ed., 1961).

84. Jackson Baker, "Saith Scalia," *Memphis Flyer*, December 19, 2013, http://www.memphisflyer.com/memphis/saith-scalia/Content?oid=3571518.

85. Zoe Tillman, "At Federalist Society, Scalia Says He Doesn't 'Live or Die' for Bill of Rights Cases," *Blog of the Legal Times*, November 19, 2012, http://legaltimes.typepad.com/blt/2012/11/at-federalist-society-scalia-says-he-doesnt-live-or-die-for-bill-of-rights-cases.html.

86. See, e.g., Daryl J. Levinson and Richard H. Pildes, "Separation of Parties, Not Powers," *Harvard Law Review* 119 (2006): 2311.

87. See 17 U.S. 316 (1819).

88. See *Nat'l Fed'n of Indep. Bus.*, 132 S. Ct. at 2622 (Ginsburg, J., dissenting) (describing the Supreme Court's pre–New Deal limits on federal power, which was permitted to reach "commercial" activities with a "direct" effect on interstate commerce but not "noncommercial" activities like "production," "mining," and "manufacturing," which had only an "indirect" effect on interstate commerce). Ginsburg notes, "These line-drawing exercises were untenable." See also *United States v. E.C. Knight Co.*, 156 U.S. 1, 12 (1895) ("Commerce succeeds to manufacture, and is not a part of it."); *Carter v. Carter Coal Co.*, 298 U.S. 238, 304 (1936) ("Mining brings the subject matter of commerce into existence. Commerce disposes of it.").

89. See, e.g., *Nat'l Labor Relations Bd. v. Jones & Laughlin Steel Co.*, 301 U.S. 1 (1937) (upholding national labor standards); *Helvering v. Davis*, 301 U.S. 619 (1937) (upholding the Social Security Act); *Wickard v. Filburn*, 317 U.S. 111 (1942) (upholding a Depression-era price-stabilization law imposing a quota on private production of wheat); *Heart of Atlanta Motel v. United States*, 379 U.S. 241 (1964) (upholding civil rights laws); and *South Dakota v. Dole*, 483 U.S. 203 (1987) (upholding law encouraging states to adopt minimum drinking age).

90. See *United States v. Lopez*, 514 U.S. 549 (1995) (striking down a law establishing gun-free school zones); *United States v. Morrison*, 529 U.S. 598 (2000) (striking down a law targeting domestic violence); *New York v. United States*, 505 U.S. 144 (1992) (striking down a law regulating state disposal of radioactive waste); and *Printz v. United States*, 521 U.S. 898 (1997) (striking down a law implementing background check system for firearm purchases). On this so-called Federalism Revolution more generally, see Mark Tushnet, *A Court Divided: The Rehnquist Court and the Future of Constitutional Law* (New York: W. W. Norton, 2005), 249–78.

91. *Nevada v. Hall*, 440 U.S. 410, 433 (1979) (Rehnquist, J., dissenting).

92. For different views on the subject, see, e.g., Randy E. Barnett, *Restoring the Lost Constitution: The Presumption of Liberty* (Princeton, N.J.: Princeton University Press, 2004); Jack M. Balkin, "Commerce," *Michigan Law Review* 109 (2010): 1; and Richard A. Epstein, "The Proper Scope of the Commerce Power," *Virginia Law Review* 73 (1987): 1387.

93. On the varieties of federalism and the different kinds of local, state, and federal relationships, see, e.g., Heather K. Gerken, "Federalism All the Way Down," *Harvard Law Review* 124 (2010): 4.

94. See, e.g., Jessica Bulman-Pozen and Heather K. Gerken, "Uncooperative Federalism," *Yale Law Journal* 118 (2009): 1256.

95. See, e.g., Randy E. Barnett, "Turning Citizens into Subjects: Why the Health Insurance Mandate Is Unconstitutional," *Mercer Law Review* 62 (2011): 608; Barnett, "Commandeering the People"; David Bernstein, "Has the Pro-ACA Side Come Up with a 'Limiting Principle'?," *Volokh Conspiracy*, March 27, 2012, http://www.volokh.com/2012/03/27/has-the-pro-aca-side-come-up-with-a-limiting-principle/; and Daivd Kopel, "Nearing the End of the Search for the Non-Existent Limiting Principles," *Volokh Conspiracy*, March 29, 2012, http://www.volokh.com/2012/03/29/nearing-the-end-of-the-search-for-the-non-existent-limiting-principles/.

96. For a theory of citizen "exit" in the context of unfavorable public policies, see Albert O. Hirschman, *Exit, Voice, and Loyalty* (Cambridge, Mass.: Harvard University Press, 1970).

97. See, e.g., *Thomas More Law Ctr. v. Obama*, 651 F.3d 529, 549 (6th Cir. 2011) (Sutton, J., concurring).

98. Publius, "Transcript and Recording of Justice Scalia on the Judiciary and Economic Liberty," *FedSoc Blog*, May 31, 2013, http://www.fedsocblog.com/blog/transcript_and_recording_of_justice_scalia_on_the_judiciary_and_economic_li/.

99. See 131 S. Ct. 2653 (2011).

100. The limits of First Amendment protection in contexts like this one are often controversial. See, e.g., Frederick Schauer, "The Boundaries of the First Amendment: A Preliminary Exploration of Constitutional Salience," *Harvard Law Review* 117 (2004): 1675.

101. See Jedediah Purdy, "The Roberts Court v. America," *Democracy: A Journal of Ideas* 23 (Winter 2012).

102. *Stop the Beach Renourishment, Inc. v. Florida Department of Environmental Protection*, 560 U.S. 702 (2010) (plurality opinion).

103. *Knox v. Serv. Emps. Int'l Union*, 132 S. Ct. 2277, 2289 (2012).

104. *Armour v. City of Indianapolis*, 132 S. Ct. 2073, 2084 (2012) (Roberts, C.J., dissenting).

105. Linda Greenhouse, "When Enough Is Enough," *New York Times*, June 13, 2012.

106. 560 U.S. 126 (2010).

107. *United States v. Kebodeaux*, 133 S. Ct. 2496, 2507 (2013) (Roberts, C.J., concurring in the judgment).

108. They have been aided in this task by sympathetic scholars. See, e.g., William Baude, "Rethinking the Federal Eminent Domain Power," *Yale Law Journal* 122 (2013): 1738.

109. For an article that offers a more comprehensive view of this trend, see Allison LaCroix, "The Shadow Powers of Article I," *Yale Law Journal* (forthcoming 2014).

3: CAMPAIGN FINANCE

1. 558 U.S. 310 (2010).

2. "Corp Constituency," *Colbert Report*, Comedy Central, aired May 11, 2011, http://www.colbertnation.com/the-colbert-report-videos/386085/may-11-2011/corp-constituency.

3. Ujala Sehgal, "The Serious Implications of Stephen Colbert's FEC Stunt," *Atlantic Wire*, May 14, 2011, http://www.theatlanticwire.com/entertainment/2011/05/stephen-colbert-federal-election-commission/37731/.

4. Catalina Camia, "Stephen Colbert's Super PAC Gets Approval," *USA Today*, June 30, 2011.

5. Dahlia Lithwick, "Colbert v. the Court," *Slate*, February 2, 2012, http://www.slate.com/articles/news_and_politics/jurisprudence/2012/02/stephen_colbert_is_winning_the_war_against_the_supreme_court_and_citizens_united_.html.

6. "Trevor Potter & Stephen's Shell Corporation," *Colbert Report*, Comedy Central, aired September 29, 2011, http://www.colbertnation.com/the-colbert-report-videos/398531/september-29-2011/colbert-super-pac—trevor-potter—stephen-s-shell-corporation.

7. "Colbert Super PAC: PARRY-with-an-A-GATE! Day 6, WOI in Des Moines Reports," *Colbert Report*, Comedy Central, aired August 18, 2011, http://www.colbertnation.com/the-colbert-report-videos/395001/august-18-2011/colbert-super-pac—parry-with-an-a-gate—-day-6—woi-in-des-moines-reports.

8. Joe Jackson, "Stephen Colbert Leads Jon Huntsman in South Carolina Poll," *Time*, January 11, 2012; Emily Yahr, "Colbert's Big Announcement: An Exploratory

Committee for 'Possible' Presidential Run, and Jon Stewart Takes Over His Super PAC," *Washington Post*, January 13, 2012.

9. Keach Hagey, "Stephen Colbert and Jon Stewart Put Super PACs in Public Eye," *Politico*, January 19, 2012, http://www.politico.com/news/stories/0112/71634 _Page2.html.

10. "Colbert Super PAC: Mitt Romney Attack Ad," *Colbert Report*, Comedy Central, aired January 16, 2012, http://www.colbertnation.com/the-colbert-report-videos /405970/january-16-2012/colbert-super-pac---mitt-romney-attack-ad.

11. "Colbert Super PAC: GOP Attack Ads & Herman Cain Ad," *Colbert Report*, Comedy Central, aired January 17, 2012, http://www.colbertnation.com/the-colbert -report-videos/406122/january-17-2012/indecision-2012---gop-attack-ads---colbert -super-pac-s-herman-cain-ad.

12. "Troubled GOP Waters & Stephen Under Attack," *Colbert Report*, Comedy Central, aired January 19, 2012, http://www.colbertnation.com/the-colbert-report-videos/406 408/january-19-2012/indecision-2012---troubled-gop-waters---stephen-under-attack.

13. Sarah Maslin Nir, "Colbert's Super PAC Raises More Than $1 Million," *New York Times*, January 31, 2012.

14. For a detailed account, see Jeffrey Toobin, *The Oath* (New York: Random House, 2012), 165–69.

15. Charlie Savage, "A Long Record on Campaign Finance, Often in Support of Regulations," *New York Times*, May 29, 2009.

16. See, e.g., *Federal Election Commission v. Wisconsin Right to Life*, 551 U.S. 449, 483 (2007) (Scalia, J., concurring); *Austin v. Michigan Chamber of Commerce*, 494 U.S. 652, 679 (1990) (Scalia, J., dissenting).

17. For an enjoyable and illuminating reflection on his time on the Court, see John Paul Stevens, *Five Chiefs: A Supreme Court Memoir* (New York: Little, Brown, 2011).

18. White House, "Statement from the President on Today's Supreme Court Decision," press release, January 21, 2010.

19. Kasie Hunt, "John McCain, Russ Feingold Diverge on Court Ruling," *Politico*, January 21, 2010, http://www.politico.com/news/stories/0110/31810.html.

20. See, e.g., Lawrence Lessig, *Republic, Lost: How Money Corrupts Congress—and a Plan to Stop It* (New York: Twelve, 2011), 290–304. Full disclosure: one of us (Larry Tribe) assisted Representative Adam Schiff of California in drafting a proposed amendment that was introduced in the 112th Congress.

21. See, e.g., Dan Eggen, "Poll: Large Majority Opposes Supreme Court's Decision on Campaign Financing," *Washington Post*, February 17, 2010.

22. See Adam Liptak, "Supreme Court Gets a Rare Rebuke, in Front of a Nation," *New York Times*, January 29, 2010.

23. Adam Liptak, "Six Justices to Attend State of the Union," *New York Times*, January 25, 2011.

24. Adam Liptak, "Former Justice O'Connor Sees Ill in Election Finance Ruling," *New York Times*, January 26, 2010.

25. "Sandra Day O'Connor Interviews John Paul Stevens," *Newsweek*, December 17, 2010.

26. Jeremy Herb, "Scalia: Don't Like Super-Pac Ads? Turn Off the TV," *Hill*, January 21, 2012, http://thehill.com/blogs/blog-briefing-room/news/205583-scalia-dont-like -super-pac-ads-turn-off-the-tv.

27. Adam Liptak, "Justice Defends Ruling on Finance," *New York Times*, February 4, 2010.

28. Associated Press, "Scalia on Unlimited Political Ads: Turn Off the TV," Fox News, January 21, 2012, http://www.foxnews.com/politics/2012/01/21/scalia-on-unlim ited-political-ads-turn-off-tv/.

29. Michelle R. Smith, "Alito Says Supreme Court Misunderstood by Media," Boston .com, September 14, 2012, http://www.boston.com/news/local/rhode-island/2012 /09/14/alito-says-supreme-court-misunderstood-media/onnoFr6jnCEhI2c3KD MX9I/story.html.

30. See generally Keith W. Olson, *Watergate: The Presidential Scandal That Shook America* (Lawrence: University Press of Kansas, 2003); Michael Schudson, *Watergate in American Memory: How We Remember, Forget, and Reconstruct the Past* (New York: Basic Books, 1993), 99; Stanley I. Kutler, *The Wars of Watergate: The Last Crisis of Richard Nixon* (New York: W. W. Norton, 1990); Anthony Corrado, *Money and Politics: A History of Federal Campaign Finance Law*, in *The New Campaign Finance Sourcebook* 7, 22 (Washington, D.C.: Brookings Institution Press, 2005); and Ciara Torres-Spelliscy, "How Much Is an Ambassadorship? And the Tale of How Watergate Led to a Strong Foreign Corrupt Practices Act and a Weak Federal Election Campaign Act," *Chapman Law Review* 16 (2012): 71.

31. "Campaign Law Washington, D.C.," *Des Moines Register*, June 14, 1975 (quoting Buckley's argument in a lower federal court).

32. Ralph K. Winter, "The History and Theory of *Buckley v. Valeo*," *Journal of Law and Policy* 6 (1997): 107–8.

33. 424 U.S. 1 (1976). For historical accounts, see Bob Woodward and Scott Armstrong, *The Brethren* (New York: Simon & Schuster, 1979), 395–400; and Richard L. Hasen, "The Untold Drafting History of *Buckley v. Valeo*," *Election Law Journal* 2 (2003): 241.

34. To be sure, the distinction for First Amendment purposes between contributions and expenditures has been aggressively criticized, by both some of the justices and many scholars. For accessible overviews, see Erwin Chemerinsky, "The Distinction Between Contribution Limits and Expenditure Limits," *SCOTUSblog* (August 12, 2013), http://www.scotusblog.com/2013/08/symposium-the-distinction-between -contribution-limits-and-expenditure-limits/; and Richard Briffault, "Coordination Reconsidered," *Columbia Law Review Sidebar* 113 (2013): 88.

35. Heather Gerken, "Keynote Address to the American Philosophical Society," Philadelphia, November 15, 2013.

36. See, e.g., Justin Levitt, "Confronting the Impact of *Citizens United*," *Yale Law and Policy Review* 29 (2010): 217; and Richard Briffault, "Corporations, Corruption, and Complexity: Campaign Finance After *Citizens United*," *Cornell Journal of Law and Public Policy* 20 (2011): 643.

37. See, e.g., Adam Winkler, "The Corporation in Election Law," *Loyola of Los Angeles Law Review* 32 (1999): 1243.

38. *Austin v. Michigan Chamber of Commerce*, 494 U.S. 652 (1990).

39. *McConnell v. Federal Election Commission*, 540 U.S. 93 (2003).

40. See, e.g., Elizabeth Garrett, "New Voices in Politics: Justice Marshall's Jurisprudence on Law and Politics," *Howard Law Journal* 52 (2009): 655.

41. See, e.g., Michael Walzer, *Spheres of Justice* (New York: Basic Books, 1983); and Ronald Dworkin, *Sovereign Virtue: The Theory and Practice of Equality* (Cambridge, Mass.: Harvard University Press, 2000).

42. See, e.g., Cass R. Sunstein, *The Second Bill of Rights* (New York: Basic Books, 2004), 1–60; John Rawls, *A Theory of Justice*, rev. ed. (Cambridge, Mass.: Belknap Press of Harvard University Press, 1999), 11–14, 229–30; and Lucy Madison, Elizabeth Warren, "There Is Nobody in This Country Who Got Rich on His Own," CBSNews, September 22, 2011.

43. Kathleen M. Sullivan, "Two Concepts of Freedom of Speech," *Harvard Law Review* 124 (2010): 144–55.

44. See also Owen M. Fiss, *The Irony of Free Speech* (Cambridge, Mass.: Harvard University Press, 1996); and Ronald Dworkin, "The Curse of American Politics," *New York Review of Books*, October 17, 1996.

45. Indeed, some scholars argue that *Citizens United* is best defended under the First Amendment freedom of the press. See, e.g., Michael W. McConnell, "Reconsidering *Citizens United* as a Press Clause Case," *Yale Law Journal* 123 (2013): 412.

46. See Richard L. Hasen, "*Citizens United* and the Orphaned Antidistortion Rationale," *Georgia State University Law Review* 27 (2011): 989.

47. See, e.g., Samuel Issacharoff, "On Political Corruption," *Harvard Law Review* 124 (2010).

48. See, e.g., Mark Leibovich, *This Town* (New York: Blue Rider Press, 2013); Thomas E. Mann and Norman J. Ornstein, *It's Even Worse Than It Looks* (New York: Basic Books, 2012); and Richard L. Hasen, "Fixing Washington," *Harvard Law Review* 126 (2012): 550.

49. Lessig, *Republic, Lost*.

50. See, e.g., Nathaniel Persily and Kelli Lammie, "Perceptions of Corruption and Campaign Finance: When Public Opinion Determines Constitutional Law," *University of Pennsylvania Law Review* 153 (2004): 119.

51. Adam M. Samaha, "Regulation for the Sake of Appearance," *Harvard Law Review* 125 (2012): 1563, 1599–1619; and Robert T. Bauer, "The Varieties of Corruption and the Problem of Appearance," *Harvard Law Review Forum* 125 (2012): 91.

52. For a contrary view, see Deborah Hellman, "Defining Corruption and Constitutionalizing Democracy," *Michigan Law Review* 111 (2013): 1386.

53. Richard Hasen, "Is 'Dependence Corruption' Distinct from a Political Equality Argument for Campaign Finance Laws? A Reply to Professor Lessig," *SSRN*, February 17, 2013. For a defense against this charge, see Lawrence Lessig, "A Reply to Professor Hasen," *Harvard Law Review Forum* 126 (2012): 61.

54. 599 F.3d 686 (D.C. Cir. 2010).

55. On the subjects discussed in this paragraph, see generally Michael S. Kang, "The Year of the Super PAC," *George Washington Law Review* 81 (2013): 1902; Richard Briffault, "Super PACs," *Minnesota Law Review* 96 (2012): 1644; Ciara Torres-Spelliscy,

"Hiding Behind the Tax Code: The Dark Election of 2010 and Why Tax-Exempt Entities Should Be Subject to Robust Federal Campaign Finance Disclosure Laws," *Nexus* 16 (2011): 59; "Lighten Our Darkness," *The Economist*, November 30, 2013; Thomas B. Edsall, "Dark Money Politics," *New York Times*, Opinionator, June 12, 2013, http://opinionator.blogs.nytimes.com/2013/06/12/dark-money-politics/; John Avlon and Michael Keller, "The Dark Money Shuffle," *Daily Beast*, September 19, 2012, http://www.thedailybeast.com/articles/2012/09/19/the-dark-money-shuffle.html; and Mike McIntire and Nicholas Confessore, "Tax-Exempt Groups Shield Politics Gifts of Business," *New York Times*, July 8, 2012.

56. Gerken, "Keynote Address to the American Philosophical Society."

57. See Thomas B. Edsall, "Billionaires Going Rogue," *New York Times*, October 28, 2012, http://campaignstops.blogs.nytimes.com/2012/10/28/billionaires-going-rogue/.

58. Michael Beckel, "Spending by Outside Groups Topped $1 Billion by Election Day," Center for Public Integrity, November 7, 2012, http://www.publicintegrity.org/2012/11/07/11789/spending-outside-groups-topped-1-billion-election-day.

59. Nicholas Confessore and Jess Bidgood, "Little to Show for Cash Flood by Big Donors," *New York Times*, November 8, 2012.

60. Michael Beckel, "Rove-Affiliated Groups Spend $175 Million, Lose 21 of 30 Races," Center for Public Integrity, November 9, 2012, http://www.publicintegrity.org/2012/11/09/11797/rove-affiliated-groups-spend-175-million-lose-21-30-races.

61. Robert Schlesinger, "Super PACs: 2012's Bond Villains or a Giant Waste of Money?," *U.S. News & World Report*, December 7, 2012.

62. Alison Frankel, "Election Results Raise Questions About Impact of *Citizens United*," Reuters, November 8, 2012, http://blogs.reuters.com/alison-frankel/2012/11/08/election-results-raise-questions-about-impact-of-citizens-united.

63. See Meghashyam Mali, "Rove: Crossroads 'Did Good Things,' Defends Super-PAC's Efforts," *Hill*, November 11, 2012, http://thehill.com/blogs/blog-briefing-room/news/267229-rove-crossroads-did-good-things-defends-super-pacs-efforts.

64. Scholars are engaged in a heated debate over whether available evidence demonstrates that the outcome of any particular election was altered by recent developments in campaign finance. While we do not purport to identify specific instances in which electoral outcomes shifted because of trends triggered by *Citizens United*, it seems to us highly likely that this has occurred in at least some races.

65. See, generally, Lessig, *Republic, Lost*; Mann and Ornstein, *It's Even Worse*; Jack Abramoff, *Capitol Punishment* (Washington, D.C.: WND Books, 2011); Hasen, "Fixing Washington"; Issacharoff, "On Political Corruption"; and Richard L. Hasen, "Lobbying, Rent-Seeking, and the Constitution," *Stanford Law Review* 64 (2012): 191.

66. Beckel, "Spending by Outside Groups Topped $1 Billion by Election Day."

67. Blair Bowie and Adam Lioz, "Billion-Dollar Democracy: The Unprecedented Role of Money in the 2012 Elections," Demos and U.S. PIRG Education Fund (2013), 8.

68. Ibid., 9.

69. "Priorities USA Action: Outside Spending Summary 2012," Center for Responsive Politics, https://www.opensecrets.org/outsidespending/detail.php?cmte=C00495861&cycle=2012; and Robert Maguire, "Obama's Shadow Money Allies File First Report,"

Center for Responsive Politics, January 8, 2013, www.opensecrets.org/news/2013/01/obamas-shadow-money-allie.html.

70. *Western Tradition Partnership, Inc. v. Attorney General*, 271 P. 3d 1 (Montana 2011).

71. Statement of Justice Ginsburg, *Am. Tradition P'ship, Inc. v. Bullock*, 132 S. Ct. 1307 (2012).

72. See Rick Hasen, "A Few Reactions About the Montana Decision," *Election Law Blog*, June 25, 2012, http://electionlawblog.org/?p=36150.

73. See, e.g., Amy Gardner and Felicia Sonmez, "Obama Dings Romney's 'Corporations Are People' Line in Official Campaign Kickoff," *Washington Post*, May 5, 2012; Burt Neuborne, "Corporations Aren't People," *Nation*, January 31, 2011; and David Kairys, "Money Isn't Speech and Corporations Aren't People," *Slate*, January 22, 2010, http://www.slate.com/articles/news_and_ politics/jurisprudence/2010/01/money_isnt_speech_and_corporations_arent_ people.html. Justice Stevens's dissent also makes the distinct argument that corporations' lack of personhood should bear on whether they are treated the same as natural persons under the First Amendment for purposes of campaign finance. See *Citizens United*, 130 S. Ct. at 972 (Stevens, J., dissenting) ("It might also be added that corporations have no consciences, no beliefs, no feelings, no thoughts, no desires. Corporations help structure and facilitate the activities of human beings, to be sure, and their 'personhood' often serves as a useful legal fiction. But they are not themselves members of 'We the People' by whom and for whom our Constitution was established.").

74. See "Elizabeth Warren Addresses DNC: 'The System Is Rigged'," *Real Clear Politics*, September 5, 2012, http://www.realclearpolitics.com/video/2012/09/05/elizabeth_warren_addresses_dnc_the_system_is_rigged.html.

75. Amy Rolph, "Seattle Woman Marries Corporation—See the Video," *Seattle Post-Intelligencer*, July 17, 2012, http://blog.seattlepi.com/thebigblog/2012/07/17/seattle-woman-marries-corporation-see-the-video.

76. "Supreme Corp.," *Daily Show with Jon Stewart*, Comedy Central, aired January 25, 2010, http://www.thedailyshow.com/watch/mon-january-25-2010/supreme-corp.

77. Mark Tushnet, *In the Balance* (New York: W. W. Norton, 2013), 264.

78. *FCC v. AT&T*, 131 S. Ct. 1177 (2011).

79. On the general topic of corporate personhood after *Citizens United*, see, e.g., Amy J. Sepinwall, "*Citizens United* and the Ineluctable Question of Corporate Citizenship," *Connecticut Law Review* 44 (2012): 575; Susanna Kim Ripken, "Corporate First Amendment Rights After *Citizens United*: An Analysis of the Popular Movement to End the Constitutional Personhood of Corporations," *University of Pennsylvania Journal of Business Law Review* 14 (2011): 209; and Ilya Shapiro and Caitlyn W. McCarthy, "So What If Corporations Aren't People?," *John Marshall Law Review* 44 (2011): 701.

80. Matt Bai, "How Much Has Citizens United Changed the Political Game?," *New York Times*, July 22, 2012.

81. See, e.g., Richard Briffault, "Campaign Finance Disclosure 2.0," *Election Law Journal* 9 (2010): 273. Justice Kennedy also discusses this point in his *Citizens United* opinion.

82. Louis D. Brandeis, "What Publicity Can Do," *Harper's Weekly*, December 20, 1913.

83. Kathleen M. Sullivan, "Against Campaign Finance Reform," *Utah Law Review* 311 (1998): 311, 326.

84. On recent debates over disclosure, see generally Michael Kang, "Campaign Finance in Direct Democracy," *Minnesota Law Review* 97 (2013): 1700; Daniel R. Ortiz, "The Informational Interest," *Journal of Law and Politics* 27 (2012): 663; Richard L. Hasen, "Chill Out: A Qualified Defense of Campaign Finance Disclosure Laws in the Internet Age," *Journal of Law and Politics* (2012): 557; and Richard Briffault, "Two Challenges for Campaign Finance Disclosure After *Citizens United* and *Doe v. Reed*," *William & Mary Bill of Rights Journal* 19 (2011): 983.

85. Kang, "Campaign Disclosure in Direct Democracy," 1706–7.

86. 130 S. Ct. 2811 (2010).

87. Ibid., 2821.

88. See Tarini Parti, "DISCLOSE Act Fails Again in Senate," *Politico*, July 16, 2012; Jordan Fabian and Alexander Bolton, "Senate Fails to Advance Campaign Finance Bill," *Hill*, July 27, 2010.

89. See, e.g., Lucian A. Bebchuk and Robert J. Jackson Jr., "Corporate Political Speech: Who Decides?," *Harvard Law Review* 124 (2010): 83.

90. *Knox v. Serv. Emp. Int'l Union*, 132 S. Ct. 2277 (2012).

91. Benjamin I. Sachs, "Unions, Corporations, and Political Opt-Out Rights After *Citizens United*," *Columbia Law Review* 112 (2012): 800.

92. Victor Brudney, "Business Corporations and Stockholders' Rights Under the First Amendment," *Yale Law Journal* 91 (1981): 235.

93. For different views, see Joel M. Gora, "Don't Feed the Alligators: Government Funding of Political Speech and the Unyielding Vigilance of the First Amendment," *CATO Supreme Court Review* (2011): 81; and Richard Briffault, "Public Funding and Democratic Elections," *University of Pennsylvania Law Review* 148 (1998): 563.

94. 132 S. Ct. 2806 (2011); and Heather K. Gerken, "Campaign Finance and the Doctrinal Death Match," *Balkinization*, June 27, 2011, http://balkin.blogspot.com /2011/06/campaign-finance-and-doctrinal-death.html.

95. See, e.g., "One Year Later: The Consequences of *Arizona Free Enterprise Club v. Bennett*," Alliance for Justice, June 15, 2012; and Adam Liptak, "Justices Strike Down Arizona Campaign Finance Law," *New York Times*, June 28, 2011.

96. Guy-Uriel Charles, "An Ideological Battle," Room for Debate, *New York Times*, September 14, 2011, http://www.nytimes.com/roomfordebate/2011/06/27/the -court-and-the-future-of-public-financing/the-courts-battle-of-ideology.

97. John Paul Stevens, "Beyond *Citizens United*," *Journal of Appellate Practice and Process* 13 (2012): 1, 2–3.

98. *Bluman v. FEC*, 800 F. Supp. 2d 281, 283 (D.C.C. 2011).

99. Richard L. Hasen, "*Citizens United* and the Illusion of Coherence," *Michigan Law Review* 109 (2011): 581, 605–10.

100. *Bluman v. FEC*, 132 S. Ct. 1087 (2012).

101. *Caperton v. A. T. Massey Coal Co.*, 129 S. Ct. 2252 (2009).

102. Michael S. Kang, "The End of Campaign Finance Law," *Virginia Law Review* 98 (2012): 1, 45–47, 56–63.

4: FREEDOM OF SPEECH

1. Bob Woodward and Scott Armstrong, *The Brethren: Inside the Supreme Court* (New York: Simon & Schuster, 2005), 239–40. The law clerk in whom Justice Stewart confided was Larry Tribe.

2. See, e.g., Frederick Schauer, "Fear, Risk, and the First Amendment: Unraveling the Chilling Effect," *Boston University Law Review* 58 (1978): 685.

3. See, e.g., Editorial, "Sordid, but Protected," *Los Angeles Times*, April 21, 2010; Adam Liptak, "A Significant Term, with Bigger Cases Ahead," *New York Times*, June 29, 2011; Greg Stohr, "Freedom of Speech Is Buttressed as U.S. Supreme Court Concludes Term," *Bloomberg*, June 28, 2011, http://www.bloomberg.com/news/2011-06 -28/speech-rights-triumph-as-u-s-high-court-limits-government-power.html.

4. Adam Liptak, "Study Challenges Supreme Court's Image as Defender of Free Speech," *New York Times*, January 8, 2012.

5. For some of the leading works on First Amendment theory, see Jeremy Waldron, *The Harm in Hate Speech* (Cambridge, Mass.: Harvard University Press, 2012); Seana Valentine Shiffrin, "A Thinker-Based Approach to Freedom of Speech," *Constitutional Commentary* 27 (2011): 283; Geoffrey Stone, *Perilous Times: Free Speech in Wartime* (New York: W. W. Norton, 2004); Robert C. Post, *Constitutional Domains: Democracy, Community, Management* (Cambridge, Mass.: Harvard University Press, 1995); Cass R. Sunstein, *Democracy and the Problem of Free Speech* (New York: Free Press, 1995); C. Edwin Baker, *Human Liberty and Freedom of Speech* (New York: Oxford University Press, 1992); Steven H. Shiffrin, *The First Amendment, Democracy, and Romance* (Cambridge, Mass.: Harvard University Press, 1990); Frederick Schauer, *Free Speech: A Philosophical Enquiry* (New York: Cambridge University Press, 1982); Robert Bork, "Neutral Principles and Some First Amendment Problems," *Indiana Law Journal* 47 (1971): 1; Thomas I. Emerson, "Toward a General Theory of the First Amendment," *Yale Law Journal* 72 (1963): 877; and Alexander Meiklejohn, "The First Amendment Is an Absolute," *Supreme Court Review* 245 (1961).

6. Frederick Schauer, "The Exceptional First Amendment" in *American Exceptionalism and Human Rights,* ed. Michael Ignatieff (Princeton, N.J.: Princeton University Press, 2009).

7. David Strauss, *The Living Constitution* (New York: Oxford University Press, 2010).

8. On Black's free speech jurisprudence, see, e.g., Harry Kalven Jr., "Upon Rereading Mr. Justice Black on the First Amendment," *UCLA Law Review* 14 (1966): 428.

9. For a contrary view of originalism generally, see Antonin Scalia, ed., *A Matter of Interpretation: Federal Courts and the Law* (Princeton, N.J.: Princeton University Press, 1997); and Steven G. Calabresi, ed., *Originalism: A Quarter-Century of Debate* (Washington, D.C.: Regnery Publishing, 2007).

10. Some suggest that this was true only of restraints on the press, not ordinary oral expression. See, e.g., Akhil Reed Amar, *The Bill of Rights: Creation and Reconstruction* (New Haven: Yale University Press, 1998). For a general history of this period, see Leonard W. Levy, *Emergence of a Free Press* (Chicago: Ivan R. Dee, 2004) (reprinting 1985 Oxford University Press edition, which in turn was a version of the

1960 Oxford edition of *Legacy of Suppression: Freedom of Speech and Press in Early American History*).

11. Ronald K. L. Collins and Sam Chaltain, *We Must Not Be Afraid to Be Free: Stories of Free Expression in America* (New York: Oxford University Press, 2011); and Michael Kent Curtis, *Free Speech, "the People's Darling Privilege": Struggles for Freedom of Expression in American History* (Durham, N.C.: Duke University Press, 2000).

12. James Morton Smith, *Freedom's Fetters: The Alien and Sedition Laws and American Civil Liberties* (Ithaca, N.Y.: Cornell University Press, 1956); and David Jenkins, "The Sedition Act of 1798 and the Incorporation of Seditious Libel into First Amendment Jurisprudence," *American Journal of Legal History* 45 (2001): 154.

13. William Lee Miller, *Arguing About Slavery: John Quincy Adams and the Great Battle in the United States Congress* (New York: Vintage Books, 1998); and Clement Eaton, "Censorship of the Southern Mails," *American Historical Review* 48 (1943): 266.

14. See Michael Kent Curtis, "Lincoln, Vallandigham, and Anti-War Speech in the Civil War," *William and Mary Bill of Rights Journal* 7 (1998): 105; and Geoffrey Stone, *Perilous Times: Free Speech in Wartime from the Sedition Act of 1798 to the War on Terrorism* (New York: W. W. Norton, 2004), 79–134.

15. Helen Lefkowitz Horowitz, *Rereading Sex: Battles over Sexual Knowledge and Suppression in Nineteenth-Century America* (New York: Knopf, 2002); David M. Rabban, *Free Speech in Its Forgotten Years* (New York: Cambridge University Press, 1997); and Margaret A. Blanchard, *Revolutionary Sparks: Freedom of Expression in Modern America* (New York: Oxford University Press, 1992).

16. Paul L. Murphy, *The Meaning of Freedom of Speech: First Amendment Freedoms from Wilson to FDR* (Westport, Conn.: Greenwood Publishing Group, 1972).

17. Paul L. Murphy, *World War I and the Origin of Civil Liberties in the United States* (New York: W. W. Norton, 1979).

18. Mark A. Graber, *Transforming Free Speech: The Ambiguous Legacy of Civil Libertarianism* (Berkeley: University of California Press, 1991), 75–121.

19. Thomas Healy, *The Great Dissent: How Oliver Wendell Holmes Changed His Mind—and Changed the History of Free Speech in America* (New York: Metropolitan Books, 2013).

20. *Abrams v. United States*, 250 U.S. 616 (1919) (Holmes, J., dissenting).

21. *Whitney v. California*, 274 U.S. 357, 375 (1927) (Brandeis, J., concurring).

22. *W. Va. State Bd. of Educ. v. Barnette*, 319 U.S. 624, 642 (1943).

23. Stone, *Perilous Times*, 311–426; and Stephen J. Whitfield, *The Culture of the Cold War* (Baltimore: Johns Hopkins University Press, 1996).

24. *Dennis v. United States*, 341 U.S. 494 (1951).

25. See, e.g., Collins and Chaltain, *We Must Not Be Afraid to Be Free*, 59–87, 134–71, 211–12, 269–91.

26. *Whitney*, 274 U.S. at 377 (Brandeis, J., concurring).

27. *Cohen v. California*, 430 U.S. 15 (1971).

28. *Holder v. Humanitarian Law Project*, 130 S. Ct. 1577 (2010).

29. *Korematsu v. United States*, 323 U.S. 214 (1944).

30. Peter Irons, *Justice at War* (Berkeley: University of California Press, 1983).
31. See, e.g., David Cole, "The First Amendment's Borders: The Place of *Holder v. Humanitarian Law Project* in First Amendment Doctrine," *Harvard Law and Policy Review* 6 (2012): 147; Erwin Chemerinsky, "Free Speech and the 'War on Terror,'" *Trial* (2011); Timothy Zick, "The First Amendment in Trans-Border Perspective: Toward a More Cosmopolitan Orientation," *Boston College Law Review* 52 (2011): 941.
32. Atul Gawande, "Hellhole," *New Yorker*, March 30, 2009.
33. Matt Stroud, "Why Are Prisoners Committing Suicide in Pennsylvania?," *Nation*, April 18, 2012.
34. *Beard v. Banks*, 548 U.S. 521 (2006).
35. Editorial, "The Youngest, Cruelest Justice," *New York Times*, February 27, 1992.
36. See *Overton v. Bazzetta*, 539 U. S. 126, 138 (2003) (Thomas, J., concurring).
37. See *Turner v. Safley*, 482 U.S. 78 (1987).
38. See *Pickering v. Board of Ed. of Township High School Dist. 205, Will Cty.*, 391 U. S. 563 (1968).
39. *McAuliffe v. City of New Bedford*, 155 Mass. 216, 220 (1892).
40. *Garcetti v. Ceballos*, 547 U.S. 410, 426 (2006).
41. See, e.g., Helen Norton, "Constraining Public Employee Speech: Government's Control of Its Workers' Speech to Protect Its Own Expression," *Duke Law Journal* 59 (2009): 1; Sheldon H. Nahmod, "Public Employee Speech, Categorical Balancing and Section 1983: A Critique of *Garcetti v. Ceballos*," *University of Richmond Law Review* (2008): 561; and Cynthia Estlund, "Harmonizing Work and Citizenship: A Due Process Solution to a First Amendment Problem," *Supreme Court Review* (2006): 115.
42. *Morse v. Frederick*, 551 U.S. 393, 397 (2007).
43. See, e.g., Brief Amicus Curiae of the Christian Legal Society in Support of Respondent, *Morse v. Frederick*, 551 U.S. 393 (2007) (No. 06-278).
44. *J.D.B. v. North Carolina*, 131 S. Ct. 2394, 2399 (2011).
45. *Miller v. Alabama*, 132 S. Ct. 2455, 2470 (2012).
46. *Brown v. Entertainment Merchants Association*, 131 S. Ct. 2729, 2742 (2011).
47. Editorial, "Joysticks and the First Amendment," *Washington Post*, October 31, 2010.
48. Antonin Scalia, "Originalism: The Lesser Evil," *University of Cincinnati Law Review* 57 (1989): 849, 864.
49. Jennifer Senior, "In Conversation: Antonin Scalia," *New York*, October 6, 2013, http://nymag.com/news/features/antonin-scalia-2013-10; and Nina Totenberg, "Justice Scalia, the Great Dissenter, Opens Up," NPR, April 28, 2008, http://www.npr.org/templates/story/story.php?storyId=89986017.
50. Adam J. White, "The Burkean Justice," *Weekly Standard*, July 18, 2011.
51. "U.S. Supreme Court Justice Samuel Alito Says Pragmatism, Stability Should Guide Court," press release, Columbia Law School, April 24, 2012.
52. On the pros and cons of rules versus standards generally, see Kathleen Sullivan, "The Justices of Rules and Standards," *Harvard Law Review* 106 (1992): 22; and Peter Schlag, "Rules and Standards," *UCLA Law Review* 33 (1985): 379.
53. *United States v. Stevens*, 130 S. Ct. 1577 (2010).

54. Frederick Schauer, "Harm(s) and the First Amendment," *Supreme Court Review* (2012): 81, 87.

55. Brief for the United States at 8, *United States v. Stevens*, 130 S. Ct. 1577 (2010) (No. 08-769).

56. See *New York Times Co. v. Sullivan*, 376 U.S. 710 (1964).

57. *McGrath v. Kristensen*, 340 U.S. 162, 178 (1950) (Jackson, J., concurring) (quoting Baron Bramwell) (internal quotation marks omitted).

58. *U.S. v. Alvarez*, 638 F.3d 666, 673 (9th Cir. 2011) (Kozinski, C.J., concurring in the denial of rehearing en banc).

59. *United States v. Alvarez*, 132 S. Ct. 2537, 2542 (2012).

60. Leading jurists abroad have called this approach a "proportionality" analysis. See Aharon Barak, *Proportionality: Constitutional Rights and Their Limitations* (New York: Cambridge University Press, 2012).

61. See Harvard Law School, "Celebrating Justice Stephen Breyer at HLS," YouTube, published on October 4, 2013, http://www.youtube.com/watch?v=NJKs5OMvqhg (segment beginning at 1:10:29).

62. *Snyder v. Phelps*, 131 S. Ct. 1207 (2011).

63. But see Steven J. Heyman, "To Drink the Cup of Fury: Funeral Picketing, Public Discourse, and the First Amendment," *Connecticut Law Review* 45 (2012): 101.

64. Editorial, "The Right to Even Ugly Free Speech," *Washington Post*, March 2, 2011.

65. See Erwin Chemerinsky, "Not a Free Speech Court," *Arizona Law Review* 53 (2011): 723. For a diverse set of views on the Roberts Court's free speech cases, see "What Are We Saying?: Violence, Vulgarity, Lies . . . and the Importance of 21st Century Free Speech," *Albany Law Review* 76 (2013): 409.

5: GUN RIGHTS

1. *Schenck v. United States*, 39 S. Ct. 247, 249 (1919).

2. See Jennifer Brown, "12 Dead, 58 Wounded in Aurora Movie Theater During Batman Premier," *Denver Post*, July 21, 2012; Dan Frosch and Kirk Johnson, "Gunman Kills 12 at Colorado Theater; Scores Wounded, Reviving Gun Debate," *New York Times*, July 21, 2012; and John Ingold, "Heroes Among Us," *Denver Post*, July 29, 2012.

3. 128 S. Ct. 2783 (2008).

4. 130 S. Ct. 3020 (2010).

5. *United States v. Masciandaro*, 638 F.3d 458, 475 (4th Cir. 2011).

6. See, e.g., Jan E. Dizard et al., eds., *Guns in America: A Reader* (New York: New York University Press, 1999); Adam Winkler, *Gunfight: The Battle Over the Right to Bear Arms in America* (New York: W. W. Norton, 2011); and Richard Hofstadter, "America as a Gun Culture," *American Heritage* 21 (1970): 4.

7. Philip J. Cook et al., "Gun Control After *Heller*: Threats and Sideshows from a Social Welfare Perspective," *UCLA Law Review* 56 (2009): 1041, 1045; and Jill Lepore, "Battleground America: One Nation, Under the Gun," *New Yorker*, April 23, 2012.

8. Lepore, "Battleground America."

9. David Hemenway, *Private Guns, Public Health* (Ann Arbor: University of Michigan Press, 2004), 69; Tom Smith, "A Call for a Truce in the DGU War," *Journal of Criminal Law and Crimonology* 87 (1997): 1462.

10. Hemenway, *Private Guns, Public Health*, 4.

11. Matthew Miller et al., "Firearms and Violent Death in the United States," in *Reducing Gun Violence in America: Informing Policy with Evidence and Analysis*, Daniel W. Webster and Jon S. Vernick, eds. (Baltimore: Johns Hopkins University Press, 2013), 3.

12. Marilynn Marchione, "Doctors Target Gun Violence as a Social Disease," Associated Press, August 12, 2012, http://usatoday30.usatoday.com/news/health/story/2012-08-11/guns-public-health/56979706/1.

13. See, e.g., Michael Cooper, "Debate on Gun Control Is Revived, Amid a Trend Toward Fewer Restrictions," *New York Times*, December 16, 2012; Adam Nagourney and Jennifer Steinhauer, "A Clamor for Gun Limits, but Few Expect Real Changes," *New York Times*, January 14, 2011.

14. Roger Ebert, "We've Seen This Movie Before," *New York Times*, July 20, 2012.

15. "Remarks by the President at Sandy Hook Interfaith Prayer Vigil," White House, December 16, 2012.

16. White House, "Now Is the Time: The President's Plan to Protect Our Children and Our Communities by Reducing Gun Violence," January 16, 2013, 13–15.

17. *Brown v. Entertainment Merchants Association*, 131 S. Ct. 2729 (2011).

18. See Dan Kahan, "Actually, Empirical Evidence Suggests a Sure Fire Way to Dramatically Lower Gun Homicides: Repeal Drug Laws," Cultural Cognition Project at Yale Law School, December 18, 2012, www.culturalcognition.net/blog/2012/12/18/actually-empirical-evidence-suggests-a-sure-fire-way-to-dram.html.

19. The literature on gun violence proposals is too vast for even a brief summary. For a few works that we have found helpful, see Webster and Vernick, *Reducing Gun Violence in America*; Hemenway, *Private Guns, Public Health*; Harry L. Wilson, *Guns, Gun Control, and Elections: The Politics and Policy of Firearms* (Lantham, Md.: Rowman & Littlefield, 2007); Bernard E. Harcourt, ed., *Guns, Crime, and Punishment in America* (New York: New York University Press, 2003); Cook, "Gun Control After *Heller*."

20. We credit Professor Adam Samaha of NYU Law School with this last pair of suggestions.

21. For a good and fair-minded introduction to the gun control debate, see Mark Tushnet, *Out of Range: Why the Constitution Can't End the Battle Over Guns* (New York: Oxford University Press, 2007).

22. See, e.g., Dan Kahan et al., "Modeling Facts, Culture and Cognition in the Gun Debate," *Social Justice Research* 18 (2005); 203. On the general subject of cultural cognition, see Dan Kahan, "Foreword: Neutral Principles, Motivated Cognition, and Some Problems for Constitutional Law," *Harvard Law Review* 125 (2011): 1.

23. This shift appears not to have lasted very long. See Bruce Drake, "A Year After Newtown, Little Change in Public Opinion on Guns," Pew Research Center, *Fact Tank*, December 12, 2013, http://www.pewresearch.org/fact-tank/2013/12/12/a-year-after-newtown-little-change-in-public-opinion-on-guns/.

24. On these debates and developments, see, e.g., Pew Research Center, "In Gun Control Debate, Several Options Draw Majority Support," January 14, 2013; Fox Butterfield, "As Expiration Looms, Gun Ban's Effect Is Debated," *New York Times*, September 10, 2004; Michael Cooper, "Debate on Gun Control Is Revived, Amid a Trend Toward Fewer Restrictions," *New York Times*, December 16, 2012; Lydia Saad, "U.S. Remains Divided Over Passing Stricter Gun Laws," Gallop, October 25, 2013, http://www.gallup.com/poll/165563/remains-divided-passing-stricter-gun-laws.aspx.

25. *United States v. Miller*, 307 U.S. 174, 178 (1939).

26. See Reva Siegel, Comment, "Dead or Alive: Originalism as Popular Constitutionalism in *Heller*," *Harvard Law Review* 122 (2008): 191; and David B. Kopel, "The Great Gun Control War of the 20th Century—and Its Lessons for Gun Laws Today," *Fordham Urban Law Journal* 39 (2012): 1527. The following paragraphs are informed by these works, as well as the other works on gun rights cited above.

27. See Siegel, "Dead or Alive"; and Jamal Greene, "Guns, Originalism, and Cultural Cognition," *University of Pennsylvania Journal of Constitutional Law* 511 (2010): 13.

28. See Tushnet, *Out of Range*.

29. Claudia Luther, "Bork Says State Gun Laws Constitutional," *Los Angeles Times*, March 15, 1989.

30. *MacNeil/Lehrer NewsHour*, PBS, broadcast December 16, 1991.

31. Sanford Levinson, Comment, "The Embarrassing Second Amendment," *Yale Law Journal* 99 (1989): 637.

32. See Tushnet, *Out of Range*, 1–72. For glimpses into a debate involving thousands of publications, see, e.g., Michael C. Dorf, "What Does the Second Amendment Mean Today?," *Chicago-Kent Law Review* 76 (2000): 291; Akhil Reed Amar, "The Second Amendment: A Case Study in Constitutional Interpretation," *Utah Law Review* (2001): 889; Eugene Volokh, "Guns and the Constitution," *Wall Street Journal*, April 12, 1999, A23; and David C. Williams, "Civic Republicanism and the Citizen Militia: The Terrifying Second Amendment," *Yale Law Journal* 101 (1991): 551.

33. See Laurence H. Tribe, *American Constitutional Law*, 3rd ed. (New York: Foundation Press, 2000), 895–903.

34. *Printz v. United States*, 521 U.S. 898 (1997).

35. *United States v. Morrison*, 529 U.S. 598, 638 n.11 (2000) (Souter, J., dissenting).

36. *Atkins v. Virginia*, 536 U.S. 304, 338 (2002) (Scalia, J., dissenting).

37. *Casey v. Planned Parenthood of Pennsylvania*, 505 U.S. 833, 981 (1992) (Scalia, J., dissenting in part).

38. Antonin Scalia, "Originalism: The Lesser Evil," *University of Cincinnati Law Review* 57 (1989): 849, 864.

39. Further insight into Justice Scalia's originalism can be found in Antonin Scalia, ed., *A Matter of Interpretation: Federal Courts and the Law* (Princeton, N.J.: Princeton University Press, 1997); and Joan Biskupic, *American Original: The Life and Constitution of Supreme Court Justice Antonin Scalia* (New York: Farrar, Straus and Giroux, 2009). See also Robert W. Bennett and Lawrence B. Solum, *Constitutional Originalism: A Debate* (Ithaca, N.Y.: Cornell University Press, 2011).

40. See, e.g., Laurence H. Tribe, "Comment," in Scalia, *A Matter of Interpretation*, 65–94; David A. Strauss, *The Living Constitution* (New York: Oxford University Press,

2010); Cass R. Sunstein, "Five Theses on Originalism," *Harvard Journal of Law and Public Policy* 19 (1996): 311; and Paul Brest, "The Misconceived Quest for the Original Understanding," *Boston University Law Review* 60 (1980): 204.

41. The leading account of this period in Supreme Court history is Jeffrey Toobin, *The Nine: Inside the Secret World of the Supreme Court* (New York: Doubleday, 2007). On Justice O'Connor, see Joan Biskupic, *Sandra Day O'Connor: How the First Woman on the Supreme Court Became Its Most Influential Justice* (New York: HarperCollins, 2009).

42. On this trend at the Court, see Barry Friedman, "The Wages of Stealth Overruling (with Particular Attention to *Miranda v. Arizona*)," *Georgetown Law Journal* 99 (2010): 1.

43. *Federal Election Commission v. Wisconsin Right to Life, Inc.*, 551 U.S. 449, 498 n. 7 (2007) (Scalia, J., concurring in part and concurring in the judgment).

44. See, e.g., Randy E. Barnett, "News Flash: The Constitution Means What It Says," *Wall Street Journal*, June 27, 2008; Christine M. Flowers, Editorial, "No Longer a Second-Class Amendment," *Philadelphia Daily News*, June 27, 2008; Post Staff Report, "Affirming the Rule of Law," *New York Post*, June 27, 2008; Editorial, "Silver Bullet," *Wall Street Journal*, June 27, 2008; Jacob Sullum et. al, "The Second Amendment Goes to Court: Civil Libertarians Respond to *D.C. v. Heller*," *Reason*, June 27, 2008, http://reason.com/archives/2008/06/27/the-second-amendment-goes-to-c.

45. *McDonald v. City of Chicago*, 130 S. Ct. 3020, 3038–40 (2010). See also Michael Kent Curtis, *No State Shall Abridge* (Durham, N.C.: Duke University Press, 1986), 52–53; and Randy E. Barnett, "Was the Right to Keep and Bear Arms Conditioned on Service in an Organized Militia?," review of *The Militia and the Right to Arms, or, How the Second Amendment Fell Silent* by H. Richard Uviller and William G. Merkel, *Texas Law Review* 83 (2004): 267–69.

46. See, e.g., Alan Gura et al., "The Tell-Tale Privileges or Immunities Clause," *CATO Supreme Court Review* (2009–2010): 163; and Josh Blackman and Ilya Shapiro, "Keeping Pandora's Box Sealed: Privileges or Immunities, the Constitution in 2020, and Properly Extending the Right to Keep and Bear Arms to the States," *Georgetown Journal of Law & Public Policy* 8 (2010): 1.

47. See generally Winkler, *Gun Fight*.

48. Cass R. Sunstein, Comment, "Second Amendment Minimalism: *Heller* as Griswold," *Harvard Law Review* 122 (2008): 246. For arguments that *Heller* truly is an originalist decision, see Randy E. Barnett, "News Flash: The Constitution Means What It Says," *Wall Street Journal*, June 27, 2008, A13; and Lawrence B. Solum, "*District of Columbia v. Heller* and Originalism," *Northwestern University Law Review* 103 (2009): 923.

49. Because the Fourteenth Amendment was ratified in 1868 and was the textual source of the ruling in *McDonald*, the decisive moment for an originalist analysis of state and local gun control measures would be 1868 rather than 1791.

50. J. Harvie Wilkinson III, "Of Guns, Abortions, and the Unraveling Rule of Law," *Virginia Law Review* 95 (2009): 253, 279.

51. *United States v. Chester*, 628 F.3d 673, 678–80 (4th Cir. 2010) (Davis, J., concurring in the judgment).

52. On some of the competing approaches to Second Amendment law that have emerged since *Heller*, see, e.g., Darrell A. H. Miller, "Text, History, and Tradition: What the Seventh Amendment Can Teach Us About the Second," *Yale Law Journal* 122 (2013): 852; Joseph Blocher, "Categoricalism and Balancing in First and Second Amendment Analysis," *New York University Law Review* 84 (2009): 375.

53. For evaluations of the historical view, see, e.g., *Heller v. District of Columbia*, 670 F.3d 1244, 1269–96 (2011) (Kavanaugh, J., dissenting); Miller, "Text, History, and Tradition"; Saul Cornell, "The Right to Carry Firearms Outside of the Home: Separating Historical Myths from Historical Realities," *Fordham Urban Law Journal* 39 (2012): 1695; Nelson Lund, "The Second Amendment, *Heller* and Originalist Jurisprudence," *UCLA Law Review* 56 (2009): 1343; "Proposals to Reduce Gun Violence: Protecting Our Communities While Respecting the Second Amendment," hearing before the Subcommittee on the Constitution, Civil Rights, and Human Rights of the Senate Judiciary Comm., 113th Cong. (2013).

54. For the origin of the phrase, see Henry Paul Monaghan, "Doing Originalism," *Columbia Law Review* 104 (2004): 32. On the practices of originalism, see H. Jefferson Powell, "Rules for Originalists," *Virginia Law Review* 73 (1987): 659.

55. Robert H. Jackson, "Full Faith and Credit—the Lawyer's Clause of the Constitution," *Columbia Law Review* 45 (1945): 1, 6.

56. *Kachalsky v. County of Westchester*, 701 F.3d 81, 91 (2d Cir. 2012).

57. This criticism of history-based arguments is not unique to the guns context. See, e.g., Matthew J. Festa, "Applying a Usable Past: The Use of History in Law," *Seton Hall Law Review* 38 (2008): 479, 507; Robert Gordon, "Sixty-First Cleveland-Marshall Fund Lecture: The Struggle over the Past," *Cleveland State Law Review* 44 (1996): 123; Martin S. Flaherty, "History 'Lite' in Modern American Constitutionalism," *Columbia Law Review* 95 (1995): 523, 525–26; William Wiecek, "Clio as Hostage: The United States Supreme Court and the Uses of History," *California Western Law Review* 24 (1987–1988): 227, 228.

58. Reacting with frustration to *Heller*'s use of history, University of Chicago Law Professor Eric Posner has remarked, perhaps with more than a little hyperbole, "Both Scalia's and Stevens' opinions are horrible messes. Scalia's parsing of the text is wooden and ludicrous. Both of them select the evidence they like and interpret it tendentiously. Neither show any feeling for history. The opinions are tedious, pompous anti-models of judicial writing, no advertisement for the method of originalism." Eric Posner, "Originalism Seminar Class 1: Heller," *Eric Posner Blog*, January 7, 2014, http://ericposner.com/originalism-seminar-class-1-heller/.

59. Siegel, "Dead or Alive."

60. See Jack M. Balkin, "Framework Originalism and the Living Constitution," *Northwestern Law Review* 103 (2009): 549; and Adam Winkler, "*Heller*'s Catch-22," *UCLA Law Review* 56 (2009): 1551.

61. *People v. Yanna*, 297 Mich. App. 137 (2012).

62. For a similar argument, see, e.g., *United States v. Skoien*, 614 F.3d 638, 640 (7th Cir. 2010).

63. See, e.g., *United States v. Booker*, 644 F.3d 12, 23 (1st Cir. 2011); *United States v. Staten*, 666 F.3d 154, 161–62 (4th Cir. 2011); *United States v. Chester*, 628 F.3d 673

(4th Cir. 2010); *United States v. Skoien*, 614 F.3d 638, 640 (9th Cir. 2010); and *United States v. White*, 593 F.3d 1199, 1206 (11th Cir. 2010).

64. See, e.g., *Crawford v. Marion County Election Board*, 553 U.S. 181 (2008).
65. Jack Balkin, "This Decision Will Cost American Lives: A Note on *Heller* and the Living Constitution," *Balkinization*, June 27, 2008, http://balkin.blogspot.com /2008/06/this-decision-will-cost-american-lives.html.
66. Siegel, "Dead or Alive."
67. Randy E. Barnett, "The Gravitational Force of Originalism," *Fordham Law Review* 82 (2013): 411, 423.
68. See, e.g., *United States v. Chovan*, 735 F.3d 1127 (9th Cir. 2013); *Booker*, 644 F.3d at 25 (1st Cir. 2011); *Kachalsky v. County of Westchester*, 701 F.3d 81, 96 (2d Cir. 2012); *United States v. Marzzarella*, 614 F.3d 85, 97 (3d Cir. 2010); *Chester*, 628 F.3d at 683 (4th Cir. 2010); *Nat'l Rifle Ass'n v. Bureau of Alcohol, Tobacco, Firearms and Explosives*, 700 F.3d 185, 205 (5th Cir. 2012); *United States v. Miller*, 604 F. Supp. 2d 1162, 1171 (W.D. Tenn. 2009); *Skoien*, 614 F.3d at 641; *Peruta v. Cnty. of San Diego*, 758 F. Supp. 2d 1106, 1117 (S.D. Cal. 2010); *United States v. Reese*, 627 F.3d 792, 802 (10th Cir. 2010); *GeorgiaCarry.Org, Inc. v. Georgia*, 764 F. Supp. 2d 1306, 1317 (M.D. Ga. 2011); *Heller v. District of Columbia*, 670 F.3d 1244, 1257 (D.C. Cir. 2011).
69. See *Peterson v. Martinez*, 707 F.3d 1197 (10th Cir. 2013) (concealed carrying); *Nat'l Rifle Ass'n of Am., Inc. v. Bureau of Alcohol, Tobacco, Firearms, & Explosives*, 700 F.3d 185, 203 (5th Cir. 2012) (sale to minors).
70. See *Zablocki v. Redhail*, 434 U.S. 374, 383 (1978); *Harper v. Va. State Bd. of Elections*, 383 U.S. 663, 670 (1966).
71. *Planned Parenthood of Se. Pa. v. Casey*, 505 U.S. 833, 874 (1992).
72. *Pa. Coal Co. v. Mahon*, 260 U.S. 393, 415 (1922).
73. *United States v. Decastro*, 682 F.3d 160 (2d Cir. 2012).
74. *Ezell v. City of Chicago*, 651 F.3d 684, 689–90 (7th Cir. 2011).
75. *Heller v. District of Columbia*, 670 F.3d 1244, 1262 (D.C. Cir. 2011).
76. On this question, see Michael C. Dorf, "Does *Heller* Protect a Right to Carry Guns Outside the Home?," *Syracuse Law Review* 59 (2008): 225.
77. *Kachalsky v. County of Westchester*, 701 F.3d 81, 94 (2d Cir. 2012).
78. *Peterson v. Martinez*, 707 F.3d 1197, 1210–12 (10th Cir. 2013).
79. *United States v. Masciandaro*, 638 F.3d 458, 475 (4th Cir. 2011).
80. *Moore v. Madigan*, 702 F.3d 933, 937, 942 (7th Cir. 2012).
81. *United States v. Booker*, 543 U.S. 220 (2005); *Rita v. United States*, 551 U.S. 338 (2007); *Gall v. United States*, 552 U.S. 38 (2007); *Kimbrough v. United States*, 552 U.S. 85 (2007).
82. *Gonzales v. Carhart*, 550 U.S. 124 (2007).
83. Adam Liptak, "Few Ripples from Supreme Court Ruling on Guns," *New York Times*, March 17, 2009, A14.
84. For arguments that *Heller* and *McDonald* will not have as big an impact on gun regulations as expected, see Mark Tushnet, "*Heller* and the Perils of Compromise," *Lewis and Clark Law Review* 13 (2009): 419; Mark Tushnet, "Permissible Gun Regulations After *Heller*: Speculations About Method and Outcomes," *University of California Law Review* 56 (2009): 1425; Michael C. Dorf, "What Regulations Will the

Supreme Court Allow? Part One: Restricting Firearms Outside of the Home," *Verdict*, December 26, 2012, http://verdict.justia.com/2012/12/26/what-gun-regulations-will-the-supreme-court-allow; Michael C. Dorf, "What Regulations Will the Supreme Court Allow? Part Two: Originalism and the Second Amendment," *Verdict*, January 2, 2013, http://verdict.justia.com/2013/01/02/what-gun-regulations-will-the-supreme-court-allow-2; Ilya Somin, "Assessing the Very Limited Impact of *McDonald* and *Heller* on Gun Regulations," *Volokh Conspiracy*, December 6, 2010, http://www.volokh.com/2010/12/06/assessing-the-very-limited-impact-of-mcdonald-and-heller-on-gun-regulations/; and Michael C. Dorf, "Does *Heller* Protect a Right to Carry Guns Outside the Home?," *Syracuse Law Review* 59 (2008): 225.

85. See Alan Rozenshtein, "The World's First 3D-Printed Gun," *Lawfare*, May 5, 2013, http://www.lawfareblog.com/2013/05/the-worlds-first-3d-printed-gun/; and Gerard N. Magliocca, "3D Printers and Guns," *Balkinization*, May 10, 2013, http://balkin.blogspot.com/2013/05/3d-printers-and-guns.html.

86. See Andy Greenberg, "State Department Demands Takedown of 3D-Printable Gun Files for Possible Export Control Violations," *Forbes*, May 9, 2013, http://www.forbes.com/sites/andygreenberg/2013/05/09/state-department-demands-takedown-of-3d-printable-gun-for-possible-export-control-violation/.

87. Glenn Adams, "Mandatory Gun Ownership Provisions Under Consideration in Communities Across the Country," *Huffington Post*, March 8, 2013, http://www.huffingtonpost.com/2013/03/08/mandatory-gun-ownership_n_2839799.html; "Kansas Community Requires Households to Have Guns," *USA Today*, November 23, 2003; and Nancy Lofholm, "Nucla Becomes Colorado's First and Only Town Mandating Gun Ownership," *Denver Post*, May 25, 2013.

88. See generally Joseph Blocher, "Rights To and Not To," *California Law Review* 100 (2012): 761; and Laurence Tribe, "Disentangling Symmetries: Speech, Association, Parenthood," *Pepperdine Law Review* 28 (2001): 641.

89. Joseph Blocher, "The Right Not to Keep or Bear Arms," *Stanford Law Review* 64 (2012): 1, 4.

90. *United States v. Arzberger*, 592 F. Supp. 2d 590 (S.D.N.Y. 2008).

91. *United States v. Portillo-Munoz*, 643 F.3d 437 (5th Cir. 2011).

92. *United States v. Verdugo-Urquidez*, 494 U.S. 259, 265, 271 (1990).

93. Note, "The Meaning(s) of 'the People' in the Constitution," *Harvard Law Review* 126 (2013): 1078.

94. *Wollschlaeger v. Farmer*, 880 F. Supp. 2d 1251 (S.D. Fla. 2012). For discussion of the Florida law and the associated legal battle, see Erin N. Marcus, "Gun Query Off Limits for Doctors in Florida," *New York Times*, August 9, 2011, D5; and Jay Weaver, "Judge Tosses Florida Ban on Doctors Asking Patients About Guns," *Seattle Times*, July 2, 2012.

95. See *GeorgiaCarry.org v. Georgia*, 687 F.3d 1244 (11th Cir. 2012) (upholding state ban on guns in places of worship); and Eugene Volokh, "Georgia Law Banning the Carrying of Guns to Church, Unless One Notifies and Gets Permission from Church Management," *Volokh Conspiracy*, July 20, 2012, http://www.volokh.com/2012/07/20/georgia-law-banning-the-carrying-of-guns-to-church-unless-one-notifies-and-gets-permission-from-church-management/.

96. See Eugene Volokh, "Implementing the Right to Keep and Bear Arms for Self-Defense: An Analytical Framework and a Research Agenda," *UCLA Law Review* 56 (2009): 1443.

97. See, e.g., *Embody v. Ward*, 695 F.3d 577 (6th Cir. 2012); *Nichols v. Brown*, 945 F. Supp. 2d 1079 (C.D. Cal. 2013); *United States v. Hart*, 726 F.Supp.2d 56 (D. Mass. 2010), *aff'd* 674 F.3d 33 (1st Cir. 2012) (not addressing Second Amendment claim); *Schubert v. City of Springfield*, 602 F. Supp. 2d 254 (D. Mass. 2009) (raising *District of Columbia v. Heller* at oral argument), *aff'd Schubert v. City of Springfield*, 589 F.3d 496, 504 (1st Cir. 2009) (declining to address Second Amendment argument due to waiver).

98. *Embody v. Ward*, 695 F.3d 577, 579 (6th Cir. 2012).

99. Mary Ann Glendon, *Rights Talk: The Impoverishment of Political Discourse* (New York: Free Press, 1991), xi.

100. On the interaction between the First and Second Amendments, see Gregory P. Magarian, "Speaking Truth to Firepower: How the First Amendment Destabilizes the Second," *Texas Law Review* 91 (2012): 49, which informs the following paragraph.

101. On the growing influence of corporate interests in elections after *Citizens United*, see Lee Fang, "Look Who's Buying the Election," *Nation*, September 17, 2012, 11; and Lawrence Lessig, *Republic, Lost* (New York: Twelve, 2011). For a suggestion that the NRA's influence also extends to judicial appointments, see Linda Greenhouse, "The N.R.A. at the Bench," Opinionator, *New York Times*, December 26, 2012, http://opinionator.blogs.nytimes.com/2012/12/26/the-n-r-a-at-the-bench/.

6: PRESIDENTIAL POWER

1. Kate Phillips, "Obama Could Hurt a Fly," *New York Times,* June 16, 2009.

2. See Daniel Klaidman, *Kill or Capture: The War on Terror and the Soul of the Obama Presidency* (New York: Houghton Mifflin, 2012); David E. Sanger, *Confront and Conceal: Obama's Secret Wars and Surprising Use of American Power* (New York: Random House, 2012).

3. Jo Becker and Scott Shane, "Secret 'Kill List' Proves a Test of Obama's Principles and Will," *New York Times*, May 29, 2012.

4. For a general account of internal separation of powers, see Neal K. Katyal, "Internal Separation of Powers: Checking Today's Most Dangerous Branch from Within," *Yale Law Journal* 115 (2006): 2314.

5. See Department of Justice White Paper, "Lawfulness of a Lethal Operation Directed Against a U.S. Citizen Who Is a Senior Operational Leader of Al-Qa'ida or an Associated Force" (2011).

6. See generally Bob Woodward, *Plan of Attack* (New York: Simon & Schuster, 2004); Jack Goldsmith, *The Terror Presidency: Law and Judgment Inside the Bush Administration* (New York: W. W. Norton, 2009); John Yoo, *War by Other Means* (New York: Atlantic Monthly Press, 2006); Jane Mayer, *The Dark Side: The Inside Story of How the War on Terror Turned into a War on American Ideals* (New York: Random House, 2009); Charlie Savage, *Takeover: The Return of the Imperial Presidency*

and the Subversion of American Democracy (New York: Little, Brown, 2007); Harold J. Krent, "From a Unitary to a Unilateral Presidency," *Boston University Law Review* 88 (2008): 523; David J. Barron and Martin S. Lederman, "The Commander in Chief at the Lowest Ebb—Framing the Problem, Doctrine, and Original Understanding," *Harvard Law Review* 121 (2008): 689, 704–11; and Christopher S. Yoo, Steven G. Calabresi, and Anthony J. Colangelo, "The Unitary Executive in the Modern Era, 1945–2004," *Iowa Law Review* 90 (2005): 601, 722–30.

7. For the view that such "signing statements" are not in themselves objectionable, see Laurence H. Tribe, " 'Signing Statements' Are a Phantom Target," *Boston Globe*, August 9, 2006.

8. See, e.g., Joseph Margulies, *Guantánamo and the Abuse of Presidential Power* (New York: Simon & Schuster, 2006); Elizabeth Drew, "Power Grab," *New York Review of Books*, June 22, 2006; Bruce Ackerman, *The Decline and Fall of the American Republic* (Cambridge, Mass.: Belknap Press, 2010); Eric A. Posner and Adrian Vermeule, *The Executive Unbound: After the Madisonian Republic* (New York: Oxford University Press, 2010); Peter M. Shane, *Madison's Nightmare: How Executive Power Threatens American Democracy* (Chicago: University of Chicago Press, 2009); David Cole, "The Emperor's Powers," *Nation*, January 9, 2006; Editorial, "Whose Privilege?," *New York Times*, April 18, 2008; Editorial, "Abuse of Executive Privilege," *New York Times*, July 1, 2007; American Bar Association, "Task Force on Presidential Signing Statements and the Separation of Powers Doctrine" (2006), http://www .americanbar.org/content/dam/aba/migrated/leadership/2006/annual/dailyjournal /20060823144113.authcheckdam.pdf.

9. See, e.g., Trevor W. Morrison, "Libya, 'Hostilities,' the Office of Legal Counsel, and the Process of Executive Branch Legal Interpretation," *Harvard Law Review Forum* 124 (2011): 62; Bruce Ackerman, "Legal Acrobatics, Illegal War," *New York Times*, June 20, 2011; Charlie Savage and Mark Landler, "White House Defends Continuing U.S. Role in Libya Operation," *New York Times*, June 15, 2011.

10. See, e.g., Rand Paul, "Obama's Unconstitutional Libyan War," *Washington Times*, June 15, 2011; Michael McConnell, "Democrats and Executive Overreach," *Wall Street Journal*, January 10, 2012; George F. Will, "Obama's Extreme Use of Executive Discretion," *Washington Post*, December 18, 2013; John Yoo, "Executive Overreach," *National Review Online*, June 15, 2012, http://www.nationalreview.com /corner/303038/executive-overreach-john-yoo; and Orin Kerr, "The Executive Power Grab in the Decision Not to Defend DOMA," *The Volokh Conspiracy*, February 23, 2011, http://www.volokh.com/2011/02/23/the-executive-power-grab-in-the -decision-not-to-defend-doma/.

11. Indeed, some scholars argue that partisanship has largely supplanted checks and balances. See Daryl J. Levinson and Richard H. Pildes, "Separation of Parties, Not Powers," *Harvard Law Review* 119 (2006): 2311.

12. *Youngstown Sheet & Tube Co. v. Sawyer*, 343 U.S. 579, 643–44 (1952) (Jackson, J., concurring).

13. For a captivating account of the *Youngstown* case, see Noah Feldman, *Scorpions: The Battles and Triumphs of FDR's Great Supreme Court Justices* (New York: Twelve, 2010), 354-68.

14. Merle Miller, *Plain Speaking: An Oral Biography of Harry S. Truman* (New York: Berkley Pub., 1974), 225–26. But see Alex Wohl, "Writing Biography in the Age of Wikipedia: Removing a Shadow from the Life of Justice Tom Clark," *SCOTUSblog*, September 23, 2013, http://www.scotusblog.com/2013/09/writing-biography-in-the-age-of-wikipedia-removing-a-shadow-from-the-life-of-justice-tom-clark/ (in this essay, a biographer of Clark expresses doubts as to the accuracy of Miller's reporting).

15. Mariah Zeisberg, *War Powers: The Politics of Constitutional Authority* (Princeton, N.J.: Princeton University Press, 2013), 5–8; Barron and Lederman, "The Commander in Chief at the Lowest Ebb," 689, 723; and Curtis A. Bradley and Trevor W. Morrison, "Presidential Power, Historical Practice, and Legal Constraint," *Columbia Law Review* 113 (2013): 1097, 1109–10.

16. John Hart Ely, *War and Responsibility* (Princeton, N.J.: Princeton University Press, 1993), 9–11; Louis Henkin, *Foreign Affairs and the U.S. Constitution* (New York: Oxford University Press, 1996), 4–5, 14–16, 21–22; Akhil Reed Amar, "Of Sovereignty and Federalism," *Yale Law Journal* 96 (1987) 1425, 1495–96; Barron and Lederman, "The Commander in Chief at the Lowest Ebb," 689, 723–25; H. Jefferson Powell, "The President's Authority Over Foreign Affairs: An Executive Branch Perspective," *George Washington Law Review* 67 (1999): 527, 530–39, 549–55; Saikrishna B. Prakash and Michael D. Ramsey, "The Executive Power Over Foreign Affairs," *Yale Law Journal* 111 (2001): 231, 233–36.

17. Scholars continue to debate the similarities and differences between Bush and Obama, even while noting that both of these presidents, though in somewhat different ways, took broad views of their power. See, e.g., David Cole, "Breaking Away," *New Republic*, December 8, 2010; David Cole, "Obama and Terror: The Hovering Questions," *New York Review of Books*, July 12, 2012; Jack Goldsmith, *Power and Constraint: The Accountable Presidency after 9/11* (New York: W. W. Norton, 2012); Jack Goldsmith, "David Cole on Obama v. Bush," *Lawfare*, December 17, 2010, http://www.lawfareblog.com/2010/12/david-cole-on-obama-v-bush/#.UuIguPbTn1x.

18. See, e.g., *Crockett v. Reagan*, 720 F.2d 1355 (D.C. Cir. 1983) (El Salvador); *Sanchez-Espinoza v. Reagan*, 770 F.2d 202 (D.C. Cir. 1985) (Nicaragua); *Conyers v. Reagan*, 765 F.2d 1124 (D.C. Cir. 1985) (Grenada); *Campbell v. Clinton*, 203 F.3d 19 (D.C. Cir. 2000) (Kosovo); *Dellums v. Bush*, 752 F. Supp. 1141 (D.C.C. 1990) (Iraq); *Pietsch v. Bush*, 755 F. Supp. 62, 64 (E.D.N.Y. 1991) *aff'd*, 935 F.2d 1278 (2d Cir. 1991) (Persian Gulf); *Kucinich v. Obama*, 821 F. Supp. 2d 110 (D.D.C. 2011) (Libya).

19. *Rumsfeld v. Padilla*, 542 U.S. 426 (2004).

20. Harold Hongju Koh, "How to End the Forever War?," speech at the Oxford Union, May 7, 2013.

21. "Remarks by the President at the National Defense University," White House, Press Release, May 23, 2013.

22. Mary Dudziak, *War Time: An Idea, Its History, Its Consequences* (New York: Oxford University Press, 2012).

23. See, e.g., Jess Bravin, *The Terror Courts: Rough Justice at Guantanamo Bay* (New Haven, Conn.: Yale University Press, 2013); Margulies, *Guantánamo and the Abuse of Presidential Power*; David Glazier, "The Development of an Exceptional Court:

The History of the American Military Commission," in Fionnuala Ni Aolain and Oren Gross, eds., *Guantánamo and Beyond: Exceptional Courts and Military Commissions in Comparative Perspective* (New York: Cambridge University Press, 2013).

24. See Jonathan Hafetz and Mark P. Denbeaux, *The Guantánamo Lawyers: Inside a Prison Outside the Law* (New York: New York University Press, 2009).

25. For an insightful overview of the cases discussed in this section, see Jenny S. Martinez, "Process and Substance in the 'War on Terror,'" *Columbia Law Review* 108 (2008): 1013.

26. See 542 U.S. 507 (2004).

27. Oral Argument in *Rumsfeld v. Padilla*, 542 U.S. 426 (2004).

28. See 542 U.S. 466 (2004).

29. Goldsmith, *Power and Constraint*, 178.

30. See, e.g., Goldsmith, *Power and Constraint*; Richard H. Fallon Jr. and Daniel J. Meltzer, "Habeas Corpus Jurisdiction, Substantive Rights, and the War on Terror," *Harvard Law Review* 120 (2007): 2029; Janet Cooper Alexander, "Jurisdiction-Stripping in the War on Terrorism," *Stanford Journal of Civil Rights and Civil Liberties* 2 (2006): 259–67; James P. Pfiffner, *Power Play: The Bush Presidency and the Constitution* (Washington, D.C.: The Brookings Institution, 2008), 100–110.

31. See 548 U.S. 557 (2006).

32. On *Hamdan*, see, e.g., George P. Fletcher, "Hamdan Confronts the Military Commissions Act of 2006," *Columbia Journal of Transnational Law* 45 (2007): 427; Harold Hongju Koh, "Setting the World Right," *Yale Law Journal* 115 (2006): 2350, 2360–68; Peter J. Spiro, "*Hamdan v. Rumsfeld*. 126 S. Ct. 2749. United States Supreme Court, June 29, 2006," *American Journal of International Law* 100 (2006): 888; Jonathan Mahler, *The Challenge:* Hamdan v. Rumsfeld *and the Fight Over Presidential Power* (New York: Farrar, Straus and Giroux, 2008).

33. John Yoo, "Sending a Message," *Wall Street Journal*, October 19, 2006.

34. For an excellent overview, see Bravin, *The Terror Courts*.

35. See, e.g., Anthony Gregory, *The Power of Habeas Corpus in America: From the King's Prerogative to the War on Terror* (New York: Cambridge University Press, 2013); Paul D. Halliday, *Habeas Corpus: From England to Empire* (Cambridge, Mass.: Harvard University Press, 2010); Stephen I. Vladeck, "The New Habeas Revisionism," *Harvard Law Review* 124 (2011): 941.

36. See Scott Sayare, "After Guantánamo, Starting Anew, in Quiet Anger," *New York Times*, May 25, 2012; Lakhdar Boumediene, "My Guantánamo Nightmare," *New York Times*, January 7, 2012.

37. See generally Linda Greenhouse, "The Mystery of Guantánamo Bay," *Berkeley Journal of International Law* 27 (2009): 1.

38. On the Suspension Clause, see, e.g., Amanda L. Tyler, "The Forgotten Core Meaning of the Suspension Clause," *Harvard Law Review* 125 (2012): 901.

39. 553 U.S. 723 (2008).

40. See, e.g., Daniel J. Meltzer, "Habeas Corpus, Suspension, and Guantánamo: The *Boumediene* Decision," *Supreme Court Review* (2008): 1; Gerald L. Neuman, "The Habeas Corpus Suspension Clause After *Boumediene v. Bush*," *Columbia Law Review*

110 (2010): 537; Eric A. Posner, "Boumediene and the Uncertain March of Judicial Cosmopolitanism," *CATO Supreme Court Review* (2009): 23.

41. See Ronald Dworkin, "Why It Was a Great Victory," *New York Review of Books*, August 14, 2008; David D. Cole, "Rights Over Borders: Transnational Constitutionalism and Guantanamo Bay," *Cato Supreme Court Review* (2007–2008): 47; Jonathan Mahler, "Why This Court Keeps Rebuking This President," *New York Times*, June 15, 2008.

42. See William Glaberson, "Judge Declares Five Detainees Held Illegally," *New York Times*, November 20, 2008.

43. See generally Benjamin Wittes et al., "The Emerging Law of Detention 2.0: The Guantánamo Habeas Cases as Lawmaking," Brookings (2011).

44. Jonathan Hafetz, "The D.C. Circuit and Guantanamo: The Defiance Reaches New Heights," *Balkinization*, November 16, 2011, http://balkin.blogspot.com/2011/11/dc -circuit-and-guantanamo-defiance.html; Jasmeet K. Ahuja and Andrew Tutt, "Evidentiary Rules Governing Guantánamo Habeas Petitions: Their Effects and Consequences," *Yale Law and Policy Review* 31 (2012): 185; and Stephen I. Vladek, "The D.C. Circuit After *Boumediene*," *Seton Hall Law Review* 42 (2011): 1451.

45. "*Boumediene*'s Legacy and the Fate of Guantánamo Detainees," panel discussion, *Lawfare*, July 17, 2012: 28–29, http://www.lawfareblog.com/wp-content/uploads/2012 /07/Transcript-from-Panel-Discussion_Boumediene.pdf.

46. *Latif v. Obama*, 666 F.3d 746, 764 (D.C. Cir. 2011).

47. Quoted in Richard Brust, "The Guantanamo Quagmire," *ABA Journal*, October 5, 2012.

48. *Esmail v. Obama*, 639 F.3d 1075, 1078 (D.C. Cir. 2011) (Silberman, J., concurring).

49. See Lyle Denniston, "Ex-Judge: *Boumediene* Is Being 'Gutted'," *SCOTUSblog*, July 17, 2012, http://www.scotusblog.com/2012/07/ex-judge-boumediene-is-being-gut ted/; and Editorial, "A Right Without a Remedy," *New York Times*, March 1, 2011.

50. Aziz Z. Huq, "What Good Is Habeas?," *Constitutional Commentary* 26 (2010): 385.

51. For a persuasive overview, see Stephen I. Vladeck, "The Passive-Aggressive Virtues," *Columbia Law Review Sidebar* 111 (2011): 122.

52. *Marbury v. Madison*, 5 U.S. 137 (1803).

53. For a canonical statement of this view, see Alexander M. Bickel, "The Passive Virtues," *Harvard Law Review* 75 (1961): 40.

54. *Al-Aulaqi v. Obama*, 727 F. Supp. 2d 1 (D.D.C. 2010).

55. *Mohamed v. Jeppesen Dataplan, Inc.*, 614 F.3d 1070, 1073 (9th Cir. 2010).

56. *DaimlerChrysler Corp. v. Cuno*, 547 U.S. 332, 341 (2006).

57. *Kucinich v. Obama*, 821 F. Supp. 2d 110, 125 (D.D.C. 2011).

58. See 133 S. Ct. 1138 (2013).

59. For reactions to the revelation of warrantless wiretapping and subsequent amendments to FISA, see Paul M. Schwartz, "Warrantless Wiretapping, FISA Reform, and the Lessons of Public Liberty: A Comment on Holmes's Jorde Lecture," *California Law Review* 97 (2009): 407; Chris Hedges, "Stop the New FISA," *Los Angeles Times*, July 11, 2008; John Cary Sims, "What NSA Is Doing . . . and Why It's Illegal," *Hastings Constitutional Law Quarterly* 33 (2006): 101; and James Risen and Eric Lichtblau, "Bush Lets U.S. Spy on Callers Without Courts," *New York Times*,

December 15, 2005. For an argument that President Bush's warrantless terrorist surveillance program was constitutional, see John Yoo, Essay, "The Terrorist Surveillance Program and the Constitution," *George Mason Law Review* 14 (2007): 565.

60. Chris Cillizza, "Who Had the Worst Week in Washington? Supreme Court Justice Antonin Scalia," *Washington Post*, June 28, 2012.

61. *Lafler v. Cooper*, 132 S. Ct. 1376 (2012); *Dorsey v. United States*, 132 S. Ct. 2321 (2012).

62. *Nat'l Fed'n of Indep. Bus. v. Sebelius*, 132 S. Ct. 2566 (2012).

63. *United States v. Alvarez*, 132 S. Ct. 2537 (2012).

64. *Arizona v. United States*, 132 S. Ct. 2492, 2510 (2012).

65. See, e.g., Tony Mauro, "Scalia Takes Flak over Arizona Dissent," *National Law Journal*, June 28, 2012; Jeffrey Toobin, "That's Just Nino: Scalia's Arizona Dissent," *New Yorker*, June 26, 2012, http://www.newyorker.com/online/blogs/comment/2012/06/antonin-scalia-dissent-immigration-arizona.html.

66. The only other Roberts Court ruling to produce such a conflict was *Medellín v. Texas*, 552 U.S. 491 (2008).

67. See generally Zachary S. Price, "Enforcement Discretion and Executive Duty," *Vanderbilt Law Review* 67 (forthcoming April 2014).

68. See, e.g., Letter from Rep. Cory Gardner to Eric H. Holder, Attorney General (September 3, 2013); Michael B. Mukasey, "Eric Holder Can't Sweep Aside Laws on Minimum Sentencing, Debate Club," *U.S. News*, August 15, 2013; Peter Suderman, "If Obamacare Is the Law of the Land, Then Why Does the Obama Administration Keep Ignoring It?," *Reason*, August 13, 2013, http://reason.com/blog/2013/08/13/if-obamacare-is-the-law-of-the-land-then; Kris W. Kobach, "The 'DREAM' Order Isn't Legal," *New York Post*, June 22, 2012; Charles Krauthammer, "The Incompetent Imperial Presidency," *Washington Post*, July 6, 2012.

69. See Jeffrey A. Love and Arpit K. Garg, "Presidential Inaction and the Separation of Powers," *Michigan Law Review* 112 (forthcoming 2014).

70. *In re Aiken County*, 725 F.3d 255, 264 (D.C. Cir. 2013).

71. Price, "Enforcement Discretion and Executive Duty."

72. The literature on this subject could fill more than a few libraries. For a few leading works, see Elena Kagan, "Presidential Administration," *Harvard Law Review* 114 (2001): 2245; Gerald E. Frug, "The Ideology of Bureaucracy in American Law," *Harvard Law Review* 97 (1984): 1276; and Richard B. Stewart, "The Reformation of American Administrative Law," *Harvard Law Review* 88 (1975): 1667.

73. Stephen G. Breyer, *Active Liberty: Interpreting Our Democratic Constitution* (New York: Knopf, 2005), 102–3.

74. On this debate, see Steven G. Calabresi and Saikrishna B. Prakash, "The President's Power to Execute the Laws," *Yale Law Journal* 104 (1994): 541; Martin S. Flaherty, "The Most Dangerous Branch," *Yale Law Journal* 105 (1996): 1725; Lawrence Lessig and Cass R. Sunstein, "The President and the Administration," *Columbia Law Review* 94 (1994): 1; and Steven G. Calabresi and Kevin H. Rhodes, "The Structural Constitution: Unitary Executive, Plural Judiciary," *Harvard Law Review* 105 (1992): 1153.

75. Quoted in Larry Engelmann, "The Way We Word: Unforgettable Quotations of 1995," *Chicago Tribune*, December 31, 1995.
76. See 130 S. Ct. 3138 (2010).
77. See Robert V. Percival, "Presidential Management of the Administrative State: The Not-So-Unitary Executive," *Duke Law Journal* 51 (2001): 963, 989; and Morton Rosenberg, "Congress's Prerogative Over Agencies and Agency Decisionmakers: The Rise and Demise of the Reagan Administration's Theory of the Unitary Executive," *George Washington Law Review* 57 (1989): 627.
78. David E. Rosenbaum, "An Advocate for the Right," *New York Times*, July 28, 2005.
79. Stephen Labaton and Jonathan D. Glater, "As a Lawyer, Court Nominee Was Considered a Skillful Advocate for Corporate Clients," *New York Times*, July 21, 2005.
80. Adam Liptak, "In His Opinions, Nominee Favors Judicial Caution," *New York Times*, July 22, 2005.
81. *City of Arlington v. FCC*, 133 S. Ct. 1863, 1878 (2013).
82. John M. Broder and Carolyn Marshall, "In Reagan's White House, a Clever, Sometimes Cocky John Roberts," *New York Times*, July 27, 2005.
83. See Richard H. Pildes, "*Free Enterprise Fund*, Boundary-Enforcing Decisions, and the Unitary Executive Branch Theory of Government Administration," *Duke Journal of Constitutional Law and Public Policy* 6 (2010): 1; Stephen Bainbridge, "The PCAOB Anti-Climax," ProfessorBainbridge.com, June 28, 2010, http://www.profes sorbainbridge.com/professorbainbridgecom/2010/06/the-pcaob-anticlimax.html; John Elwood, "*Free Enterprise Fund*: The *Lopez* of Separation of Powers Doctrine," *Volokh Conspiracy*, June 28, 2010; and Richard H. Pildes, "The *Free Enterprise* Decision: A Symbolic Victory for the 'Unitary Executive Branch' Vision of the Presidency, but of Limited Practical Consequence," *Balkinization*, June 28, 2010, http://balkin.blogspot.com/2010/06/free-enterprise-decision-symbolic.html.
84. Paul Clement, "*Free Enterprise*: Doctrinal Shift or Snoozefest?," *Slate*, June 29, 2010, http://www.slate.com/articles/life/the_breakfast_table/features/2010/supreme _court_breakfast_table/free_enterprise_doctrinal_shift_or_snoozefest.html.
85. Breyer, *Active Liberty*, 103.
86. *Olmstead v. United States*, 277 U.S. 438, 485 (1928) (dissenting opinion).

7: PRIVACY

1. The full quotation, "The Supreme Court is nine scorpions in a bottle," furnished the title and opening epigraph of Noah Feldman's brilliantly conceived biography of Justices Felix Frankfurter, William O. Douglas, Hugo L. Black, and Robert H. Jackson. See Feldman, *Scorpions: The Battles and Triumphs of FDR's Great Supreme Court Justices* (New York: Twelve, 2010). Feldman notes that while the quotation is "often attributed to Oliver Wendell Holmes Jr., . . . there is no evidence Holmes ever said it or anything like it" (437 n. 1). He adds that the metaphor, in all likelihood first applied to the Court of that era by Yale Law School's Alexander Bickel, can be traced back to J. Robert Oppenheimer's vivid 1953 description of the arms race between the U.S. and the Soviet Union as a life-and-death struggle between "two

scorpions in a bottle, each capable of killing the other, but only at the risk of his own life." This book's focus is entirely different: our point in using the phrase isn't the fragile peace generated by mutually assured destruction but the shared concern about privacy generated by how the scorpions find themselves in the same translucent predicament: they are all *in a bottle*.

2. Feldman, *Scorpions*.

3. Quoted in ibid., 398.

4. Dahlia Lithwick, "Her Honor," *New York Magazine*, November 27, 2011.

5. Adam Liptak, "This Bench Belongs in a Dugout," *New York Times*, May 31, 2010.

6. Joan Biskupic, "Ginsburg, Scalia Strike a Balance," *USA Today*, December 25, 2007.

7. See Erwin Chemerinsky and Eric J. Segall, "Supreme Court Should Lift Its Blackout," *Los Angeles Times*, March 22, 2012; Kenneth W. Starr, "Open Up High Court to Cameras," *New York Times*, October 3, 2011; and Adam Cohen, "Why Won't the Supreme Court Allow TV Cameras?," *Time*, November 21, 2011.

8. Adam Liptak, "Bucking a Trend, Supreme Court Justices Reject Video Coverage," *New York Times*, February 19, 2013.

9. *Cameras in the Court*, C-SPAN, http://www.c-span.org/The-Courts/Cameras-in-The -Court (last visited December 3, 2013).

10. Ibid.

11. Ibid.

12. See Stephen Breyer, *Active Liberty: Interpreting Our Democratic Constitution* (New York: Knopf, 2005); Antonin Scalia, ed., *A Matter of Interpretation: Federal Courts and the Law* (Princeton, N.J.: Princeton University Press, 1998); Sonia Sotomayor, *My Beloved World* (New York: Knopf, 2013); and Clarence Thomas, *My Grandfather's Son: A Memoir* (New York: HarperCollins, 2007).

13. Adam Liptak, "Court Is 'One of Most Activist,' Ginsburg Says, Vowing to Stay," *New York Times*, August 25, 2013.

14. See, e.g., Todd Ruger, "Alito Defends 'Citizens' in Speech to Federalist Society," *Blog of the Legal Times*, November 16, 2012, http://legaltimes.typepad.com/blt/2012/11/ alito-defends-citizens-in-speech-to-federalist-society.html.

15. "Souter Won't Get a Taste of His Own Medicine," NBCNews.com, March 15, 2006, http://www.nbcnews.com/id/11827131/#.Up6UH2RDtwo; *Kelo v. New London*, 545 U.S. 469 (2005).

16. See Adam Liptak, "Chief Justice Defends Peers on Health Law," *New York Times*, January 1, 2012.

17. Alison Frankel, "From Aspen: Justice Kagan Calls Surveillance Cases 'Growth Industry,'" Reuters, July 1, 2013, http://blogs.reuters.com/alison-frankel/2013/07/01/from -aspen-justice-kagan-calls-surveillance-cases-growth-industry/.

18. For an excellent introduction, see Wayne R. LaFave et al., *Principles of Criminal Procedure: Investigation*, 2nd ed. (St. Paul, Minn.: West, 2009).

19. The following discussion of the nature of privacy rights is informed by the work of many excellent scholars. See, e.g., Daniel J. Solove, *Nothing to Hide: The False Trade-off between Privacy and Security* (New Haven, Conn.: Yale University Press, 2011); Anita L. Allen, *Unpopular Privacy: What Must We Hide?* (New York: Oxford Uni-

versity Press, 2011); Daniel Solove, *Understanding Privacy* (Cambridge, Mass.: Harvard University Press, 2008); David Lyon, *Surveillance Studies: An Overview* (Malden, Mass.: Polity Press, 2007); Charles Fried, *An Anatomy of Values* (Cambridge, Mass.: Harvard University Press, 1970); Julie E. Cohen, "What Privacy Is For," *Harvard Law Review* 126 (2013): 1904; Neil M. Richards, "The Dangers of Surveillance," *Harvard Law Review* 126 (2013): 1934; and James Q. Whitman, "The Two Western Cultures of Privacy: Dignity Versus Liberty," *Yale Law Journal* 113 (2004): 1151.

20. Jason Collins (with Frank Lidz), "Why NBA Center Jason Collins Is Coming Out Now," *Sports Illustrated*, April 29, 2013.

21. Alexander Solzhenitsyn, *Cancer Ward*, trans. Nicholas Bethell and David Burg (New York: Farar, Straus and Giroux, 1991), 192.

22. Alexander Pope, *An Essay on Criticism* (St. Louis, Mo.: Washington University Press, 1962).

23. *Stanley v. Georgia*, 394 U.S. 557, 565 (1969) (holding that the Constitution forbids the seizure in one's home even of concededly obscene material that is unprotected by the First Amendment when it is an object of purchase or sale).

24. *Brinegar v. United States*, 338 U.S. 160, 180 (1949) (Jackson, J., dissenting).

25. Deborah Nelson, *Pursuing Privacy in Cold War America* (New York: Columbia University Press, 2001), xi.

26. George Orwell, *1984* (London: Sacker & Warburg, 1949).

27. Charles Duhigg, "How Companies Learn Your Secrets," *New York Times*, February 16, 2012.

28. See the sources cited above surveying the privacy rights literature, as well as Richard A. Posner, "Privacy Is Overrated," *New York Daily News*, April 28, 2013; and William J. Stuntz, "Against Privacy and Transparency," *New Republic*, April 17, 2006.

29. Benjamin Franklin, *Poor Richard's Almanack* (1735), reprinted in *The Oxford Dictionary of Quotations*, 2nd ed. (London: Oxford University Press, 1959), 211.

30. See, generally, Kenneth A. Bamberger and Deirdre K. Mulligan, "Privacy on the Books and on the Ground," *Stanford Law Review* 63 (2011): 247; Edward J. Janger and Paul M. Schwartz, "The Gramm-Leach-Bliley Act, Information Privacy, and the Limits of Default Rules," *Minnesota Law Review* 86 (2001): 1219; and Daniel J. Solove, "Privacy Self-Management and the Consent Dilemma," *Harvard Law Review* 126 (2013): 1880.

31. Glenn Greenwald, "NSA Collecting Phone Records of Millions of Verizon Customers Daily," *Guardian*, June 5, 2013, http://www.theguardian.com/world/2013/jun/06/nsa-phone-records-verizon-court-order; and Glenn Greenwald et al., "Edward Snowden: The Whistleblower Behind the NSA Surveillance Revelations," *Guardian*, June 9, 2013, http://www.theguardian.com/world/2013/jun/09/edward-snowden-nsa-whistleblower-surveillance.

32. On the role of statutory privacy protections, see, e.g., Erin Murphy, "The Politics of Privacy in the Criminal Justice System: Information Disclosure, The Fourth Amendment, and Statutory Law Enforcement Exemptions," *Michigan Law Review* 111 (2013): 485.

33. *Katz v. United States*, 389 U.S. 347 (1967); and *Olmstead v. United States*, 277 U.S. 438, 464 (1928).

34. For a recent article that describes this dynamic, see Orin S. Kerr, "An Equilibrium-Adjustment Theory of the Fourth Amendment," *Harvard Law Review* 125 (2011): 476.

35. *Smith v. Maryland*, 442 U.S. 735 (1979).

36. See Stephen J. Schulhofer, *More Essential Than Ever* (New York: Oxford University Press, 2012); and Sonia K. McNeil, "Privacy and the Modern Grid," *Harvard Journal of Law and Technology* 25 (2011): 199. For a debate on the merits of the third-party doctrine, compare Orin S. Kerr, "The Case for the Third-Party Doctrine," *Michigan Law Review* 107 (2009): 561; with Erin Murphy, "The Case Against the Case for Third-Party Doctrine," *Berkeley Technology Law Journal* 24 (2009): 1239.

37. Dahlia Lithwick and Steve Vladeck, "Taking the 'Meh' Out of Metadata," *Slate*, November 22, 2013, http://www.slate.com/articles/news_and_politics/jurisprudence/2013/11/nsa_and_metadata_how_the_government_can_spy_on_your_health_political_beliefs.html.

38. Federal courts hearing challenges to NSA programs have debated *Smith*'s continued relevance and proper application. Compare *Klayman v. Obama*, 2013 WL 6571596 (D.D.C. Dec. 16, 2013), with *ACLU v. Clapper*, 2013 WL 6819708 (S.D.N.Y. Dec. 27, 2013).

39. *United States v. Jones*, 132 S. Ct. 945 (2012).

40. *Florida v. Jardines*, 133 S. Ct. 1509 (2013).

41. What count as "physical intrusions" and therefore as "searches" under Scalia's historical approach may, however, depend on advances in technology. Just as the technology of aviation had become sufficiently commonplace by late in the previous century to prevent airborne observation with the naked eye of marijuana growing in an open field from constituting a "search" under *Katz*—see *California v. Ciraolo*, 476 U.S. 207, 215 (1986)—so the technology of thermal imaging had not yet become sufficiently routine to prevent its use to "see" through the walls of a private home from constituting a "search" under the same test early in this century. See *Kyllo v. U.S.*, 533 U.S. 27, 39 n. 6 (2001) (Scalia, J.).

42. See, e.g., Orin S. Kerr, "The Mosaic Theory of the Fourth Amendment," *Michigan Law Review* 110 (2012): 311.

43. See ibid. at 315–20.

44. *United States v. Pineda-Moreno*, 617 F.3d 1120, 1124, 1126 (9th Cir. 2010) (Kozinski, C.J., dissenting from denial of rehearing en banc).

45. *People v. Weaver*, 12 N.Y.3d 433, 441–42 (2009).

46. See Kerr, "Mosaic Theory."

47. See 133 S. Ct. 1958 (2013).

48. Cyrus Vance, "Taking DNA from All Criminals Should Be Standard Procedure," *New York Times*, January 23, 2012.

49. *United States v. Kincade*, 379 F.3d 813, 843 (9th Cir. 2004) (en banc) (Reinhardt, J., dissenting).

50. *District Attorney's Office v. Osborne*, 557 U.S. 52 (2009).

51. See, e.g., Orin Kerr, "A Few Thoughts on *Maryland v. King*," *Volokh Conspiracy*,

June 3, 2013, http://www.volokh.com/2013/06/03/a-few-thoughts-on-maryland-v
-king-2/.

52. *City of Ontario v. Quon*, 130 S. Ct. 2619 (2010).

53. See Julie Samuels et al., "Collecting DNA at Arrest: Policies, Practices, and Implications" Urban Institute (May 2013), 24, http://www.urban.org/publications
/412831.html.

54. See, e.g., Paul E. Tracy and Vincent Morgan, "Big Brother and His Science Kit:
DNA Databases for 21st Century Crime Control?," *Journal of Criminal Law and
Criminology* 90 (2000): 635; Paul M. Monteleoni, "DNA Databases, Universality,
and the Fourth Amendment," *New York University Law Review* 82 (2007): 247;
D. H. Kaye and Michael E. Smith, "DNA Identification Databases: Legality,
Legitimacy, and the Case for Population-Wide Coverage," *Wisconsin Law
Review* 2003 (2003): 413; Henry T. Greely et al., "Family Ties: The Use of DNA
Offender Databases to Catch Offenders' Kin," *Journal of Law, Medicine & Ethics*
34 (2006): 248.

55. *United States v. Kincade*, 379 F.3d 813, 873 (9th Cir. 2004) (en banc) (Kozinski, J.,
dissenting).

56. See Jill Lawless, "Spread of DNA Databases Sparks Ethical Concerns," Associated
Press, July 12, 2013, http://news.yahoo.com/spread-dna-databases-sparks-ethical
-concerns-072535306.html; Peggy Noonan, "Privacy Isn't All We're Losing," *Wall
Street Journal*, June 14, 2013; and James B. Rule, "The Price of the Panopticon," *New
York Times*, June 12, 2013, A27.

57. See William C. Sammons and Lydia S. Hu, "Embracing DNA Collection as a Routine Booking Procedure," *Jurist*, July 11, 2013, http://jurist.org/sidebar/2013/07
/sammons-hu-routine-booking-procedure.php; Eric Posner, "DNA at the Supreme
Court: The Case for a Universal Database," *Slate*, March 5, 2013, http://www.slate
.com/articles/news_and_politics/view_from_chicago/2013/03/dna_at_the
_supreme_court_the_case_for_a_universal_database.html; Texas Department of
Public Safety, "DNA Database Helping Texas Law Enforcement Solve Crimes,"
press release, December 12, 2012; and Michael Seringhaus, "To Stop Crime, Share
Your Genes," *New York Times*, March 15, 2010.

58. See, e.g., Julie Samuels et al., "Collecting DNA from Arrestees: Implementation
Lessons," *NIJ Journal* (June 2012): 18, https://www.ncjrs.gov/pdffiles1/nij/238484.
pdf; Erin Murphy, Comment, "License, Registration, Cheek Swab: DNA Testing
and the Divided Court," *Harvard Law Review* 127 (2013): 161, 167–68; *Haskell v.
Harris*, 727 F.3d 916 (9th Cir. 2013); and Joseph Goldstein, "Police Agencies Are
Assembling Records of DNA," *New York Times*, June 12, 2013, A1.

59. See Murphy, Comment, "License, Registration, Cheek Swab," 161; Mark Hansen,
"Crime Labs Under the Microscope After a String of Shoddy, Suspect and Fraudu-
lent Results," *ABA Journal*, September 1, 2013; Brian Resnick, "The United States
Has a Huge Backlog of Untested DNA Evidence," *National Journal*, August 6,
2013; and Jason Silverstein, "The Dark Side of DNA Evidence," *Nation*, March 27,
2013.

60. *United States v. Kincade*, 379 F.3d 813, 871 (9th Cir. 2004) (en banc) (Kozinski, J.,
dissenting).

61. Marc D. Rayman, *Dawn Journal*, Jet Propulsion Laboratory (September 30, 2007), http://dawn.jpl.nasa.gov/mission/journal_9_30_07.asp.

62. See *Whalen v. Roe*, 429 U.S. 589 (1977); and *Nixon v. Administrator of General Services*, 422 U.S. 425 (1977).

63. *Doe v. City of New York*, 15 F.3d 264 (2d Cir. 1994) (HIV status); *Plante v. Gonzalez*, 575 F.2d 1119 (5th Cir. 1978) (financial records of state senators); *York v. Story*, 324 F.2d 450 (9th Cir. 1963) (nude photographs); and *Tucson Woman's Clinic v. Eden*, 379 F.3d 531, 551 (9th Cir. 2004) (abortion clinics).

64. *NASA v. Nelson*, 131 S. Ct. 746 (2011).

65. *Nelson v. NASA*, 530 F.3d 865 (9th Cir. 2008).

66. See, e.g., *Marsh v. Cnty. of San Diego*, 680 F.3d 1148, 1153 (9th Cir. 2012); *Douglas v. Dobbs*, 419 F.3d 1097, 1101 (10th Cir. 2005); and *Denius v. Dunlap*, 209 F.3d 944, 955 (7th Cir. 2000).

67. On this geometric methodology of constitutional analysis, see Laurence H. Tribe, *The Invisible Constitution* (New York: Oxford University Press, 2008), 157–63.

68. "To Young Lawyers Section of the Washington State Bar Association," in Melvin I. Urofsky, ed., *The Douglas Letters: Selections from the Private Papers of Justice William O. Douglas* (Bethesda, Md.: Adler & Adler, 1987), 162.

69. Letter from Oliver Wendell Holmes Jr. to Harold J. Laski (March 4, 1920), in Mark DeWolfe Howe, ed., *Holmes-Laski Letters: The Correspondence of Mr. Justice Holmes and Harold J. Laski* (Cambridge, Mass.: Harvard University Press, 1953), 248, 249.

8: RIGHTS FOR SALE

1. Simon James and Chantal Stebbings, eds., *A Dictionary of Legal Quotations* (New York: Macmillan, 1987), 103 (quoting Clarence Darrow).

2. This quotation, or a close variant, is commonly attributed to Justice Holmes. See, e.g., Edward W. Knappman, ed., *Watergate and the White House* (New York: Facts on File, 1973–74), 100.

3. Thomas Jefferson, *The Autobiography of Thomas Jefferson, 1743–1790, Together with a Summary of the Chief Events in Jefferson's Life*, ed. Paul Leicester Ford (Philadelphia: University of Pennsylvania Press, 2005), 90–91.

4. Benjamin Franklin, *Poor Richard's Almanack* (December 1733).

5. See American Bar Association, *Model Rules of Professional Conduct* (2011).

6. 531 U.S. 533 (2001).

7. *Rust v. Sullivan*, 500 U.S. 173 (1991). One of us (Larry Tribe) represented the losing doctors in the Supreme Court.

8. Erik W. Stanley, "LBJ, the IRS, and Churches," *Regent University Law Review* 24 (2012): 237.

9. See, e.g., *Hill v. Lockhart*, 474 U.S. 52 (1985); *Santobello v. New York*, 404 U.S. 257 (1971); and *Brady v. United States*, 397 U.S. 742 (1970). But compare *United States v. Jackson*, 390 U.S. 570 (1968).

10. See *South Dakota v. Dole*, 483 U.S. 203 (1987).

11. *Agency for Int'l Dev. v. Alliance for Open Soc'y Int'l, Inc.*, 133 S. Ct. 2321 (2013).

12. Commonly attributed to Mark Twain. See John Robert Colombo, "A Said Poem," in *Neo Poems* (Winlaw, B.C.: Sono Nis Press, 1970), 46.

13. See Jackson Lears, *Rebirth of a Nation: The Making of Modern America, 1877–1920* (New York: HarperCollins, 2009).

14. See Susan Jacoby, *Freethinkers: A History of American Secularism* (New York: Henry Holt, 2004), 286–87; David Manwaring, *Render Unto Caesar: The Flag-Salute Controversy* (Chicago: University of Chicago Press, 1962), 2–8; and Leonard A. Stevens, *Salute! The Case of the Bible vs. the Flag* (New York: Coward, McCann & Geoghegan, 1973), 22–25. This paragraph is informed by these works.

15. *Minersville Sch. Dist. v. Gobitis*, 310 U.S. 586 (1940).

16. *Jones v. Opelika*, 316 U.S. 584 (1942) (Black, Douglas, and Murphy, JJ., dissenting).

17. *West Virginia State Board of Education v. Barnette*, 319 U.S. 624 (1943).

18. *Wooley v. Maynard*, 430 U.S. 705 (1977).

19. See 133 S. Ct. 2321 (2013).

20. *AID*, quoting *Barnette*.

21. When asked about his judicial role models in connection with his confirmation hearing for appointment to the Court of Appeals for the D.C. Circuit, Chief Justice Roberts remarked, "I admire the judicial restraint of Holmes and Brandeis, the intellectual rigor of Frankfurter, the common sense and pragmatism of Jackson, the vision of John Marshall." See *Confirmation Hearing on Federal Appointments: Hearing Before the Senate Comm. on the Judiciary*, 108th Cong. 437–38 (2003).

22. See, e.g., *Engel v. Vitale*, 370 U.S. 421 (1962); and *Abbington v. Schempp*, 374 U.S. 203 (1963). The issues posed by official prayers in public settings have been addressed in the past—see *Marsh v. Chambers*, 463 U.S. 783 (1983) (upholding such prayers at the start of legislative sessions principally on the basis of an unbroken history of initiating congressional sessions in that manner)—and continue to puzzle the Court. See, e.g., *Town of Greece v. Galloway*, No. 12-696 (prayers, usually Christian in character, routinely recited at start of every town meeting) (argued November 6, 2013).

23. See Laurence H. Tribe, "Disentangling Symmetries: Speech, Association, Parenthood," *Pepperdine Law Review* 28 (2001): 641, 644.

24. Elena Kagan, "Evening Lecture," *SCOTUSblog*, October 17, 2007, http://www.sco tusblog.com/wp-content/uploads/2010/04/Kagan-speech_WestPoint.pdf.

25. 547 U.S. 47 (2006).

26. See, e.g., Sylvia Law, "Civil Rights Under Attack by the Military," *Washington University Journal of Law & Policy* 7 (2001): 117; and Robin Ingli, "Gays in the Military: A Policy Analysis of 'Don't Ask, Don't Tell' and the Solomon Amendment," *Hamline Journal of Public Law and Policy* 20 (1998): 89.

27. See, generally, Robert I. Correales, "Don't Ask, Don't Tell: A Dying Policy on the Precipice," *California Western Law Review* 44 (2008): 413; Kathi Westcott and Rebecca Sawyer, "Silent Sacrifices: The Impact of 'Don't Ask, Don't Tell' on Lesbian and Gay Military Families," *Duke Journal of Gender Law and Policy* 14 (2007): 1121; and Aaron Belkin and Geoffrey Bateman, eds., *Don't Ask, Don't Tell: Debating the Gay Ban in the Military* (Boulder, Colo.: Lynne Rienner Publishers, 2003).

28. See Tobias Barrington Wolff, "Political Representation and Accountability Under

Don't Ask, Don't Tell," *Iowa Law Review* 89 (2004): 1633; and Tobias Barrington Wolff, "Compelled Affirmations, Free Speech, and the U.S. Military's Don't Ask, Don't Tell Policy," *Brooklyn Law Review* 63 (1997): 1141. On the policy's violation of equality, see Louis J. Virelli III, "Don't Ask, Don't Tell, Don't Work: The Discriminatory Effect of Veterans' Preferences on Homosexuals," *John Marshall Law Review* 38 (2005): 1083; and Kenji Yoshino, "Assimilationist Bias in Equal Protection: The Visibility Presumption and the Case of 'Don't Ask, Don't Tell,'" *Yale Law Journal* 108 (1998): 485. Though several federal district court judges found that Don't Ask, Don't Tell violated Equal Protection, every circuit court to consider the Equal Protection challenge to Don't Ask, Don't Tell rejected it. See, e.g., *Able v. United States*, 880 F. Supp. 968, 980 (E.D.N.Y. 1995), *vacated*, 88 F.3d 1280 (2d Cir. 1996). Despite her prior position, in her capacity as the Solicitor General Kagan urged President Obama to defend "don't ask, don't tell" against constitutional attack—an unpopular view in the administration and one that Obama rejected, though Kagan earned the president's respect for her advocacy and for her willingness to disagree with him. See Jeffrey Toobin, *The Oath* (New York: Doubleday, 2012), 222–23.

29. Sonia Sotomayor, *My Beloved World* (New York: Knopf, 2013), 196–252.

30. Ibid., 203.

31. See, e.g., Morton J. Horwitz, *The Warren Court and the Pursuit of Justice* (New York: Hill & Wang, 1999), 91–98; Melvin I. Urofsky, *The Warren Court: Justices, Rulings, and Legacy* (Santa Barbara, Calif.: ABC-CLIO, 2001), 156–81; Michal R. Belknap, *The Supreme Court and Criminal Procedure: The Warren Court Revolution* (Thousand Oaks, Calif.: CQ Press, 2011).

32. *United States v. Jones*, 132 S. Ct. 945, 954–57 (2012) (Sotomayor, J., concurring).

33. *J.D.B. v. North Carolina*, 131 S. Ct. 2394 (2011).

34. *Perry v. New Hampshire*, 132 S. Ct. 716, 730–40 (2012) (Sotomayor, J., dissenting).

35. *Mario Dion Woodward v. Alabama*, No. 15-5380 (November 18, 2013) (dissent from denial of certiorari).

36. A vast literature addresses plea bargaining. See, e.g., Stephanos Bibas, "Incompetent Plea Bargaining and Extrajudicial Reforms," *Harvard Law Review* 126 (2012): 150; William J. Stuntz, "Plea Bargaining and Criminal Law's Disappearing Shadow," *Harvard Law Review* 117 (2004): 2548; Stephanos Bibas, "Plea Bargaining Outside the Shadow of Trial," *Harvard Law Review* 117 (2004): 2463, 2469–86; William J. Stuntz, "The Pathological Politics of Criminal Law," *Michigan Law Review* 100 (2001): 505, 520, 528, 536–38, 550–52, 571–72; and Albert W. Alschuler, "Plea Bargaining and Its History," *Columbia Law Review* 79 (1979): 1, 33–42.

37. *Lafler v. Cooper*, 132 S. Ct. 1376 (2012); see also *Missouri v. Frye*, 132 S. Ct. 1399 (2012).

38. On the history of plea bargaining, see, e.g., George Fisher, *Plea Bargaining's Triumph: A History of Plea Bargaining in America* (Stanford, Calif.: Stanford University Press, 2003).

39. See, e.g., *Bordenkircher v. Hayes*, 434 U.S. 357 (1978).

40. *Lafler*, 132 S. Ct. at 1387.

41. Jordan Fabian, "Obama's Healthcare Plan Nixes Ben Nelson's 'Cornhusker Kick-

back' Deal," *Hill*, February 22, 2010, http://thehill.com/blogs/blog-briefing-room /news/82621-obama-healthcare-plan-nixes-ben-nelsons-cornhusker-kickback -deal; Lawrence R. Jacobs and Theda Skocpol, *Health Care Reform and American Politics: What Everyone Needs to Know* (New York: Oxford University Press, 2010), 51, 55, 186; and John E. McDonough, *Inside National Health Reform* (Berkeley: University of California Press, 2012), 151.

42. Robert Pear and David M. Herszenhorn, "Obama Hails Vote on Health Care as Answering 'the Call of History,'" *New York Times*, March 22, 2010, A1.

43. Don Walton, "Nelson Welcomes Role as Swing Vote," *Lincoln Journal Star*, September 3, 2009.

44. *N.F.I.B. v. Sebelius*, 132 S. Ct. 2566, 2601–2608 (2012); see also Samuel R. Bagenstos, "The Anti-Leveraging Principle and the Spending Clause After *NFIB*," *Georgetown Law Journal* 101 (2013): 861; and Mitchell N. Berman, "Coercion, Compulsion, and the Medicaid Expansion: A Study in the Doctrine of Unconstitutional Conditions," *Texas Law Review* 91 (2013): 1283.

45. See *Printz v. United States*, 521 U.S. 898, 918–22, 928, 935 (1997); *New York v. United States*, 505 U.S. 144–69 (1992); Lynn A. Baker, "Conditional Federal Spending After *Lopez*," *Columbia Law Review* 95 (1995): 1911, 1913–18; Jack M. Balkin and Sanford Levinson, "Understanding Constitutional Revolution," *Virginia Law Review* 87 (2001): 1045, 1058–59; Vicki C. Jackon, "Federalism and the Uses and Limits of Law: *Printz* and Principle," *Harvard Law Review* 111 (1998): 2180, 2211–12.

46. For commentary on the wide-ranging implications of the Spending Clause portion of the *Health Care Case*, see Bagenstos, "The Anti-Leveraging Principle and the Spending Clause After *NFIB*," 861; Eloise Pasachoff, "Conditional Spending After *NFIB v. Sebelius*: The Example of Federal Education Law," *American University Law Review* 62 (2013): 577; Kevin Russell, "Civil Rights Statutes Put at Risk by Health Care Decision," *SCOTUSblog*, June 29, 2012, www.scotusblog.com/2012 /06/civil-rights-statutes-put-at-risk-by-health-care-decision; and Jonathan H. Adler, "Could the Health Care Decision Hobble the Clean Air Act?," *Percolator Blog*, July 23, 2012, http://www.percolatorblog.org/2012/07/23/could-the-health -care-decision-hobble-the-clean-air-act.

47. For judicial perspectives on the function of dissents, see Diane P. Wood, "When to Hold, When to Fold, and When to Reshuffle: The Art of Decisionmaking on a Multi-Member Court," *California Law Review* 100 (2012): 1445; and William J. Brennan Jr., "In Defense of Dissents," *Hastings Law Journal* 37 (1986): 427.

48. See Seth Stern and Stephen Wermiel, *Justice Brennan: Liberal Champion* (New York: Houghton Mifflin Harcourt, 2010) 409–33; and Justice Thurgood Marshall, "Remarks on the Death Penalty Made at the Judicial Conference of the Second Circuit," *Columbia Law Review* 86 (1986): 1.

49. For an engaging and comprehensive overview, see Evan J. Mandery, *A Wild Justice: The Death and Resurrection of Capital Punishment in America* (New York: W. W. Norton, 2013).

50. *McCleskey v. Kemp*, 481 U.S. 279, 320 (1987) (Brennan, J., dissenting).

51. *Callins v. Collins*, 510 U.S. 1141, 1145 (1994) (Blackmun, J., dissenting); Linda Greenhouse, *Becoming Justice Blackmun* (New York: Times Books, 2005): 174–81.

52. David Garland, *Peculiar Institution: America's Death Penalty in an Age of Abolition* (Cambridge, Mass.: The Belknap Press of Harvard University Press, 2010).
53. *Printz v. United States*, 521 U.S. 898 (1997).
54. Ibid., 976–78 (Breyer, J. dissenting).
55. Dennis G. Smith and Edmund F. Haislmaier, "Medicaid Meltdown: Dropping Medicaid Could Save States $1 Trillion," Heritage Foundation, December 1, 2009, http://www.heritage.org/research/reports/2009/11/medicaid-meltdown-dropping -medicaid-could-save-states-1-trillion.
56. *South Dakota v. Dole*, 483 U.S. 203 (1987).
57. *Annual Fourth Circuit Court of Appeals Conference,* C-SPAN television broadcast, June 25, 2011.
58. See, e.g., Neal K. Katyal, "*Hamdan v. Rumsfeld*: The Legal Academy Goes to Practice," *Harvard Law Review* 120 (2006): 65.
59. Adam B. Cox and Adam Samaha, "Unconstitutional Conditions Questions Everywhere: The Implications of Exit and Sorting for Constitutional Law and Theory," *Journal of Legal Analysis* 5 (2013): 61, 64–69; Philip Hamburger, "Unconstitutional Conditions: The Irrelevance of Consent," *Virginia Law Review* 98 (2012): 479–91; Frederick Schauer, "Too Hard: Unconstitutional Conditions and the Chimera of Constitutional Consistency," *Denver University Law Review* 72 (1995): 989, 992–96; Cass R. Sunstein, "Why the Unconstitutional Conditions Doctrine Is an Anachronism (with Particular Reference to Religion, Speech, and Abortion)," *Boston University Law Review* 70 (1990): 593, 595–604; Kathleen M. Sullivan, "Unconstitutional Conditions," *Harvard Law Review* 102 (1989): 413, 1428–42; and Richard A. Epstein, "The Supreme Court, 1987 Term—Foreword: Unconstitutional Conditions, State Power, and the Limits of Consent," *Harvard Law Review* 102 (1988): 4, 28–102.
60. *Speiser v. Randall*, 357 U.S. 513 (1958).

9: MAKING RIGHTS REAL

1. Major League Baseball, *Official Baseball Rules: 2013 Edition.*
2. Chad Finn, "Obstruction Call Is a Tough Way to Lose, but Red Sox Have to Get Out of Their Own Way," *Boston Globe*, October 26, 2013.
3. *Confirmation Hearing on the Nomination of John G. Roberts, Jr. to Be Chief Justice of the United States: Hearing Before the S. Comm. on the Judiciary*, 109th Cong. 55–56 (2005) (statement of John G. Roberts Jr.).
4. "Transcript: Day Two of the Roberts Confirmation Hearings," *Washington Post*, September 13, 2005 (quoting Senator Cornyn).
5. "Transcript: Day One of the Roberts Hearings," *Washington Post*, September 13, 2005 (quoting Senator Brownback).
6. Aaron S. J. Zelinsky, "Essay: The Justice as Commissioner: Benching the Judge-Umpire Analogy," *Yale Law Journal Online* 119 (2010): 113, 118.
7. Mark Tushnet, *In the Balance: Law and Politics on the Roberts Court* (New York: W. W. Norton, 2013); Jeffrey Toobin, "No More Mr. Nice Guy," *New Yorker*, May 25, 2009; Michael J. Gerhardt, "Constitutional Humility," *University of Cincinnati Law Review* 76 (2007): 23; Arnold H. Loewy, "Chief Justice Roberts (A Preliminary

Assessment)," *Stetson Law Review* 40 (2011): 763; Gene Nichol, "Trumping Politics: The Roberts Court and 'Judicial' Review," *Tulsa Law Review* 46 (2011): 421 and Senator Charles E. Schumer, keynote address to the American Constitution Society, July 27, 2007, http://www.schumer.senate.gov/Newsroom/record.cfm?id=280107&&year=2007&.

8. Lee Epstein, William M. Landes, and Richard A. Posner, "How Business Fares in the Supreme Court," *Minnesota Law Review* 97 (2013): 1431; Erwin Chemerinsky, "The Roberts Court at Age Three," *Wayne Law Review* 54 (2008): 947, 962–66; Erwin Chemerinsky, "Justice for Big Business," *New York Times*, July 1, 2013; Editorial, "First Monday," *New York Times*, October 3, 2010; and James Vicini, "Courts Sides with Business in Key Decisions," Reuters, July 2, 2008, http://www.reuters.com/article/2008/07/02/us-usa-business-court-idUSN0236698320080702.

9. Geoffrey R. Stone, "The Roberts Court, Stare Decisis, and the Future of Constitutional Law," *Tulsa Law Review* 82 (2008): 1533; Neil S. Siegel, "Umpires at Bat: On Integration and Legitimation," *Constitutional Commentary* 24 (2007): 701; Patricia J. Williams, "The Roberts Court's Civil Rights Denialism," *Nation*, July 2, 2013; Noah Feldman, "John Roberts Just Ended the Civil-Rights Era," *Bloomberg.com*, June 25, 2013, http://www.bloomberg.com/news/2013-06-25/the-civil-rights-era-ended-today.html.

10. Erwin Chemerinsky, "Closing the Courthouse Doors," *Denver University Law Review* 90 (2012): 317, 326-30; Thomas K. Clancy, "The Irrelevancy of the Fourth Amendment in the Roberts Court," *Chicago-Kent Law Review* 85 (2010): 191; Erwin Chemerinsky, "Supreme Court's Conservative Majority Is Making Its Mark," *Los Angeles Times*, October 4, 2010; and Adam Liptak, "Court Under Roberts Is Most Conservative in Decades," *New York Times*, July 20, 2010.

11. See, e.g., Michael C. Dorf, "Recent Supreme Court Rulings May Show Hostility to Civil Rights, Even on the Part of Almost All of the Court's Liberals," *Verdict*, April 23, 2013, http://verdict.justia.com/2012/04/23/recent-supreme-court-rulings-may-show-hostility-to-civil-rights-even-on-the-part-of-almost-all-of-the-courts-liberals.

12. See, e.g., *Conley v. Gibson*, 355 U.S. 41 (1957); *Monroe v. Pape*, 365 U.S. 167 (1961); *Gideon v. Wainwright*, 372 U.S. 335 (1963); *NAACP v. Button*, 371 U.S. 415 (1963); *Cooper v. Pate*, 378 U.S. 546 (1964); *Flast v. Cohen*, 392 U.S. 83 (1968); *Goldberg v. Kelly*, 397 U.S. 254 (1970); *Bivens v. Six Unknown Named Agents*, 403 U.S. 388 (1971); *Monell v. Department of Social Services*, 436 U.S. 658 (1978).

13. Clare Cushman, *Courtwatchers: Eyewitness Accounts in Supreme Court History* (Lanham, Md.: Rowman & Littlefield, 2011), 114. Although Cushman specifies 1972, the Mets and Reds faced off in 1973.

14. See *Flood v. Kuhn*, 407 U.S. 258, 262 (1972); and Bob Woodward and Scott Armstrong, *The Brethren* (New York: Simon & Schuster, 1979), 190–91.

15. Nina Totenberg, "Justice Sotomayor Takes Swing at Famed Baseball Case," NPR, May 23, 2013, http://www.npr.org/2013/05/23/186314129/justice-sotomayor-takes-swing-at-famed-baseball-case.

16. Neal A. Lewis, "On a Supreme Court Prospect's Resume: 'Baseball Savior,'" *New York Times*, May 14, 2009.

17. Anthony DiComo, "Justice Sotomayor Throws Out First Pitch," MLB.com, September 26, 2009, http://newyork.yankees.mlb.com/news/article.jsp?ymd=20090926&content_id=7169594&c_id=nyy&vkey=news_nyy.

18. Tony Mauro, "Justice Alito, Phillies Phanatic," *Blog of Legal Times*, October 31, 2008, http://legaltimes.typepad.com/blt/2008/10/justice-alito-phillies-phanatic.html.

19. Transcript of Oral Argument at 16, *Am. Needle, Inc. v. Nat'l Football League*, 130 S. Ct. 2201 (2010) (No. 08-661).

20. Bruce Weber, "Umpires v. Judges," *New York Times*, July 11, 2009 (quoting umpire Gary Cederstrom).

21. Richard A. Posner, "The Role of the Judge in the Twenty-first Century," *Boston University Law Review* 86 (2006): 1049, 1051, 1054.

22. See Theodore A. McKee, "Judges as Umpires," *Hofstra Law Review* 35 (2007): 1709, 1717–18.

23. Richard Hasen, "Scholarship Highlight: End of the Supreme Court-Congress Dialogue?," *SCOTUSblog*, January 29, 2013, http://www.scotusblog.com/2013/01/scholarship-highlight-end-of-the-supreme-court-congress-dialogue.

24. John G. Roberts, "2013 Year-End Report on the Federal Judiciary," 12.

25. Lani Guinier, "Foreword, Demosprudence Through Dissent," *Harvard Law Review* 122 (2008): 4, 7 (quoting Kennedy in response to a student's question).

26. See Neil S. Siegel, "Umpires at Bat: On Integration and Legitimation," *Constitutional Commentary* 24 (2007): 701.

27. "The Supreme Court: Ends a Busy Term, Draws a Heavy Fire," *Time*, June 25, 1956.

28. "The Nomination of Elena Kagan to Be an Associate Justice of the Supreme Court of the United States: Hearing Before the S. Comm. on the Judiciary," 111th Cong. 203 (2010) (statement of Elena Kagan, to be an associate justice of the Supreme Court of the United States).

29. Jeffrey Toobin, *The Oath* (New York: Doubleday, 2012), 227.

30. *Republican Party of Minn. v. White*, 536 U.S. 765, 777, 778 (2002).

31. For an excellent overview of this subject, see Mark Tushnet, *In the Balance: Law and Politics on the Roberts Court* (New York: W. W. Norton, 2013), 187–214.

32. Jeffrey Rosen, "Supreme Court, Inc.," *New York Times*, March 16, 2008; Editorial, "Business Reigns Supreme," *Washington Post*, July 1, 2007.

33. Epstein, Landes, and Posner, "How Business Fares in the Supreme Court," 1450.

34. Adam Liptak, "Justices Offer Receptive Ear to Business Interests," *New York Times*, December 18, 2010; http://www.nytimes.com/2010/12/19/us/19roberts.html?pagewanted=all&_r=0.

35. Rosen, "Supreme Court, Inc."

36. U.S. Chamber of Commerce, "Chamber's Litigation Center Celebrates 30th Anniversary," press release, September 12, 2007, http://www.uschamber.com/press/releases/2007/september/chambers-litigation-center-celebrates-30th-anniversary.

37. Adam Chandler, "Cert.-Stage Amicus 'All Stars': Where Are They Now?," *SCOTUSblog*, April 4, 2013, http://www.scotusblog.com/2013/04/cert-stage-amicus-all-stars-where-are-they-now.

38. A vast literature of articles and op-eds debates these matters. See, e.g., Richard

Epstein, "The Myth of a Pro-Business SCOTUS," Hoover Institute, Foundry, July 9, 2013, http://www.hoover.org/publications/defining-ideas/article/151391; Ramesh Ponnuru, "Supreme Court Isn't Pro-Business, But Should Be," *Bloomberg*, July 4, 2011, http://www.bloomberg.com/news/2011-07-05/supreme-court-isn-t-pro-busi ness-but-should-be-ramesh-ponnuru.html; Adam Liptak, "Corporations Find a Friend in the Supreme Court," *New York Times*, May 4, 2013; Adam Liptak, "Justices Offer Receptive Ear to Business Interests," *New York Times*, December 18, 2010; Robin S. Conrad, "The Roberts Court and the Myth of a Pro-Business Bias," *Santa Clara Law Review* 997 (2009); David L. Franklin, "What Kind of Business-Friendly Court? Explaining the Chamber of Commerce's Success at the Roberts Court," *Santa Clara Law Review* 1019 (2009); Sri Srinivasan and Bradley W. Joondeph, "Business, the Roberts Court, and the Solicitor General: Why the Supreme Court's Recent Business Decisions May Not Reveal Very Much," *Santa Clara Law Review* 1103 (2009); Kenneth W. Starr, "The Roberts Court and the Business Cases," *Pepperdine Law Review* 541 (2008); Jonathan H. Adler, "Getting the Roberts Court Right: A Response to Chemerinsky," *Wayne Law Review* 983 (2008); and Erwin Chemerinsky, "The Roberts Court at Age Three," *Wayne Law Review* 947 (2008).

39. Aspen Ideas Festival, "Justice Elena Kagan at the Aspen Ideas Festival," YouTube, June 29, 2013, https://www.youtube.com/watch?v=DC_PVDsYKg.

40. David Spanier, *Total Chess* (New York: E. P. Dutton, 1984), 203 (quoting Koestler).

41. On the subject of Supreme Court decision making, see, generally, Richard L. Pacelle Jr. et al., *Decision Making by the Modern Supreme Court* (New York: Cambridge University Press, 2011); Thomas H. Hammond et al., *Strategic Behavior and Policy Choice on the U.S. Supreme Court* (Stanford, Calif.: Stanford University Press, 2005); and Lee Epstein and Jack Knight, *The Choices Justices Make* (Washington, D.C.: CQ Press, 1998).

42. The discussion that follows over the next several pages is informed by the work of many scholars, including Arthur R. Miller, "Simplified Pleading, Meaningful Days in Court, and Trials on the Merits: Reflections on the Deformation of Federal Procedure," *New York University Law Review* 88 (2013): 286; Myriam Gilles, "Killing Them with Kindness: Examining 'Consumer-Friendly' Arbitration Clauses After *AT&T Mobility v. Concepcion*," *Notre Dame Law Review* 88 (2012): 825; Myriam Gilles and Gary Friedman, "After Class: Aggregate Litigation in the Wake of *AT&T Mobility v. Concepcion*," *University of Chicago Law Review* 79 (2012): 623; Margaret H. Lemos, "Aggregate Litigation Goes Public: Representative Suits by State Attorneys General," *Harvard Law Review* 126 (2012): 486; David L. Noll, "Rethinking Anti-Aggregation Doctrine," *Notre Dame Law Review* 88 (2012): 649; Judith Resnik, "Fairness in Numbers: A Comment on *AT&T v. Concepcion, Wal-Mart v. Dukes, and Turner v. Rogers*," *Harvard Law Review* 125 (2011): 78; and Myriam Gilles and Gary Friedman, "Exploding the Class Action Agency Costs Myth: The Social Utility of Entrepreneurial Lawyers," *University of Pennsylvania Law Review* 155 (2006): 103.

43. Miller, "Simplified Pleading, Meaningful Days in Court, and Trials on the Merits," 286, 301.

44. *AT&T Mobility LLC v. Concepcion*, 131 S. Ct. 1740, 1744 (2011).

45. See *Am. Express Co. v. Italian Colors Rest.*, 133 S. Ct. 2304 (2013); *Compucredit Corp. v. Greenwood*, 132 S. Ct. 665 (2012); *Marmet Health Care Ctr., Inc. v. Brown*, 132 S. Ct. 1201 (2012); *Stolt-Nielsen, S.A. v. AnimalFeeds Int'l Corp.*, 130 S. Ct. 1758 (2010); *Rent-A-Center, W., Inc. v. Jackson*, 130 S. Ct. 2772 (2010).

46. For discussions of arbitration in *Concepcion* and more generally, see Resnik, "Fairness in Numbers"; Gilles, "Killing Them with Kindness"; and Theodore Eisenberg et. al., "Arbitration's Summer Soldiers: An Empirical Study of Arbitration Clauses in Consumer and Nonconsumer Contracts," *University of Michigan Journal of Law Reform* 41 (2008): 871.

47. Tushnet, *In the Balance*, 204.

48. See 133 S. Ct. 2304 (2013).

49. *Wal-Mart v. Dukes*, 131 S. Ct. 2541 (2011).

50. For another Roberts Court case that has made it much harder to certify classes, see *Comcast Corp. v. Behrend*, 133 S. Ct. 1426 (2013).

51. *Ashcroft v. Iqbal*, 556 U.S. 662 (2009); *Bell Atl. Corp. v. Twombly*, 550 U.S. 544 (2007).

52. *Kiobel v. Royal Dutch Petrol. Co.*, 133 S. Ct. 1659 (2013).

53. See, e.g., *Daimler AG v. Bauman*, No. 11-965, 2014 WL 113486 (2014); *Goodyear Dunlop Tires Operations, S.A. v. Brown*, 131 S. Ct. 2846 (2011); *J. McIntyre Mach., Ltd. v. Nicastro*, 131 S. Ct. 2780 (2011).

54. Benjamin Disraeli, *Tancred* (London: Henry Colburn, 1847), 129.

55. *Zivotofsky ex rel. Zivotofsky v. Clinton*, 132 S. Ct. 1421 (2012).

56. See *Zivotofsky v. Secretary of State*, 571 F.3d 1227 (D.C. Cir. 2009).

57. For discussions of the importance of remedies in civil rights litigation, see Erwin Chemerinsky, "Closing the Courthouse Doors to Civil Rights Litigants," *University of Pennsylvania Journal of Constitutional Law* (2003): 537, 546; Pamela S. Karlan, "Disarming the Private Attorney General," *University of Illinois Law Review* 183 (2003): 207; Judith Resnik, "Constricting Remedies: The Rehnquist Judiciary, Congress, and Federal Power," *Indiana Law Journal* 78 (2003): 223; Daryl J. Levinson, "Making Government Pay: Markets, Politics, and the Allocation of Constitutional Costs," *University of Chicago Law Review* 67 (2000): 345; John C. Jeffries Jr., "Compensation for Constitutional Torts: Reflections on the Significance of Fault," *Michigan Law Review* 88 (1989): 82, 84.

58. *Marbury v. Madison*, 5 U.S. 137 (1803).

59. See 131 S. Ct. 1350 (2011). The following discussion is informed by Susan A. Bandes, "The Lone Miscreant, the Self-Training Prosecutor, and Other Fictions: A Comment on *Connick v. Thompson*," *Fordham Law Review* 80 (2011): 715; and David Rittgers, "*Connick v. Thompson*: An Immunity That Admits of (Almost) No Liabilities," *Cato Supreme Court Review* (2010): 203.

60. See also Joshua Matz, "The Supreme Court, 2010 Term—Leading Cases," *Harvard Law Review* 125 (2011): 331.

61. See, e.g., Pamela S. Karlan, "What's a Right Without a Remedy," *Boston Review*, March 1, 2012.

62. See, e.g., *Stanton v. Sims*, 134 S. Ct. 3 (2013).

63. See generally Michael T. Kirkpatrick and Joshua Matz, "Avoiding Permanent

Limbo: Qualified Immunity and the Elaboration of Constitutional Rights from Saucier to Camreta (and Beyond)," *Fordham Law Review* 80 (2011): 643; John C. Jeffries Jr., "The Right-Remedy Gap in Constitutional Law," *Yale Law Journal* 109 (1999): 87, 90; John M. M. Greabe, "Mirabile Dictum!: The Case for 'Unnecessary' Constitutional Rulings in Civil Rights Damages Actions," *Notre Dame Law Review* 74 (1999): 403, 405; and Richard H. Fallon Jr., "Some Confusions About Due Process, Judicial Review, and Constitutional Remedies," *Columbia Law Review* 93 (1993): 309, 338.

64. See generally Bandes, "The Lone Miscreant."

65. Dahlia Lithwick, "Cruel but Not Unusual," *Slate,* April 1, 2011, www.slate.com /articles/news_and_politics/jurisprudence/2011/04/cruel_but_not_unusual.html.

66. *Kansas v. Marsh*, 126 S. Ct. 2516, 2533 (2006) (Scalia, J., concurring).

67. See, e.g., Pamela S. Karlan, "The Paradoxical Structure of Constitutional Litigation," *Fordham Law Review* 75 (2007): 1913; Myriam E. Gilles, "In Defense of Making Government Pay: The Deterrent Effect of Constitutional Tort Remedies," *Georgia. Law Review* 35 (2001): 845; and Richard H. Fallon Jr. and Daniel J. Meltzer, "New Law, Non-Retroactivity, and Constitutional Remedies," *Harvard Law Review* 104 (1991): 1731, 1788.

68. See 384 U.S. 436 (1966).

69. See, e.g., David Gray, "A Spectacular Non Sequitur: The Supreme Court's Contemporary Fourth Amendment Exclusionary Rule Jurisprudence," *American Criminal Law Review* 50 (2013): 1; Justin F. Marceau, "The Fourth Amendment at a Three-Way Stop," *Alabama Law Review* 62 (2011): 687; and Jonathan Witmer-Rich, "Interrogation and the Roberts Court," *Florida Law Review* 63 (2011): 1189.

70. See *Herring v. United States*, 555 U.S. 135 (2009). For criticism of *Herring*, see Jennifer E. Laurin, "Trawling for *Herring*: Lessons in Doctrinal Borrowing and Convergence," *Columbia Law Review* 111 (2011): 670; Albert W. Alschuler, "*Herring v. United States*: A Minnow or a Shark?," *Ohio State Journal of Criminal Law* 7 (2009): 463; Wayne R. LaFave, "The Smell of *Herring*: A Critique of the Supreme Court's Latest Assault on the Exclusionary Rule," *Journal of Criminal Law and Criminology* 99 (2009): 757. For a discussion of the implications of *Herring,* see Claire Angelique Nolasco et. al., "What *Herring* Hath Wrought: An Analysis of Post-*Herring* Cases in the Federal Courts," *American Journal of Criminal Law* 38 (2011): 221, 224.

71. The volume of commentary both supporting and opposing Supreme Court rulings mandating the exclusion of illegally obtained evidence, see *Weeks v. United States*, 232 U.S. 383 (1914); *Mapp v. Ohio*, 367 U.S. 643 (1961), is too vast to summarize here. For a sample of illuminating writing on the topic, see, e.g., Akhil Reed Amar, "Against Exclusion (Except to Protect Truth or Prevent Privacy Violations)," *Harvard Journal of Law & Public Policy* 20 (1997): 457; Yale Kamisar, "On the 'Fruits' of *Miranda* Violations, Coerced Confessions, and Compelled Testimony," *Michigan Law Review* 93 (1995): 929; Akhil Reed Amar, "Fourth Amendment First Principles," *Harvard Law Review* (1994): 757; Carol S. Steiker, "Response, Second Thoughts About First Principles," *Harvard Law Review* 107 (1994): 820.

72. For an argument that the exclusionary rule, on the contrary, is not of recent vintage but "was well established in the regular practices of Founding-era judges and

lawyers" and accordingly has deep originalist roots, see Roger Roots, "The Originalist Case for the Fourth Amendment Exclusionary Rule," *Gonzaga Law Review* 45 (2009/10): 1.

73. *United States v. Leon*, 468 U.S. 897, 941 (1984).

74. Henry J. Friendly, "The Bill of Rights as a Code of Criminal Procedure," 53 *California Law Review* 53 (1965): 929, 951.

75. See 130 S. Ct. 2250 (2010). For a discussion of the history of *Miranda* and the "heavy blow" dealt to the doctrine in *Berghuis v. Thompkins*, see Yale Kamisar, "The Rise, Decline, and Fall (?) of *Miranda*," *Washington Law Review* 87 (2012): 965. See also Barry Friedman, "The Wages of Stealth Overruling (with Particular Attention to *Miranda v. Arizona*)," *Georgetown Law Journal* 99 (2010): 1.

76. See *Dickerson v. United States*, 530 U.S. 428 (2000) (Scalia, J., dissenting).

77. "According to most estimates, about four-fifths of the civil legal needs of the poor, and two- to three-fifths of the needs of middle-income individuals, remain unmet," Deborah L. Rhode, *Access to Justice* (New York: Oxford University Press, 2004), 3. See also Rebecca L. Sandefur and Aaron C. Smyth, "Access Across America: First Report of the Civil Justice Infrastructure Mapping Project," American Bar Foundation (October 7, 2011). The situation is even more dire with respect to the needs of all but the wealthy for competent criminal defense. See, e.g., Rhode, *Access to Justice*, 122–44.

78. *Gideon v. Wainwright*, 327 U.S. 335 (1963). See Stephen B. Bright and Sia M. Sanneh, "Fifty Years of Defiance and Resistance After *Gideon v. Wainwright*," *Yale Law Journal* 122 (2013): 2150; Lincoln Caplan, "The Right to Counsel: Badly Battered at 50," *New York Times*, March 10, 2013; Laura Parker, "Lack of Public Defenders May Free Accused Felons," *USA Today*, February 14, 2006; Committee on Legal Aid & Indigent Defendants, American Bar Association, "Gideon's Broken Promise: America's Continuing Quest for Equal Justice" (2004); and Mary Sue Backus and Paul Marcus, "The Right to Counsel in Criminal Cases, A National Crisis," *Hastings Law Journal* 57 (2006): 1031.

79. U.S. Department of Justice, "Attorney General Eric Holder Speaks at the White House Forum on Increasing Access to Justice," April 16, 2013, www.justice.gov/iso /opa/ag/speeches/2013/ag-speech-1304161.html.

80. See Rhode, *Access to Justice*, 3.

81. For broader discussions of presidential secrecy, see, e.g., Mark J. Rozell, *Executive Privilege: Presidential Power, Secrecy, and Accountability* (Lawrence: University Press of Kansas, 2010); and David E. Pozen, "The Leaky Leviathan: Why the Government Condemns and Condones Unlawful Disclosures of Information," *Harvard Law Review* 127 (2013): 512.

82. See Department of Justice White Paper, "Lawfulness of a Lethal Operation Directed Against a U.S. Citizen Who Is a Senior Operational Leader of Al-Qa'ida or an Associated Force" (2011), 1.

83. Adam Liptak, "The Case of the Plummeting Supreme Court Docket," *New York Times*, September 28, 2009, A18; and Ryan J. Owens and David A. Simon, "Explaining the Supreme Court's Shrinking Docket," *William and Mary Law Review* 53 (2012): 1219.

84. *Buck v. Thaler*, 132 S. Ct. 32 (2011) (Sotomayor, J., dissenting from denial of certiorari); *Hodge v. Kentucky*, 133 S. Ct. 506 (2012) (Sotomayor, J., dissenting from denial of certiorari); *Pitre v. Cain*, 131 S. Ct. 8 (2010) (Sotomayor, J., dissenting from denial of certiorari).

85. Adam Liptak and Allison Kopicki, "Approval Rating for Justices Hits Just 44% in New Poll," *New York Times*, June 7, 2012, A1; and "Supreme Court's Favorability Edges Below 50%," Pew Research Center, July 24, 2013, www.people-press.org/2013/07/24/supreme-courts-favorability-edges-below-50/.

86. Stephen Breyer, "Statement Concerning the Supreme Court's Front Entrance," May 3, 2010, http://www.supremecourt.gov/orders/journal/jnl09.pdf#page=807.

EPILOGUE

1. For a fascinating discussion of the relationship between culture and the Court, see Robert C. Post, "Foreword: Fashioning the Legal Constitution: Culture, Courts, and Law," *Harvard Law Review* 117 (2003): 4.

2. See, e.g., Michael J. Klarman, "How *Brown* Changed Race Relations: The Backlash Thesis," *Journal of American History* 81 (1994): 81.

3. See Martha Minow, *In Brown's Wake: Legacies of America's Educational Landmark* (New York: Oxford University Press, 2010).

4. See Reva B. Siegel, "Foreword: Equality Divided," *Harvard Law Review* 127 (2013): 1.

5. William Faulkner, *Absalom, Absalom* (New York, Random House, 1966), 266.

6. See Gerald N. Rosenberg, *The Hollow Hope: Can Courts Bring About Social Change?*, 2nd ed. (Chicago: University of Chicago Press, 2008).

7. For a critical survey of these arguments, see Linda Greenhouse and Reva B. Siegel, "Before (and After) *Roe v. Wade*: New Questions About Backlash," *Yale Law Journal* 120 (2011): 2028.

8. A lively scholarly debate still rages over judicial interventions into the same-sex marriage field. See, e.g., Michael Klarman, *From the Closet to the Altar* (New York: Oxford University Press, 2012); Rosenberg, *The Hollow Hope,* 339–419; William N. Eskridge Jr., "Backlash Politics: How Constitutional Litigation Has Advanced Marriage Equality in the United States," *Boston University Law Review* 98 (2013): 275; Scott L. Cummings and Douglas NeJaime, "Lawyering for Marriage Equality," *UCLA Law Review* 57 (2011): 1235; Thomas M. Keck, "Beyond Backlash: Assessing the Impact of Judicial Decisions on LGBT Rights," *Law and Society Review* 43 (2009): 151; and Carlos A. Ball, "The Backlash Thesis and Same-Sex Marriage: Learning from *Brown v. Board of Education* and Its Aftermath," *William and Mary Bill of Rights Journal* 14 (2006): 1493. See also Laurence H. Tribe, "Structural Due Process," *Harvard Civil Rights–Civil Liberties Law Review* 10 (1975): 269, 290–321.

9. *Herbert v. Kitchen*, No. 13A687 (Order of January 6, 2014).

10. *McCullen v. Coakley*, No. 12-1168.

11. *Hill v. Colorado*, 530 U.S. 703 (2000). See Kathleen M. Sullivan, "Sex, Money, and Groups: Free Speech and Association Decisions in the October 1999 Term," *Pepperdine Law Review* 28 (2001): 723, 734–38; "Symposium: Professor Michael W. McConnell's Response," *Pepperdine Law Review* 28 (2001): 747.

12. In its 2012 term, the Court granted one such case but later dismissed it as improvidently granted. See *Cline v. Oklahoma Coalition for Reproductive Justice*, No. 12-1094.

13. *Town of Greece v. Galloway*, No. 12-969.

14. *Sebelius v. Hobby Lobby Stores*, No. 13-354.

15. *National Labor Relations Board v. Noel Canning*, No. 12-1281.

16. *Bond v. United States*, No. 12-158.

17. Winston Churchill, "The Russian Enigma," BBC radio address, October 1, 1939.

18. See Lani Guinier, "Foreword: Demosprudence Through Dissent," *Harvard Law Review* 122 (2008): 4.

19. Pamela S. Karlan, "Out of Alignment," *Boston Review*, December 23, 2013.

20. Robert Pogue Harrison, *Gardens: An Essay on the Human Condition* (Chicago: University of Chicago Press, 2009), 100.

ACKNOWLEDGMENTS

In writing this book, we have benefited in innumerable ways from the support and thoughtful reactions of our families, friends, and colleagues. Their encouragement, candid feedback, constructive criticism, and insightful suggestions are reflected in every page of our exploration of the Roberts Court and the Constitution.

We are particularly grateful to those who read and commented on the whole manuscript: Michael Dorf, Sam Harbourt, Jason Harrow, Andrew Kaufman, Aaron Kotler, Philip Mayor, Mark Rosenbaum, Jarrod Schaeffer, Zachary Shemtob, Vivek Suri, and Mark Tushnet. We are also deeply indebted to those who offered invaluable counsel either on our book proposal at the outset or on individual chapters as we progressed: Jack Balkin, Aharon Barak, Randy Barnett, Josh Blackman, Tristan Duncan, Erin Earl, Cormac Early, Heather Gerken, Patrick Gudridge, Rick Hasen, David Hemenway, Justin Levitt, Anna Lvovsky, Erin Monju, Judith Resnik, Alan Rozenshtein, Peter Rubin, Rachel Sachs, Adam Samaha, Steven Shiffrin, Eugene Volokh, Lauren Weinstein, and Ernest Young.

We owe special thanks to Dean Martha Minow of Harvard Law School, who offered marvelous feedback on several chapters and was immensely supportive of this entire project. We also owe a special debt of gratitude to Larry's longtime faculty assistant, Kathy McGillicuddy. Kathy's genius for organization, technological savvy, and tremendous personal warmth made her a vital part of our team.

Over the past two years, we have been privileged to work with a stellar group of dedicated research assistants. It is our pleasure to thank them for their hard work and many contributions: Sam Barr, Andrew Chan, Samuel Cortina, Bryce Daigle, Christopher Ferro, Elizabeth Finley, Jon Gould, Greg Halperin, Caitlin Halpern, Brett Kalikow, David Korn, Nina Kovalenko, Natacha Lam, Michael Mencher, and Allison Trzop.

Ever since he first cast a vote of confidence in this book, John Sterling of Henry Holt and Company has made it better in every way. We are lucky to have benefited from his enthusiasm and editorial acumen—and from excellent work by everyone else at Henry Holt, notably including our copy editor Bonnie Thompson and our production editor Christopher O'Connell. We also thank our agent Ike Williams and his associate Katherine Flynn of the Kneerim, Williams & Bloom Agency for their wise and expert guidance.

We express special gratitude to Elizabeth Westling, who has read and reread the manuscript with unflagging care and made countless insightful suggestions from the perspective of a historian and a humanist rather than that of a lawyer. We thank her not only for her contributions as a careful and insightful reader but also for helping to set this whole book in motion.

Finally, we hasten to add the usual disclaimer that, much as we benefitted from the help of our friends, all errors are our own.

From Larry Tribe: I want to thank the generations of remarkable students who have taught me at least as much as I have taught them, and my colleagues—past and present—at Harvard Law School and Harvard University for their generous friendship and collegiality. To the score of people it is not possible to acknowledge here and to my family, especially my son Mark, my daughter Kerry, and my brother Shurka, who have tolerated and encouraged my preoccupation with this project and others that preceded it: I owe you more than I can express in words, something I trust you'll understand when you learn that I'm dedicating this book to you (and to my grandchildren Isabel, Sadie, Eno, and Emit) with all my love.

Although it is not customary to express gratitude to one's coauthor, I must. Without my former constitutional law student, longtime research assistant, former head teaching fellow, and recent collaborator and friend, Joshua Matz, I could not have written this book.

Finally, I must add a special, personal note of thanks to Elizabeth: she made this book possible, was invariably supportive and loving (and always candid!) as my partner and muse, and she has inspired me every step of the way.

From Joshua Matz: First and foremost, I thank my family, especially my parents and grandparents. It is impossible to overstate how much their support, advice, and encouragement have meant to me, both in writing this book and in so many other ways. Through years in which I largely vanished into two judicial clerkships and the world of the Roberts Court, my family has been a constant source of strength and inspiration. So I thank Merri and Ned Braunstein, Bill and Marie Matz, Genna and Jake Matz, Neil and Terri Matz, and Barbara and Jerry Tack—to whom I dedicate this book with love.

I have been lucky in my young career to benefit from the wisdom, knowledge, and guidance of many mentors: Susan Staub, Irwin Katz, and Robert Wilson before college; Warren Breckman, Sarah Igo, Peter Struck, Michael Weisberg, and Liliane Weissberg at the University of Pennsylvania; and Lawrence Goldman at Oxford University. At Harvard Law School, I was privileged to learn from many great scholars, including David Barron, Richard Fallon, Noah Feldman, Martha Field, Jody Freeman, Jacob Gersen, Nancy Gertner, Jon Hanson, Judge Brett Kavanaugh, Michael Klarman, Jed Shugerman, Matthew Stephenson, Carol Steiker, William Stuntz, and Mark Tushnet. Their lessons complemented my work with the incredibly talented attorneys at Equality Advocates Pennsylvania, the Federal Defender of New York, the Innocence Project, Neufeld Scheck & Brustin, the Public Citizen Litigation Group, and *SCOTUSblog*. I have also learned much from the time I have been fortunate enough to spend clerking for two truly great judges: Judge J. Paul Oetken of the Southern District of New York and Judge Stephen Reinhardt of the U.S. Court of Appeals for the Ninth Circuit.

Finally, I must follow Larry in breaking custom and thank him for being such a remarkable mentor, friend, and coauthor. Like so many of his students before me—and like many more still to come—I credit Larry with bringing the Court and the Constitution to life in my mind. He is a true giant of the law, one of its greatest scholars, professors, and practitioners, and I have been humbled by the opportunity to work with him. He is also a kind and generous man, and a wonderful friend and coauthor. Because words would otherwise fail me, I will simply say to him, "Thank you."

INDEX